V&R

Refo500 Academic Studies

Edited by
Herman J. Selderhuis

Volume 50

Charles P. Arand / Erik H. Herrmann /
Daniel L. Mattson (eds.)

From Wittenberg to the World

Essays on the Reformation and its Legacy in Honor of Robert Kolb

Vandenhoeck & Ruprecht

With 3 Figures

Bibliographic information published by the Deutsche Nationalbibliothek
The Deutsche Nationalbibliothek lists this publication in the Deutsche Nationalbibliografie; detailed bibliographic data available online: http://dnb.d-nb.de.

ISSN 2198-3089
ISBN 978-3-525-53126-6

Typesetting by 3w+p GmbH, Rimpar
Printed and bound by Hubert & Co. GmbH & Co. KG BuchPartner,
Robert-Bosch-Breite 6, D-37079 Göttingen

Printed in the EU.

Fig. 1: Robert Kolb

Contents

Abbreviations

1521 Loci	Philip Melachthon, *Loci communes theologici* of 1521. Lowell J. Sartre, trans., revisions by Wilhelm Pauck, The Library of Christian Classics 19, ed., Wilhelm Pauck. Philadelphia: Westminster Press, 1969.
1543 Loci	Philip Melanchthon, *Loci communes rerum theologicarum* of 1543. English translation: *Loci communes* 1543, trans., J.A.O. Preus. St. Louis: Concordia, 1992.
1555 Loci	Philip Melanchthon, 1555 *Loci Communes*, trans. and ed., Clyde L. Manschreck. New York: Oxford University Press, 1965.
AC	Augsburg Confession.
Ap	Apology of the Augsburg Confession.
Asm	Smalcald Articles.
BenshH	*Bensheimer Hefte*. Göttingen.
BGLRK	*Beiträge zur Geschichte und Lehre der Reformierten Kirche.*
BSLK	*Die Bekentnisschriften der evangelisch-lutherischen Kirche.* Eleventh edn. Göttingen: Vandenhoeck & Ruprecht, 1992.
BSELK	*Die Bekenntnisschriften der Evangelisch-Lutherischen Kirche*, Vollständige Neuedition. ed., Irene Dingel. Göttingen: Vandenhoeck & Ruprecht, 2014.
CR	*Corpus Reformatorum.* Vol. 1–28: *Philippi Melanthonis Opera quae supersunt omnia.* ed., C.G. Bretschneider and H.E. Bindseil. Halle: C.A. Schwetschke 1834–60. Vol. 29–87: *Ioannis Calvini Opera quae supersunt omnia.* ed., W. Baum/E. Cunitz/E. Reuss. Braunschweig: C.A. Schwetschke et filius, 1863–1900. Vol. 88– *Huldreich Zwinglis Sämtliche Werke.* ed., Emil Egli et al. Leipzig: Heinsius, 1905–
DH	Heinrich Denzinger, *Enchiridion symbolorum definitionum et declarationum de rebus fidei et morum, verbessert, erweitert, ins Deutsche übertragen [...].* ed., Peter Hünermann. Freiburg i.Br./Basel/Rom/Wien: Herder, 2017 (1854).
ESV	English Standard Version. Wheaton, IL: Good News Bibles, 2001.
FC SD	Solid Declaration of the Formula of Concord.
FKDG	*Forschungen zur Kirchen- und Dogmengeschichte.*
fol.	folio
HAB	*Herzog August Bibliothek. Wolfenbüttel.*
HAST	*Handbuch systematischer Theologie.*
HZ	*Historische Zeitschrift.* 1859–2006. Oldenbourg: Wissenschaftsverlag/Akademie Verlag.

KiO.M	*Kirche im Osten. Monographienreihe.* Stuttgart.
KuD	*Kerygma und Dogma.* Göttingen: Vandenhoeck & Ruprecht.
KW	Robert Kolb/Timothy J. Wengert, ed. *The Book of Concord: The Confessions of the Evangelical Lutheran Church.* Minneapolis: Fortress Press, 2000.
LC	Luther's Large Catechism.
LD	*Luther Deutsch.* Göttingen: Vandenhoeck & Ruprecht.
LH	*Luther Handbuch.* ed., Albrecht Beutel. Tübingen: Mohr Siebeck, 2005.
LI	The Leipzig Interim, Robert Kolb, trans., in *Sources and Contexts of the Book of Concord.* ed., Robert Kolb and James A. Nestingen. Minneapolis: Fortress Press, 2001, 183–184.
LKW	*Lutherische Kirche in der Welt.* Jahrbuch des Martin-Luther-Bundes.
LStRLO	*Leucorea Studien zur Geschichte der Reformation und der Lutherischen Orthodoxie.* ed., Matthias Asche/Heiner Lück/Manfred Rudersdorf/Markus Wriedt. Leipzig: Evangelische Verlagsanstalt.
LuThK	*Lutherische Theologie und Kirche.* ed., Fakultät der Lutherischen Theologischen Hochschule, Oberursel.
LthK	*Lexikon für theologie und Kirche.* Freiburg i.Br.: Herder.
LW	Luther's Works: American Edition. Vol. 1–30: ed., Jaroslav Pelikan. St. Louis: Concordia, 1955–76. Vol.31–55: ed., Helmut Lehmann. Philadelphia/Minneapolis: Muhlenberg/Fortress Press, 1957–86; Vol. 56–82: ed., Christopher Boyd Brown. St. Louis: Concordia, 2009–.
MBW	*Melanchthons Briefwechsel.* ed., Heinz Scheible. 10+ vol. Stuttgart: Frommann/Holzboog, 1997–.
OUH	*Oberurseler Hefte.* ed., Fakultät der Lutherischen Theologischen Hochschule, Oberursel.
NIV	Holy Bible: New International Version, International Bible Society, 1973, 1978, 1984.
QuM	*Quellen und Materialien.*
SC	Luther's Small Catechism.
SVRG	*Schriften des Vereins für Reformationsgeschichte.* Marburg: Fachbereich Evangelische Theologie, Philipps-Universität.
TRE	*Theologische Realenzyklopädie.* 36 vol. ed., Gerhard Müller/Horst Balz/Gerhard Krause. Berlin: De Gruyter, 1976–2004.
VD16	*Verzeichnis der im deutschen Sprachbereich erschienenen Drucke des XVI. Jahrhunderts.* 25 vol. ed., Irmgard Bezzel. Stuttgart: Hiersemann, 1983–2000.
VIEG	*Veröffentlichungen des Instituts für Europäische Geschichte Mainz.* ed., Irene Dingel. Göttingen: Vandenhoeck & Ruprecht.
VLAR	*Veröffentlichungen der Luther-Akademie Ratzeburg.* Erlangen: Luther-Akademie.
W^2	*Dr. Martin Luthers sämtliche Schriften.* 25 vol. ed., Johann Georg Walch, Jena, 1740–1753. *Nachdruck der zweiten, überarbeiteten Auflage,* St. Louis, 1880–1910, Groß Oesingen, 1986.
WA	*D. Martin Luthers Werke: Kritische Gesamtausgabe.* 73 vol. in 85. Weimar: H. Böhlau, 1883–.
WABr	*D. Martin Luthers Werke: Briefwechsel.* 18 vol. Weimar: H. Böhlau, 1930–.
WADB	*D. Martin Luthers Werke: Deutsche Bibel.* 12 vol. in 15. Weimar: H. Böhlau, 1906–
WATR	*D. Martin Luthers Werke: Tischreden.* 6 vol. Weimar: H. Böhlau, 1912–21.

Introduction – The Editors

With this Festschrift, we pay tribute to a man who has an impact upon the lives and professional careers of many of us as well as the readers of this volume.

Dan, Erik, and I have known Dr. Robert Kolb for varying lengths of time and in different capacities. Dan has known Bob the longest, stretching back to the days when he and Bob were classmates at Concordia College, St. Paul (1960). Erik and I became personally acquainted with Bob when he arrived as a professor at Concordia Seminary twenty-four years ago. By that time, Bob had already established himself as a leading Reformation scholar. Despite his incredibly busy speaking and writing schedule, he took a young colleague (Chuck) and student (Erik) under his wings. In doing so, he has shaped Chuck's reading of the Lutheran Confessions and Erik's study of the history and theology of Luther down to the present day.

To introduce this volume, we share a few thoughts here with which, I suspect, our contributors and many of our readers will readily relate followed by a slightly more formal biography of Bob's life that will provide a context for his work.

An Appreciation

We cannot do justice the life and work of Robert Kolb without making a few personal reflections about Bob and his significant impact upon us as students, teachers, scholars, pastors, and churchmen as well as his pastoral guidance for many of the people who sit in the pews of our churches every Sunday.

Collegial Collaborations

When Bob arrived at Concordia Seminary, he brought with him a way of doing theology that he had learned – as he would frequently say – from his sixteenth-century friends (how many of us have not heard Bob remark with a straight face, "I have a friend who says …" and that friend turns out to be Martin Luther or

Nicholas von Amsdorf or Spannenberg or dozens of other friends who are over 500 years old!). But there was truth to what Bob had said. He has spent much time studying how theologians in Wittenberg worked together to give us what he came to call, "The Wittenberg way of doing theology." And it is simply this. Theology is not done in isolation; it is a collaborative affair. It is not an individual event; it is a team effort.

Bob has embodied throughout his life what he learned from his sixteenth-century friends and modeled for his students and colleagues. Many of us in this volume have found Bob to be a stimulating conversational partner who is incredibly generous with his time. He has read our drafts, edited our articles, and given us his feedback to our ideas and thoughts. Perhaps most important, he has always encouraged us to pursue a line of research or develop an idea and to publish! And Bob always seemed so positive and agreeable in his comments. But as many of us have perhaps discovered on more than one occasion, Bob would make a comment and it was not until the next day that we realized, "Wait, that wasn't a compliment … it was a criticism!"

Bob's collaborative way of doing theology, not only with his sixteenth-century friends or his Missouri Synod colleagues, has extended across denominations and around the globe. His conversational and collaborative approach to theology has extended to ecumenical discussions with people holding different positions and arguments. As he often reminded us, one must listen, as well as talk. His goal was always to work together so as to sharpen each other's thinking, the articulation of the faith, and the proclamation the Gospel.

Throughout his work and conversations, Bob has modeled for us all how to be teachers and confessors of the faith. He has shown us how teaching and writing can be scriptural and orthodox to the core – without being stifling or stultifying. For Bob, confessing is not about repristinating the past either in its questions or its formulations. And theology is not a set quantity of data. Instead, confessing the faith is as much about carrying on a conversation (listening and chatting) with people today and translating into their language God's own words. He would listen to how people described the human experience today and learn from their experiences. Meeting them where they are, Bob would translate the Gospel into language to which they could relate: God giving us in Christ a new identity, eternal security, and meaning for life. Bob's theology is both down to earth and refreshing as he encourages us to see how Reformation theology continually opens up new possibilities for engaging our culture today with the Word of God.

Theological Contributions

A quick look at his bibliography will reveal Bob's many contributions across a wide array of subjects. But which are his most important and influential works? We will leave that for you to decide. I have a hunch we each will have our favorite candidates. But there are a few consistent threads in his work that are worth highlighting.

One of Bob's greatest and most lasting contributions both to Luther studies and the church lies with his recapturing Luther's distinction of "Two Kinds of Righteousness." As the Reformation marked a turn in some ways toward anthropology with its emphasis on original sin, free will, faith, and good works, Bob's insights into Luther's two kinds of righteousness provided a way to describe and reflect theological anthropology. By considering the human creature within two different relationships (*coram deo* and *coram mundo*), each of which has a fundamentally different foundation, Bob provided a resource to the church, resolving some longstanding conundrums in Lutheran theology. These included, "How do you talk about the Christian life without infringing on justification?" "How can we think about the relationship of justification?"

Closely related to the above, is Bob's emphasis upon the Word of God. Here he moved beyond a simple discussion of different ways in which that expression is used (Christ, Gospel, Scripture) to two emphases. The first is that God is above all a God of conversation. As he expressed it one time, "God is a chatterbox all through the Bible." And this emphasis on conversation (with its mutual hearing and speaking) provided a way for him to speak both about God's relationship to us as well as our relationship to each other. The second lies in his emphasis on the performative character of the Word of God, namely, it does what it says. This provided a further way to see the unity of Scripture from God's work of creating to God's work of making all things new with his justifying word. As God embeds his word in his creatures for temporal life, so he embeds it again in creation as means (water, bread and wine) for eternal life. And with that, he gives us a picture of the church that is not defined by institution and ritual as it is by word and faith.

Perhaps not as readily recognized as a contribution to Reformation studies lies what we might call Bob's theological recovery of the significance of the First Article (creation) for all of theology. Although the topic of creation was often relegated to only being about a question of origins, Bob revived it as presupposition and hence the *cantus firmus* for all the theological *loci* of the Christian faith. Of course, he learned this from his good friend, Martin Luther, whose teaching on justification by faith also marked a turn toward the earthly and the well-being of all who live in God's creation. After all, that's where our works belong – down here on earth – as Bob would quip when contrasting Luther's teaching with that of Aquinas and Biel. And it is this world for which God has created us and redeemed us.

The Life and Work of Dr. Robert Kolb

Many readers may be less familiar with the biography of Dr. Kolb than they are with his writings. The following offers a little context for reading his work and appreciating his contributions as well getting a sense of both the breadth and depth of his thought.

Student and Studies

We begin the record of his education, work, and accomplishments with undergraduate studies at Concordia St. Paul (CSP) in 1959, just after his youth and childhood spent in Fort Dodge, Iowa. We will not mention that the Ft. Dodge high school must have been one of the most unusual public high schools in the US in the late 1950s, offering multiple years of Latin instruction. We will have to depend on Bob to fill us in with tales of the beginnings and his Scandinavian and German ancestry or memories of summer jobs in the Hormel factory, working his way through school, and tasting the fresh Spam along with the whole crew at the plant!

After two years at CSP, Robert continued his studies for the ministry at Concordia Sr. College, Ft. Wayne, and received his Bachelor of Arts in 1963. At both St. Paul and Ft. Wayne he prepared for his writing and editing career as editor of the student newspapers. Entering Concordia Seminary, St. Louis, he continued to excel in scholarship and writing.

His graduation year at Concordia Seminary, and vicarage at Rochester, Michigan, were enhanced by his marriage to Pauline Ansorge on August 14, 1965. She was a Minnesota pastor's daughter he had met at CSP. With her quiet strength and faithful assistance, Pauline has been "my rib" to Bob throughout his multifaceted career. At Concordia Seminary Kolb received a Master of Divinity in 1967, and the Master of Sacred Theology degree in 1968.

Continuing his graduate studies at the University of Wisconsin—Madison, Robert Kolb earned a Master's degree in 1969 and his Doctor of Philosophy in the field of history in 1973, studying under the late Robert M. Kingdon, one of the premier Reformation scholars of the twentieth century. He was ordained a pastor of the Lutheran Church—Missouri Synod in 1972. He returned to St. Louis to continue his research in the Reformation era and serve as the Executive Director of the Center for Reformation Research from 1972–1977.

Recognizing the achievements of Robert Kolb in a variety of fields, the following institutions have granted him honorary Doctor of Letters degrees: Valparaiso University in 2000, Concordia University, St. Paul in 2005, and Concordia University, Irvine in 2008 and Comenius University in Bratislava in 2018. Kolb has also been awarded research grants from European universities for study abroad.

Teacher and Professor

Dr. Robert Kolb was called to teach at his alma mater, Concordia University, St. Paul, inspiring a generation of students (1977–1993) in the religion and history departments. Students selected him "Professor of the Year" repeatedly to affirm his impact on their lives. Professor Kolb became Chairman of the Religion Department, and from 1990–1991 served as acting president of CSP.

From time to time, he accepted the challenge of serving as guest lecturer or visiting professor at institutions such as Valparaiso, Ohio State, Wisconsin, Luther Seminary, and Concordia Seminary.

Devoted to Christ's mission mandate to reach out to all the world, Robert Kolb began visiting and teaching in support of the mission of the church in many countries. His first mission trip was in 1980, leading a missionary retreat in Jos, Nigeria, and visiting mission stations there. He grasped new opportunities to teach in Eastern European seminaries in the post-Soviet era. To date he has now lectured at more than forty educational venues on five continents, in countries including Nigeria, India, Latvia, Estonia, Norway, Sweden, Russia, Czech Republic, Canada, Switzerland, the UK, and Germany. Never a stranger in Germany, he has spent a part of every year at the Herzog August Bibliothek in Wolfenbuettel, and has been a visiting faculty member (*Gastdozent*) at Lutherische Theologische Hochschule in Oberursel, Germany, since 1996. He is probably the only professor at an American seminary whose wristwatch is permanently set to German time.

His role as a visiting missionary connects to his call to Concordia Seminary, St. Louis in 1993 as Director of the Institute for Mission Studies and Missions Professor in systematic theology. He has had an enormous impact on the seminary student body (nearly everyone has a Kolb story) and has directed the research of a steady stream of graduate students. As a member of the Seminary faculty, he spent about half of each year traveling to Lutheran institutions worldwide, often from his German base, to teach, preach, and represent the seminary and The Lutheran Church—Missouri Synod at conferences and meetings.

Scholar and Author

Robert Kolb is probably best known for his prolific written work. As a foremost authority on the Reformation, and post-Reformation period, on Martin Luther and his colleagues, and on Lutheran theology, Dr. Kolb has written scholarly and practical books, articles, and reviews, as well as recorded presentations on tapes, videos, and other media. Of major importance is *The Book of Concord: The Confessions of the Evangelical Lutheran Church,* also known as Kolb-Wengert (KW), appearing in 2000. Because of the sheer volume of Robert Kolb's writings, it is risky to start naming his books in this short biography. *The Christian Faith: A Lutheran Exposition; For All the Saints, Changing Perceptions of Martyrdom and Sainthood; Luther and the Stories of God; Speaking the Gospel Today; Martin Luther: Confessor of the Faith; Martin Luther as Prophet, Teacher, and Hero; Luther's Heirs Define His Legacy,* and *Teaching God's Children His Teaching* are books you will find among the hundreds of works on the bibliographic list of Kolb writings in this volume. Some of his books have been translated into other languages, especially for people in the places where he has taught.

He has been co-author of many books and made contributions in dictionaries, encyclopedias, and other collected works. Beyond writing, he has edited or co-edited numerous scholarly editions. Recently, Dr. Robert Kolb has collaborated on the massive work, a new German critical edition of the Lutheran Confessions. As the editor of the *Katechismen* portion, he is the first non-German to participate so significantly in such a monumental work.

The influence of Kolb in telling the stories of the Reformation and explaining the Christian faith has proliferated through the numerous articles published in journals. Among the prestigious journals where his writings appear are *The Harvard Theological Review, The Lutheran Quarterly, Church History, The Sixteenth Century Journal, Renaissance Quarterly,* and *Concordia Journal,* and many other journals throughout the world. He was associate editor or co-editor of *The Sixteenth Century Journal* from 1973–1997; and has been a co-editor of *Missio Apostolica* (now known as *Lutheran Mission Matters*) since 1996.

For those of us who know Bob well, he is just one of the guys. It is easy to forget or not realize how well regarded he is outside of our Lutheran boundaries and how he has been an admirable witness to the Lutheran faith beyond Lutheran circles. A personal anecdote illustrates this well. When my daughter was going through clinicals in Maryland for her nurse anesthesia program she was working in an operating room with a surgeon who also happened to be on the board for a seminary on the east coast. Knowing that her father was a pastor/professor, he mentioned that he had been reading a wonderful book on the Reformation by a Dr. Robert Kolb. My daughter exclaimed, "Oh, you mean uncle Bob?" She said that his jaw dropped as he uttered in awe, "You know Dr. Kolb?" It is easy to take for granted Bob's influence not only upon Luther scholars, but upon many others who are just interested in the Reformation and its theology—CPA.

Churchman

Robert Kolb's distinguished career includes membership on important commissions and scholarly organizations. He served on the Commission on Theology and Church Relations (CTCR) of The Lutheran Church—Missouri Synod beginning in

1984 and continuing as chair of CTCR from 1990–1992. He served as president of the Sixteenth Century Studies Conference (1981–1982) and president of the Society for Reformation Research (1994–1996). Since 1993 he has been a member of the Continuation Committee of the International Congress for Luther Research. On multiple committees at Concordia Seminary, even after retiring in 2008, the Rev. Dr. Robert A. Kolb continues to influence and encourage his colleagues. As his instruction and example has impacted another generation of students at the Seminary, Kolb has inspired those with whom he works here and abroad not only to strive for greater service to God but to find the joy of the Lord in daily living.

Whether you know the scholar Dr. Kolb, Professor Kolb, Rev. Kolb, the author and editor Robert A. Kolb, or just Bob Kolb, it is the same amiable and honorable man whom we honor with this festschrift. We thank God for his life and work.

Concordia Seminary,
St. Louis, MO, USA.
31 October 2017.
Charles P. Arand, Erik H. Herrmann
and Daniel L. Mattson

From Wittenberg

L'ubomír Batka

Luther's Exposition of Psalms 1–25 at Coburg (1530)

For Martin Luther, the Book of Psalms was the *kleine Biblia,*[1] a never-ending source of divine wisdom which he cherished during his entire life. As he believed the psalms to be texts inspired by the Holy Spirit, in Luther's understanding they contain the word of God and theological doctrine applicable to the life of every individual in any era. Luther returned to the exposition of psalms throughout his life. In a later period such exposition can be found in the *Exposition of Psalms 1–25*, which Luther wrote at Coburg in 1530. Even though this exposition, in terms of its length, does not compare to Luther's extensive lectures, such as the first and second lecture on the psalms (*Dictata super Psalterium,* 1513–1516, and *Operationes in Psalmos,* 1519–1521), it still is an authentic theological work of the Reformer. The work dates back to the time of the Diet of Augsburg and offers a valuable textual basis for a more detailed theological analysis, which has not until now been the subject of research. The analysis of Luther's theology will make it possible to compare Luther's theological thought revealed here with other expositions of the first psalms.

The analysis will be divided into three sections based on the doctrine of Trinity[2] as God the Father, Son and the Holy Spirit speaking. Although Luther does not specifically address the Trinitarian doctrine in the *Exposition of Psalms 1–25*, which can be explained by the shortness of this piece and its context, we will use the thesis of Oswald Bayer to support such structure in this article: "The divine being communicates itself with final validity as a gift and testamental promise in which he himself gives himself to us fully and completely."[3] Bayer offers an alternative for a theology of the Trinity other than an attempt at specifying the timeless relationship between the Father, Son and the Spirit on the

1 WADB 10: 99.24–25.

2 Luther's theology of the Trinity has in recent years become the subject of several studies. The most important ones are listed in Hans-Martin Barth, *Die Theologie Martin Luthers. Eine kritische Würdigung* (Gütersloh: Gütersloher Verlagshaus, 2009), 217, fn. 81.

3 Oswald Bayer, *Gott als Autor: Zu einer poietologischen Theologie* (Tübingen: Mohr Siebeck, 1999), 144.

one hand, or an assumption of subsequently following epochs of the Father, Son and the Spirit on the other hand. Oswald Bayer develops the idea of the so-called "poetological theology," which sees God as the "Poet," thus capturing "the identity of divine speech and action; in his spoken action and performing speech [God] is a poet."[4] Thus laid out, a depiction of God's actions with regard to the actions of God the Father, the Son and the Holy Spirit can be supported by Luther's comment on Psalm 9:7 in *Operationes*, which states that "in the Holy Scripture one has to pay more attention to the verbs than to the nouns, if one wants to understand the Spirit."[5]

In the first section, this article will relate the context in which Luther wrote the exposition. The subsequent three sections will then introduce the character of divine action and the final part will focus on the word of God in relation to man and his spiritual life. It will offer a glance at the praxis of living out one's faith and following Christ in a communicative character based on the word of God. It can be assumed that this procedure will reveal Luther's theology also in the Coburg exposition of psalms.

1. Historical Context

In 1530, Luther was staying at the Coburg fortress, "the southernmost watch point of the Duchy of Saxony,"[6] as he was unable to attend the diet at Augsburg due to the imperial ban. For five months, from Easter until early October, Luther dedicated himself on this personal "Mount Sinai" to theological and exegetical work: the psalms and the prophets.

Short expositions of the first 25 psalms, entitled *Exposition of Psalms 1–25*, also known as the "Coburg Psalms,"[7] were no mere spiritual exercises of the reformer. During his time at Coburg, Luther suffered from health complications

4 Bayer, *Gott als Autor*, 144: "*Um das, was im kritischen Bezug zur Metaphysik und Mythologie zu bedenken ist, positiv zu benennen, gebrauche ich den Gottestitel des 'm das, w, von dem das nizäno-konstantinopolitanische Glaubensbekenntnis redet. Dieser Titel sagt eindrücklich die Identität von Gottes Reden und Handeln; in seinem sprechenden Werk und wirksamen Sprechen ist er 'konst.*"

5 WA 5: 298.11–13. By "*intelligendo spiritu*" Luther actually means the "meaning of the text."

6 Hans Schwarz, *Martin Luther. Úvod do života a diela nášho reformátora* (Liptovský Mikuláš: Tranoscius, 1999), 33. Luther's stay at Coburg is described in Martin Brecht, *Martin Luther: Shaping and Defining the Reformation 1521–1532, vol. 2* (Minneapolis: Fortress Press, 1994), 372–384. Cf. Walter von Loewenich, *Martin Luther: The Man and His Work* (München: List, 1986), 318–329. In 1530 Luther used new edition of the Book of Psalms from Faber Stapulenzis *Quincuplex Psalterium* (1509).

7 Von Loewenich, *Martin Luther*, 324. We know the exact dates when Luther dictated his comments: May 4–6, 11, 14–17, 31, June 1–3, 13, 26, 27, July 1, 10, 13, 17, 18, 22, September 25. and the Exegesis of Ps. 25,12–22, on January 2. in 1531. They were published in 1559.

(headaches).[8] Additionally, Luther was going through spiritual struggles as he tried to comfort his close collaborator, J. Jonas, whose newborn son had died,[9] and W. Link of Nuremberg whose daughter had passed away.[10] He was also deeply troubled by the news of his own father's passing (June 5). According to the testimony of Luther's secretary, Veit Dietrich, who was staying with Luther at Coburg, Luther overcame the difficulties by praying the psalms.[11]

He also became concerned about the church-political situation. It is, therefore, typical of this exposition to link the meaning of particular psalms with the events of his time:[12] the delivery of the reformational confession of faith at Augsburg on June 25,[13] the August Confutation of the Augsburg Confession and subsequent theological and political negotiations. Luther was also troubled by the news of Turkish invasions in 1530. Here, too, Luther found a wellspring of strength and comfort in the psalms (Ps 23:2, Ps 25:3). Dietrich Korsch portrays the situation as "theological tension within Reformation itself [...] between the subjective authenticity of faith and the teaching office established by church regulations."[14]

From among the first 25 psalms, Luther was especially moved by Psalms 2, 8[15], 14[16], 19[17] and 22.[18] It can be said that interpretation of the psalms as prophecies of events unraveling during Luther's time gained prominence here. This adaptation of the psalms to fit his own context drew on the assumption that the psalms are written using "general" or "universal" language and can, therefore, be applied to diverse situations in any given time.[19]

8 WABr 5: 316.1–317, 20n. (May 12, 1530, No. 1566).

9 WABr 5: 318 (May 15, No.1567); WA 31.1: 287.14–17.

10 WABr 5: 349 (June 5, No. 1583).

11 WABr 5: 377 (19. June 1530, Nr. 1595). Heinrich Bornkamm, *Luther in Mid-Career, 1521-1530* (Philadelphia: Fortress Press, 1983), 676, fn. 68. Personal notes in WABr 5:373 (19. June 1530, Nr. 1593) and WATR 6: 369.14–23 (Nr. 7075).

12 WA 31.1: 294.13–17. See for instance WA 31.1: 299.5–8 (Elector George and the Emperor). WA 31.1: 299.11–16 (Luther and Cardinal Cajetan). WA 31.1: 299.19–26 (John Hus). Cf. Ps 17. H. v. Schubert says: "All experience he has gathered up to this point resurface as he meditates on the text and becomes an illustration of God's great deeds as well as deeply ingrained ungodly attitudes of his enemies." Hans Schubert, "*Luther auf der Koburg*," in D. Knolle, *Lutherjahrbuch 1930*, 129.

13 WA 31.1: 289.29–34; WA 31.1: 309.32–24; WA 31.1: 311.28–33; WA 31.1: 373.14–16; WA 31.1: 368.21–22; WA 31.1: 354.19–20; WA 31.1: 355.32–33; WA 31.1: 374.16–17; WA 31.1: 378.16–18.

14 Dietrich Korsch, "*Sic sum. Der Theologie Martin Luther auf der Veste Coburg 1530*," in Dietrich Korsch and Leppin Volker, *Martin Luther – Biographie und Theologie* (Tübingen: Mohr Siebeck, 2010), 183.

15 WA 31.1: 288.2–3.

16 It talks about "the article of justification" (WA 31.1: 310.21–22).

17 It says "everything that could only be said of the gospel" (WA 31.1: 345.28–29).

18 Due to prophesies about the suffering of Jesus Christ (WA 31.1: 353.12–13). Luther accepted without any change Stapulensis' view that David is a prophet (WA 31.1: 353.21–23; WA 31.1: 359.28).

19 WA 31.1: 338.13–35.

The parallels between the content of psalms and real-life examples serve as comparisons. Later expositions of psalms reveal that Luther did not yield to the tendency toward a radical contextualization of the psalms, but offered theologically rich – timeless – interpretations.

During the time of *Operationes*, the question of authority in the Church with regard to Rome became of great importance. Luther placed emphasis on the authority of the Scripture. Between 1522 and 1525, the issue of authority regained importance, owing to the so-called "Radical Reformation."[20] Once again, the issue was which authority was to determine the content of one's faith. The heterogeneous "movement" of those known as *Schwärmer*,[21] with spokespeople such as A. Karlstadt and H. Denck, leaders like T. Müntzer and L. Hätzer, and followers such as the "Zwickau prophets" were connected by several ideas they held in common. Among them was Augustine's *De spiritu et litera*, and a work of German mysticism, *Theologia Deutsch*.[22] In addition to legalistic tendencies in terms of spiritual emphasis, and antiauthoritarian, even anarchist, conduct in the sphere of public law and authorities, the "inner word" became the ultimate authority which inspired new prophecies and was seen as free from the things of this world. Not even the authority of the Scripture was spared from this "blowing of the Spirit." The "mute God" living in "dead Letters"[23] was replaced by an immediate encounter with the Spirit in the exegete, preacher and listener. For T. Müntzer, for instance, "true faith" is based in personal experience of "communicating with God" resting on an "open heart" and it is "the most personal work of a God who reveals himself to one willing to believe."[24]

These events changed Luther's views and he stopped publicly praising *Theologia Deutsch*. At the same time, from 1522 when he wrote the *Wartburg Postil*, a

20 Scott H. Hendrix, *Recultivating the Vineyard: The Reformation Agendas of Christianization* (Lousville; London: Westminster John Knox Press, 2004), 97–121.

21 WA 31.1: 315.21–23; WA 31.1: 346.23–24.

22 Karl-Heinz Zur Mühlen, "*Heiliger Geist und Heilige Schrift bei Thomas Müntzer*," in Johannes Brosseder and Athina Lexutt, *Reformatisches Profil: Studien zum Weg Martin Luthers und der Reformation* (Göttingen: Vandenhoeck & Ruprecht, 1995), 139–150. Zur Mühlen summarizes the difference to Luther's emphasis on 273–274. Cf. Martin Wernisch, *Mystika a reformace: Theologia Deutsch, text a dejinný kontext* (Praha: Vyšehrad, 2007), 99–114; Albrecht Beutel, *Luther Handbuch*, 139–142. Volker Leppin concludes that Karlstadt accepts from Tauler "defining impulses," especially the reference to the connection between "*Gelassenheit, Kreuz und Leiden*." Volker Leppin, "*Mystisches Erbe auf getrennten Wegen: Überlegungen zu Karlstadt und Luther*," 153–169 in Christoph Bultmann, *Luther und das monastische Erbe* (Tübingen: Mohr Siebeck, 2007), 166.

23 Zur Mühlen, "*Heiliger Geist und Heilige Schrift bei Thomas Müntzer*," 265.

24 Walter Elliger, *Außenseiter der Reformation: Thomas Müntzer* (Göttingen: Vandenhoeck & Ruprecht, 1975), 11. Müntzer leaning towards mysticism is also discussed in Reinhard Schwarz, "*Thomas Müntzer und die Mystik*," in Siegfried Brauer and Helmar Junghans, *Der Theologe Thomas Müntzer. Untersuchungen zu seiner Entwicklung und Lehre* (Göttingen: Vandenhoeck & Ruprecht, 1989), 139–142.

strong emphasis on *verbum externum* is felt in a conscious rejection of the Augustinian hermeneutic of *litera* and *spiritus*. The *Exposition of Psalms 1–25* does not provide the opportunity to historically anchor Luther's development. However, research findings are summarized by Albrecht Beutel,[25] who also offers a systematic view of "Divine speech" in the foursome of *verbum aeternum*, the word that God is from time eternal, *verbum creatum*, the word by which the world was created, *verbum scriptum*, in which God reveals himself, and *verbum praedicatum*, through which God comforts and exhorts in sermons and sustains in death.[26] Essentially, this is the relation between *verbum aeternum* and *verbum externum*. How this relation has been understood by Luther in his *Exposition to Psalms 1–25* will be shown in the following lines.

2. Father Rules by Righteousness

In the Coburg Psalms (Ps 2), similarly to *Operationes*, Luther emphasizes the creative power of God's word. God "does everything by word."[27] When God speaks, things happen. And this is true despite the fact that God "creates all *ex nihilo*,"[28] as Luther adds when discussing Ps 9.

Although God himself is hidden from human sight, he allows man to know him as a Creator who gives everything by his grace. He "is righteous, makes righteous, rules in righteousness and bestows righteousness."[29] However, this righteousness is not a mere passive character of God, it is communicated in the realm of divine word.

Adam is the first one given the mandate to rule over the creation (Ps 8:8–9), but because of sin this role is passed on to the new Adam, Jesus Christ.[30] Similarly to *Operationes*, Luther does not take God's blessings to mean a physical "abundance of possessions." Although in specific instances blessings can be physical, Luther never finds this issue as central to his exegesis. Blessings are present in the life of one who lives by the power of the word of God in faith, love, teaching, delight,

25 Beutel, *Luther Handbuch*, 385–394. Compare this also with note 254 and the bibliography it contains. Beutel adds: "*Durchschaut man die nicht zu zählenden Stellen, an denen Luther nach 1525 auf das Verhältnis von Wort und Geist bzw. von verbum externum und verbum internum zu sprechen kommt, so wird rasch deutlich, dass sich an der soteriologisch begründeten Konzentration auf das äußere, mündliche Wort im Wesentlichen nichts mehr geändert hat.*" Beutel, *Luther Handbuch*, 397.

26 Beutel, *Luther Handbuch*, 364 (see also 362–371).

27 WA 31.1: 267.4–5.

28 WA 31.1: 291.12–13; WA 31.1: 291.20.

29 WA 31.1: 290:19–22.

30 WA 31.1: 287.34–36.

perseverance, and endurance. Blessings are related to finding and retaining eternal life.

Further, it needs to be said that when comparing the exposition of Psalm 1 with that in *Operationes*, Luther abandoned the notion of a "listening" and "communicating" creation.[31] This is confirmed in such an exemplary verse as Psalm 19:1, when in both interpretations, Luther understands "the firmament" as "ministers"[32] of the gospel in this world. The Creation doctrine draws on the communicative relation between man and the Creator, who speaks to man and calls him to gratitude for all he has been given by God.[33] Luther's overall focus is on man *coram deo* rather than the whole of creation.

In Luther's Coburg interpretation of psalms we can see a shift in the *hamartiological* emphasis and his definition of the fundamental human sin, viewed through the prism of unbelief in God and his words: "The one who rejects the word rejects all, including God, whose word it is."[34] Man without the word is "corrupt in unbelief."[35] Luther shifts this to the universal level, stating that "all fight against faith" and "we each want to be our own God."[36] Such deeply hostile attitude of man toward God underlies Luther's understanding of original sin, which is, in Luther's theological system, more serious than sinful deeds. In Luther's commentary on Ps 25:11 a more detailed treatment of the original sin, *peccatum originis*, is found. It is *peccatum radicale et capital,*[37] which cannot be escaped. The evil of sin and the evil of man is manifested specifically in this sin rather than in sinful deeds. The "evil" of sin consists in that the man of God becomes "a child of wrath, sin and death."[38] Sin lays snares that lead to one's damnation. Thus, sin becomes an inescapable power for man: "Our heart is our own enemy and our greatest enemy."[39] In the same way the perpetrators of the original sin become external danger for another sinner.[40]

Coram deo sin is a trespass against the Law, therefore it remains true that "the whole world ... is guilty before God, for none is righteous and when [the world] has lost Christ, there is no salvation or grace, all is evil and damned."[41] In

31 WA 5: 34.3–11.
32 WA 31.1: 339.26. Cf. WA 5: 541.26–542.6. Here taken to mean those endowed with ecclesiastical office.
33 WA 31.1: 288.17–20.
34 WA 31.1: 308.4–5. Cf. WA 31.1: 308.10.
35 WA 31.1: 294.9–11.
36 WA 31.1: 272.11–19; WA 31.1: 307.28–29.
37 WA 31.1: 379.16–17.
38 WA 31.1: 294.9–11.
39 WA 31.1: 344.26. Cf. WA 31.1: 344.34–35.
40 WA 31.1: 345.26–27. In addition to the heart as the inner enemy, there are enemies external to ourselves, e.g. false teachers, the flesh and the devil.
41 WA 31.1: 307.24–27. Cf. WA 31.1: 312.38.

Operationes, Luther discovers a reference to the etymological basis of the word *man* (*enosh*) as the one who "forgets."[42] In the Coburg Psalms, however, Luther discusses man in terms of the Hebrew *enosh* only briefly, so that, unfortunately, he remains in the theoretical plane, without further developing the Hebrew meaning of the word theologically.

From what has been said, therefore, it follows that unbelief as "non-faith" is the basic characteristic of sin: "Without faith all are sinners – great sinners."[43] At the same time, there is a certain tension between Luther's "unbelief in the word" and "unbelief in Christ." However, as it remains true that just as God, so also Christ is accessible to man only in God's word, this tension fades. The sin of unbelief in the word of God in reality means that one starts to rely on his own *Werkgerechtigkeit*, the sin thus showing itself in the form of breaking God's first commandment. Man's sin thus effectively doubles itself.[44] "All teachers who stand outside the gospel are proud"[45] and this gives rise to hypocrisy and deception. Those who are proud seemingly seek the *gloria Christi*, but under this guise do no more than seek their own glory.[46] In contrast to one's own righteousness is faith in God's first commandment, connected with faith in God who helps the sinner because of his own kindness: "That is the first commandment, having a merciful God."[47] This line of thought leads to a paradoxical state in which sin is maximized where there is no mention of it and man does not know it or negates it. On the other hand, sin ceases to exist exactly where it is maximized: "God loathes sinners, those sinners who do not want to be sinners. Even though we are all sinful, not all want to be sinners. Those who recognize themselves as sinners have God."[48] This corresponds to the interpretation of Ps 1:4 where Luther distinguishes between what seems to be great *coram hominibus*, that is *coram deo* "dust" and "nothing," because they do not have the Spirit.[49] Even though the term *theologia crucis* does not appear in the *Exposition of Psalms 1–25*, it can be assumed that this essential form of piety, recognizing divine actions *sub contratio* had become a steady component of Luther's theology.[50]

---

42 WA 5: 269.32–35

43 WA 31.1: 308.36.

44 WA 31.1: 272.33–273.2. Cf. WA 31.1: 277.11–12; WA 31.1: 279.12; WA 31.1: 279.33; WA 31.1: 280.7; WA 31.1: 288.20.

45 WA 31.1: 345.1; WA 31.1: 345.12–14.

46 WA 31.1: 345.4–5.

47 WA 31.1: 281.14.

48 WA 31.1: 377.27–29.

49 WA 31.1: 265.17–19.

50 This view is held by R. Kolb who supports his conclusion by an analysis of Luther's expositions from 1532/1533 AD, *In XV Psalmos graduum*, where Luther speaks of the theology of the cross as "our theology" (WA 50.3: 193.6–7, 19–20), and who points out that basic principles, such as *deus absconditus/deus revelatus*, God's revelation in Christ's death on the

Finally, it can be said that in *Operationes* Luther understood faith in God as a type of affection towards God from which follows a proper attitude toward the word of God. The argument can be made that ten years later the word of God gains prominence as reflected in the statement: "Whoever is without the word of God is without faith, and thus without God and the truth."

To summarize, it can be concluded that in 1530 Luther's main emphasis shifts to the preached word as *viva vox* – external word (*verbum externum*), which comes from the outside, from God, through the lips of the minister. In this case the original sin means that every person exists in a continuous struggle between faith and unbelief, negating the primacy of the word of God, either as a tendency towards false teaching, pride, self-righteousness, disrespect with regard to the word of God, mockery of the word, lack of interest in the word, boasting, or as teaching and spreading a false gospel, lies, etc.[51] Luther's interpretation of Psalm 6 sees the consequence of this state before God in that it equates life without the word of God with a life without faith, hope, worship, salvation, and thus also without thanksgiving and praise. This state means that man becomes the object of God's wrath and meets God as a "harsh judge" (*strenger Richter*).[52] For unbelief leads to despair, despair to blasphemy and mockery of God. And that is, in Luther's view, in existential or dogmatic sense, hell. Sin leads man to total destruction of himself. In contrast, Luther can state: Whoever has faith and hope dwells in heaven. In the present time, only in faith and hope, but in the eschaton for real.

3. The Son Becomes Present in the Word

In the Coburg *Psalms* Luther focuses on Christ and the office of his word. While *Operationes* included references to Christ in a broader scope of salvation history, from the creation until the last judgment and eternal reign, ten years later (1530) this broad scope is disappearing. In *Operationes*, for instance, Luther interprets Psalm 2 in a prophetic-historical sense, relating it to the Passover events in the life of Jesus Christ; in his Coburg interpretation, however, Luther does not see Psalm

cross, the necessity of trusting in God's word, God's actions *sub contratio* and day-to-day repentance as a Christian's struggle with Satan, had remained from the period of the Heidelberg disputation and become Luther's hermeneutical instrument in all of his work. Robert Kolb, "Luther's Theology of the Cross: Fifteen Years after Heidelberg; Lectures on the Psalms of Ascent," *Lutheran Quarterly* 61/1, (2010): 85. For theology of the cross, see Hubert Blaumeiser, *Martin Luthers Kreuzestheologie* (Paderborn: Bonifatius, 1995). Von Loewenich, *Luthers theologia crucis* (Witten: Luther Verlag, 1982). Alister McGrath, *Luther's Theology of the Cross: Martin Luther's Theological Breakthrough* (Oxford: Blackwell Publishers, 1985).

51 WA 31.1: 286.21–22. Cf. Ps 12. WA 31.1: 303.34–15; WA 31.1: 308.32–33.

52 WA 31.1: 284.13–14.

2 primarily as a prophecy about the historical Jesus Christ. Starting with Christ and the office of his word, Luther looks at the relevance of Jesus for his own contemporaries, thus reacting to the rejection of evangelical reformation on the part of Rome and the "*Schwärmer.*" Rejection of Christ's word is a rejection of Christ.[53]

What the two mentioned interpretations of Psalm 2 hold in common is an emphasis on the Christological teaching of two natures found in the person of Jesus Christ.[54] From the beginning, there has been unity between the Father and the Son: "Whoever wants to serve God should worship the Son alone. And whoever disrespects the Son also disgraces the Father."[55] The Father, by his authority, called Jesus his "Son" and the apostles did also correctly identify Jesus as the Son of God and the Son by nature.[56] Thus, Jesus is by his nature a true and eternal God,[57] begotten in eternity.[58] His is the whole world according to his divine nature, as well as on the basis of the prophetic word of the Holy Spirit.[59]

God the Father introduces the man Jesus,[60] born without sin[61] as the King of the earth.[62] His kingdom is a "dominion of order and righteousness."[63] As it is a spiritual kingdom, it is not limited by space and spans the entire territory of the earth. Christ's reign is not to be understood as an analogy to earthly rule according to human understanding. After all, this does not even seem as plausible when considering the "historical" Jesus. It can only be understood "by faith and through the word."[64] God becomes present in the Word.

On the other hand, quite typically for the entire emphasis of the Coburg *Psalms*, Christ's spiritual reign is not to be understood in a spiritualist sense only,

53 He makes the same argument in the opening of his exposition of Psalm 5 (WA 31.1: 276.3–9).

54 It is interesting to see the change in his interpretation of Ps 2:6. In *Operationes* Luther treats "Mount Sion" as a synecdoche, based also on its etymology, as the church. (WA 5: 269.1–272.24). Ten years later, this verse is interpreted as a testimony of Christ's true human nature (WA 31.1: 267.37–268.2).

55 WA 31.1: 269.5–6. Cf. WA 31.1: 293.21–22.

56 WA 31.1: 267.28–30.

57 WA 31.1: 267.30.

58 WA 31.1: 268.1.

59 WA 31.1: 268.9–11. Although the connection between the economic and immanent Trinity is not explicitly stated, it is present in Luther's theological thought. Reiner Jansen puts it as follows: "*aus der Offenbarungstrinität wird die imanente Trinität als Bedingung ihrer Möglichkeit erschlossen. […] Theologiegeschichtlich neu ist vor allem die starke Betonung der ökonomischen Trinität, die zu einer Widerbelebung des trinitarischen Denkens führte.*" Reiner Jansen, *Studien zu Luthers Trinitätslehre* (Frankfurt a. Main: Peter Lang, 1976), 225.

60 WA 31.1: 267.23–24.

61 WA 31.1: 357.2.

62 WA 31.1: 267.13–14; WA 31.1: 350.20–21.

63 WA 31.1: 290.1.

64 WA 31.1: 268.18–19. Cf. WA 5: 49.34–36 which states that man should not only find delight in faith and hope, but should also understand them. The same view is voiced in WA 5: 54.9–12.

as though Christ's reign was limited to the stirring of godly hearts. There are many points in this interpretation of psalms that emphasize that the reign of God and the man Jesus Christ is connected with the word: "the kingdom of Christ is in the word and in the spiritual realm."[65] Again, it is true here that Luther does not mean the "inner word of God, the Holy Spirit in a man's heart," but *externum et vocale verbum.*[66] Just as Jesus was a preacher, so too is he the "king of the word" (*rex verbalis*).[67] By his word, Christ does away with the "wisdom of man" and "Moses" and expects that people will accept his word with reverence and joy.[68] This word of Christ is here, more than in *Operationes*, portrayed as the word of the gospel which shall be preached to the entire world.[69] The message of the gospel is "true worship"[70] because it expresses rejoicing over, faith in, and gratitude toward the Son of God.[71] It is, therefore, evident that ministers are not meant to be preaching anything other than the gospel. (As this is *viva vox*; Luther is interested in the voice of man and not of the "voice of the firmament," Ps 19.)

This emphasis on the external word corresponds to a certain extent with the structure of what appeared in *Operationes* as the "theology of the cross." Even though – as it has already been pointed out – the term "theology of the cross" does not appear in this interpretation, the notion of God's hidden saving act on the cross, central to Luther's interpretation in *Operationes*, is still present. Specifically, in Ps 8:5–6: The King is the one "crucified and glorified, dead and risen." Everyone who sees him thinks that "God has turned his face away from him and sees him not." In reality, God remembers him and is with him.[72] Similarly, in Ps 9, which Luther counts among the victory psalms, lauding the victory of the church, God's power is not evidenced by brute strength, but active under the guise of weakness: "through those killed, it kills the living, and through martyrs it brings damnation down on the tyrants."[73]

65 WA 31.1: 285.8; WA 31.1: 334.29.

66 WA 31.1: 362.1.

67 WA 31.1: 362.2–3.

68 WA 31.1: 268.27–32. Luther does not treat joy as a negligible thing. The opposite of joy, sadness, is a serious threat to man's spiritual life. Sadness is dangerous for a young man, "devouring all his senses," making him "sleepy and lazy." It cannot be overcome in any other way besides trusting in "God's mercy and his promises" (WA 31.1: 306.29–307.17). Christ is a king who rules in joy against sin, hell and the devil (WA 31.1: 349.22–25).

69 WA 31.1: 339.14.

70 WA 31.1: 343.6.

71 WA 31.1: 285.14–16; WA 31.1: 288.15–16; WA 31.1: 301.6; WA 31.1: 313.31–314.1.

72 WA 31.1: 287.8–20; WA 31.1: 297.30; WA 31.1. 373.10–12. For more on the Coburg interpretation of Ps 8 see the study by Horst Beintker, "*Gottverlassenheit und Transitus durch den Glauben. Eine Erschließung der Anfechtungen des Menschen Jesus nach Luthers Auslegungen der Psalmen 8 und 22,*" *Evangelische Theologie* 45 (1985): 115–117.

73 WA 31.1: 288.12–13. Por. WA 31.1: 293.12–14.

Luther's views at this time can be explained in the following way: To have God means to have his word and to have his word means to have God. This is realized in the person of Jesus Christ as the Word of God. Where there is Christ, the gospel is being preached. When one believes the gospel, one joins the kingdom of Christ, as in Christ the statement is completely true: "*Natura verbi esse servare nos.*"[74] According to the gospel, there are three places God can surely be found: "In the Gospel, there are three faces: baptism, in which God makes himself known as present, then the visible word, and the sacrament of the altar."[75] This statement has a fundamental theological value as it means that "[God] should only be sought where he has placed himself, otherwise he cannot be found, and he can only be found in his word."[76] However, this could also be said the other way around: when God turns away from man, lost are all the "promises of salvation," "the word of grace and salvation," and man is left to his own defenses in the fight against the devil.[77] This state can also be identified using the theological phrase "wrath of God."

4. The Holy Spirit Is Being Added to the Word

The fact cannot be overlooked that in his *Exposition to Psalms 1–25*, Luther makes less mention of the Holy Spirit than he had in *Operationes.* This can be explained by Luther's own commentary (Ps 19:7): "And this text about the preached word with Christ speaks against the hordes [of fanatics] who want to have the Holy Spirit without the word."[78] The same line of thought is upheld by Luther in Ps 19:11 with reference to Müntzer, who, when interpreting the psalm, "did much speculate, but only about the Spirit, against the external word."[79] As discussions of the Holy Spirit were misused on the part of the enthusiasts, Luther chooses to emphasize the Christocentric aspect of the teaching of righteousness together with the preached gospel of Christ's word. As has already been stated, Christ and his kingdom are overall, and that is why he can affect people without limitations of time and space. This is how he takes care of the believers. However,

74 WA 31.1: 344.19.
75 WA 31.1: 372.31–33.
76 WA 31.1: 327.22–24.
77 WA 31.1: 281.7–11; WA 31.1: 306.13–16.
78 WA 31.1: 341.31–32.
79 WA 31.1: 343.33–34. To Müntzer, the measure of the Spirit was the presence of good fruit. See WA 31.1: 343, note 7., publ. J. Agrikola, *Müntzer's interpretation of Ps 18 in Wittenberg in 1525.* An explicit treatment of the understanding of *verbum internum* in the theology of Karlstadt and Müntzer can be found in Karl-Heinz Zur Mühlen, *Nos extra nos, Luthers Theologie zwischen Mystik und Scholastik* (Tübingen: Mohr Siebeck, 1972), 244–258.

does this apply in the same way to the work of the Holy Spirit? Is Luther deliberately steering clear of the subject of the Holy Spirit?

Luther's theological system, with its emphasis on the external word as the deciding criterion, can be seen from the abovementioned interpretation of Ps 19:2: "The heavens are telling the glory of God." Luther interprets word "glory" to mean "gospel" and "the firmament" as "ministers."[80] It follows from this that "ministers preach the gospel of Jesus Christ" and according to the gospel the idea of "New prophets" is not valid; the Spirit addresses spiritual words directly to the heart of man. Still, we do not find in Luther's interpretations any diminishing of the importance of the Holy Spirit, but rather a specific form of seeking to understand the meaning of the text that agrees with the overall meaning of the Scripture in the sense: *was Christen treibet.* Thus, Luther is more interested in how "the Holy Spirit adds" and "adds grace to that,"[81] when man listens to the word (Luther has in mind listening with our physical ears), than in reflecting on the work of the Spirit guiding the minds of the biblical authors (the inspiration of the Scripture is practically not mentioned at all in the Coburg *Psalms*). In his commentary on Ps 23, Luther makes a statement which points to his reference to the prophetic inspiration of king David through the Holy Spirit.[82] The apparent tension which arises here with regard to restricting the work of the Spirit in new prophets versus old prophets is not discussed here by Luther.

A new characteristic feature should be mentioned here that appears in 1530. It is Luther's emphasis on the authorities and the world order. Luther rejects any spiritual endeavor which seeks to overturn the foundations of the social system. Essentially, he finds such in monks on the one hand, and fanatics on the other hand. The monks do not respect marriage and worldly authorities.[83] By this he

80 WA 31.1: 339.27.

81 WA 31.1: 264.26–27. Cf. WA 31.1: 269.9–10.

82 WA 31.1: 353.21–23. One cannot claim that Luther refrains from speaking about the Holy Spirit because of the *Schwärmer.* When looking at his later disputes, for instance, with the Antinomians, it is obvious that the article concerning the Holy Spirit still played an important role. More truth is perhaps reflected in the statement: "*Es gibt jedoch bemerkenswerte Ähnlichkeiten in Luthers Äußerungen über die verschiedenen Personen der Gottheit. [...] In Luthers Äußerungen zur Pneumatologie hat man eine Analogie zur Christologie erkannt, ja man hat sogar von einem 'inkarnatorischen' Charakter der Pneumatologie Luthers gesprochen.*" in Pekka Kärkkäinen, *Luthers trinitarische Theologie des Heiligen Geistes* (Mainz: Philipp von Zabern, 2005), 134.

83 WA 31.1: 342.18–21; WA 31.1: 346.4–5. Wolfgang Breul comes to an interesting conclusion regarding Luther's marriage and its relation to the peasants' revolts (1525). Breul states that for Luther marriage is instituted by God and thus perceives his own entering into marriage as "a sign of the new gospel order", signifying "the end of a spiritual state." Luther's marriage was thus a "theological sign," not because of stubbornness, but rather because of the "peasants' revolt." Wolfgang Breul, "*Es ist verloren der geystlich standt,*" in Dietrich Korsch and Volker Leppin, *Martin Luther – Biographie und Theologie* (Tübingen: Mohr Siebeck, 2010), 166. Hans-Martin Barth presents two reasons why Luther rejected the peasants' revolts:

means celibacy and removing the management of monasteries from the jurisdiction of princes. As for the fanatics, although Luther does not state specific facts, when considering the chiliastic moments of Müntzer's visions and Anabaptist pacifism[84] it can be assumed that the emphasis on the worldly regiment is in place here.

Luther's attitude towards authorities is revealed in his exposition of Psalm 20. Luther goes into quite some detail concerning four things that regard the authorities: God finds delight in authorities, God protects the authorities, it is necessary to pray for the authorities, and this "state" is very demanding.[85] The devil is an enemy of the authorities, as he does not tolerate rest and peace. Authorities create peace for those who can benefit from it. However, the authorities themselves cannot find rest and peace. This is an imitation of God's reign in this world.[86] Even in his interpretation of the well-known Ps 23 Luther takes into account the two-fold nature of authority: the minister's office (*ministerio verbi*) of the church and worldly government (*politia*).[87] The Lord is the shepherd on both the spiritual and the earthly plane. If God acts in the sphere of worldly government and uses it as an instrument to do his will, how much more does the same apply to the Church.

The emphasis on the *verbum externum* was already clearly articulated in *Operationes*, as seen in Luther's commentary on Ps 2:11. The preached word – as the word of the cross – served a two-fold purpose in bringing into question the sinner's (self-)righteousness and in working for the salvation of those who believe the word (1 Cor 1:21). Ten years later, in 1530, this aspect of the external form of the message becomes the alpha and omega of Luther's theological thought. Christ "exercises his power solely through 'the mouth, speech, and words.'"[88] All the while it remains true that the minister's own abilities, similarly to *Operationes* (WA 5: 258.27–31), are irrelevant and remain in the background. Within the context of Ps 8:3 Luther interprets the phrase "little children" once again as

"*seine im Römerbrief (Röm 13) begründete Sicht der Obrigkeit und seine Ablehnung einer Mystik, sie ohne Bibel, ja ohne Christus auskommen kann. […] die Ablehnung der Müntzerschen Mystik ergab sich für ihn zwangsläufig aus seinem Verständnis des Evangeliums.*" Barth, *Die Theologie Martin Luthers*, 84.

84 M. Wernisch aptly summarizes that the Müntzerian movement entails revolutionary and separatist tendencies, which resulted in "sectarianism which knew no tolerance and which could not be tolerated." Martin Wernisch, *Politické myšlení evropské reformace* (Praha: Vyšehrad, 2011), 70 (cf. 69–76). The chiliastic resolution to Christianize Europe as shared by Müntzer, Hut, Hoffman, Rothmann and the Münster Melchiorites is discussed by Hendrix, *Recultivating the Vineyard*, 108.

85 WA 31.1: 345.33–346.1.

86 WA 31.1: 346.1–8.

87 WA 31.1: 367.19–20.

88 WA 31.1: 285.26–27. Therefore it is possible to call the gospel "God's power," in the same vein as Paul did, which is an argument that already appeared in *Operationes* (WA 5: 537.21).

meaning "ministers of God's word." Thus, he is voicing the idea that their power and the power of their office does not dwell with them alone, but rather in the power of the word that they preach. For this reason, that they alone are weak, the power of the word becomes more obvious (1 Cor 1:27).[89] It is not the words of the holy man that bring a blessing, but rather that holy words are a blessing to man.

Ministers are, similarly to *Operationes,*[90] instruments of God's working. They draw on what they have received and their mission can be compared to being the protectors of the purity of the word,[91] rather than those who create the word. This means they are called to "speak nothing but truth and to stay away from false sermons and words, to take nothing away from the word and not to corrupt the word." In order for them not to "corrupt the Scripture" they need God's highest grace.[92]

When commenting on Ps 12:7 in *Operationes,* Luther expresses the idea that apart from interpreting the Scriptures there is another way in which God speaks to man, where no interpretation of the Scriptures is involved. It is good to remind ourselves of Luther's statement made in *Operationes* that "all that God says through man, whether learned or not, even without the use of Scripture, as he spoke through the apostles and still speaks through those who belong to him"[93] is the word of God. This stream of thought has been abandoned by Luther in his *Exposition of Psalms 1–25* written at Coburg and his attitude can be summed up in the words of Hans Schwarz: "Luther does say that only people led by the Holy Spirit can interpret Scripture. This Spirit, however, comes to them through Scripture alone."[94]

Without going back to the idea of "twittering" (*garrire*) *expresis verbis,* Luther does essentially remain faithful to this notion and even expands it by adding the aspect of the poetic ability of man: "It is a great grace when man delights in

89 WA 31.1: 286.9–10; WA 31.1: 331.16–19. In spite of this, Luther expects ministers to be "pious" (*fromm*) WA 31.1: 303.29–30.

90 WA 5: 257.17; WA 5: 258,1–2.

91 Philipp Melanchthon says in Chapter 3 of *Loci communes* "*De lege*" that rather than being a "teacher" he wants to be a "reminder" of what is found in the Scripture because the Scripture is the "wellspring" and contains "sweeter," "purer," and "more reliable" words than the theological works of men. He likens "commentaries" to puddles of mud. This statement captures the point of the Renaissance "*ad fontes*" on the one hand, and the essence of the how Reformation understood ministerial – even teaching – activities on the other hand. Philipp Melanchthon, *Loci communes 1521,* 2nd ed., Lateinisch-Deutsch. transl. H.G. Poehlmann, (Gütersloh: Gütersloher Verlagshaus, 1993), 98–101.

92 WA 31.1: 311.19–24. Cf. WA 31.1: 342.32–343.2. Pure gospel, a term that appears in so prominent a place as AV 7, (*das lauter rein Euangelium*) means "without falsehood" (*kein falsch*) and "without hypocrisy" (*heucheley*), "untainted by any human tradition" (*nullis traditionibus hominum contaminatum*). It is similar to "pure actions." WA 31.1: 343.9–11.

93 WA 5: 379.8–10.

94 Hans Schwarz, *Martin Luther,* 114.

listening to the word [of God], writes poems about it, speaks [*schwetzet*] and sings about it."[95] This is a broad understanding of the word of God: "meditation," "preaching," "writing," "reading."[96] As can be seen, all these verbs relate to the "outward" manner of dealing with the word. We can even say that the essence of evangelical spirituality is being formed here. Such man is a "pious man."[97] The words of Ps 19 offer Luther a chance to underline that the message of the gospel is not limited by space, time, or language ("the gospel needs to be preached in German, Saxon, Bavarian, Swabian, etc.").[98]

The decisive factor is that preaching should be truly based on God's word, for only then can the preacher say with peace of mind: "Thus says the Lord!"[99] To avoid any misunderstanding, Luther's attitude should not be understood as operating *ex opere operato*. Similar to *Operationes*, once again Luther continues to stress that preaching needs to be followed by prayer, as another way of "external" manipulation of the word: "*Orare est secundum opus post praedicationem.*"[100] What the prayer does is refer to the will of God and leave room for the Holy Spirit to act as and when he pleases, where word has been preached. For "prayer causes our preaching to have effect."[101] The Holy Spirit is added to the word in a way that reminds one of the statement made by J. Hilburg that "the Spirit and the word are effective only when they are connected like two poles in the electric circuit. An electric circuit is only closed when both connecting cords are present. This is something Luther continually emphasized, especially later, during his fight against the *Schwärmer*."[102]

It is necessary to deal in greater detail with the question of the place where the preaching should take place in the process of salvation. While in *Operationes* the content of the preaching alternated between "law," "gospel," and "grace," ten years later this distinction is replaced by the pair: "law" and "gospel." A more articulated distinction between the functions of the law and the gospel is another

95 WA 31.1: 264.19–21.
96 WA 31.1: 292.32–33.
97 WA 31.1: 264.25.
98 WA 31.1: 340.24–25.
99 WA 51: 517.5–16.
100 WA 31.1: 363.7.
101 WA 31.1: 276.13–14; WA 31.1: 345.4–8.
102 Johannes Hilburg, *Luther und das Wort Gottes in seiner Exegese und Theologie dargestellt auf Grund seiner Operationes in psalmos 1591/21 in Verbindung mit seinen früheren Vorlesungen.* (Marburg-Lahn: self-published, 1948), 111: "*[Hierbei ist besonders zu beachten], daß Geist und Wort nur in Verbindung zueinander wirksam sind wie die Pole eines elektrischen Stromes. Der Stromkreis ist nur dann geschlossen, wenn beide Verbindungsdräthe vorhanden sind. Das hat Luther vor allem später im Kampf gegen die Schwärmer mit allem Nachdruck betonen müssen.*"

important characteristic of Luther's later period.[103] This could be expressed in the following manner: what seemed as "*Doppelwerk* of the gospel" in *Operationes*, is transformed here into "*Doppelwerk* of the word" (as law and gospel).

Of the law, Luther speaks in the following manner: God does not judge according to appearance, but considers the "motives of one's heart" (*affectiones*) and "thoughts" (*cogitationes*). As a "harsh judge" (*strenger Richter*), he knows the thoughts man harbors in his heart and the tendencies he leans toward.[104] His judgment consists of two aspects: "to save the innocent" and "to destroy the guilty ones."[105] Such statements faithfully capture the weight Luther attributes to God's judgment and are more than a part of Luther's idiolect. They have an inseparable share in his theological thought. Law is an instrument of God's judgment in that it convicts man of sin. The guilt, as *reatus*, should be understood as part of the divine judgment. The Law of Moses is unchanging (*ohne Wandel*), by which Luther means that some of its parts correspond to the natural law and thus remain valid without change. In his Coburg exposition, Luther is concerned primarily with the effect of law (towards salvation). *Ohne Wandel* refers to the fact that law cannot make people perfect, nor does it comfort man's soul, but rather oppresses it.[106]

If the judgment is "to save the innocent," the questions arises: What does Luther see as innocence? A significant change can be seen in comparison with *Operationes*, where Luther interprets Ps 4:6 ("sacrifice of righteousness") as "admission and confession of sins," i.e., "the opposite of self-righteous deeds."[107] In a later interpretation, however, it is understood as "faith." Not that Luther is abandoning his criticism of human deeds misused in the process of salvation! Especially in his interpretation of Ps 5, Luther vehemently sets himself against deeds of righteousness. In a manner typical for him, Luther generalizes and calls into question the faith of papists, monks, Turks, Jews, fanatics, and "all who do not believe"[108] because theirs is a religion of deeds. "They do not have the word of God, they do not teach it, and therefore they do not keep it either."[109] Clearly, in

---

103 WA 31.1: 353.18–20. In his suffering, Christ brought "the end of law and the beginning of the gospel," which marks a clear-cut distinction between the functions of the law and the gospel.

104 WA 31.1: 284.4–6; WA 31.1: 302.30–33.

105 WA 31.1: 284.13–14; WA 31.1: 323.19–23.

106 WA 31.1: 342.6–9. See as well WA 31.1: 342.2–5.

107 WA 5: 114.22–25. Cf. WA 5: 114.28–29. The heart must accept, the mouth confess, and man must prove himself by his deeds.

108 WA 31.1: 277.33–34. Ps 5:9 contains a reference to the Strasbourg apostates. Luther might be referring to the events surrounding his *Brief an die Christen zu Straßburg wider den Schwärmergeist*. See Brecht, *Martin Luther*, vol. 2, 163–165.

109 WA 31.1: 295.16–17; WA 31.1: 307.32–308.2. There is a shift here from the rhetoric of *Operationes*, where Luther addresses general ignorance with regard to "God" in Ps 14. Ten years later, he moves toward "the word of God." His note that "whoever rejects the word of

the Coburg *Psalms* Luther departs from *Operationes,* in which he made clear references to specific teachings of the scholastic school. In the Coburg exposition these are not present; instead one can find here a greater tendency to make sweeping statements and generalizations regarding the opinions of his "opponents."

In 1530, Luther expresses his unswerving conviction that the law and its observance is not the path to righteousness. The true church teaches that people "are justified without deeds, through faith in Christ."[110] The gospel is the message that "we are saved and reconciled through Christ's blood alone." This message turns the glory of this world into *nihilum,*[111] but that is not the main role of the gospel. The gospel is a creative word, giving life where there was no life. "We live by promise alone that God finds delight in us and that he has given us his beloved Son for our reconciliation."[112]

In the Coburg exposition, the subject of "reconciliation" is present along with thoughts on the connection between Christ's suffering and human sin. Without further clarification, Luther states: "Christ suffered for our sins and because of our sins."[113] In another place, where Luther claims: Through his suffering, Christ has "earned" salvation and in his resurrection, he "paid back" the debt,[114] it can be asserted that Christ's death appears as the bearing of the "punishment" reserved for "guilty sinners." The weight of Christ's suffering is portrayed as dramatically as it had been ten years earlier. Christ's deep humiliation, so that he gave up all honor in the eyes of this world, to be trampled as a worm,[115] signifies the greatest suffering, rejection, mockery, celebration and triumph of his enemies.[116] Nowhere in Luther's words is it indicated that Christ's death is of significance in relation to the "calming of God's wrath." In the foreground stands the substitutionary nature of his death. It is not possible to fit all of Luther's statements into a single "theory of salvation." We can find statements, for instance, that might imply that Luther has in mind Abelard's theory of the so-called "moral influence," when he says that Jesus Christ "teaches people to fear God and trust God and love one another and bear the cross, and [thus] reinstates righteousness and order."[117] In Ps 19:6 a reference is found to Jesus as the bride-

God also rejects God himself" bridges over the two interpretations. It confirms the claim that in 1530 Luther puts greater emphasis on *verbum externum.* WA 31.1: 332.27–30.

110 WA 31.1: 277.9.

111 WA 31.1: 339.31–340.1. Luther bases his claim on the argument that the glory of the world is sin, evil, and shame and we cannot speak of human effort and deeds before God.

112 WA 31.1: 277.11–12.

113 WA 31.1: 354.32–33.

114 WA 31.1: 313.26–27.

115 WA 31.1: 355.29 34.

116 WA 31.1: 356.19–20.

117 WA 31.1: 290.5–7. On the one hand, Luther states that one cannot know God without "faith"

groom: "the Son of righteousness" and "the bride" he takes to be his wife. Although Luther does not directly speak here of a "joyful exchange," in this interpretation he does not refer in these words to "man" (or "Mary"), but "the church," which he adorns with a hidden joy.[118] The statement that Jesus is our brother (Ps 22:23) also appears to be a variant of the joyful exchange, as implied in it is the claim that all that is his also belongs to the believers.[119]

As has already been said, the main emphasis of Luther's claims is directed toward the subject of righteousness. God is, therefore, the "God of righteousness," because it is by his grace that he "justifies in sin and comforts in suffering."[120] With regard to the terminology, the term "salvation" is absent. It can, however, be said that the gospel is an instrument of salvation in the sense that it has the power to "comfort" and bring joy. "It perfects people and comforts them, ridding the heart of sad thoughts, and it is true and certain."[121] The righteousness that the psalms address is "no small righteousness" (*valde tenuis iustitia*), nor is it the righteousness of the "lawyers," as regards the seven commandments of the second tablet of the Law (*valde tenuis iustitia*), but rather "the great righteousness of God."[122]

In agreement with what has been said so far concerning faith and unbelief, it is understandable that faith gains crucial importance in the process of justification. In the same way as his interpretation of the first commandment in the *Small Catechism*, Luther explains what faith means: "to believe God by having trust, faith and hope in Him."[123] Trust, which attributes everything to God on the basis of the message of the gospel concerning God's merciful affection for sinful people as shown and realized in Jesus Christ, shifts the whole weight of the saving action to God.

The reason why this is so is quite understandable too. The conviction of the radical nature of the original sin remains unchanged during Luther's stay at Coburg. In this interpretation of the psalms, the "indelible" nature of the original sin gains ground. There is only one medicine against the original sin, to live *sub gratia*,[124] for sin remains in man even after baptism, even though man believes. The difference is that sin remains but "is no longer master over us." A believing

(WA 31.1: 332.30–31), on the other hand, he claims that one cannot know God without "the word" (WA 31.1: 333.6). As faith comes from the word, it can be said that the word is superior.

118 WA 31.1: 341.11–14.

119 WA 31.1: 361.6–8.

120 WA 31.1: 272.29–30. Cf. WA 31.1: 273.2–4.

121 WA 31.1: 342.9–12.

122 WA 31.1: 290.2–4. WA 31.1: 372.11–12.

123 WA 31.1: 274.20–21. The legal and theological justice is also mentioned in WA 31.1: 347.22–30. Cf. WA 31.1: 290.8: "*Iustitia autem est credere.*" Cf. WA 31.1: 303.15.

124 WA 31.1: 379.24–25.

man rules over it, but in reality, this means an everyday struggle for the rest of one's life.

From the point of view of this world, but also from that of those "too spiritual," faith delimited in this way appears as weak. The remaining sin seemingly negates the power of God's word (and the sacraments). Luther reflects on these objections, replying in turn that faith on this earth cannot be absolute. He supports his theological stance by referring to Rom 7:23 and stating: "if Paul speaks thus, so too should we."[125] Luther saw Rom 7 as proof that sin remains rooted even in a Christian's life. Paul did not speak here of the will of the natural man before he believes. As man can never free himself from sin completely, he has to pray that God would not "count" against him the sin that remains.[126] In *Operationes* Luther offers an important thesis: "the cross is our theology."[127] In his Coburg interpretation, however, this claim shifts its meaning to the context of justification: "*Hoc est theologia nostra, sicut oramus: 'Dimitte nobis debita nostra.'* "[128] By this he means that the original sin remains, but God no longer "counts" it against people (*non imputat*). In contrast, if man is unwilling to admit his own sinfulness, God "counts" it against him.[129] A crucial question offers itself here whether we are dealing with a shift in Luther's teaching on justification towards an "imputation" or "forensic" theory. The text of the exposition of psalms does not offer a clear answer. The lasting nature of the original sin and objections that this is a case of weak faith lead Luther to consider the nature of faith. He remarks that even though our faith is weak (*infirmes*), it is not untrue (*unechter*).[130] This is not his statement concerning his own faith. He means it as a general remark in the sense: The weakness of faith does not call into question its existence, and thus even small faith is sufficient for salvation. Small faith is not inferior to "unswerving" faith, as though it were deficient with regard to God's "crediting" Christ's righteousness to us. The point of imputative aspect of justification is to maximize divine action and minimize man's share. It is understandable that with regard to fanatics, Luther attempts to define the essence of justification in a way that would be understood quite the opposite way: not by claiming righteousness as one's own or as having been completed.

125 WA 31.1: 379.12–13.
126 WA 31.1: 344.31–33. WA 31.1: 345.12–17.
127 WA 5: 176.32: "*Crux sola est nostra Theologia.*"
128 WA 31.1: 379.35–36.
129 WA 31.1: 379.33–35.
130 WA 31.1: 331.17.

5. The Believer Teaches Correctly

In the *Exposition of Psalms 1–25* we can notice two lines of emphasis on the typical attitudes toward the word of God in the psalms. In Luther's view, the word of God is not only being preached in the psalms, but it is also being taught and expressed as both "message" and "doctrine." This connection between preaching and doctrine (*doctrina*) is closer in the Coburg exposition than in *Operationes*. What the two have in common is the gospel.[131] Pure doctrine (*pura doctrina*), in Luther's view, is like pure gospel, meaning "without falsehood" (*kein falsch*) and "without hypocrisy" (*heucheley*), "without contamination by human tradition" (*nullis traditionibus hominum contaminatum*).[132] Good doctrine, as Luther says, is like evergreen leaves because it offers counsel, teaching, and consolation for everyone,[133] in which once again the similarity between "doctrine" and the "message" of the gospel becomes evident. Luther does not offer a specific example of a "pure" doctrine. At first sight, it is a category that is hard to grasp. The criterion of whether or not the content is pure, correct, and good, is the efficacy toward the good and for the benefit of mankind. Although Luther does not specifically make this claim, the analogy with the work of the gospel applies here in that merely formal reference to the letter is not sufficient. With doctrine, too, the goal is the salvation of mankind. The analogy cannot be made, however, with regard to the status of the two, as the word of God is principially superior to doctrine. Doctrine is thus aimed toward mankind, not God.

For a better understanding of Luther's train of thought a comparison with what Luther perceives as the opposite, i. e., false doctrine, can be helpful. Sects do not remain in the position of a "student" (and listener to the word of God), and thus do not remain in the "service" and in "office," by which Luther means the office of the true word (*officio recti verbi*).[134] Sectarianism and division is seen by Luther as confirmation of the absence of pure word (and the Spirit who gives unity). Once again it is confirmed that the word is superior to doctrine.[135]

But, in the world around us we can encounter also blasphemy, represented by tyrants, enemies, persecutors, but also one's own sinfulness, as the believer's faith

131 WA 31.1: 285.10–11.

132 WA 31.1: 342. 32–343.2.

133 WA 31.1: 264.30–31. For Luther's understanding of doctrine see the study from Richard Bucher, *The Ecumenical Luther: The Development and Use of His Doctrinal Hermeneutic* (St. Louis: Concordia Publishing House, 2003), 19–59.

134 WA 31.1: 265.20–22; WA 31.1: 301.2–4.

135 This is also confirmed by the statement that "the devil can often snatch away the Scripture with a single word" (WA 31.1: 305.24–25. Cf. WA 31.1: 312.24. WA 31.1: 368.18–20). The point here is that the primary problem rests in the understanding of God's word rather than discussing human interpretations.

and hope enter a struggle.[136] According to Luther, blasphemy is such speech that aims to call into question the trustworthiness of God's word in a brute manner. Luther compares such words to the poisonous words causing *tribulatio verbi.* If false doctrine is not good because it does not offer good counsel, teaching, and delight, so blasphemy is not good because it torments the soul of the believer.[137] If a man should lose faith and hope, if he should not have the word and stop calling out to God, he would be in a state that can be likened to "hell."

Despite all this, the cross is part of every Christian's life, it leads to "exercising one's faith," which teaches one "to trust God."[138] We can assume here that this emphasis on external struggles and the experience of the cross should be viewed against the "internalized" experience of God as spoken of by Müntzer. Unlike mysticism, in which divine presence is evidenced by feelings of delight, Müntzer spoke of the living voice of God in the Son of God as the suffering Lamb of God. Suffering as the process of purification is of importance, but it occurs as the "internal" voice of God.[139] "To be able to trust God when all is well is no great achievement. But in suffering, when things do not go well? It could be seen as the chastening rod and to say in those times: Dear father, that is a feat."[140] If a Christian were to flee suffering, he cannot find Christ. Christ also went through the "experience of suffering," was strengthened by the word of God to the extent that he "endured" in suffering, learned "obedience" and became the first true doctor [of theology].[141] A variant of the theology of cross can be found in Luther's

136 WA 31.1: 280.18–21. This experience (*experientia*) can be likened to death and can thus be seen as superior to Scholastic dialectics without "experience." When analyzing the interpretation of Ps 6, H. C. Knuth concludes that this view was held by Luther from 1517 until his statements at the table in 1530, as well as the *Coburg Psalms* (WA 31.1: 281.3–5). Hans Christian Knuth, *Zur Auslegungsgeschichte von Psalm 6.* (Tübingen: Mohr Siebeck, 1971), 222. The developments in Luther's translation of Ps 6 starting with the *Exposition of the Seven Penitential Psalms* (1517) are discussed by Heinz Bluhm, "The Evolution of Luther's Translation of the First Penitential Psalm," in Heinz Bluhm, *Studies in Luther. Luther Studien* (Frankfurt a. Main: Peter Lang, 1987), 109–122.

137 WA 31.1: 270.18–25; WA 31.1: 273.13–14. Even though the ungodly do not fear God, this does not mean they have no fear. They are afraid of other things. Fear is a common symptom of unbelief (WA 31.1: 309.24–29).

138 WA 31.1: 269.21–24. Cf. WA 31.1: 290.14–16; WA 31.1: 305.11–20; WA 31.1: 314.12–18; WA 31.1: 315. Luther teaches in the same vein in *Operationes: "Crux probat omnia"* (WA 5: 179.31).

139 Schwarz, "Thomas Müntzer und die Mystik," in Bräuer, *Der Theologe Thomas Müntzer*, argues (291): "*Werden die äußeren Vermittlungen des geistlichen Lebens von den Mystikern relativiert, so werden sie bei Müntzer zum Gegenstand von scharfer Polemik. An zwei Fronten kämpft er gegen äußere Vermittlungen des Geistwirkens Gottes, an der einen Front gegen die altgläubige Berufung auf objektiv sakramentale Geistvermittlung, an der anderen Front gegen die Wittenberger Berufung auf eine den Heiligen Geist vermittelnde und den Glauben weckende Verkündigung des Evangeliums.*"

140 WA 31.1: 269.26–28.

141 WA 31.1: 317.5–12.

claims stating that the faithless do not suffer the cross but live in pleasures. As soon as trust in God's word is found, so too is the cross, suffering, hatred, jealousy, slander, shame, sad thoughts, blasphemy.[142] This line of thought has to do with Luther's historical experience. In *Operationes,* experience (*experientia*) is used to mean spiritual struggles; ten years later these struggles are "externalized." They appear from outside and take place in the external sphere. It would be right to ask, however, if Luther's view might not be merely a simplified interpretation of reality, or perhaps a negative twist of the "joyful exchange" in the world. If there is a theological model that led Luther in this direction, it could be the notion that "divine action takes place *sub contraria.*" Often it seems that God loves the world, which receives many gifts from God, and forgets about his own.[143]

An example from the natural world that Luther gives of a farmer who feeds his swine better than his son despite the fact that he loves his son more, while the fattened pig is readied for slaughter, is intended to comfort the "sons."[144] We can assume that Luther did not intend to evoke such theological consequences from this statement that would imply that God leads this world for the benefit of those who belong to him. The point here is rather that God, not man, enacts judgment on the enemies. The enemies are primarily "enemies of the word." Judgment over them takes place in no other manner than through the word.[145] Victory means that the enemies will "descend into hell." What seems at first a harsh and unacceptable wish is endowed with a spiritual meaning. Descent into hell means the realization of one's sin and the judgment of God, which leads to repentance and turning of the enemies (of the word) to the word, faith and righteousness: "I do not want them to perish, but be reformed: I want them to confess their sins."[146]

God will enact his judgment, but not immediately. For a Christian, therefore, two things remain – "prayer" and "faith" – which are needed in all suffering. The connection of two "mighty weapons" also helps in that faith protects from despair and prayer give strength to overcome suffering.[147] Prayer, even if it takes on

142 WA 31.1: 320.13–18.

143 To be abandoned by God means to be abandoned by all that belongs to God (life, wisdom) and thus also to remain in all that belongs to man (death, sin, guilt, folly) (WA 31.1: 353.33–354.3).

144 WA 31.1: 273.29–37. This can be seen from the statement: "*Das thut er seinen Heiligen, die er lieb hat.*" Cf. WA 31.1: 276.2–3.

145 WA 31.1: 292.29–293.1. Cf. WA 31.1: 304.7–305.3.

146 WA 31.1: 293.11–12.

147 WA 31.1: 271.8–9. Cf. WA 31.1: 272.25–26; WA 31.1: 276.13–14. Even with regard to false teaching, there is no "weapon" apart from "*verbum externum and vehemens oratio.*" WA 31.1: 321.22–30. The same is true of managing worldly affairs and successful actions of the authorities (WA 31.1: 346.18–20).

the form of a complaint (Ps 6, Ps 23), is necessary as "the devil is too strong, the body too weak, and the world too evil" for man to stand.[148]

Faith protects from despair, thus where there is faith, there is hope. When Luther speaks of hope in this exposition, it is obvious that he is no longer thinking in terms of the categories of "theological virtues" and sees "hope" as giving up wanting to see (thus hoping).[149] Faith itself does not need to see. Its essence lies not in itself, for it is the faith in the "friendly word" of God.[150] The word here is *dabar* – word and deed, so only a word is needed and man can live again – this is the power no human words have, because it is by the word of God that "everything is sanctified, [...] without the word of God nothing is holy."[151] This statement captures not only the the essence of Christian life *coram hominibus*, but also *coram deo*. The word of God is at the center of Luther's theology even in the *Exposition of Psalms 1–25*.

6. Conclusion

It is typical for Luther's theology found in his *Exposition of Psalms 1–25* at Coburg to interpret the psalms in relation to the events he was experiencing. At the forefront is interpretation of the psalms as prophecies of events unfolding in Luther's own time. The troubled events surrounding the *Schwärmer* movement and the Peasants' War changed Luther's direction of thought in that he gave up publicly praising *Theologia Deutsch* and turned his attention to the relation between *verbum aeternum* and *verbum externum*.

Increasingly, Luther is growing interested in man before God (*coram deo*), and creation as such recedes into background. In his exposition written at Coburg, one can see a shift in the *hamartiological* emphasis and in defining human sin not only as unbelief in God and Jesus Christ, but rather as a state of unbelief in God and his word. The word of God and the theology of the word of God do not serve as the foundation for a theoretical theological discourse. The word of God gains primacy in the sense that anyone who does not have the word of God is without faith and thus without God and the truth. In contrast, to have God means to have his word, and to have his word means to have God.

Implied here is the connectedness of Luther's theology of the word to the person of Jesus Christ. Where there is Christ, there the gospel is being preached to the people. If one believes the gospel, he belongs in Christ's kingdom, because

148 WA 31.1: 322.20.
149 WA 31.1: 274.22–23.
150 WA 31.1: 275.11–13. Cf. WA 31.1: 275.26.
151 WA 31.1: 263.11–12.

in Christ the statement is completely true: "*Natura verbi esse servare nos*"(WA 31.1: 344.19). Even though *Exposition of Psalms 1–25* does not feature the term *theologia crucis*, we can argue that this essential form of piousness recognizing God's actions *sub contratio* has become a steady part of Luther's theology. Sin is greatest where no mention is made of it and man does not know it or negates it. On the other hand, sin disappears there where its realization is maximized. This dialectic is related to a more emphatic distinction between the functions of the word of the law and the gospel, which is another important characteristic of Luther's later period.

The law turns the glory of the world into "nothing." The main office of the word of the gospel is to create and bring life to where there is none. Trust, which attributes everything to God based on the gospel message of God's gracious affection for sinful people as made known and realized in Jesus Christ, shifts the weight of the entire saving action to God in Trinity. The Trinitarian aspect of God's speaking is inseparable from the language of the Scripture in this interpretation. Owing to growing spiritualist misuse, however, we can see Luther taking greater care when discussing the Holy Spirit. Knowing God in Trinity is connected to the written word of the Scripture. On the other hand, the Spirit gives the right interpretation of the word.

God's word is the only guarantee of true hope and true life. The nature of the external form of the message becomes, in this period, the alpha and omega of Luther's theological thought. Christ rules "by word alone." At the same time, it remains true that the abilities of the minister are irrelevant, but remain in the background. It is not true that the words of a holy man are a blessing, but rather that holy words are a blessing to man. Thus, it is understandable that Luther emphasizes a broadly conceived discussion of the word of God as "meditation," "preaching," "writing," "reading," and all other "external" methods of dealing with the word. We can say that we are talking here about the essence of evangelical spirituality.

The second central aspect of dealing with God's word on the part of the believers is *doctrina*. The connection between preaching and doctrine in the Coburg exposition is much closer than in *Operationes*. What is new here is the emphasis on authorities and worldly order. Luther rejects all spiritual efforts which undermine the foundation of social order. God finds delight in authorities, protects them; it is a challenging "state" for which one should pray. Not only in this sphere, but also on the personal level spiritual struggles can be found. Luther's emphasis on external struggles and the experience of the cross must be viewed against the backdrop of an "internalized" experience of God as spoken of by Müntzer. If a Christian were to flee from (external) suffering, he would not be able to find Christ. Christ, too, went through the "school of suffering," was strengthened by God to the point that he endured suffering, learned obedience and became a true doctor [of theology]. The communicative character of the life form of faith and following Christ is based on the word of God, which alone is the instrument of God's righteous reign, the Son's presence and the work of the Holy Spirit in the world. The word of God is at the center of Luther's theology in the *Exposition of Psalms 1–25* (1530).

Amy Nelson Burnett

"Instructed with the Greatest Diligence Concerning the Holy Sacrament"

Communion Preparation in the Early Years of the Reformation

> The people are instructed more regularly and with the greatest diligence concerning the holy sacrament, to what purpose it was instituted, and how it is to be used, namely, as a comfort to terrified consciences. In this way, the people are drawn to Communion and the Mass.[1]

So asserted the Augsburg Confession in 1530, in response to charges that the Lutherans had abolished the Mass. Most readers see in this statement an allusion to the evangelical catechisms that were produced from the mid-1520s on. The catechism was a new genre: a short work, usually printed in octavo format, that used question and answer to teach children the rudiments of the Christian faith, defined as the Apostles' Creed, the Lord's Prayer, the Ten Commandments, and the two evangelical sacraments of baptism and the Lord's Supper.[2] Cheaply produced, used to the point of disintegration, and not valued enough to be preserved in library collections, these pamphlets are among the most ephemeral of early printed works.[3] A number of catechisms are extant in only one copy, and it is virtually certain that others have disappeared without a trace. At the other end of the spectrum, Luther's Large and Small Catechisms, first published in the spring of 1529, would become especially important for shaping evangelical religious instruction over the course of the sixteenth century.[4]

1 KW, 68.

2 Foundational for understanding the development of the evangelical catechism through the 1520s is the source edition and "summarizing presentation" of Ferdinand Cohrs, *Die evangelischen Katechismusversuche vor Luthers Enchiridion,* 4 vols. in 2 (Olms: Hildesheim, 1978; repr. of Berlin, 1900–1907). Cohrs limited his catechism edition to material intended for the instruction of children, however, which has made it more difficult for later scholars to see the influence of other types of religious instruction on the development of the genre.

3 On the low survival rate of popular literature more generally, Andrew Pettegree, *The Book in the Renaissance* (New Haven: Yale University Press, 2010), 333–334.

4 On Luther's catechisms, see especially Albrecht Peters, *Kommentar zu Luthers Katechismen,* edited by Gottfried Seebass, 4 vols. (Vandenhoeck & Ruprecht: Göttingen, 1990–1994). Older but still valuable are Johannes Meyer, *Historischer Kommentar zu Luthers Kleinem Katechismus* (Güterlsoh: Bertelsmann, 1929), and Johann Michael Reu, *Dr. Martin Luther's Small*

Scholars have long been interested in the links between late medieval religious literature and the new evangelical catechisms. The fifteenth century witnessed an outpouring of vernacular religious works circulating first in manuscript, then in print. Echoing an argument made by Bernd Moeller in his pioneering study of popular piety on the eve of the Reformation, Werner William-Krapp has even suggested that, due to the production of religious literature in the vernacular, the well-read laity were often better educated than the local clergy.[5] Although there was a broad spectrum of religious material, studies have tended to focus on the treatment of the Apostles' Creed, the Lord's Prayer, and the Ten Commandments, which formed the core of the later Catechism.[6] Already in the eighth century the church required all Christians to learn the Creed and Lord's Prayer; during the later Middle Ages the Ten Commandments increasingly came to be used as a way to aid Christians in making their mandatory yearly confession to a priest.[7] At the end of the Middle Ages, preachers and theologians also listed a variety of other things Christians should know, such as the Ave Maria, the commands of the church (for example, the requirement to confess and receive communion at Eastertime), the seven deadly sins, and the names of the sacra-

Catechism: A History of Its Origin, Its Distribution and Its Use. A Jubilee Offering (Chicago: Wartburg Publishing House, 1929), as well as the lengthy introduction to both catechisms in WA 30.1: 426–474. Most of the items included in David Daniel and Charles P. Arand, "A Bibliography of the Lutheran Confessions: Luther's Small and Large Catechism," *Sixteenth Century Bibliography* 28 (1988): 111–135, take Luther's catechisms as their starting point, and there is very little on earlier catechetical literature.

5 Robert J. Bast, *Honor Your Fathers: Catechisms and the Emergence of a Patriarchial Ideology in Germany 1400–1600* (Leiden: Brill, 1997), 1–32; Rudolf Padberg, *Erasmus als Katechet* (Freiburg i.Br.: Herder, 1956), 22–44; Werner Williams-Krapp, "The Erosion of a Monopoly: German Religious Literature in the Fifteenth Century," in R. Blumenfeld-Kosinski, D. Robertson and N. Bradley Warren, ed., *The Vernacular Spirit: Essays on Medieval Religious Literature* (New York: Palgrave, 2002), 239–259; cf. Bernd Moeller, "Piety in Germany around 1500," in S. Ozment, ed., *The Reformation in Medieval Perspective* (Chicago: Quadrangle Books, 1971), 50–75.

6 Older discussions of catechization in the later Middle Ages and the early Reformation reflect the confessional bias of their participants. From the Catholic side, Franz Falk described a number of catechetical works in "*Der Unterricht des Volkes in den katechetischen Hauptstücken am Ende des Mittelalters,*" *Historisch-politische Blätter* 108 (1891): 553–560, 682–694, and 109 (1892): 81–95, 721–731. Representative of the Lutheran dismissal of late medieval catechetical efforts are Ernst Ernst and Johann Adam, *Katechetische Geschichte des Elsasses bis zur Revolution* (Strasbourg: Bull, 1897), 5–12, and Reu, *Luther's Small Catechism*, 1–6, both of which acknowledge the existence of this literature but deny its effectiveness.

7 Cohrs, *Katechismusversuche* 4: 229–234; John Bossy stresses Jean Gerson's importance for the growing importance of the Ten Commandments, "Moral Arithmetic: Seven Sins into Ten Commandments," in Edmund Leites, ed., *Conscience and Casuistry in Early Modern Europe* (Cambridge: Cambridge University Press, Paris, Editions de la Maison des Sciences de l'Homme, 1988), 214–234.

ments, but there was no general agreement that this additional material had the same status as Creed, Commandments, and the Lord's Prayer.

In the early years of the Reformation, evangelical preachers continued to center catechetical instruction on the three "chief parts" of Creed, Commandments, and Lord's Prayer. It is striking that the evangelical sacraments were not a part of this instruction. Luther preached on the Creed, Commandments, and Lord's Prayer even before the beginning of the Reformation, and he continued to do so regularly through the early 1520s, but he did not consider the sacraments in conjunction with his catechetical sermons.[8] There was no discussion of the Lord's Supper or baptism in the first evangelical devotional books for the laity or in schoolbooks for children. Luther's *Little Prayer Book,* first published in 1522 and expanded and regularly reprinted thereafter, contained catechetical material in addition to prayers, but its earliest versions had nothing on the sacraments.[9] In addition to the Creed, Commandments, Lord's Prayer, and Ave Maria, Melanchthon's 1523 *Enchiridion* contained lengthy scripture passages and proverbs from classical sources for schoolboys to memorize, but it, too, was silent concerning the sacraments. The situation outside of Wittenberg was no different. A catechetical broadsheet printed in Zurich in 1525 listed the Commandments, Creed, Lord's Prayer, and Ave Maria, while a Strasbourg broadsheet from the same year gave only the Ten Commandments with an explanation.[10]

How then did discussion of the sacraments come to be included in the Lutheran catechism? Their addition to the traditional catechetical triad of Creed, Commandments, and Lord's Prayer has generally been associated with the outbreak of disagreements with both Sacramentarians and Anabaptists in the mid-1520s. These controversies certainly played a role, but there was another factor that encouraged the addition of a section on the Lord's Supper to the evangelical catechism. Luther's rejection of the Catholic Mass and his new understanding of the Lord's Supper meant that pastors had to come up with some way to help their parishioners prepare to receive the sacrament in an evangelical way. For this they employed a genre popular during the later Middle Ages, the guide to communion preparation. An examination of how communion was discussed in catechetical literature published through the first half of the 1520s shows how this genre was first adapted for evangelical use and then included in

8 See the summary of Luther's early catechetical activity in Meyer, *Historischer Kommentar,* 46–49, and the more detailed listing in Georg Buchwald, *Die Entstehung der Katechismen Luthers und die Grundlage des grossen Katechismus* (Leipzig: Wigand, 1894), V–XI.

9 Michael Beyer, "*Martin Luther Betbüchlein,*" *Lutherjahrbuch* 74 (2007): 29–50. On the *Betbüchlein* as a catechetical text, Timothy J. Wengert, "Wittenberg's Earliest Catechism," *Lutheran Quarterly* 7 (1993): 247–260; Johannes Schilling, "5. *Katechismen,*" in Albrecht Beutel, ed., *Luther Handbuch* (Tübingen: Mohr Siebeck, 2005), 305–312.

10 All three works are listed in Cohrs, *Katechismusversuche* 1: 17–64, 117–127.

early catechisms. It also offers a very vivid demonstration of how Luther's understanding of the Lord's Supper was disseminated among the literate laity.

Throughout the Middle Ages, the laity were taught the faith through sermons, rituals, and the decorative program of church buildings, but the rise in literacy and the invention of the printing press in the fifteenth century significantly increased the importance and the availability of the written word for religious instruction.[11] Printed materials were aimed at two different audiences. Professional works for the clergy, such as pastors' manuals, confessors' manuals, and sermon collections, provided some guidance to those responsible for teaching the laity, whether publicly through preaching or individually in hearing confessions.[12] For those men and women who could read and could afford to buy books, German presses produced devotional works – not only Latin books of hours but also vernacular works such as *The Soul's Consolation* (*Seelentrost*), a collection of Bible stories and exempla grouped according to the Ten Commandments compiled in the mid-fourteenth century; the Viennese Augustinian Stephan von Landskron's *The Road to Heaven* (*Himmelstraß*) from 1465, Dietrich Kolde's *Fruitful Mirror for Christians*, first printed in 1470, and *The Little Garden of the Soul* (*Hortulus Animae*) a popular prayer book published in Latin and quickly translated into German. All of these works were frequently reprinted into the sixteenth century.[13]

11 According to Williams-Krapp, 80 % of the manuscripts and printed works of the fifteenth century were religious in nature, "The Erosion of a Monopoly," 239.

12 For a broad overview of such literature, Franz Machilek, "*Einführung. Beweggründe, Inhalte und Probleme kirchlicher Reformen des 14./15. Jahrhunderts (mit besonderer Berücksichtigung der Verhältnisse im östlichen Mitteleuropa),*" in Winfried Eberhard and Franz Machilek, ed., *Kirchliche Reformimpulse des 14./15. Jahrhunderts in Ostmitteleuropa, Forschungen und Quellen zur Kirchen- und Kulturgeschichte Ostdeutschlands* 36 (Cologne: Böhlau, 2006), 1–121, esp. 66–70. More specialized studies include Peter A. Dykema, "Handbooks for Pastors: Late Medieval Manuals for Parish Priests and Conrad Porta's Pastorale Lutheri (1582)," in R. J. Bast and A. C. Gow, ed., *Continuity and Change: The Harvest of Late Medieval and Reformation History. Essays Presented to Heiko A. Oberman on His 70th Birthday* (Leiden: Brill, 2000), 143–162; Dorothea Roth, *Die mittelalterliche Predigttheorie und das Manuale curatorum des Johann Ulrich Surgant, Basler Beiträge zur Geschichtswissenschaft* 58 (Basel: Helbing & Lichtenhahn, 1956); Thomas N. Tentler, *Sin and Confession on the Eve of the Reformation* (Princeton: Princeton University Press, 1977); Anne T. Thayer, *Penitence, Preaching and the Coming of the Reformation*, St. Andrews Studies in Reformation History (Aldershot: Ashgate, 2002).

13 Johannes Geffcken, *Der Bildercatechismus des fünfzehnten Jahrhunderts und die catechetischen Haupstücke in dieser Zeit bis auf Luther* (Leipzig: Weigel, 1855); Margarete Schmitt, *Der Grosse Seelentrost. Ein niederdeutsches Erbauungsbuch des vierzehnten Jahrhunderts, Niederdeutsche Studien* 5 (Cologne: Böhlau, 1959); Gerardus Johannes Jaspers, *Die Hymelstrasz: mit einer Einleitung und vergleichenden Betrachtungen zum Sprachgebrauch in den Frühdrucken (Augsburg 1484, 1501 und 1510)* (Amsterdam: Rodopi,1979); M. Consuelo Oldenbourg, *Hortulus animae: (1494)–1523. Bibliographie und Illustrationen* (Hamburg: Hauswedell, 1973). An English translation of Kolde's work is contained in Denis Janz, *Three*

In a survey of late medieval French religious literature, Geneviève Hasenohr concludes that such works emphasized ascetic morality and devotion, meditation, and the recitation of memorized prayers, and there was little discussion of theology.[14] The same might be said of religious works in German. Much of the religious instruction these works provided came in the form of lists that could be memorized relatively easily: not only the Ten Commandments but also the seven deadly sins, the six acts of mercy, the seven virtues, the seven gifts of the Holy Spirit, and so on. The *Hortulus Animae*, for instance, listed the seven sacraments but gave no explanation of any of them.[15] With regard to the Eucharist, these books aimed chiefly at deepening the readers' devotion, and they included prayers to recite before, during, and after communion, as well as those to be said at various points in the Mass, especially at the elevation of the host.

It is wrong to assume that the laity were not taught about the sacrament of the altar, however. Lay men and women were most likely to learn about the Eucharist in two ways, both connected with Lateran IV's requirement that all Christians were to confess their sins and receive communion at Eastertime. The first was through preaching, especially the sermons held on Maundy Thursday and the feast of Corpus Christi. In his study of medieval preaching on the Eucharist, Willi Massa described several themes that come to the fore in these sermons: the sacrifice of the Mass, the presence of Christ's body and blood in the consecrated elements, the proper preparation for communion, the fruit of receiving the sacrament, and the relationship between sacramental and spiritual communion. Preachers also discussed the mystical union with Christ and the saints imparted through communion, and they commended the practice of frequent communion.[16]

Reformation Catechisms: Catholic, Anabaptist, Lutheran (New York: Edward Mellen Press, 1982), 31–130.

14 Geneviève Hasenohr, "Religious Reading Amongst the Laity in France in the Fifteenth Century," in Peter Biller and Anne Hudson, ed., *Heresy and Literacy, 1000–1530*, Cambridge Studies in Medieval Literature 23 (Cambridge: Cambridge University Press, 1994), 205–221.

15 *Hortulus Animae* (Strasbourg, 1505): list of the sacraments, fol. CLVII; prayers for communion, beginning fol. CLIX–CLXIII; Thomas Lentes, "Counting Piety in the Late Middle Ages," in B. Jussen, ed., *Ordering Medieval Society: Perspectives on Intellectual and Practical Modes of Shaping Social Relations* (Philadelphia: University of Pennsylvania Press, 2000), 55–87. Cohrs alludes to this literature in his judgment that medieval instruction on the sacraments consisted only in being able to list them, *Katechismusversuche*, 4: 274–275.

16 Willi Massa, *Die Eucharistiepredigt am Vorabend der Reformation. Eine material-kerygmatische Untersuchung zum Glaubensverständnis von Altarssakrament und Messe am Beginn des 16. Jahrhunderts als Beitrag zur Geschichte der Predigt, Veröffentlichungen des Missionspriesterseminars St. Augustine, Siegburg* 15 (St. Augustin: Steyler Verlag, 1966), 63–212; see also Charles M.A. Caspers, "*Magister Consensus: Wessel Gansfort (1419–1489) und die Geistliche Kommunion*," in Fokke Akkerman, et al., ed., *Northern Humanism in European Context, 1469–1625: From the "Adwert Academy" to Ubbo Emmius*, Studies in Intellectual

The second way the laity were instructed about the Eucharist was through tracts intended to help them prepare for their mandatory annual confession and communion.[17] Those printed on the eve of the Reformation were not entirely distinct from sermons, for preachers might adapt the contents of their sermons on the sacrament for publication. This was the case with two pamphlets on communion preparation published in the spring of 1518, Martin Luther's *Sermon on Worthy Preparation for the Sacrament of the Eucharist*, and Kaspar Güttel's *Most Fruitful Pamphlet on Adam's Works and God's Grace [...]Preached During the Most Holy Lenten Season.* Güttel, the prior of the Augustinian convent in Eisleben, claimed that he was only repeating the points made by Johann Staupitz in a series of sermons delivered in Nuremberg the previous year on confession, penance, and receiving the sacrament.[18] Two other pamphlets published the same year were written for specific audiences. The Strasbourg schoolmaster Hieronymus Gebwiler wrote his 1518 *Brief Exhortation Useful for Those Desiring to Go to Holy Communion* in Latin for schoolboys.[19] Anton Engelbrecht, a chaplain in Basel's cathedral, wrote his *Reverent Teaching on the Venerable Sacrament* for Countess Helena von Lüppfen in response to her request for advice on how to prepare to receive the sacrament.[20] An even lengthier work was the anonymous *On the Venerable Sacrament of the Body of Christ Jesus, with Wholly Necessary and Lovely Instruction*, published in Nuremberg in 1514.[21] With the exception of

History 94 (Leiden: Brill, 1999), 82–98. *The Road to Heaven* discusses many of these themes as well, Jaspers, Hymelstrasz, fol. 146r–161r.

17 Ronald K. Rittgers summarizes a number of works intended to help the laity make a full confession and discusses the theology that underlay them, but he does not consider the connection between confession and communion, *The Reformation of the Keys: Confession, Conscience and Authority in Sixteenth-Century Germany* (Cambridge, Mass: Harvard University Press, 2004), 25–40.

18 *Jhesus. Ein fast fruchtbar buchlein von Adams wercken/ vnd gottes genadē mit vnterricht wie recht beichten/ busszen/ vnd das hochwirdigst Sacrament selig tzu entpfahen im Augustiner Closter tzu sandt Anne vor Eisleben dise heiligste fasten gepredigt vnd gegeben* (Leipzig: Lotter, 1518), fol. A3r-v, VD16: G 3982. The work also contains the earliest extant version of Luther's *Short Explanation of the Ten Commandments* (WA 1: 247–256).

19 *Exhortatio admodum brevis sacram communionem adire cupientibus haud inutilis* (Strasbourg: Prüß, 1518), VD16: G 602. The tract was reprinted in 1520, VD16: ZV 6424.

20 Anton Engelbrecht, *Ein andechtige leer von dem hochwyrdigen sacrament* (Basel: Petri, 1518), VD16: ZV 5019; dedication fol. a1v.

21 *Von dem Hochwirdigen Sacrament des fronleichnam Cristi Jesu mit gar notdürfftigen vnd schönen vnderweyssungen* (Nuremberg: Peypus, 1514), V 2493. It is tempting to think that the treatise might have been intended for nuns in a Nuremberg convent. It certainly demands a high level of vernacular literacy, and its discussion of sins to avoid focuses on gossip and ostentatious dress, both associated especially with women, fol. F7v. On the importance of Observant religious orders for the spread of vernacular religious literature in the fifteenth century, Werner Williams-Krapp, "*Literaturlandschaften im späten Mittelalter,*" in idem, *Geistliche Literatur des späten Mittelalters, Spätmittelalter, Humanismus,* Reformation 64 (Tübingen: Mohr Siebeck, 2012), 29–34.

Luther's sermon, which will be discussed below, all of these pamphlets can be seen as popularizations of scholastic teaching on the sacrament, and their authors cited a range of authorities from Augustine and Chrysostom to Peter Lombard, Thomas Aquinas, and Jean Gerson.[22]

Since these pamphlets were concerned specifically with communion rather than with the Mass as a whole, they did not discuss the sacrifice of the Mass, but they addressed the remaining topics that Massa found in his examination of Eucharistic sermons, starting with the doctrine of transubstantiation. The Nuremberg pamphlet opened with the words, "for this is my body," followed by a prayer acknowledging that the visible bread was Christ's body because Christ had said so.[23] Gebwiler briefly summarized scholastic teaching on the sacrament, emphasizing the conversion of the elements and explaining the doctrine of concomitance – that Christ's body in the consecrated host also contained his blood – used to justify communion in one kind. Engelbrecht and Güttel also defended communion in one kind, and Güttel warned against the "Hussite poison" of lay communion in both kinds. All three authors reminded their readers that the unconsecrated wine received after communion was only wine and not Christ's blood; Güttel noted that "a large part of the ignorant people" believed that they received the sacrament from the unconsecrated chalice.[24] Engelbrecht did not explain the doctrine of transubstantiation, but he clearly assumed it in describing the miracle of Christ's coming in the sacrament even though the senses were deceived by the forms of bread and wine. He also stressed that recipients must have firm faith that Christ was truly and substantially contained in the sacrament.[25]

The right way to prepare for receiving the sacrament was a concern of all four pamphlets. The three vernacular pamphlets emphasized that no one was worthy to receive the sacrament through his or her own merit, but one should nevertheless prepare diligently for communion. The emphasis on human unworthiness is strongest in Güttel, who advocated sacramental confession to counter

22 The shortest of these, Gebwiler's *Exhortatio*, cites only Lombard's *Sentences*, fol. A4r. The marginalia of Güttel's pamphlet refer to Augustine, Chrysostom, Gerson, Gregory the Great, Thomas Aquinas, and canon law. Engelbrecht cites Lombard's *Sentences*, Chrysostom, Albertus Magnus, Gregory the Great, Bernard of Clairvaux, Anselm, Thomas Aquinas, and Bonaventure, while the Nuremberg pamphlet frequently cites Thomas Aquinas, as well as Augustine, Ambrose, Chrysostom, Bernard, Gregory the Great, and Bonaventure.

23 *Von dem Hochwirdigen Sacrament*, fol. A2r-v.

24 Gebwiler, *Exhortatio*, fol. A4r-A5r; Engelbrecht, *andechtige leer*, fol. f3v-f4r; Güttel, *fruchtbar buchlein*, fol. H1r-H3r. On the use of unconsecrated wine to rinse the mouths of communicants after receiving the host, Amy Nelson Burnett, "The Social History of Communion and the Reformation of the Eucharist," *Past and Present* 211 (2011): 77–119, esp. 86, 94; Heinrich Müller-Diersfordt, "*Abendmahl under beiderlei Gestalt in rheinischen Gemeinde vor der Reformation*," *Monatshefte für Rheinische Kirchengeschichte* 2 (1953): 33–38, 176–178.

25 Engelbrecht, *andechtige leer*, fol. c4r, e2r.

inborn tendencies to sin. The other two authors were more positive, teaching a form of worthiness obtained through external purity and internal devotion. Christians were to make a full confession to their priest, trust in God's grace, feel sorrow for sin, and have an earnest desire to reform one's life. Engelbrecht encouraged those who felt unworthy to desire the sacrament as medicine against spiritual sickness, and he taught the nominalist position that to those who did what they could, God would do his part and give grace. In his brief booklet Gebwiler did not address subjective feelings of unworthiness, but he, too, advocated a complete sacramental confession, and he advised those who remembered a forgotten sin to postpone their communion until after they had confessed it to a priest. He was also most concerned with teaching the importance of outward purity. Christians were to fast before receiving communion, and he recommended cleansing the mouth two or three times the evening before communicating to ensure that no food remained.[26]

To those who still felt unworthy, the Nuremberg author advised abstention from the sacrament, for one could still communicate spiritually. The other, shorter pamphlets did not discuss spiritual communion, but the Nuremberg pamphlet devoted several pages to the difference between spiritual and sacramental communion and the relationship between the two. It concluded that although spiritual communion was good, sacramental communion was better and more fruitful, and it described at length the spiritual benefits brought by sacramental communion. These included strength to avoid future sin, rekindled love of God, and a desire to do good.[27] All three vernacular treatises contained prayers for communion intended to promote internal devotion and salutary reception of the sacrament.

Taken together with Massa's study of late medieval preaching on the Eucharist, these pamphlets make it difficult to uphold the assertion that the church did little to teach the laity about the sacrament. While one might question the extent to which these ideas filtered down to an illiterate rural population, there are sufficient indications that, between regular preaching and access to vernacular publications, literate laymen and women were regularly exposed to the church's teaching on the Eucharist. The Augsburg Confession's statement about the Lord's Supper must therefore be understood not as implying that the medieval church's instruction about communion was nonexistent, but rather that it was

26 Güttel, *fruchtbar buchlein*, fol. A3v-B2r; *Von dem Hochwirdigen Sacrament*, fol. B6v-C2v; Engelbrecht, *andechtige leer*, fol. c1r-v, d4r-v; Gebwiler, *Exhortatio*, A2v-A3v.

27 *Von dem Hochwirdigen Sacrament*, fol. A3r-B5r, c7rr-D2v. D8v-E2r, F1r-v, H5vv-H8v. On medieval discussions of spiritual communion, Burnett, "Social History;" in Heinz R. Schlette, *Die Lehre von der geistlichen Kommunion bei Bonaventura, Albert dem Grossen, und Thomas von Aquin*, *Münchener theologische Studien. II. Systematische Abteilung* 17 (Munich: Hueber, 1959).

both wrong and inadequate. Luther asserted as much in his 1523 Maundy Thursday sermon, when he criticized those who only emphasized belief in the presence of Christ's body and blood and did not teach what the sacrament was or why one should receive it.[28]

Luther's criticism prompts us to take a closer look at how he taught his hearers to receive communion. Luther regularly preached on the sacrament during Holy Week in order to help people prepare for their Easter communion, and there is an almost complete set of those sermons through the decade of the 1520s. Moreover, Luther's early sermons on communion were frequently reprinted, making his ideas far better known than those of any other reformer. In essence, these pamphlets functioned both as model communion sermons that could be imitated by other preachers and as guides instructing the laity on how to prepare for worthy communion.

Luther's 1518 *Sermon on Worthy Preparation for the Sacrament of the Eucharist* was his first published discussion of the sacrament. He began his sermon in a traditional way, by pointing out that it was necessary to confess all manifest mortal sins, although he countered any undue scrupulosity by saying that no one could confess those sins he or she was unaware of. Like the other authors, he focused on fear of receiving the sacrament unworthily, but unlike them he did not prescribe ways to purify oneself in preparation for communion; in fact, he condemned those who approached the sacrament relying on the completeness of their confession and trusting in their own worthiness. Instead, Luther stated, feeling unworthy was the best preparation one could make for communion. The faith necessary for worthy reception was defined not as belief that the consecrated host was Christ's body but instead as trust that the recipient would obtain God's grace. This faith alone made one pure and worthy, because it relied on Christ's words.[29] Luther's emphasis on faith and his rejection of any other type of preparation beyond sacramental confession set his advice apart from that given by his contemporaries.[30]

In contrast to the *Sermon on Worthy Preparation*, Luther's 1519 *Sermon on the Venerable Sacrament of the Holy True Body of Christ* was probably never

28 *Eyn Sermon am grunen donnerstag* (1523), WA 12: 476–478. For more on this sermon, see below.

29 WA 1: 329–334.

30 In fact, Luther's advice on how to prepare to receive the sacrament was fairly close to that of his mentor Johann von Staupitz, as recorded in a summary of the latter's sermons in Nuremberg. Staupitz told his hearers that no one could make himself sufficiently worthy, but that only God could give such worthiness. Communicants should prepare through repentance, confession, and intention to reform, as well as through meditation on Christ's passion, and then approach the sacrament trusting that God would make them worthy; J.F. Knaake, *Johann von Staupitzens sämmtliche Werke*. Vol. 1: *Deutsche Schriften* (Krausnick: Potsdam, 1867), 32–33.

preached. It was instead one of three "sermons" on the sacraments that the Reformer published towards the end of that year. If anything, his pamphlet was more traditional than the 1518 sermon in emphasizing the unity among believers created by the sacrament.[31] By the time this sermon was published, however, the conflict over indulgences was causing Luther to rethink not just sacramental confession but the entire sacramental system, and the revolutionary nature of his new ideas would become apparent in 1520.[32] Luther's Holy Week sermon from that year was expanded and published in July as *A Sermon on the New Testament, That is, on the Holy Mass*, and the main ideas were repeated and sharpened in his *Prelude to the Babylonian Captivity of the Church*, published in November.

Luther now defined a sacrament as God's promise joined with a sign. God always acted first in giving his promises, and he added a physical sign so that people would not doubt that promise.[33] Applying this new understanding of a sacrament to the Mass, Luther focused on Christ's words, "this is my body, given for you for the forgiveness of sins." This promise was the new testament put into effect by the death of Christ the testator, and Christ's body and blood under the forms of bread and wine were the signs given to confirm that promise. Worthy preparation for communion consisted in faith in Christ's death, a desire for forgiveness, and trust in God's promise even if one felt unworthy. Finally, if the heart of the sacrament was found in Christ's words, "this is my body, given for you for the forgiveness of sins," then those words should not be mumbled in Latin but must be spoken aloud and explained in a sermon so that the laity could hear the promise they contained.[34]

In his Maundy Thursday sermon for 1521, Luther emphasized a corollary of his new understanding. Since desire for forgiveness was an essential part of worthy preparation for communion, those who did not feel such desire should not approach the Lord's Table, even if the pope commanded it. Communion should be left free to those who felt driven by their need for forgiveness. Those who did feel such need, however, would be drawn to communicate frequently.[35]

31 WA 2: 738–758; LW 35: 49–73.

32 Wolfgang Schwab, *Entwicklung und Gestalt der Sakramententheologie bei Martin Luther, Europäische Hochschulschriften: Reihe 23, Theologie* 79 (Frankfurt/M: Lang, 1977), 77–232.

33 It was precisely this lack of a physical sign that caused Luther to reject confession as a sacrament in his treatise *On the Babylonian Captivity of the Church*, WA 6: 572, although he continued to regard the priest's word of absolution as almost sacramental in nature.

34 *Sermo de Testamento Christi*, WA 9: 445–449; *Ein Sermon von dem neuen Testament*, WA 6: 353–378, LW 35: 79–111; *De Captivitate Babylonica Ecclesiae Praeludium*, WA 6: 502–526, LW 36: 19–57.

35 *In Die Coena Domini Sermo*, WA 9: 640–649; published as *Sermon von der würdigen Empfahung des heiligen wahren Leichnams Christi*, WA 7: 692–697. The editor suggests that the longer manuscript form may have been expanded, while the printed edition reflects the disposition of the sermon without Luther's polemic, although I find the printed sermon to be

The understanding of the Lord's Supper that Luther articulated in 1520 and 1521 would be repeated and refined in his Invocavit sermons from 1522 as well as in his Holy Week sermons over the next few years. In most of these sermons he repeated his definition of a sacrament as the joining of divine promise to an external sign. Although he rejected mandatory confession and communion, he taught that both should be sought out by Christians seeking assurance that they had been forgiven. Worthy preparation for communion required acknowledging one's sinfulness and having faith in Christ's promise of forgiveness, while reception of the sacrament consoled a troubled conscience and strengthened faith. Luther increasingly emphasized that Christians should know the words with which Christ instituted the Supper and that they should appropriate for themselves the promise, "given for you."[36]

Although it is unlikely that many people had access to all of Luther's published sermons so that they could understand fully his new understanding of the Mass and the proper preparation for communion, each pamphlet said enough that a reader would be able to grasp the basics. And the likelihood that a curious reader could learn of Luther's view was high, given the large number of reprints in the vernacular for each of the printed sermons.[37] Unlike the other treatises on communion preparation published in 1518, which probably had little impact beyond the local level, Luther's *Sermon on Worthy Preparation* was diffused widely, with nine imprints in the original Latin and fourteen in German translation. It was also included in Froben's collection of Luther's Latin works published in 1518 and reprinted in Strasbourg the following year.[38] There were fifteen

more polemical. The sermon was given only a few days before Luther left for the Diet of Worms, and unless he gave the outline for the sermon to the printer immediately after preaching it, the text must have been provided by someone else. Aside from length, the chief difference between the two texts is that the printed version is more critical of the church's requirement of annual confession, while the manuscript version devotes more space to what constituted worthy preparation for communion. I am inclined to think that the manuscript version reflects Luther's sermon as preached more faithfully than the printed version.

36 1522 Maundy Thursday sermon, WA 10/3: 68–71; Sermons 6–8 of the 1522 Invocavit sermons (published in 1523), WA 10/3: 48–64; 1523 sermons for Maundy Thursday and Easter Monday, WA 12: 476–505; 1524 Palm Sunday and Maundy Thursday sermons, WA 15: 490–506; see also his sermon for Laetare 1523, which was not printed, WA 11:65–67.

37 The large number of reprints of Luther's sermons on the Lord's Supper is one aspect in the dominance of Luther's works among all pamphlets printed through 1525, Mark U. Edwards, *Printing, Propaganda, and Martin Luther* (Berkeley: University of California Press, 1994), 14–28 ; as well as those specifically on the sacrament, Amy Nelson Burnett, *Karlstadt and the Origins of the Eucharistic Controversy: A Study in the Circulation of Ideas*, Oxford Studies in Reformation Theology (New York: Oxford University Press, 2011), 37–40.

38 Imprints of Luther's sermon, VD16: L 3407–3409, L 5975–5996, ZV 19419. Of the other pamphlets on communion preparation discussed above, only Gebwiler's *Exhortatio* was reprinted, in 1520; VD16: ZV 6424.

imprints of the 1520 *Sermon on the New Testament.*[39] Although it was written in Latin, the *Babylonian Captivity* also appeared in five German imprints. The Maundy Thursday sermon from 1521 was published eight times, the Invocavit sermons were printed six times, and the Maundy Thursday sermon from 1522 appeared in fourteen imprints.[40] The initial Wittenberg printing of Luther's 1523 *Sermon Preached [...] on Maundy Thursday* was reprinted in Nuremberg and Breslau with its original title, but competing printers in Augsburg gave more explicit titles to their reprints: *A Sermon on the Reception and Preparation for the Venerable Body of Jesus Christ*, and *A Sermon on the Fruit and Use of the Holy Sacrament.*[41] Luther also expanded that Maundy Thursday sermon into a foreword for his sermons preached on Easter Monday and on the Sunday after Easter, which were then printed in Hagenau with the title, *Order and Instruction about What One Should Do (with Those who Want to Receive the Venerable Sacrament). Also Two Christian Sermons Concerning Christ's Resurrection and the Chief Article of our Faith.*[42] This expanded pamphlet inspired the title given to two 1524 reprints of the Easter Monday sermon: *A Sermon on the Chief Article of our Faith.*[43] Last but not least, the two sermons from Holy Week 1524 were expanded and published under the title, *A Sermon on Confession and the Sacrament.* The resulting pamphlet would be printed six more times over the next year; it was also published once in Latin translation.[44] Assuming an average print run of 1500

39 VD16: L 6401–L 6415.

40 VD16: L 6567–6574, L 3630–3635, L 4817–4830.

41 VD16: L 6058–6060; the variant titles were drawn from the two parts of the sermon: The *Sermon von der Empfahung und Zubereitung des hochwürdigen Fronleichnam Jesu Christi* was printed by Ramminger in 1524 (VD16: L 6061); it was reprinted in Zwickau the same year. The *Sermon von der frucht vnd nutzparkayt des hayligen Sacraments* was printed by Ulhart (L 6062), also in 1524; it was reprinted in Nuremberg the same year with a slightly abbreviated title (L 6063).

42 *Ordenung vnd Bericht wie es furterhin (mit ihnen so das Hochwirdig Sacramentempfahen wollen) gehalten sol [...]*, VD16: L 5572. Johannes Setzer, who printed the Hagenau pamphlet, came to Wittenberg in the summer of 1522 to study medicine and returned to Hagenau in March 1523 to take over the press of his father-in-law, Thomas Anselm; Heinz Scheible, "*Melanchthons Verhältnis zu Johannes Setzer,*" in Heinz Scheible, ed., *Aufsätze zu Melanchthon*, Spätmittelalter, Humanismus, Reformation 49 (Tübingen: Mohr Siebeck, 2010), 309–316. He therefore was not in Wittenberg when the Maundy Thursday sermon was preached (on 2 April), but this earlier contact is probably what prompted Luther to send him the expanded sermons. According to VD16, Setzer published nine works in 1523, all but one of them from Wittenberg (not only Luther's *Ordenung und Bericht* but also works of Melanchthon, Justus Jonas, and Nicolas von Amsdorf); see also Frédéric Hartweg, "*Lutherdrucke in Hagenau,*" in Günter Vogler, ed., *Martin Luther. Leben—Werk—Wirkung* (Berlin: Akademie Verlag, 1986), 367–375, and Karl Steiff, "*Johannes Setzer (Secerius), der gelehrte Buchdrucker in Hagenau,*" *Centralblatt für BIbliothekswesen* 9 (1892): 297–317.

43 The pamphlets were reprinted in Breslau (VD16: L 6149) and Nuremberg (L 6150].

44 *Eyn Sermon von der Beycht vnd dem Sacrament* (Wittenberg: Lufft, 1524), VD16: L 6465–6472.

copies per imprint, there were over 117,000 copies of one of these sermons circulating by the end of 1524.

Luther's communion sermons would also reach a wider audience through the incorporation in other often-reprinted works. The 1524 Palm Sunday sermon was included in the expanded version of Luther's *Little Prayer Book* published in 1525 and in several editions thereafter, including the Latin translation of 1529.[45] Both this sermon and the original, shorter version of the 1523 Maundy Thursday sermon were incorporated into Luther's church postil as well.[46] In this format they would continue to be reprinted and became models for Lutheran preaching on communion for the rest of the sixteenth century.[47] Even more so than the earlier Holy Week sermons, which were reprinted in the year or so after their first printing and then disappeared from the market, these two sermons perpetuated a stage in Luther's discussion of the Lord's Supper that predated the outbreak of the Eucharistic controversy and so did not contain the same accents and emphases as his later works.

Luther was not the only author to describe how one should prepare for evangelical communion. Just as important as his publications in the early 1520s were the works of others who picked up and passed on his ideas. During Luther's time at the Wartburg, his colleagues continued his publication offensive. Philipp Melanchthon did his part by shaping his discussion of the sacraments according to Luther's definition of promise and sign in the first edition of his *Loci Communes*, published at the end of 1521. There he asserted that receiving communion brought neither forgiveness nor justification, for only faith could justify. Instead, it confirmed to troubled consciences the forgiveness and justification imparted by faith.[48]

More importantly, Andreas Bodenstein von Karlstadt published his own advice for communion preparation, *On the Recipients, Signs and Promise of the Holy Sacrament*, in the summer of 1521; the pamphlet was printed four more times before the end of the year. Like Luther, Karlstadt argued that faith was the only thing necessary for worthy communion, and those who truly felt their sins

---

The pamphlet also included a sermon on Christian freedom in the matter of fasting that was preached at the beginning of Lent.

45 WA 10/2: 355–369; VD16: there were two imprints before 1530 (VD16: L 4097, 4099). On the development of the *Betbüchlein*, Christopher Boyd Brown, "Devotional Life in Liturgy, Hymns, Music, and Prayer," in Robert Kolb, ed., *Lutheran Ecclesiastical Culture, 1550–1675* (Leiden: Brill, 2008), 205–258, esp. 237–240.

46 The 1523 sermon was printed in Roth's *Sommerpostil*, WA 21:162; the 1524 sermon in the 1525 *Fastenpostil*, WA 17.2: 246.

47 John Frymire, *The Primacy of the Postils: Catholics, Protestants, and the Dissemination of Ideas in Early Modern Germany*, Studies in Medieval and Reformation Traditions 147 (Leiden: Brill, 2010), 29–32, 535–543.

48 CR 21: 208–211, 221–222.

should feel driven to receive the sacrament. Using the familiar metaphor of the Eucharist as medicine for the soul, he argued that those who sought that medicine first had to acknowledge their sickness and desire healing from Christ, who came to save sinners. Karlstadt also emphasized the promise of forgiveness in the sacrament as its most important part. Christians should grasp the sign as that which assured them of God's promise.[49] Karlstadt repeated some of this advice in the sermon he preached on Christmas Day 1521 before distributing the sacrament in both kinds to his hearers; that sermon was printed four times over the course of 1522.[50]

Authors outside of Wittenberg incorporated and passed on Luther's advice for communion preparation in their own treatises as well. These works spread Luther's basic understanding of the Lord's Supper but diluted it by combining it with ideas from other sources, especially the late medieval emphasis on spiritual communion.[51] In his 1521 *Useful Sermon on the True Evangelical Mass* the Ulm preacher Johannes Diepold explained that the sacrament was Christ's testament and promise, and that Christians were made worthy to receive the sacrament by faith in that promise. He condemned those preachers and confessors who terrified people by saying they had to confess all their sins and prepare for the sacrament with various exercises. To those who objected that the emphasis on faith alone encouraged people to approach the sacrament without due reverence, Diepold responded that those who did not believe God's promise and repent of their sins should abstain from communion. Those who did have faith, though, received the sacrament spiritually. Without such faith and spiritual communion, physical reception of the sacrament was useless.[52]

Jakob Strauss was even harsher in his condemnation of "false preachers" who insisted that Christians make a complete confession of all their sins along with their circumstances in order to be pure enough to receive the sacrament. His *Comforting, Reasonable Teaching on the Word of Paul, One Should Examine Himself and Then Eat from the Bread and Drink from the Cup,* originated as the Maundy Thursday sermon delivered to his congregation in Hall in the Tyrol. Proper preparation for communion, according to Strauss, was to have un-

49 *Von den Empfahern: zeychen: vnd zusag des heyligenn Sacraments fleysch vnd bluts Christi* (Wittenberg, 1521), VD16: B 6239; English translation in Amy Nelson Burnett, ed., *The Eucharistic Pamphlets of Andreas Bodenstein von Karlstadt* (Kirksville, MO: Truman State University Press, 2011), 21–48; Burnett, *Karlstadt,* 13–15.

50 *Predig Andresen Boden. Von Carolstatt [...] von empfahung des heiligen Sacraments* (Wittenberg: Schirlentz, 1522); VD16 B 6185; English translation in Burnett, *Eucharistic Pamphlets,* 78–88. Karlstadt's other two eucharistic pamphlets of 1521 did not directly discuss the issue of communion preparation.

51 Burnett, *Karlstadt,* 40–48.

52 Johann Diepold, *Ein nützlicher Sermon [...] von der rechten evangelischen Meß* (Augsburg: Nadler, 1522), VD16: D 1433–1441; there was also a 1527 reprint.

doubting faith that Christ's body and blood were present and given to communicants to renew the effects of his passion and death, and to believe that only Christ's death made one pure and free of sin. Worthiness consisted in the exercise of faith, not in human contrition and confession. If their priest barred them from sacramental communion, Christians should be satisfied with the spiritual communion given by Christ. To aid them, Strauss outlined the five points one must believe in order to communicate spiritually: that Christ's body and blood were present in the bread and wine, that Christ took on body and blood to save Adam and his descendants, that his body was given and his blood shed for the recipient, that Christ was present in the sacrament to confirm his promise to forgive sins, and that Christ gave himself to eat and drink to all who received the sacrament in true faith.[53]

The Augsburg preacher Urbanus Rhegius published not only an *Instruction how a Christian Should Act So That He Obtains the Fruit of the Mass and Goes to God's Table in a Christian Way* (1522) but also two Corpus Christi sermons from 1521 and 1523 that were strongly influenced by Luther's understanding of the sacrament. The Mass was Christ's testament, confirmed by his death, and Christ's words spoken by the priest over the bread and wine were a promise made to all Christians. Through the sacrament, consciences were consoled, and those who received the sacrament were incorporated into Christ's spiritual body and shared all things with their fellow believers.[54]

The significance of these works was increased by their broad diffusion: Diepold's *Sermon* went through nine imprints, including one in Low German, in 1522–1523, while Strauss's *Comforting, Reasonable Teaching* was printed six times in 1522. Portions of it were also published in 1524 as *A Lovely and Dear Instruction for Considering and Receiving the Precious, Most Holy Body of Christ and Receiving His Rosy Blood*, and that same year the Jena pastor Martin Reinhart published the final section, on spiritual communion, under his own name as *Instruction How a Pious Christian Should Act during the Papist Mass*; this pamphlet was reprinted six times.[55] Of Rhegius's three pamphlets, only his 1523

53 Jakob Strauss, *Ein trostliche verstendige leerüber das Wort Sanct Pauli [...]* (Erfurt: Maler, 1522); VD16: S 9504–9509.

54 *Vnterricht wie sich ain Christen mensch halten sol das er frucht der Meß erlang vnd Christlich zuo gotz tisch ganng* (Augsburg: Grimm & Wirsung, 1522), VD16: R 1994; *Ain Sermon von dem Hochwirdigen sacrament des Altars* (Augsburg: Otmar, 1521), VD16: R 1969; *Vom hochwürdigen Sacrament des altars vnderricht was man auß hayliger geschryfft wissen mag* (Augsburg: Ruff, 1523), VD16: ZV 1394.

55 Diepold's *Sermon*, VD16: D 1433–1441; the work was also reprinted as an anonymous work in 1527 in Nuremberg, N 2062. Strauss's pamphlet, *A Comforting, Reasonable Teaching*, VD16: S 9504–9509; Reinhart's pamphlet, *Vnderrichte wie sich ein frumer Christ bey den Papistischen Messen [...] halten soll*, VD16: R 948–951, ZV 13045, ZV 16307, and ZV 24291.

Instruction on the Venerable Sacrament was immediately reprinted, but all of his pamphlets taught the same general understanding of the sacrament.

Less important for spreading the new understanding of the sacrament but worth noting in comparison to earlier guides for communion preparation are two pamphlets by anonymous or little-known authors. *A Short and Christian Instruction on Receiving the Venerable Sacrament Worthily*, published in Basel in 1522, grew out of a sermon on communion. The anonymous author avoided any polemic or statements that would identify him with either side, such as defining the sacrament as promise and sign or expressly endorsing transubstantiation, and he explicitly refused to address the controversy concerning communion in both kinds and the church's specific requirements concerning how the sacrament was to be administered and received. Instead, he concentrated on ideas that were held by both Luther and his opponents, although his statements reflected Luther's priorities. Communicants were to guard themselves against receiving the sacrament only because they were commanded to do so but should approach the table out of their own love and desire. The author also warned against overscrupulosity: Christians should not abstain from communion if a drop of water inadvertently fell into their mouth or they bit off and swallowed a fingernail on the day of communion. They were to guard against thinking that they were not pure enough to receive the sacrament but should instead acknowledge that they were sick and look to the Lord for healing. Finally, they were to let their consciences rest on God's promise to forgive their sins. Through the sacrament they would see their faith confirmed and be assured of forgiveness. The best preparation for communion was to remember the Lord's passion, to believe firmly in the promise of forgiveness, and to be united in brotherly love with others.[56]

Martin Bryßgawer's *How One Should Confess, Receive the Sacraments, Hold Mass and Adore the Sacrament in a Christian Way*, published in 1524, was more openly evangelical. Bryßgawer condemned as presumption the belief that one must be pure in order to receive the sacrament, which he described as medicine for sin. From the definition of a sacrament as Christ's word joined with the signs of his body and blood, Bryßgawer distinguished between spiritual and inner communion, received at any time through faith in Christ's promise, and the

56 *Eyn kurtze vnnd Christliche vnderrichtung wirdig zu empfahen das Hochwirdig sacrament* (Basel: Curio, 1522), VD16: K2675–2676. The reference to a sermon suggests that the author was one of the three evangelical preachers active in Basel at that time. Both Wilhelm Reublin and Wolfgang Wissemberg had reputations for polemical preaching and provocative acts that make their authorship unlikely. The author was probably the third preacher, the Franciscan Johannes Lüthardt, who had reason to suppress his name, for in 1522 his superiors in the order suspected the Basel Franciscans of sympathizing with the Lutheran heresy; Amy Nelson Burnett, "The Reformation in Basel," *Companion to the Swiss Reformation*, ed., Amy Nelson Burnett and Emidio Campi (Leiden: Brill, 2016).

physical and external sacrament received to strengthen faith. Christians should receive the sacrament whenever they felt oppressed by their sin and desired consolation, and not according to the calendar. They were to examine themselves to see that they not only believed that Christ's body and blood were under the bread and wine but that his body and blood were given and shed for their sins. The preparation necessary to receive the sacrament was trust in God's word and love of neighbor, since it was called communion.[57]

Printers also helped diffuse this evangelical advice by producing their own pamphlets and broadsheets on how to prepare for communion. Reinhold Schwarz has illustrated this development in his discussion of two works, a broadsheet with the heading, *A Christian Confession Drawn from Holy Scripture*, published in Nuremberg in 1524, and an anonymous pamphlet published in Basel, *How a Christian Should Make a Daily Confession to God from His Heart. What Form and Faith We Should Hold Concerning the Testament and Table of Christ.*[58] The format of the two works – both publications required only one sheet of paper – suggests that the printers hoped to make a profit by putting together simple guides to help the laity as they prepared for their yearly confession and communion. The Basel pamphlet was made even more attractive by the title page woodcut of communion in both kinds, against a backdrop of Christ and his disciples at the Last Supper.[59]

The broadsheet reproduced the five prerequisites of spiritual communion listed by Strauss together with two prayers and a short question and answer passage on the sacrament taken from another work first published in 1524, the

57 Martin Bryßgawer, *Wie man Christlicher weysz beichten: Sacrament entpfahen: Messz halten/ vnd das Sacrament anbetten sol* (Strasbourg: Schwan, 1524), VD16: B8821, fol. C4r-D2v. The dedication to Markgraf Ernst of Baden urged the prince to support the spread of the Gospel in his lands, fol. A1v-A2r.

58 Reinhard Schwarz, "*Abendmahlsgemeinschaft durch das Evangelium, obwohl der Tisch des Herrn 'durch menschliche Irrung versperrt ist'*," *Lutherjahrbuch* 59 (1992): 38–78. The pamphlet, *Wie ein Christen mensch ein tegliche beicht vnnd bekantnus gegen got vn hertzen sol thuon/ gezogen auß der geschrifft. Mit was gestalt vnd glauben wir vns sollen halten gegen dem Testament vnd disch Christi*, does not give printer or date. According to VD16, the printer was Thomas Wolff. The date is given as 1526, which was probably assigned in reliance on Emil Weller, *Repertorium typographicum: die deutsche Literatur im ersten Viertel des sechzehnten Jahrhunderts: im Anschluss an Hains Repertorium und Panzers deutsche Annalen* (Hildesheim: Olms, 1961), no. 4032. This late date is highly unlikely, though, since the pamphlet shows no indication of the impact of the Eucharistic controversy, which Wolff promoted by his other publications: in Oct. 1524, he printed two of Karlstadt's pamphlets initiating that controversy, and in 1526 he printed two Eucharistic pamphlets by Oecolampadius. According to Schwarz (49, n. 33), the editors of VD16 judged on the basis of the font used that the pamphlet may have been printed in 1524, a date that is much more probable.

59 The woodcut is reproduced in Schwarz, "*Abendmahlsgemeinschaft*," 51, and Burnett, "Social History of Communion," 104.

anonymous *Comforting Disputation in Question and Answer Form.*[60] The text of the broadsheet formed the first part of the Basel pamphlet. According to Schwarz, the remaining two sections of the pamphlet were original but heavily dependent on Luther's *On the Misuse of the Mass*, published in 1522. These two sections, along with the two prayers from the broadsheet, would also be included in a reprint of Rhegius's 1523 Corpus Christi sermon, *Instruction on the Venerable Sacrament of the Altar*, published in Leipzig in 1525.[61] While Schwarz attributes the inclusion of these sections in the 1525 imprints to Rhegius, it is far more likely that the decision to reprint the pamphlet with the additional material was made by the printer. Like the Basel pamphlet, the Leipzig reprint of Rhegius's pamphlet included a woodcut of communion in both kinds with a backdrop of the Last Supper.

The expanded version of Rhegius's pamphlet must have been a popular success, for it was printed four times in 1525 and once in 1526 by three different Leipzig printers.[62] The pamphlet also underwent a change in format. While the original sermon had been printed in quarto, the size most common for pamphlets, the later reprints were all published in octavo, the format most common for devotional literature. Like the broadsheet and the anonymous Basel pamphlet, the Leipzig pamphlets were produced for a market that printers hoped would be profitable. The frequent reprinting of this work suggests there was significant popular demand for such communion preparation guides, and it reminds us that printers could play a more significant role in the diffusion of evangelical works than the authors themselves.

These pamphlets indicate that Luther's redefinition of the sacrament as Christ's testament and his new understanding of what constituted worthiness when receiving communion spread broadly in the first half of the 1520s, although his ideas were modified to reflect elements of late medieval teaching on communion. The chief continuity of these evangelical pamphlets with their late medieval predecessors consisted in their practical emphasis. In every case, the author was concerned not with what readers should know about the sacrament but with how they should prepare to receive it. With the exception of Rhegius's

60 *Ein trostliche disputation/ auff frag vnd antwuort gestellet/ Von zwayen Handtwercks mennern/ den Glauben/ vnd die lieb/ auch andere Christenliche leer betreffend/ auch form wie einer den andern Christenlich vnderweysen sol/ gantz nützlich zuo den artickeln Do. Vrbani Regij vnd Gretzingers* (Nuremberg: Gutknecht, 1524), VD16: T 2024.

61 Schwarz attributes the pamphlet to Heinrich Öttinger in Magdeburg, but VD16 does not list a Magdeburg imprint for the pamphlet. Based on his description, Schwarz probably used the imprint of Nickel Schmidt, ZV 13199.

62 VD16: ZV 13191–13192, ZV 13198–13200. It should be noted that Duke Georg had forbidden the publication of evangelical works in his lands. With these pamphlets, the printers spread evangelical ideas by using a traditional format that would not draw the attention of the censors.

works and the *Comforting Disputation*, the evangelical pamphlets contained very few attacks on the Mass. Such polemic was considered inappropriate for works intended specifically to help people prepare for communion. There was also no questioning of the presence of Christ's body and blood in the elements. Where this was not stated explicitly, it was implicit in the terminology used.

The evangelical pamphlets differed from their late medieval predecessors, however, by following Luther's understanding of communion. In describing proper preparation, the pamphlets shifted the focus from the communicants' actions to their attitude or spiritual disposition: it was their faith in God's promise of forgiveness, not their own ascetic practices or the ritual purity bestowed in sacramental confession, that made Christians worthy to receive the Supper. Like Luther, the authors were critical of those preachers who defined proper preparation only in terms of outward actions, such as making a complete confession of all sins or not allowing anything to enter the mouth or stomach before communion. Evangelical authors stressed that individuals should feel impelled to receive communion by their awareness of their sins, and as the chief benefit of communion they emphasized the assurance that those sins were forgiven. Finally, they broke with scholastic teaching about communion and followed Luther in describing the Supper as Christ's testament, as the joining of word and sign, and in focusing on Christ's words of institution that promised forgiveness of sin.

All of these works were written for the literate laity, and a few of them were in question and answer form, which has caused them to be seen as forerunners to the evangelical catechisms that began to be published in 1525.[63] Unlike the later catechisms, however, they were intended for meditation, not for easy memorization. Both their length and the sophistication of their language made them unsuitable for those who were barely literate or could not read at all. It was therefore all the more significant, then, when Luther's understanding of proper preparation for communion was put into question and answer form. In conjunction with the pre-communion examination instituted in Wittenberg at the end of 1523, the Wittenbergers drew up five questions concerning the meaning and purpose of the sacrament. These questions were included in a 1525 Wittenberg reprint of Luther's 1523 Maundy Thursday sermon and in two Wittenberg reprints of the *Comforting Disputation in Question and Answer Form*.[64] They

63 See, for instance, Reinhard Schwarz, "*Abendmahlsgemeinschaft*," 62–63; Wengert, "Catechism," 250–252.

64 *Ordenung vnd Bericht*, 1525 Wittenberg imprint, VD16: L 5575, the *Comforting Disputation* bore the slightly revised title of *Eyn trostlich gesprechbüchleyn*; VD16: T 2035–2036. The questions have been attributed to Luther by modern scholars, but some sixteenth-century imprints associated them with Johannes Bugenhagen. As Wittenberg's parish pastor and so the one who examined individuals before communion, it seems more probable that Bugenhagen wrote the questions and answers.

would be both reprinted and imitated elsewhere. From here it was a natural step for evangelical authors to add questions concerning communion to their catechisms. The section of Petrus Schultz's 1527 *Booklet in Question and Answer Form* devoted to the Lord's Supper had the superscript, "Formula of Question and Answers for Those Who Want to Receive the Sacrament." In his *Catechism* of 1528, Andreas Althamer stated that he included his discussion of the sacrament not so much for children, who were not allowed to receive communion until they were old enough to examine themselves according to St. Paul's admonition, but "for the sake of simple priests and the laity."[65] Luther's inclusion of a section on the sacrament of the altar in his catechisms not only endorsed this development; it set the standard that later catechism authors would imitate.

Although a few authors published separate guides for communion preparation in the later 1520s,[66] by the 1530s the genre had virtually disappeared. Instruction for receiving the sacrament worthily had been subsumed within the evangelical catechism. In the transitional years of the early Reformation, however, the pamphlets on communion preparation filled a perceived need for popular religious instruction. As is often the case in history, the Augsburg Confession's assertion that people were diligently instructed concerning the sacrament obscures a more complex story of adaptation and development.

65 Cohrs, *Katechismusversuche*, 2: 226 (Schultz), 3:32 (Althamer).

66 For instance, Urbanus Rhegius, *Prob zu des Herrn nachtmal für die eynfelttigen* (Augsburg: Steiner, 1528), VD16: R 1870, and Wenzeslaus Linck, *Vnterrichtung der kinder/ so zu Gottes tische wöllen geen* (Nuremberg: Gutknecht, 1528), VD16: L 1836.

Mary Jane Haemig

Living in the Light of the End: Reformation Sermons on Advent 2

The study of sermons has enriched reformation studies by considering how the reformers' insights were conveyed to the general populace. This essay examines the key emphases of Lutheran sermons for the second Sunday in Advent in reformation Germany. It focuses on gospel sermons published in postils between 1530 and 1580, looking particularly at postils published at least three times during that period.[1] It considers Lutheran preachers other than Martin Luther.

1 This essay was originally presented as a paper at the Sixteenth Century Studies Conference, Fort Worth, Texas, October 29, 2011. My thanks to all who offered comments and suggestions. These postils include the following. Printing statistics are derived from *Verzeichnis der im Deutschen Sprachbereich Erschienenen Drucke des XVI. Jahrhunderts* compiled by the Bavarian State Library, Munich, and the Herzog-August Bibliothek, Wolfenbüttel (Stuttgart: Anton Hiersemann, 1983–1995) (VD16) and from John Frymire, *The Primacy of the Postils: Catholics, Protestants, and the Dissemination of Ideas in Early Modern Germany* (Leiden: Brill, 2010). Appendices 1 and 2, 454–523 (Frymire). In counting editions listed in VD16, I have only counted those postil editions that were published between 1530 and 1580 and included the Advent sermons. My purpose here is not to provide an exact count of editions (though I hope my information is accurate) but rather to show that these were postils that were published frequently and, presumably, were used frequently.
Johannes Brenz, *Auszlegung Aller Euangelien un Episteln So man durchs gantze Jar auff einen jeden Sontag/ auch auff gewo(e)hnlichen Festen und Feyertagen in der Kirchen pflegt zu Predigen [...]* (Frankfurt/Main, 1572). VD16 lists eleven printings before 1580: B7591–7594 (Latin) and B7822, 7824, 7826, 7829, 7831–7833 (German). Frymire lists thirteen editions between 1550 and 1588.
Antonius Corvinus, *Kurtze und einfeltige Auslegung der Episteln und Euangelien/ so auff die Sontage und furnemisten Feste durchs gantze Jar [...]* (Wittenberg, 1539). VD16 lists 41 printings of the gospel sermons in German, Latin, and low German before 1580: C5348–5360, C5375, C5379–5384, C5387–5392, C5395, C5397–C5402, C5404, C5407–5409, ZV 27960, ZV3924, ZV26705, ZV3921. Frymire lists 42 editions between 1535 and 1591 and notes "The majority of editions had appeared by 1550" FN 51, 477.
Christoff Fischer, *Auszlegung der Euangelien/ so man auff die Sontage in der Christlichen Kirchen zu handeln pfleget/ Vom Advent bis auff Ostern [...]* (Smalcald: Michael Schmuck, 1573). VD16 lists five printings before 1580: V1595–1597, V1600, V1602. Frymire lists three editions, with the winter postil published between 1570 and 1576 and the summer between 1572 and 1577.
Johannes Gigas, *Postilla der Sontag Euangelien und etlicher Festen* (Stettin: Johan. Eicherns

Much of the scholarly work of Robert Kolb has focused on reformers other than Luther, the many pastors and theologians who were influenced by and who in turn shaped a "Wittenberg Theology."

The lectionary gospel text for Advent 2 was Luke 21: 25–36. In it Jesus speaks of signs that the kingdom of God is near, "Signs in sun and moon and stars, and upon the earth distress of nations in perplexity at the roaring of the sea and the waves, men fainting with fear and with foreboding of what is coming on the world; for the powers of the heavens will be shaken" (v. 25–26). These signs will precede his coming in the clouds with power and glory (v. 27). Jesus tells his listeners that when these things begin to take place they should lift up their heads for their salvation is near. He admonishes them not to be "weighed down with dissipation and drunkenness and cares of this life" (v. 34) but to "watch and pray" (v. 36) in anticipation of this event.

While the sermons examined spend varying amounts of time on descriptions of the signs of the end times – and some even find parallels in their own time – their primary focus is not on these terrible signs nor on scaring listeners into

---

Druckerey, 1570). VD16 lists six printings before 1580: H3230–3233, H3236, ZV22784. Frymire lists eight editions for the winter postil, the last published in 1596.

Johannes Habermann, *Postilla/ Das ist/ Auslegung uber die Sontags Euangelia/ vom Advent bis auff Ostern* (Wittenberg: Clement Schleich, 1581). VD16 lists three printings before 1580 (1574, 1578, and 1578), H52–H54. Frymire lists seven editions between 1575 and 1600.

Caspar Huberinus, *Postilla Deutsch: Uber alle Sontagliche und der Fu(e)rnemsten Fest Euangelien/ Durchs gantze Jar* (Wittenberg: Peter Seitzen Erben, 1557). VD16 lists eleven editions: H5394–5396, H5398–5399, H5403–5405, H5411, H5413–5414. Frymire lists eleven editions of the winter postil between 1545 and 1571.

Johannes Mathesius, *Postilla/ Oder Auszlegung der Sontags Euangelien űber das gantze jar.* (Nuremberg: Ulrich Neuber and Johann vom Bergs Erben, 1565). VD16 lists five printings before 1580, M1533–1535, M1538 and ZV10506. Frymire lists fourteen editions between 1565 and 1614, nine of them before 1580.

Simon Musaeus, *Postilla. Das ist Auszlegung der Euangelien/ so uber alle Son(n)tage/ vom Advent bis auff Ostern [...]* (Eisleben: Gaubisch, 1567). VD16 lists four printings before 1580, M5045–5047, M5052. Frymire lists eight editions between 1567 and 1590.

Simon Pauli, *Postilla. Das ist Auszlegung der Episteln und Euangelien/ an Sontagen und fu(e)rnemesten Festen [...] Das Erste Teil/ vom Advent/ bis auff Ostern* (Magdeburg: Kirchner, 1572). VD16 lists eight printings of the gospel postil before 1580, P996, P999–1001, P 1014–1016, ZV12222. Frymire lists twelve editions between 1567 and 1591.

Erasmus Sarcerius, *Auslegunge uber die euangelia der Sontage/ Von dem ersten des Advents/ bis auff der heiligen Dreyfaltigkeit tage* (1552). VD16 lists three printings before 1580: S1718–1720. Frymire lists six editions between 1538 and 1561.

Johann Spangenberg, *Auszlegunge der Episteln und Euangelien/ auff alle Sontage und fu(e)rnembsten Fest/ durchs gantze Jar* (Nu(e)rnberg: 1567). Frymire lists 47 editions between 1543 and 1620.

Johann Wigand, *Postilla/Ausslegung der Euangelien, so man durch das gantze Jar auff einen jeden Sontag und fu(e)rnemste Fest [...]* (Ursel: Nicolaus Henricus, 1569). VD16 lists six printings before 1580: W2825–2826, W2828, W2830, W2832, W2835. Frymire lists five editions between 1565/66 and 1570.

beliefs or behaviors. Rather, Lutheran preachers used this text to comfort their listeners and enable them to live with hope and confidence in light of the coming end and judgment. They wanted them to watch and pray rather than fear and tremble. Four features of these sermons support this thesis. First, the organization of the sermons shows a clear emphasis on consolatory elements over threatening elements. Second, even in the discussion of the signs of the end times the preachers emphasize consolatory elements over threatening elements. Third, the sermons emphasize the consolation both explicit and implicit in Christ's coming judgment. Especially their commentary on the verse (28) "Now when these things begin to take place, look up and raise your heads because your redemption is drawing near" makes this clear. Fourth, the sermons' discussion of the admonition (v. 36) to watch and pray sees these activities as appropriate responses to the hope and confidence in which the Christian lives.

First, the organization of the sermons shows a clear emphasis on consolatory elements over threatening elements. These preachers organized their sermons either verse by verse or thematically. As the century progressed, most preachers organized their sermons thematically. While not all preachers organized their sermons explicitly (point one, point two, etc.,) they all had a recognizable progression of thought.

Sermons on the Advent 2 text typically started with discussion of the signs of the end times and the certainty of Christ's coming in judgment. They then moved to discussing why this should be comforting rather than frightening to Christians and then to how Christians should live in anticipation of this arrival of Christ. Johannes Gigas (1514–1581) illustrates this typical progression of thought, using three points to organize his sermon:[2]

1. What signs tell us that the Last Day certainly is near
2. Why Christians should not fear or be disturbed by this day and its signs
3. How we should conduct ourselves in these miserable last days

Johannes Habermann (1516–1590), Simon Pauli (1534–1591), and Johannes Wigand (1523–1587) used almost exactly the same three points to organize their sermons. The other Lutheran preachers, while perhaps dividing their sermons into more points, also progressed through the text by discussing first the signs, then the consolatory aspects of those signs, and then the question of what to do. The preachers never left listeners with threatening signs only. Rather these signs

2 Gigas, 7r.
1. *Bey welchen Zeichen abzunemen sey/ dasz der Ju(e)ngste tag gewislich fu(e)r der Thu(e)r und nahe ist.*
2. *Warumb Christen fu(e)r diesem tage/ und den vorgehenden Zeichen/ sich nicht fu(e)rchten/ noch entsetzen sollen.*
3. *Wie wir uns in diesen letzten elenden zeiten verhalten sollen.*

became the prelude to discussion of the consolation offered by God's deeds on that day.

Second, the preachers emphasized that the signs of the end times were actually a source of consolation rather than fear for the Christian. All preachers discussed the signs described in the biblical text, some relatively briefly, others in great detail. The signs are of several kinds: in nature, in human history, in human perceptions and emotional lives. While some preachers acknowledged other explanations for these events, all see them as (nonetheless) signs given by God to warn of the last coming. Simon Pauli, for example, said that although solar eclipses have natural causes, they are also intended to be signs of misfortune.[3]

For some, the signs give opportunity for offering specific comfort to the listeners.

Antonius Corvinus (1501–1553) specifically rejected putting "a long explanation" of the signs into his sermon, noting that if we remain in faith, no sign or terror can harm us. Then he named the signs but related each one to Christ's care for us. Taking an expanded version of the text from Luke 21, Corvinus noted that Luke says first that many false prophets will come and mislead people. This is shocking, especially because they come in the name of Christ. But Corvinus told his listeners to behold the care of Christ for them and to do what he says, namely don't believe them. The second sign, gluttony and drunkenness also is opportunity for Christ to show his care for us; he says to guard yourselves against that. The third sign, that the gospel will be preached in all places, was evident in Corvinus' time "for we must confess that in many hundreds of years the gospel has never been so purely preached as now."[4]

---

3 Pauli, 18r. *Ob wol aber die finsternissen der Sonnen jre ursachen haben in der natur/ sintemal die Sonne von Gott also erschaften/ das sie vorfinstert wird/ wenn in newen Liecht der Mond sich gerad unter sie setzet/ un(d) also jr liecht auffnimet/ und demselbigen wehret/ das es nicht zu den Menschen// so an gewissen o(e)rtern auff der Erden sind/ komen noch scheinen kan/ und deerwegen von den Mathematicis viel Jar zuvor ehe sie geschehen / ko(e)nnen zuku(e)nfftig auff gewisse Jar/ Monat/ Tag/ Stunde und Minuten verku(e)ndiget werden. So bedeuten sie dennoch allzeit grosse straffen und unglu(e)ck / wie die Historien von anfang her solchs bezeugen [...] Weil auch Sonn/ Mond und Stern/ von Gott erschaffen sind/ das sie nicht allein Tage und Jare/ sondern auch Zeichen geben sollen/ wie Gene. 3 ausdru(e)cklich geschrieben stehet/ so ists gewis auch aus Gottes Wort/ das die Finsternissen an der Sonnen und Mond zeichen sind/ die allzeit etwas sonderliches von grossem unglu(e)ck bedeuten [...].*

4 Corvinus, 6v. *Doch wir wo(e)llen auffs ku(e)rtzest die zeiche/ so Lucas erzelet/ besehen/ auff das jederman wissen mu(e)ge/ wie fern sie geschehen sein/ oder noch geschehen sollen. Auffs erst sagt er/ das viel falscher Propheten komen/ und viel verfu(e)ren werden. O wie schrecklich ist das/ dieweil sie im namen Christi komen sollen. Aber sihe hie an die sorgfeltigkeit Christi fur dich/ und thue/ was er dich heisset/ so wirds kein not haben/ Nolite credere/ sagt er/ Gleubt jnen nicht. Hieher geho(e)rt der Endechrist/ mit seiner falschen lere/ und eusserlichem Gottes dienst/ davon die 2. Epistel zum Tessa. 2. sagt. Zum andern/ wird aus den worten Luce klar/ das fressen und sauffen/ grosse sorge fur zeitlich gut/ einreissen werden/ Da sorgt Christus abermal fur uns/ und sagt/ Hu(e)tet euch. Zum dritten/ Sol das Euangelion allenthalben gepredigt werden/ Solchs*

Almost all dealt with the question of *when* this event will occur. Though none had an answer, most explained why God does not want us to know when. Some emphasized the mercy in not knowing exactly when. Simon Musaeus (1521 or 1529–1576) commented that at other times when God wanted to send great punishment and change to the world, he foretold exactly when this would happen. But God has not revealed to any person either the timing of the Last Day or of one's death. Musaeus then said, "Such happens for the best so that we do not, on account of certainty, delay our repentance."[5] Johannes Brenz (1499–1570) described to his listeners both the absolute certainty of the last judgment and the absolute uncertainty of when this will occur. The reason God keeps the time of this event hidden is that he wants to keep us in our vocations, that is, he wants us to engage in our present vocation rather than seek to discover future things *(nach ku(e)nfftigen sachen gru(e)blen und forschen)*.[6]

Some preachers pointed out that while the signs are consolatory for the believer, they are cause for despair to the unbeliever. Erasmus Sarcerius (1501–1559) made much of the signs of the end times. The signs are useful for those who have faith, for they learn that when the signs appear they should lift up their heads and know their salvation is near. They should be happy and not despair concerning present signs or the coming of the Lord. But the godless should learn that they will not gain anything other than grief and sadness from the signs and the coming of Christ. For them, the signs and the coming of Christ produce despair.[7]

---

sehen wir itzt furaugen/ also/ das wir bekennen mu(e)ssen/ das es inn viel hundert jaren/ nie so rein gepredigt worden sey/ als eben itzt. Zum letzen/ sol/ Sonn/ Mond/ und die Stern/ jren natu(e)rlichen schein verlieren/ Auch sol folgen beku(e)mmernis der vo(e)lcker/ furchte der dinge/ so uber die welt komen sollen/ Rauschen des Meers/ bewegung der himelkreffte/ und was denn von Christo der zeichen mehr werden verku(e)ndiget. Wolan da hastu die zeichen und ho(e)rst/ das si komen mu(e)ssen. Auch hastu geho(e)rt/ das sie denen/ so inn Christo sein/ nicht fast schrecklich sein werden/ Demnach gedencke/ das du Christum hie im glauben ergreiffest/ als einen Herrn/ der fur dich sorget/ der dich so treulich warnet/ und bey dir/ bis an das ende der welt bleiben wil/ So wird dir kein ding schedlich sein.

5 Musaeus, 6v. *Die dritte eigenschfft des ju(e)ngsten Tages/ beruhet in der offenbarung der zeit wenn er komen sol. Da ists one sonderlichen rath nicht geschehen/ das got in andern sachen gemeiniglich/ wenn er eine grosse straff und enderung uber die Welt schicken hat wollen/ hat ers offt so genaaw zuvor geoffenbaret/ das er auch den tag ausgedruckt hat/ wenn es geschchen solte. (examples) Aber vom ju(e)ngsten Tage/ ja auch von eines jglichen Menschen tod/ hat er niemand weder jar/ tag noch stunde wollen offenbaren [...] Solchs ist uns zum besten geschehen/ das wir nicht aus sicherheit unsere Busse auffschieben [...].*

6 Brenz, 24. *daneben aber die zeit solcher zukunfft verborgen behalten/ darumb/ auff das ser uns allweg in unserm Beruff und ampt behielt/ und uns gewehnet/ dasz wir unsern gegenwertigen beruff viel mehr unterstu(e)nden auszzurichten/ den dasz wir nach ku(e)nfftigen sachen gru(e)blen und forschen wolten.*

7 Sarcerius, D5r. *Der sechste artickel helt uns fu(e)r den entlichen nu(e)tzen der zeichen Christi von dem Ju(e)ngsten tage/ und von der zukunfft des Herrn/ fu(e)r die Gottseligen/ auff das dises hieraus lernen/ wie sie inen diese zeichen sollen zum troste nutz machen. Das sollen sie also thun/ das sie auffsehen sollen/ jre heupter auffheben/ und wissen das ire erlo(e)sunge herzu*

Frequently the preachers opined that the signs are meant as an admonition to repentance. Caspar Huberinus (1500–1553) remarked that the signs in the heavens serve the purpose of admonishing and warning the godless and unrepentant so that the evil people in the world do not live so confidently in dissipation, without fear of God. Because they do not want to hear and be warned by God's Word through public preaching, they must be admonished by strange wondrous signs to repent, so that on the last day they have no excuse.[8]

In discussing the signs, Lutheran preachers' primary emphasis was not scaring the listeners into compliance with a code or into behaving a certain way. Both the placement of the discussion of the signs – always early in the sermon – and the amount of space devoted to them – which varies but seldom outweighs the subsequent statements of consolation and encouragement – make this clear. Lutheran preachers were not trying to produce fear of one's ultimate fate, nor were they trying to produce good works that would stave off that fate. They were not trying to scare listeners, but already to convey the consolation, hope and confidence, offered by the promise of this Last Day.

Third, the preachers made clear to their listeners that Christ's coming will accomplish good things and therefore is consoling, not frightening, to the Christian. What Christ does was described in different ways. For these preachers Christ did come to judge, but not merely to judge. Johannes Brenz made this clear in his two sermons. In the first sermon he talked of Christ bringing both judgment and the restoration of all things. The day on which Christ comes is a day "on which all chaos and disorder in this world will be destroyed and all matters brought again to their proper condition." Brenz recognized that great disorder also persisted in the fact that, even though Christ is preached as the one who overcomes sin, death, and the devil, these are still powerful. He assured his listeners that this disorder will be changed when Christ comes. Christ will also put into proper order the affairs of the world so that although people now oppress

nahet. Sie sollen derhalben als den fro(e)lich und gutter dinge sein/ sich nicht betru(e)ben von wegen der gegenwertigen zeichen/ oder der zukunfft des Herren.

Aus dem gegential haben die Gottlosen hie zu lernen/ das sie an den zeichen der zukunfft des Herrn/ und an seiner aukunfft selbs/ nichts werden haben/ den allein ursache zu hertzleid und betru(e)bnis.

Was lernen wir nu aus diesem sechsten artickel?

Das die zukunfft des Herrn Jhesu Christi den Gottseligen wird tro(e)stlich sein. Und widerumb den Gotlosen [v] beschwerlich/ verdrieslich/ und eine ursache zur verzweifflung.

8 Huberinus, C2v. *Zum sechsten/ ist hie weiter von den zeichen des firmaments zu mercken/ das dieselbigen von Gott dem HERRN/ den unbusfertigen und Gottlosen zur vermanung/ warnung und furcht Gottes/ geschehen/ auff das die bo(e)sen Leut in der Welt/ nicht so sicher und vermessen leben/ on allen scheuh und gotes forcht. Denn dieweil sie nicht wo(e)llen ho(e)ren/ annemen/ und sich warnen lassen/ durch Gottes Wort/ durch o(e)ffentliche predig/ so mu(e)ssen sie durch die seltzame wunderbarliche zeichen/ zur Buss vermanet werdn/ auff das [C3r] sie am Jungsten tag keine entschu(e)ldigung furwenden mo(e)gen/ jres Gottlosen lebens halben […].*

each other and take things wrongfully, this will change when he comes.[9] In his second sermon, Brenz repeated the theme of Christ as the one who restores order to chaos. God himself had to come to judge and re-order things because no king or kaiser could do away with the great disorder and dissipation in this world.[10] Brenz continued to paint a vivid picture of Christ the judge and reconciler. Brenz emphasized that God did not choose a tyrant or an angel to judge us but rather his only son Jesus Christ.

> Who is this Christ? Is he not a mediator, a savior, an advocate and a protector? Yes, why should we then worry about this judgment, especially as our Lord Christ has given us certain means and a certain way through which we come to our eternal advocate and protector, such means is faith in him.[11]

9 Brenz, 19. *Und ist eben diese zeit unnd der tag/ auff den christu swider komen wird/ welchen wir auch den Ju(e)ngsten tag nennen/ ein solche zeit/ unnd ein solcher tag/ auff welchem alle zerru(e)ttung und unordnung dieser welt abgethan/ und alle sachen widerumb in ihren rechten stand unnd wesen gebracht werden. Wir sehen/ das viel/ ja unzalbarlich unordnung sich in dieser welt zutregt...Aber solche unordnung wirdt nicht ehe auffho(e)ren / dann bisz der Ju(e)ngste tag kompt. Also great disorder that one preaches Christ has overcome sin and the devil but we see these are still powerful. This disorder wil not be removed until the Ju. Tag. Comes. Also, great disorder that one preaches Christ has overcome and destroyed death, but death still takes both the good and the evil – but such disorder will not be made right until this day comes. Also, in outer worldly affair, great disorder. Citizens oppresss each other and take for themselves what is others. What should one do? One cannot get rid of it. Also gehet es auch alles unordentlich untereinander hie inn dieser Welt/ aber es wirdt alles verichtet werden auff dem gemeinen grossen Reichstag/ den Christus auff den Ju(e)ngsten tag halten wirdt/ dessen musz man mit gedult erwarten.*

10 Brenz, 22. *Weil nuh (sprich ich) solchs die ho(e)chste gro(e)ste unordnung und zerru(e)ttung ist/ die also in dieser welt sich eingetrungen/ und durch keinen Ko(e)nig oder Kayser (wie gewaltig er auch sey) abgethan/ und verrichtet werden kan/ so musz not halben noch ein gemein Gericht Gottes vorhanden sein/ in dem Gott selbs alle ding recht anricht und ordne.*

11 Brenz, 26. *Was aber die andern die gleich wol an solche zukunfft gleuben/ aber sich doch hefftig dafu(e)r fo(e)rchten/ belangt/ ist es zwar kein wunder/ dasz sie sich von wegen der erkanntnis jrer Su(e)nd/ fu(e)r Gottes gericht forchten/ und besorgen. Das ist aber ein wunder/ dasz wir nicht bedencken noch lernen wo(e)llen/ durch wen Gott solchs sein Gericht exequiren/ un(d) verwalten wo(e)lle. Den Gott wil nicht fu(e)r sich selbs on einigen Mittler execution unnd vollstreckung thun/ so wil er auch hierzu zu solchem Gericht/ nicht einen Tyrannen zum executorn und verwalter haben/ auch keinen Engel nicht/ Sondern er wil hierzu brauchen seinen eingebornen Son Jhesum Christum/ wie Christus selbs solches meldet Johannis am 5. Der Vatter hat dem Son alles Gericht ubergeben. Und an einem andern ort/ Mir ist geben aller gewalt im Himmel und auff Erden/ u. Wer ist denn Christus? ist er nit ein Mitler/ ein Heyland/ ein Fu(e)rsprech unnd Schutzherr? Ja/ was wo(e)llen wir uns denn vor diesem Gericht besorgen/ sintemal unser HERR Christus uns ein gewis mittel/ und ein gewissen weg fu(e)r gestellt hat/ dardurch wir jn zu unserm ewigen fu(e)rsprechen und schutz oder Schirmherrn uberkommen mo(e)gen/ solches Mittel ist der glaub an jn/ und ein rechter gehorsam des glaubens. Denn das ist gewis (wie er selbs sagt) Wer da glaubt an den Eingebornen Son Gottes/ der hat das ewig Leben/ und kompt nicht in das gericht.*

Simon Musaeus described three changes that Christ will bring on the last day. First, Christ will destroy heaven and earth as if it were an old unstable house, and make a new heaven and earth. Second, all humans, dead and alive, good and bad, will be changed and receive either eternal death or eternal life. Third, judgment will come but Christ will deal differently with the faithful and the unfaithful.[12]

Johannes Wigand made clear that when Christ comes he will redeem us from all evil. He noted that in this world the righteousness of Christ is already accounted to Christians, so what do they still need? His answer is that while they now have Christ as a protector against the devil, in this life they still have a powerful enemy and tyrant, namely, original sin, that harms and plagues their natures. And the godless world still drives the pious to fear and suffering. For this reason, Christ says that the complete redemption is near, in which the pious are redeemed completely from the power and rule of sin and made again into the image of God. They will be freed entirely from the ways of the devil and the evil world and received body and soul into the kingdom of God.[13]

Repeatedly Lutheran preachers emphasized that the coming of Christ is consoling to his own. Johann Mathesius (1504–1565) said he would tell listeners why Christ comes to judge so that they would not fear this "happy day," our

---

12 Musaeus, 6r. *Die ander eigenschafft des ju(e)ngsten Tages beruhet auff dreien grosmechtigen enderungen/ die Christus mit dem ju(e)ngsten Tage sol anrichten/ umb welcher willen auch Petrus Act. Iii den ju(e)ngsten Tag nennet/ Diem restitutionis omnius, das ist/ einen tag/ da alles herwider gebracht werd/ was Gott von der Welt an/ durch den Mund aller seiner Propheten geredt hett/ wie alles viel besser sol werden [...] Die erste enderung sol Christus anrichten/ an dem grossen gebew des Himels und der Erden/ wie er selber hie sagt: Himel und Erden werden vergehen [...].*
Die ander enderung Christi am ju(e)ngsten tage / sol geschehen an allen menschen/ todten und lebendigen [...] quotes Paul I Thes. 4 *Aus diesen worten ist klar/ das alle Menschen/ todte und lebendige/ gute und bo(e)se/ werden also geendert werden/ und solche Naturen bekommen/ das sie nimmermehr werden vergehen ko(e)nnen/ sondern in ewigkeit bleiben/ Es geschehe gleich im ewigen tode/ oder im ewigen leben [...]* 6v *Die dritte enderung Christi am Ju(e)ngsten tage/ ist das Gericht mit seiner folge und execution/ davon man auff den 26. Sontag nach Trinitatis pflegt sonderlich und nach der lenge zu handeln. Alhie aber ist gnut/ so viel zu wissen/ das Christus ungleicher weise am ju(e)ngsten Gericht/ mit den Gleubigen und Ungleubigen werde umbehen [...].*

13 Wigand, 30. *Item / Ob sie gleich Christum haben zu einem Schutzherrn / wider den Teuffel/ So haben sie doch/ so lang sie hie leben/ noch injnen einen gewaltigen Feind und Tryannen/ der mit nichten feyret/ Nemlich/ Die Erbsu(e)nde/ welche jre natur noch sto(e)cket blo(e)cket und plaget. Darnach so peiniget und martert der Teuffel die frome und Gottsfu(e)rchtige/ am allermeisten der Su(e)nde halben/ welche in jnen noch uberig ist/ wie Petrus in der ersten im 5. Capit. Bezeuget.*
Uber das/ so treibet die Gottlose Welt die Fromen in angst und not/ peiniget sie auff das herteste und scherpffste/Derhalben sagt Christus/ Das die volkomene und gentzliche Erlo(e)sunge nahe sey/ in welcher die Fromen gantz und gar von dem gewalt und herschung der Su(e)nden/ erlo(e)set/ und dem bilde Gottes wider gleich werden. Item/ da werden sie von des Teuffels und der bo(e)sen Welt umbtreibung und beleidigung gentzlich erlediget und gefreiet/ und mit Leib und Seele in das Reich Gottes an und auffgenomen werden.

blessed hope. While it is a terrible day for those who are against the gospel, the Christians realize that the son of God comes to rescue the faithful from sin and death, to wipe out their misery, to turn their mourning into eternal joy, to bring them to eternal rest and regeneration, to place and restore them into their promised inheritance and possession, and to establish an eternal jubilee year.[14] He also told them they will reign with Christ in heaven and earth, as true princes of heaven.[15] Similarly, Christoph Fischer (1519–1598) made clear that for Christians the Last Day is nothing to fear.

It is a great consolation that the Last Day is a day of redemption and not of imprisonment, a day of enlivening and not of suffocating (*nicht der erstickung/ sunder der quicken*), for us Christians. All will be set in proper order, we will be fully redeemed and transferred from the kingdom of faith into the kingdom of sight. We will escape all misfortune and tears. All of our suffering will be turned to eternal joy.[16]

The preachers often used Christ's command "Lift up your heads" to express and summarize the hope and consolation that Christ's coming in judgment will give to the Christian. Johannes Spangenberg (1484–1550) linked the words "lift up your heads" to a great reversal that will take place on the day of Christ's coming:

14 Mathesius, 15v. *Zum vierdten/ wenn jr nun die wunder unnd treffliche historien habt von dem Ju(e)ngsten tage/ solt jr Layen hie sonderlich mercken/ warum der Herze Christus zum gerichte kommet/ damit jr fu(e)r diesem fro(e)lichen tage/ als unser selige hoffnung/ nicht erschrecket wie die gleyszner/ welche gar harte wort auszdem Propheten Sophonia/ mit unverstand von diesem tro(e)stlichen tage singen [...].*
Wir Christen aber die wir uns dises gerechten heylandes/ und der gerechtigkeyt seines blutes tro(e)sten/ sollen hie ho(e)ren/ warumb der Son Gottes dises gericht hegen/ unnd zum andernmal widerkommen will/ Nemlich/ das er die glaubigen ausz su(e)nde und todt errette/ jnen alle zeher und elende abwische/ jre trawrigkeyt in ewige freude verwandele/ sie ausz iren rebern und verborgem lebenin die ewige ruhe und erquickung bringe/ und sie wider in jr altes unnd [16r] verheissen erbe und besitzung restituire und einsetze/ und ein ewigs/ frey unnd Jubel jar anrichte.

15 Mathesius, 18r. *Hierausz sollet jr nun heut disen vierdten Artickel lernen/ wesz halben der Herre Jesus zum gericht kommen wirdt/ Nemlich/ das e runs erlo(e)sen/ und inn sein ewige ruhe einfu(e)ren/ und alle erquicken/ und in unser alt erbe/ oder inn die versprochne gu(e)ter/ als der rechte Josua/ einweysen/ und ein ewigs frey/ Jubel und freud jar auszru(e)ffen wirdt/ da wir von aller beschwerde unnd menschen dienstbarkeyt befreyet/ ewigklich mit jm in gleychen ehren und herrligkeyt herrschen und regiren im Himel und in Erden/ als rechte Himelsfu(e)rsten/ und mitgenossen aller seiner gu(e)ter.*

16 Fischer, A7r. *Aus der massen ein herrlicher trost ist dis/ das der Ju(e)ngste tag nicht ein tag der Gefengnis/sondern der erlo(e)sung/ nicht der erstickung/ sondern der erquickung/ uns Christen sein sol/ da alles wider zu recht gebracht wird/ wir auch vollko(e)mlich erloset/ und aus dem Reich des Glaubens in das Reich des schawens transferirt udn versetzt werden/ allem unglu(e)ck entlauffen/ all threnen von unserm angesicht/ all unser leid in ewige frewde verwandelt werden sollen [...].*

> Christ makes clear how we should prepare for his coming, as if he were to say 'You poor little ones, you have suffered much in this world for my sake, now look up at him whom you have trusted. Where are those now who persecuted you? Where is now their great pomp and vanity? Have they not all been disgraced in body and soul? Behold, now your cross and suffering shall be at an end and their eternal misfortune and damnation begin. Do not let my power and glory shock you. They are not against you but for you.'[17]

Others voiced similar sentiments. Caspar Huberinus said that "Lift up your heads" is comforting for those with little courage. Our salvation, not our condemnation, is near.[18] Simon Pauli, in commenting on "Lift up your heads," described the work of Christ in coming, bringing us to freedom, and leading us into the kingdom of his Father. Pauli used the words of Revelation 7 and 21, "God will wipe away all our tears, we will not hunger or thirst, death will be no more, nor suffering" to describe this day.[19]

In sum, Lutheran preachers emphasized that the coming of Christ is cause for rejoicing, not for fear, a reason to be consoled rather than terrified. Listeners were to "lift up their heads," filled with hope and certainty that the Last Day would bring them good things.

Fourth, the preachers' discussion of the admonition in verse 36 to watch and pray saw these activities as appropriate responses to the hope and confidence in which the Christian lives. The preachers asserted that such watching is not passive but involves love in action. Antonius Corvinus noted,

> The Lord closes his sermon with the little words watch [and] pray. How should we watch? We should have fervent, burning, living faith that is active in love, as the five young women had. For *watch* means this, as *sleep* means to despise God's word, to remain in unbelief and not do anything good.[20]

---

17 Spangenberg, 13v. *ER zeigt an/ wie wir uns zu seiner Zukunfft bereiten sollen/ als solt er sagen/ Du armes heufflin/ hast viel inn dieser Welt umb meinet willen mu(e)ssen leyden/ Nun sihe auff den/ dem du vertrawet hast. Wo findt sie nun/ die dich verfolget haben? Wo ist nun jr grosser pracht unnd stoltz? Sind sie nicht alsampt an leyb und Seel zu schanden worden? Sihe/ jetzund sol dein Creutz und elend ein ende haben/ und jr ewiges unglu(e)ck unnd verdamnusz angehen/ Lasz dich mein gewalt unnd herrligkeyt nicht schrecken. Sie ist nicht wider dich/ sondern fu(e)r dich.*

18 Huberinus C2r.

19 Pauli, 20v. *Da Gott der HERR wird abwischen alle Threnen von unsern augen/ da wir nicht mehr werden hungern noch du(e)rsten/ da der Tod nicht mehr wird sein/ noch leid/ noch geschrey/ noch schmertzen/ kein frost/keine hitze/ da wir nicht werden bedu(e)rffen der Sonnen/ noch des Monden/ das sie uns scheinen/ denn die herrligkeit des HERRN wird uns erleuchten/ un(d) unser leuchte wird sein das Lamb Gottes Jesus Christus/ Apoca. Cap. 7 und 21.*

20 Corvinus, 7r. *Aber die Christen haben acht auff diese ziet [...][der Herr] beschleusset seine predigt mit dem wo(e)rtlein/ Vigilate/Wachet/ Wie sollen wir aber wachen? Hitzigen/ brenneden/ lebendigen glauben sollen wir haben/ so durch die liebe thetig sey/ wie die fu(e)nff klugen Jungfrawen gehabt haben/ Denn durch wache(n) / wird solchs bedeut/ Wie wiederumb schlaffen heisset Gottes wort verachten/ im unglauben bleiben/ und nichts guts thun.*

Johannes Spangenberg used almost identical language to Corvinus, saying that "to watch" means a fervent burning, living faith, that is active in love and helps the neighbor.[21]

Some preachers specifically mentioned that such watching involved remaining in one's vocation. Anticipation of the end times should not cause one to leave one's everyday pursuits but rather to carry them out with renewed vigor. Simon Pauli devoted two pages to the admonition to watch and pray. He defined "watching" as paying attention to one's vocation, and to the blessedness which consists in diligently and properly carrying it out, so that one is worthy at any time to receive the Lord Jesus Christ. Prayer is a wall and armor against all misfortune so that one can avoid the awful things that will happen before the Last Day and can, with right faith and good conscience, greet the Lord Christ, the judge of the living and the dead.[22] He described six reasons to watch and pray: First, Christ's command here; second, the example of the flood which tells us that the last day will surely come even if delayed; third, the fact that Christ will judge all, regardless of their earthly status; fourth, the present time and the signs reported in it, from which one can be convinced that the last day is near; fifth, the fact that the exact hour of the Lord's appearance is uncertain; and sixth, eternity, in which those blessed by God will have eternal joy and glory while the godless will be burned and tortured in eternal fire.[23]

Preachers also described behavior to avoid. Johannes Habermann contrasted gluttony and worry with the proper behavior of watching and praying. His third

---

21 Spangenberg, 13v. *Es heyst einen hitzigen/ brennenden/ lebendigen glauben haben/ der durch die liebe tha(e)tig ist/ Gott fu(e)r augen hat/ und dem Nechsten hilfft/ wie die fu(e)nff klugen Jungfrawen/ Martth. 25.*

22 Pauli, 21r. *Wacker sein/ ist ein auff sehen haben auff seinen Beruff/ und auff die Gottseligkeit/ sich vleissig darin vornemen lassen/ also / das man im [v] glauben/ Gottes furcht/ und gutem gewissen bereit ist/ allezeit/ alle stund/ und alle augenblick/ den HERRN Christum wirdig zu empfahen. Das Gebet aber/ so eine Maur und eine Brustwehr ist/ wider alles unglu(e)ck/ bitter gewrich und embsich/ das man allem ubel welchs fu(e)r dem Ju(e)ngsten tage wird vorher gehen/ entfliehen/ und mit rechtem glauben und gutem gewissen den HERRN christum/ den Richter der Lebendigen und der todten empfahen mo(e)ge.*

23 Pauli, 21v. *Die Erste ursache ist/ Des Herrn Christi Befehl/ davon allhie stehet: So seid nu allezeit wacker und betet […] Die Ander ursache ist/ das Exempel der Sindflut/ Nemlich das der Ju(e)ngste tag gewisse komen wird/ obwol die zeit lang wehret […]Die Dritte ursche ist/ der Richter Christus/ der ohn ansehen der Personen mit gerechtigkeit richten wird/all Keiser/ Ko(e)nige/ Fu(e)rsten/ Graven/ Freyherrn/ Edeleut/ Bu(e)rgermeister/ Ratsverwandten/ Bu(e)rger/ Bauren/ Gelerte/ Ungelerte/ Herrn/ Knechte/ Frawen/ Megde/ Reich/ Arm/ Alt und Jung […] Die Vierde ursache ist die gegenwertige [22r] zeit/ und die zeichen droben gemeldet/ daraus man gewis kan uberzeuget werden/ das der Ju(e)ngste tag itzt fu(e)r der thu(e)r und fu(e)rhanden sey…Die fu(e)nffte ursache ist/ die ungewisse stunde/ darin der HERR wird erscheinen/ davon allhie melding geschiehet […] Die sechste ursache ist/ die ewigkeit/ so nimer kein ende hat/ darin die Gottseligen ewige freude und herrligkeit haben werden/ die gottlosen aber/ durch ewiges feur/ werden gebrent/ gequelet und gemartert werden […].*

point began by warning against the two vices of gluttony and immersion in the cares of this life. Then he contrasted these to the proper activities of watching and praying. To watch is to engage God's word in a fresh and lively fashion, to hear and learn it without complaint or laziness and not grow weary of it. To pray means that we zealously and ceaselessly call on God in this last dangerous time for a blessed journey home out of this miserable life, for a blessed end, that we may flee all the misfortune of this world, that we may overcome all misfortune and stand with joy before the judgment seat of Jesus Christ our Lord.[24]

Johannes Gigas sought to strike a balance between proper behavior and avoiding problematic behavior, declaring,

> We should behave according to Christ's rules (Matthew 6). Pray diligently, work faithfully and carry out our proper vocation, remain silent, and commit all things to our heavenly father [...] We can surely, in God's name, eat, drink, and be merry with good friends, for God gives us wine and beer for our thirst, health, and joy (Psalm 104, Sirach 32, 1 Tim. 5 etc.) Only let all things happen in the fear of God and without harming our offices and that we do not drink ourselves into a stupor.[25]

Lutheran preachers did not use this opportunity to say much about prayer. Those who commented saw prayer as helping to preserve the believer in faith. Johannes Wigand noted that Christ admonishes us to pray so that those who fear God commit themselves to God and let him rule us, so that we do not fall into sin or grow stubborn and contrary but rather are ready at all times to appear before the judgment seat of Christ.[26]

---

24 Habermann, 38r. *Wacker sein heist Frisch und keck sich uben inGottes [v] wort/ dasselbige one verdrus und one faulheit ho(e)ren und lernen/ dabey verharren / und desselbigen nicht uberdru(e)ssig werden/ sondern wachen als die trewen Knechte/ die auff iren Herrn warten/ wie Christus spreicht Luc. 12. Lasset ewer Lenden umbgu(e)rtet sein/ und ewer Liechte brennen/ [...].*
Beten geho(e)ret auch zu der bereitschafft auff diesen tag des HErrn/ das wir embsig und on unterlas zu Gott ruffen/ in dieser letzten/ gefehrlichen zeit/ umb eine selige heimfart aus diesem elenden leben/ umb ein seliges ende/ das wir mu(e)gen entfliehen allem unglu(e)ck in dieser Welt/ das ist/ auff das wir alles unglu(e)ck mo(e)gen uberwinden/ und mit frewden stehen fu(e)r dem Richterstuel Jhesu Christi unsers HErrn/ Denn wirdig sein/ heist allhie so viel/ als ko(e)nnen entfliehen.

25 Gigas, 10v. *[...] wir sollen uns nach Christi REgeln halten/ Matth. 6. Fleiszig beten/ getrewlich arbeiten/ und unsers ordentlichen beruffs warten/ fein still sein/ unnd unserm himlischen Vater alles befehlen/ den den rechten Segen und Regen gibt/ Psalm 127. Etc. Wir mu(e)gen wol in Gottes namen essen/ trincken/ und bey guten freunden fro(e)lich sein/ den Gott gib uns Wein un(d) Bier/ fu(e)rn durst/ zur gesundheit und freude/ Psalm 104. Syrach 32. 1 Tim. 5 etc. Alleine das alles in Gottes furcht und on ergernis unsers Ampts geschehe/ und das wir uns nicht unsinnig unnd zu Narrn sauffen [...].*

26 Wigand, *Betet. Es thut der Herr Christus auch dis stu(e)ck hinzu/ auff das die Gottsfu(e)rchtige mit stetigem Gebet sich got befehlen und ergebe(n)/ das derselbige uns regiere/ auff das wir nicht in grewlichen Su(e)nde un(d) Laster fallen/ noch halstarrig und widerspenstig seien/ Sondern alle stund un(d) augenblick bereit und geru(e)st fu(e)r de(n) Richstul Christi zuer-*

Lutheran preachers warned their listeners against falling from the true faith. Erasmus Sarcerius hinted that some in his time had failed to "watch and pray." He admonished his listeners to watch and pray so that they, in the desperate times that will precede the Last Day, do not fall into sin and stubbornly remain in the kingdom of the antichrist or, after escaping from it, again join it. Sarcerius reported that many in his day had thought they found peace in falling away from the truth, but these will really find in the end only fear and trembling.[27]

These Lutheran messages contrast sharply with Roman Catholic sermons preached on the same Sunday and text. Roman Catholic preachers in this era used this text to scare listeners. A common theme was that those who had not been convinced by the Advent 1 sermon, a gentle invitation to live appropriately in light of the coming of Christ, would need to be scared by the signs and threats of Advent 2. While a lengthy comparison of Lutherans and Roman Catholics is a topic for another time, such comparison makes possible a fuller appreciation of Lutheran emphases.

For Lutheran preachers, Luke's story of signs and catastrophes preceding Christ's coming to judgment, and that coming to judgment itself, were not cause for fear but rather for hope on the part of the faithful. Rather than trying to scare their listeners, they used this text as an opportunity to build hope and confidence that the merciful God would take care of the believer.

---

scheinen/ Den(n) diss ist das aller gro(e)ssest und fu(e)rnemste ding/ Den(n) wen(n) Christus komen wird/ so werden alle ding/ die in dieser Welt sind/ auffho(e)ren un(d) ein ende nemen. Welche nu werden Busse gethan/ Gottes Word vleissig geho(e)ret/ und sch des Abendmals des Herrn gebrauchet haben/ die werden in die ewige freude Eingehen. Welche aber gantz und gar in den sorgen dieser Welt sind ersoffen gewesen/ der Volseufferey nachgehenget/ Gottes Wort und das heilige Abendmal verachtet haben/ dieselbigen werden solcher Gu(e)ter mangeln/ auch unaussprechliche grosse Straffe/ marter und pein dem dem Hellischen fewer erfaren mu(e)ssen.

27 Sarcerius, D4r. *Was lernen wir nu aus diesem vierden artickel?*
Das wir wachen und beten sollen/ auff das wir nicht von wegen vorstehender not/ die sich in den letzten zeiten fu(e)r dem Ju(e)ngsten tage werden zutragen/ in ergernis fallen/ und hieraus ursache nemen/ bey dem reich des Antichrists zuverharren/ oder so wir darvon abgefallen wider darzu tretten. Wie den von vielen heutiges tages geschicht in dem sie vermeinen ruhe zufinden durch jren abfal von der warheit/ so doch hernach ire angst und bangigkeit aller ersten recht angehet.

Scott Hendrix

Martin Luther's Bauernkrieg[1]

The following summary of the Peasants' War was written in 1525 on the title page of Martin Luther's Admonition to Peace.

> In the year 1525 a horrible spilling of blood was caused by a widespread peasants' war. Almost every region of Germany rebelled against the authorities with the result that about 200,000 peasants were woefully slain. It reached Alsace, Franconia, the Rhineland, the Black Forest, the Nördlingen crater,[2] Thuringia, Meissen, Swabia, and elsewhere. In the rebellious towns and countryside more than 300,000 people were killed by the sword and other weapons. O God, please forgive us and have mercy on us.[3]

The number of casualties was much too high, but even for today the extent of the war was accurately portrayed—if we include under "elsewhere" the action in Austria and skirmishes outside the areas that are named. The number of dead is now estimated to be fewer than 100,000.[4] The author was well aware that the revolution of 1525, as Peter Blickle renamed it, was a war fought with deadly weapons and not a feud among farmers wielding hayforks.[5]

1. The summary was probably inscribed on the front of Luther's *Admonition to Peace* in order to protest Luther's condemnation of rebelling peasants or to confirm that Luther was right to warn peasants and princes against using vio-

1 The original German text of this essay was delivered on June 3, 2013, at the Westfälische Wilhelms-Universität Münster in a series of lectures sponsored by the Exzellenzcluster "Religion und Politik." I wish to thank Dr. Iris Flessenkämper and her colleagues for the invitation and Dr. Hauke Christiansen (Ratzeburg) for improving the original German. The essay has been translated and revised by the author.

2 The *Ries*, a large crater in south-central Germany about 50 miles north of Augsburg.

3 Martin Luther, *Ermanunge zum fride auff die zwolff artickel der Bawerschafft in Schwaben.* (Wittenberg, 1525). HAB Wolfenbüttel Sign. 131.6 Theol. (16).

4 Modern scholars estimate the number of dead to be no more than 75,000 or 0.5 % of the population of the Holy Roman Empire in 1525. See Thomas Robisheaux, "Peasants' War, German," in *Europe 1450 to 1790: Encyclopedia of the Early Modern World*, vol. 4 (New York: Charles Scribner's Sons, 2004) 432–436.

5 Peter Blickle, *Der Bauernkrieg: Die Revolution des Gemeinen Mannes* (Munich: C.H. Beck, 1998), 41–54.

lence. Be that as it may, this lamentation over the war's losses set next to the title of Luther's pamphlet highlights how little influence the Reformer exercised over the tragedy of 1525. Luther predicted what would happen if peasants and princes chose violence over negotiations: "an endless shedding of blood in German lands."[6] But the ink was scarcely dry on *Admonition to Peace* when the Thuringian phase of the war ended with the slaughter of 5,000 or more commoners outside Frankenhausen on May 15, 1525.

No intervention by Luther could have prevented the slaughter. That statement cannot be proven, of course, but it is probable in the form that Albrecht Beutel phrased it: "All in all, there is no reason to believe that anything different would have happened during the Peasants' War if Luther had remained silent or expressed himself differently."[7] Nevertheless, Luther's name is often mentioned in the same breath with the revolution, even though he lived just outside the war zone and wrote about it only near the end. A competent portrayal of the historical event is possible without mentioning Luther at all, but twenty-five years ago Winfried Schulze expressed the view that prevailed: "How is it possible to give an account of the Peasants' War without mentioning Luther's stance, commenting on it, and finally condemning him?"[8] No one has ever said that about Urban Rhegius, who lived much closer to the action, or about Rhegius's pamphlet on *Leibeigenschaft* to which Luther referred in *Admonition to Peace.*[9]

It is hard to resist mentioning Luther because of his words at the conclusion of the pamphlet, *Against the Robbing and Murdering Hordes of Peasants*, words once more highlighted and condemned in a recent biography as *ungeheuerliche Aussagen:*[10]

> Therefore, dear lords, here is an opportunity to save, rescue, and help. Have mercy on these poor people. Let whoever is able stab, smite, slay. If you die in doing it, good for you! A more blessed death can never be yours; for you die while obeying the divine commandment in Romans [13] and in loving service of your neighbor, whom you are saving from the bonds of hell and the devil. I beg everyone who can to flee from the

6 *Ermahnung zum Frieden auf die zwölf Artikel der Bauernschaft in Schwaben* (1525), in WA 18: 329; LW 46: 40.

7 Albrecht Beutel, *Martin Luther: Eine Einführung in sein Leben Werk und Wirkung* 2. Aufl. (Leipzig: Evangelische Verlagsanstalt, 2006), 121.

8 Winfried Schulze, *Deutsche Geschichte im 16. Jahrhundert 1500–1618* (Frankfurt am Main: Neue Historische Bibliothek, 1987), 103.

9 Urban Rhegius, *Von Leibaygenschafft odder knechthait wie sich Herren unnd aygen leut Christlich halten sollend* (Augsburg and Leipzig, 1525); Luther, *Ermahnung zum Frieden*, in WA 18: 327. See Michael Schuft, *Urbanus Rhegius—Von Leibeigenschaft und Knechtheit* (Norderstedt: GRIN Verlag, 2008); see also Robert Kolb, "The Theologians and the Peasants: Conservative Evangelical Reactions to the German Peasants' Revolt," *Archive für Reformationsgeschichte* 69 (1978): 103–131.

10 Heinz Schilling, *Martin Luther: Rebell in einer Zeit des Umbruchs* (Munich: C.H. Beck, 2012), 309.

> peasants as from the devil himself. Those who do not flee, I pray that God will enlighten and convert. As for those who refuse to be converted, God grant them neither fortune nor success. [...] Let anyone who thinks this is too harsh remember: rebellion is intolerable and the destruction of the world is to be expected every hour.[11]

These words color almost every treatment of Luther and the revolution even though he had little to do with the conflict. Moreover, these words were not directed against all peasants. Luther distinguished the "robbing and murdering" peasants from those who only foolishly or unwillingly joined Müntzer's force and, assumed Luther, could still refuse to fight. Luther made the distinction because of a three-week journey through Thuringia that ended only ten days before Frankenhausen. He learned that Thomas Müntzer was recruiting allies for a violent revolt, but he also learned that not everybody supported Müntzer and that not every recruit, like inexperienced soldiers today, could envision what lay ahead. Looking back after six years, Luther claimed that more than once he was in danger of life and limb,[12] and indeed that was possible. When the routes taken by Luther during the last half of his journey are matched to documented instances of pillaging by peasant bands, Luther might have witnessed enough mayhem to feel personally threatened and to convince him that the social order was collapsing.[13]

Luther's sympathy for the naïve and unwilling recruits enabled him to distinguish between peaceful and militant peasants; and his conviction that German society might not survive a revolution led to harsh words against the rebelling peasants. There was another trigger, however, in addition to the theological and historical motives, something personal, which made Luther unload his anger on the peasants. He not only feared the consequences of a war but he was also personally confronted by a reformation very different from the one he envisioned. By 1525 the reformation advocated by Luther and his colleagues was still emerging. They did not know exactly what shape a church separated from Rome and its bishops would take; and until after Elector John succeeded Frederick in May 1525, the reforms implemented so far had received no official sanction from the authorities in Electoral Saxony. Luther was, however, certain of one thing: he did not want a reformation that resulted from a violent revolution. With Thomas Müntzer and his followers in Thuringia, that was exactly what he faced.

2. Reformation without revolution – Luther did not always have that conviction. He arrived at it step by step between 1521 and 1525. At Worms it was not yet present because Luther and his colleagues were only beginning to envision a

---

11 *Auch wider die räuberischen und mörderischen Rotten der anderen Bauern* (1525), in WA 18: 361; LW 46: 54–55.

12 *Warnung an seine lieben Deutschen (1531)*, in WA 30.3: 279; LW 47: 15.

13 Christiane Griese, "*Luthers Reise ins Aufstandsgebiet vom 16.4.1525 bis zum 6.5.1525,*" *Mühlhäuser Beiträge zu Geschichte, Kulturgeschichte, Natur und Umwelt* 12 (1989): 34–35.

Christendom without the pope. Luther knew in 1521 that most of the estates at the Diet were deeply afraid of a revolution by the commoners in their domains. Before Luther was invited to the Diet, a proposal from Emperor Charles V to condemn Luther unheard was defeated by the estates because it might incite rebellion. During his first hearing, Luther was warned that the writings he was asked to recant might lead to a popular uprising. The next day, after he refused to repudiate what he had written, Luther responded to that warning:

> From what I have said it should be clear that I have carefully considered the threat that my teaching might cause divisions, strife, peril, and excessive zeal. For me, however, it is a great joy to observe that the word of God has caused both zealotry and discord. God's word is both the cause and the occasion of that strife and always leads down that road, as Jesus said (Matt 10:34): 'I did not come to bring peace but the sword.'[14]

The man who wrote harsh words against the rebelling peasants in 1525 was in April of 1521 a happy fomenter of discord.

At the Wartburg Luther changed his tune. During a brief visit incognito to Wittenberg in early December of 1521, he could easily have witnessed the public disturbances that were happening around him. Soon after his return to the Wartburg, he published *A Sincere Admonition to all Christians to Guard Against Insurrection and Rebellion.* It appeared, he said, that the commoners would no longer put up with the injustices they suffered and had "good reason" to resort to violence.[15] Luther's source was the pamphlet *Karsthans*,[16] one of the inflammatory writings he might have seen in Leipzig during the journey to Wittenberg. He reported to Spalatin: "I was worried about the violent conduct of some of our followers and have determined to issue a public exhortation on that subject as soon as I return to my wilderness [the Wartburg]."[17] Luther was worried about broader unrest than what he might have seen in Wittenberg, but his *Sincere Admonition* did not endorse the violence he wrote might be justified. For the commoners, there was no legitimate use of force without an order from the authorities. Therefore, "we must calm the minds of the commoners and tell them to abstain from the words and also the passions which led to insurrection." Those who understood my teaching aright, he promised, would never start a rebellion. No insurrection was ever right no matter how just the cause it sought to promote. And for himself: "I am always on the side of those who suffer from an

14 *Verhandlungen mit D. Martin Luther auf dem Reichstage zu Worms* (1521), in WA 8: 834–835; LW 32: 111.

15 *Eine treue Vermahnung M. Luthers zu allen Christen, sich zu hüten vor Aufruhr und Empörung* (1522), in WA 8: 676; LW 45: 57.

16 See Thomas Neukirchen, *Karsthans: Thomas Murners "Hans Karst" und seine Wirkung in sechs Texten der Reformationszeit* (Heidelberg: Universitaetsverlag Winter, 2011).

17 Luther to Spalatin, ca. December 5, 1521, in WABr 2: 410, n. 5.

insurrection and against those who start the rebellion regardless of the reason, because the result can only be innocent bloodshed and damage."[18]

At the end of 1521, Luther was no longer delighting in the strife his teaching might cause. And by the middle of 1523 he was reinforcing his main point: genuine Christians would not start an insurrection, but if their faith was threatened, they could express resistance without violence. Moreover, the sword was given to princes, but Christian princes must not think they ruled mainly by force,[19] although two years later at Frankenhausen they found it necessary to use force – with Luther's approval. In a treatise entitled *Temporal Authority*, Luther argued that true Christians did not need for themselves the sword or laws passed by civil authority to protect and serve the commonweal; rather they abided by the laws of civil rulers only for the sake of others. It was Luther's way of resolving the conflict between the nonresistance of Matt 5:39 and obedience to civil authority in Rom 13:1: "At one and the same time, you satisfy God's kingdom inwardly and the kingdom of the world outwardly."[20]

3. Before the Peasants' War, Luther's stance – reformation without revolution – was further strengthened by his conflict with Thomas Müntzer. Five years younger than Luther, Müntzer born in Stolberg, a picturesque town twenty-five miles from Mansfeld where Luther grew up. From 1517 to 1519 Müntzer studied on and off in Wittenberg, but Luther's influence on him has never been pinpointed. Müntzer could hardly avoid the calls for reform emanating from Luther and his colleagues,[21] but it did not take long for the contrast between his idea of reform and Luther's view to become evident.[22] As a pastor in Zwickau (1520–1521) Müntzer clashed with senior clergy, one of whom, Egranus, was close to Luther. When Müntzer was summoned to appear before the Zwickau council for inciting unrest, he fled the town. After six months in Prague, where his theology of the end times became more pronounced, Müntzer moved around until accepting a pastorate in 1523 at Allstedt. He wrote a German liturgy for St. John's parish and drew crowds to his sermons by admonishing them to prepare for the last days. His message was direct: A new spirit-filled church of the elect must replace the current feeble and decaying Christendom of the godless.[23] The dif-

18 *Eine treue Vermahnung*, in WA 8: 680; LW 45: 62–63.

19 *Von weltlicher Oberkeit, wie weit man ihr Gehorsam schuldig sei*, in WA 11: 271–272; LW 45: 118.

20 *Von weltlicher Oberkeit*, in WA 11: 255; LW 45: 96.

21 Helmar Junghans, "*Thomas Müntzer als Wittenberger Theologe*," in *Der Theologe Thomas Müntzer*, ed., Siegfried Bräuer and Helmar Junghans (Göttingen: Vandenhoeck & Ruprecht, 1989), 267–270.

22 Leif Grane, "*Thomas Müntzer und Martin Luther*," in *Bauernkriegs-Studien, Schriften des Verein fur Reformationsgeschichte* 82, 2/83, ed., Bernd Moeller (Gütersloh 1975), 74–77.

23 Günter Vogler, "*Thomas Müntzer – Irrweg oder Alternative? Plädoyer für eine andere Sicht*," *Archive für Reformationsgeschichte* 103 (2012): 11–40.

ference between the elect and the godless was the quality of their faith. According to Müntzer, the ungodly sought a faith without deprivation and suffering just as Luther, whom Müntzer called the "soft-living flesh at Wittenberg,"[24] was doing. True faith, however, sought the "bitter Christ" and stood ready to suffer with him.[25] In order to fortify the elect and separate them from the ungodly, Müntzer bound the elect into a new covenant that was sealed with the rainbow from the story of Noah and the flood.

Müntzer and Luther quickly realized their differences – especially after Müntzer and his followers allegedly burned down the Mallerbach chapel near Allstedt. The chapel, a popular pilgrimage destination dedicated to the Virgin Mary, belonged to a Cistercian convent. The Saxon authorities sought the arsonists without success and asked the town council of Allstedt for assistance. A letter formulated in all likelihood by Müntzer was sent to Duke John declaring that the town council refused to cooperate; but he practically admitted that Allstedt citizens had set the fire, because "the poor pilgrims who came to the chapel failed to realized they were venerating and praying to the devil who had assumed Mary's name." Since our people, argued Müntzer, had caused no harm to the common good, the princes should stop defending the idolatrous monks and nuns and do their duty, that is, punish the ungodly with the sword and protect the godly, who were, of course, Müntzer's cohort of the elect.[26]

4. When Luther received a report of the letter's content, he responded with his own *Letter to the Princes of Saxony concerning the Rebellious Spirit.* It was the Reformer's first public declaration of combat with critics from his own ranks.[27] The entire tract was directed at Müntzer, and it contains the key to Luther's harsh reaction to the rebelling peasants, including his so-called *ungeheuere Aussagen.*

Luther was convinced that Müntzer was planning not only a public demonstration but a violent revolution against the authorities. With that in mind Luther encouraged the Saxon princes to imagine the outcome if Müntzer succeeded in winning over most of the populace.[28] To prevent that, Luther for the first time urged the princes to take the initiative with force:

---

24 Thomas Müntzer, *Hoch verursachte Schutzrede und antwwort wider das Gaistlosze sanfft lebende fleisch zu Wittenberg* (Nuremberg, 1524).

25 Thomas Müntzer, *Schriften und Briefe, kritische Gesamtausgabe*, ed., Gunther Franz (Gütersloh: Gütersloher Verlagshaus, 1968), 222.22–23.

26 *Rat und Gemeinde zur Allstedt* to Herzog Johann, ca. June 14, 1524, in *Thomas-Müntzer-Ausgabe*, vol. 2, *Briefwechsel* 76 (Leipzig: Evangelische Verlagsanstalt, 2010), 252–256.

27 Siegfried Bräuer, "*Die Vorgeschichte von Luthers 'Ein Brief an die Fürsten zu Sachsen von dem aufrührerischen Geist,'*" *Lutherjahrbuch* 47 (1980): 40.

28 *Ein Brief an die Fürsten zu Sachsen von dem Aufrührerischen Geist* (1524), in WA 15: 212; LW 40: 51.

> Your Graces should not sleep or be idle. For God will want and require an answer if the power of the sword is carelessly used or regarded. Nor would your Graces be able to give account to the people or to the world if you tolerated and endured violence and rebellion.[29]

Luther was afraid, however, that Müntzer would convince the princes that he was driven by the Spirit and was therefore justified in using force at his pleasure. To preclude that possibility, Luther reminded the princes that Müntzer had a hand in burning down the Mallerbach Chapel: "It must be an evil spirit if it can only prove its legitimacy by destroying churches and cloisters and setting the saints on fire. The worst villains on earth could do that especially if they were protected with certainty against meeting resistance."[30]

For Luther, however, it was not enough to attack the unjustified use of force by Müntzer. It was necessary to attack Müntzer himself, whom Luther regarded as his rival in securing the support of the princes. Several factors led Luther to this opinion. In Luther's homeland, the county of Mansfeld, he was alerted by friends in 1524 that Müntzer was winning adherents.[31] Shortly thereafter, Müntzer delivered a sermon at Allstedt in the presence of Duke John and his son, John Frederick. In the sermon Müntzer styled himself a new Daniel who, like the Old Testament prophet, was showing princes their duty and interpreting for them the end times. It was the same duty that Müntzer, on behalf of the Allstedters, claimed in the letter to Duke John, but this time with an ominous proof text (Deut 13:10): "Stone to death those who try to turn you away from the Lord your God."[32] Müntzer's prophetic calling and aggressive determination forced Luther to revise his views of using force. At Worms he had declared that preaching God's word always led to strife and upheaval, but now he warned that a violent rebellion would not advance the reformation but severely damage it. In 1524 he concluded: "We who are engaged in the ministry of the word are not allowed to use force. Ours is a spiritual conflict in which we wrest hearts and souls from the devil."[33]

5. Luther came to view Müntzer as a rival because his call for violence threatened Luther's own divinely inspired mission to reform Christendom only by the nonviolent preaching of God's word. In Luther's eyes Müntzer was an upstart, who claimed to be inspired by the Spirit to establish a spotless church of the elect through a revolution that annihilated the ungodly. Müntzer's revolution

29 *Ein Brief an die Fürsten zu Sachsen*, WA 15: 213; LW 40: 51–52.

30 *Ein Brief an die Fürsten zu Sachsen*, WA 15: 213; LW 40: 52.

31 Siegfried Bräuer, "*Bauernschaft in der Grafschaft Mansfeld-Fiktion und Fakten*," in *Martin Luther und der Bergbau im Mansfelder Land*, ed., Rosemarie Knape (Eisleben: Stiftung Luthergedenkstätten in Sachsen-Anhalt, 2000), 121–157.

32 Michael Baylor, ed., *The German Reformation and the Peasants' War: A Brief History with Documents* (Boston: Bedford/St. Martin's, 2012), 72.

33 *Ein Brief an die Fürsten zu Sachsen*, in WA 15: 219; LW 40: 57.

would undermine Luther's reformation. Luther sought first to disqualify Müntzer's claim to divine direction by contrasting Müntzer's refusal to face a neutral audience with Luther's defense of his views in hostile circumstances at Augsburg, Leipzig, and Worms.[34] By asserting the superiority of his own judgment, Luther then attacked Müntzer's claim to spiritual guidance:

> I am sure that we who have and acknowledge the gospel, even though we are poor sinners, have the right spirit, or as Paul says [Romans 8:23], 'the first fruits of the Spirit,' even if now we do not have the fullness of the Spirit. [...] For we know what faith is, and love, and the cross; and we can learn no greater thing on earth than faith and love. Hence we can know and judge what doctrine is true or not true, and whether it is in accordance with the faith or not. We know this lying spirit [Müntzer] and are convinced that he will disregard scripture and the spoken word of God and abolish the sacrament of the altar and baptism.[35]

Finally, after making his case that the princes should support his reformation and not Müntzer's revolution, Luther requested them to take the same action that one year later he urged against the rebelling peasants, only not so ruthlessly:

> I have humbly entreated your Graces to deal earnestly with such ranting and raving, so that in this matter we act only according to the word of God as is fitting for Christians. Only thus can we guard against the sparks of rabble-rousing, to which the mob is otherwise all too inclined. Even though they brag they are full to overflowing with ten holy spirits, they are not Christians if they want to overrun God's word and use their fists rather than suffer and endure everything.[36]

6. The Saxon authorities did not take action against Müntzer until May of 1525 when the threat of sedition and revolution became obvious. In April Luther saw the mounting unrest during his tour of Thuringia and in person asked Duke John to prepare his troops for battle.[37] On the way home, Luther urged his friend and relative, John Rühel, to prevent Count Albrecht of Mansfeld from going soft on the peasants. Even if they numbered several thousand, the peasants were still robbers and murderers who aimed to establish a new social order against God's commandment. Luther must have heard someone assert that the peasants were not following Müntzer, for he wrote: "No one except their god, the devil, will believe them when they deny any connection to Müntzer."[38] It was a sure sign of divine wrath, wrote Luther already in *Admonition to Peace*, that God was sending

34 *Ein Brief an die Fürsten zu Sachsen*, in WA 15: 214; LW 40: 53–54.

35 *Ein Brief an die Fürsten zu Sachsen*, in WA 15: 216; LW 40: 55.

36 *Ein Brief an die Fürsten zu Sachsen*, in WA 15: 220–221; LW 40: 59.

37 For local conflicts in Thuringia, see Volkmar Joestel, *Ostthüringen und Karlstadt: Soziale Bewegung und Reformation im mittleren Saaletal am Vorabend des Bauernkrieges (1522–1524)* (Berlin, Schelzky & Jeep, 1996), 24; Günter Vogler, ed. , *Bauernkrieg zwischen Harz und Thüringer Wald* (Stuttgart: Steiner, 2008), 182, 309.

38 *Luther to Rühel, May 4, 1525*, in WABr 3: 480, 482; LW 49: 109, 111.

among us "many false teachers and prophets," who were seducing the peasants. One of those "murder-prophets" was Müntzer, on whom Luther squarely blamed the anticipated bedlam.[39] Eleven days before Frankenhausen, as violence was breaking out in Thuringia, Luther still regarded Müntzer as the chief culprit.

That did not change after Frankenhausen. Exactly three months after the battle, Luther reported to John Briessmann in Königsberg: "Müntzer and the peasants have done much damage to the gospel here [in Wittenberg] and have revived the spirits of the papists to such a degree that we have to build all over again."[40] In 1526, after warning that God would punish wrongdoers unless they repented and made amends, Luther commented that even Müntzer and the peasants would have to agree.[41] Three years later, Luther maintained that the Turk was "Muntzerian," for he tolerated no gradations of government such as princes, dukes, counts, etc. What else had Müntzer sought but to become a new Turkish emperor?[42] Luther could not get over how narrowly defined was reformation as he viewed. The association of Müntzer with the peasants and the narrow escape from Müntzer's fantasy was so strong that Luther's *Bauernkrieg* turned into a *Müntzerkrieg*, which lasted beyond the failed revolution of 1525.

Luther's war with Müntzer was not just a battle over theology and politics; it was directed *ad hominem* against Müntzer as a rival for whom reform was a violent revolution. Luther was not the only Wittenberger to blame Müntzer for the revolt. Philip Melanchthon learned about Frankenhausen only three days after the fact and regretted the slaughter; but he was gratified by the capture of Müntzer, whom he accused of seducing the common folk with empty promises.[43] The *Histori Thome Muntzers*, edited by Melanchthon, described Müntzer as devil-possessed, presumptuous, a teacher of blasphemy, and instigator of the peasant revolt.[44] In 1572, Cyriakus Spangenberg relied on the *Histori* when he labeled Müntzer a "restless, overambitious spirit" and ringleader of the revolt in Thuringia.[45]

7. It must be said, however, that Müntzer was not the only ambitious and self-centered reformer in Electoral Saxony. Luther himself expressed similar traits. Before he was called a lackey of the princes, Luther condemned the uprisings as machinations of the devil directed personally at him. The devil plainly wanted

39 *Ermahnung zum Frieden*, in WA 18: 294, 296; LW 46: 19–21.

40 *Luther to Briessmann, August 15, 1525*, in WABr 3: 555; LW 49: 123.

41 *Ob Kriegsleute auch in seligem Stande sein können* (1526), in WA 19: 647; LW 46: 121.

42 *Vom Kriege wider die Türken* (1529), in WA 30.2: 125, 128; LW 46: 80, 183.

43 "Melanchthon to Camerarius, May 19, 1525," MBW.R 1: 193–194 (no. 403); CR 1, 744.

44 Michael Beyer et al., ed., *Melanchthon Deutsch*, 2 vols. (Leipzig: Evangelische Verlagsanstalt, 1997) 1:288–307. See Heinz Scheible, "*Die Verfasserfrage der Histori Thome Muntzers,*" in *Aufsätze zu Melanchthon*, ed., H. Scheible (Tübingen: Mohr Siebeck, 2010) 328–341.

45 Bräuer, "*Bauernkrieg in der Grafschaft Mansfeld – Fiktion und Fakten,*" 122.

him dead and would turn the world upside down to achieve his goal: "I am convinced," wrote Luther, "that because of me the devil makes such a mess of the world."[46] Luther made that grandiose statement because he believed himself to be an apostle called by God for a new mission; and for the success of that mission he was accountable to God alone. Luther came to that conclusion while he was at the Wartburg. It was a new calling that replaced his monastic vows, a topic he was pondering and writing about in a treatise dedicated to his father. The new identity and purpose for himself was summed up as allegiance to a new superior: "I am a still a monk and yet no longer a monk; I am a new creature, not of the pope, but of Christ." Then, addressing his father directly, Luther wrote:

> I am sending you this book so that you can see how Christ, with such prodigious signs and might, has released me from these vows and blessed me with such abundant freedom that, although he has made me a servant of all, I am yet subject to no one but him alone. For Christ is my immediate bishop, abbot, prior, lord, father, and master. I no longer acknowledge any other.[47]

That divine calling and the accountability that accompanied it made Luther immune to the criticism of his harsh book against the peasants. Only three days after the execution of Müntzer, Luther learned from Amsdorf that he was being mocked as a toady of the princes. He responded that Satan had honored him often in this way and continued:

> Even if all the peasants had been killed, that would have been better than if the princes and the magistrates had died. Why? Because the peasants took up the sword without God's command. The consequence of that evil can only be the satanic devastation of God's kingdom and of the world.[48]

Two weeks later, Luther used his divine calling as a defiant defense of the harsh judgment:

> What a howling I have caused with my book against the peasants! Everything God has done through me is forgotten! Masters, papists, and peasants have lined up against me and threatened to kill me. Never mind if they are so crazy and foolish. I will try harder to make them more so. I will throw off my previous life as a papist and present myself to God as a new creature.[49]

"Everything God has done through me." Making that statement required an unusually strong sense of divine calling coupled with a certain egoism that permitted Luther to feel little accountability to others. In his chronicle of Luther's life, Johann Cochlaeus recognized that personal flaw as soon as he read Luther's

46 Luther to John Rühel, May 4 or 5, 1525, in WABr 3: 481.
47 *De votis monasticis Martini Lutheri iudicium*, in WA 8: 575–576; LW 49: 335–336.
48 Luther to Amsdorf, May 30, 1525, in WABr 3: 517–518; LW 49: 113–114.
49 Luther to his Mansfeld friends, June 15, 1525, in WABr 3: 531.

words: "I am certain that my word is not mine but the word of Christ; accordingly, my mouth is also the mouth of Christ whose word it speaks."[50] Cochlaeus wrote: "Who would be willing to believe Luther after hearing such arrogance?"[51]

Nevertheless, Luther's conviction of having a divine calling was not the cause of the Peasants' War. Rather, revolt of the commoners was an enormous challenge to his divine calling. First came the conflict with Müntzer, who also boasted of a divine calling to bring about reformation through revolution. Then Luther realized that he had little influence on either the peasants or the princes. He could not prevent a bloody revolution that would undermine his ideal of a reformation without violence. The only way for Luther to accept this limited power was to place guilt on the devil and interpret the devil's action as a personal test for himself.

8. It was also a test of the way in which Luther related religion and politics. The reformer Luther defined religion as the "affair of Christ" (*die Sache Christi*) or the gospel, which he summarized as salvation alone through Christ. He was bewildered by the evidence that not everyone who heard the good news rejoiced in the same freedom that he felt. The ideal religious life which that freedom made possible consisted not of self-centered fear and striving but of faith and love, as he described it at the end of *Freedom of a Christian:*

> The upshot of everything so far is: Christians live not in themselves but in Christ and in others – in Christ through faith and in others through love. Through faith they are lifted above themselves to God and from God they are lowered through love below themselves while all the time remaining in God and God's love.[52]

For Luther that picture could not contain rebellion or violence of any sort. They could only result from an intrusion of the devil.[53] Luther's followers were to get busy with a more important task:

> Spread the holy gospel, and help others spread it; teach, speak, write, and preach that human laws are nothing; urge people not to enter the priesthood, the monastery, or the convent, and hinder them from so doing; encourage those who have already entered to leave; give no more money for bulls, candles, bells, votive tablets, and churches; rather tell them that a Christian life consists of faith and love.[54]

It turned out, however, that the reformation was not only the affair of Christ as Luther envisioned it but also a political affair through and through. Luther's ideal of a nonviolent reformation leading to a life of faith and love was not possible in

50 *Eine treue Vermahnung*, in WA 8: 683; LW 45: 67
51 Johann Cochlaeus, *Historia Martini Lutheri*, trans. Johann Hueber (Ingolstadt, 1582), 241, 244.
52 *Von der Freiheit eines Christenmenschen* (1520), in WA 7: 38; LW 31: 371.
53 *Eine treue Vermahnung*, in WA 8: 681; LW 45: 67–68.
54 *Eine treue Vermahnung*, in WA 8: 683–684; LW 45: 68.

the real world and in the end was violated by Luther himself. He espoused a theology of the boundless mercy of God, but after Frankenhausen he was accused of teaching "bloodshed without mercy."[55] Luther sought refuge from that charge in the whole word of God:

> If we are to preach the word of God, we have to include in our sermons the texts that announce the wrath as well as the mercy of God. We have to preach about hell and heaven and about the godly and the ungodly, so that for both groups we help to promote the word, work, and judgment of God that results in punishing the evildoers and protecting the godly.[56]

Luther did not notice the irony: Thomas Müntzer could have written exactly the same sentences. The only difference was: For Müntzer the godly were also those who were willing to kill the ungodly. In contrast, Luther's advice to the peasants was: "If you seek mercy, then do not mingle with the rebels but instead respect the authorities and do good."[57]

That advice came too late. Luther's *Bauernkrieg*, through which he hoped to save a reformation without violence, ended with violence that he endorsed. Some historians have argued that the Peasants' War permanently damaged the evangelical movement by weakening its popularity and momentum. That argument presumes that one could know beforehand how the Reformation would develop otherwise. We now know that in the territories of those princes who prevailed at Frankenhausen – Electoral Saxony, Hesse, and eventually Ducal Saxony – the Reformation was promoted and established. Whether or not that was a success depends on how one judges the relationship of religion and politics. The same must be said of Luther's *Bauernkrieg*. Did his approval of violence to quash a revolution sacrifice the Christian ideal of freedom through faith and love? What appears to be certain is the religious and political cost of a clash between two religious leaders, like Müntzer and Luther, who nurtured resolutely opposing views of what it meant to be called by God to reform church and society.

55 *Ein Sendbrief von dem harten Büchlein wider die Bauern (1525)*, in WA 18: 388; LW 46: 68–69.
56 *Sendbrief von dem harten Büchlein*, in WA 18: 386–387; LW 46: 66.
57 *Sendbrief von dem harten Büchlein*, in WA 18: 386; LW 46: 66.

Erik H. Herrmann

Conflicts on Righteousness and Imputation in Early Lutheranism

The Case of Georg Karg (1512–1576)

> The Law of God exact he shall fulfill
> Both by obedience and by love, though love
> Alone fulfill the Law; thy punishment
> He shall endure by coming in the Flesh
> To a reproachful life and cursed death,
> Proclaiming Life to all who shall believe
> In his redemption, and that his obedience
> Imputed becomes theirs by Faith, his merits
> To save them, not their own, though legal, works.
>
> (John Milton, *Paradise Lost,* 12. 393–410)

In the second half of the sixteenth century much of the intra-Lutheran disputes centered on Luther's theological legacy, especially doctrines related to justification and the relationship of faith and works. The third article of the *Formula concordiae* represents two such disputes. Normally, one thinks of this article, *de iustificatione*, as a rebuke of the theology of Andreas Osiander and his view that the righteousness of justification is the indwelling of Christ's divine nature in the believer. But another lesser known controversy is also addressed; namely, that of Georg Karg and whether justification requires the imputation of Christ's obedience to the law, his so-called "active obedience." One of the implications of this debate was the introduction of a new way of talking about justification that arguably reframed Luther's concept of righteousness, especially the righteousness of faith.

However one assesses Luther's theological development, along with the various witnesses to his Reformation discovery or breakthrough,[1] it is impossible to

1 The chief witnesses to Luther's theological breakthrough are in his preface to his collected Latin writings in 1545, WA 54: 185–186; a table talk from 1542/43, WATr 5: 210, 6f., no. 5518; and a letter to Johannes Staupitz in 1518 which speaks in a strikingly similar way but about *poenitentia* rather than *iustitia*; WA 1: 524–527. In 2008, Martin Lohrmann published an additional witness from Johannes Bugenhagen's commentary on Jonah from 1550; "A Newly

give a full account without dealing with the concept of "righteousness." The most famous source – the end of his preface to his collected Latin writings in 1545 – centers on his attempt to understand the Pauline concept of *iustitia Dei*, the righteousness of God. His struggle hinged on a particular interpretation of Rom 1:17 which, he maintained, was commonly held among his teachers; namely, that the phrase *iustitia Dei* referred to "the formal or active righteousness with which God is righteous and punishes the unrighteous sinner."[2] For the scholastic there was a distinction between righteousness, on the one hand, and grace or mercy on the other.[3] The door was opened, however, when Luther understood the Pauline phrase not as a standard by which God judges the sinner, but rather as God's gift given to the one who has faith, "the passive righteousness with which the merciful God justifies us by faith."[4] Righteousness and mercy were the same. He found the same basic notion of righteousness as a gift in Augustine,[5] though he admitted that certain aspects of the insight needed to be more clearly developed, especially regarding *imputation.* In particular, Luther understood the imputation of righteousness through faith as the full and complete divine act of justification grounded in the new creation established by the death and resurrection of Christ.

Furthermore, this righteousness was, at a fundamental level, of another kind than the righteousness of the law. The former was, with respect to the person, passive – a divine gift in which God must always remain the subject and the believer the object. The righteousness of the law, on the other hand, was an active righteousness, i.e., an activity and work by the human subject. And even if that work was animated by virtues flowing from a new heart, it was nevertheless of this other kind.

Robert Kolb has especially argued for the centrality of this distinction for Luther's way of thinking,[6] underscoring that Luther himself maintained that such a distinction between the two kinds of righteousness lay at the heart of what he called, "our theology":

> This is our theology by which we teach a precise distinction between these two kinds of righteousness, the active and the passive, so that morality and faith, works and grace, secular society and religion may not be confused. Both are necessary, but both must be

Discovered Report of Luther's Reformation Breakthrough from Johannes Bugenhagen's 1550 Jonah Commentary," in *Lutheran Quarterly* XXII (2008): 324–330.

2 WA 54: 185, 18–20; LW 34: 336.

3 Cf. Comments on Psalm 51:14, 1532; WA 40 II: 444.36–445.29.

4 WA 54: 186, 5f; LW 34: 337.

5 Cf. Augustine, *De spiritu et litera* I, ix, x, 15–16.

6 See especially Robert Kolb, "Luther on the Two Kinds of Righteousness; Reflections on His Two-Dimensional Definition of Humanity at the Heart of His Theology," in *Lutheran Quarterly* XIII (1999): 449–466; Charles Arand and Robert Kolb, *The Genius of Luther's Theology: A Wittenberg Way of Thinking for the Contemporary Church* (Grand Rapids: Baker Academic, 2008).

> kept within their limits. [...] We set forth two worlds, as it were, one of them heavenly and the other earthly. Into these we place these two kinds of righteousness, which are distinct and separated from each other. The righteousness of the Law is earthly and deals with earthly things [...]. [Christian righteousness] has nothing to do with the righteousness of the Law or with earthly and active righteousness. But this righteousness is heavenly and passive. We do not have it of ourselves; we receive it from heaven. We do not perform it; we accept it by faith, through which we ascend beyond all laws and works.[7]

Such a sharp and thorough-going distinction is an important point of divergence from Luther's scholastic predecessors. In spite of the vast distance of God and human beings, scholastic theology still sought to find some point of continuity between God and the human subject, even if that continuity could only be approximated by way of *analogia.*[8] Thus, for matters soteriological, the difference between the righteousness achieved, say through Aristotelian ethics, and the righteousness of God was set largely in quantitative rather than qualitative terms. Divine righteousness was higher, purer than human righteousness, but it was not, fundamentally, of another kind. Scholastics could debate whether such was the case out of necessity or by condescension, but they were generally in agreement that the substance of the righteousness of the law and the goal of the righteousness of faith were the same. The latter was a realization of the former, albeit through the habitual exercise of virtue through the power of divine grace.

But for Luther, the person *coram deo* must exist in a *qualitatively* different manner than the person *coram hominibus.* This is how Luther understood the Pauline difference between faith and the law: "Now it is evident that no one is justified before God by the law, for 'The righteous shall live by faith.' *But the law is not of faith [...]*" (Gal 3:10–11). A person's relationships *coram hominibus* are many but all fall under the law, broadly conceived, and its righteousness.[9] The human creature's relationship to God, however, is necessarily *passive* – she is the object of the divine initiative with *faith* or trust in God the only fitting correlative. And this distinction holds not only for soteriology but is grounded in the fabric of creation – even Edenic humanity lived before God by such a passive righteousness. It is thus not only absurd but the height of impiety to attempt to turn God into the object of human initiative and make such activity constitutive for the

7 WA 40. I: 45, 24f; LW 26: 7–8.

8 Cf. Wilfried Joest, *Ontologie der Person bei Luther* (Göttingen: Vandenhoeck & Ruprecht, 1967), 56f. Also on 122f, Joest demonstrates how Luther's critique of traditional ontology is explicitly connected to soteriology in his Heidelberg Disputation, theses 19f.

9 However, the first commandment, understood rightly, actually describes the *coram deo* relationship, and therefore stands apart from the works of the Second Table. Cf. Albrecht Beutel, "*Luthers Auslegung des ersten Gebotes*" in *'Ich bin der Herr, dein Gott' – Das erste Gebot in säkularisierter Zeit. Veröffentlichungen der Luther-Akademie e.V. Ratzeburg,* Band 24, ed. Joachim Heubach (Ratzeburg: Luther-Akademie, 1995), 65–108.

divine/human relationship. One might say that the root of sin is a kind of collapsing of the two types of relationships into a single righteousness of the law.[10] But *faith* is different. Only faith, which suffers God to give and act, to create and recreate can define humanity *coram deo*. And because such action and recreation has come to full expression in the cross and resurrection, the righteousness of faith is the very deliverance from sin, death, and hell that are found in Christ who has joined himself to the believer.

Luther already began developing this distinction over against scholastic theology in his Romans lectures (1515–1516), speaking of two kinds of justification.[11] While he would subsequently change and clarify his terminology, the basic thrust of the distinction remained constant throughout his writings.[12] On the one hand, Luther's teaching on righteousness was a central characteristic of the new evangelical theology in Wittenberg – especially when he spoke about righteousness as a distinction of the law from the gospel.

Still, the core difference between faith and works was not always grasped or appreciated. Melanchthon is a good example of one who could utilize the distinction to great effect, but could also be less clear about whether the passivity of faith is a fundamental characteristic of righteousness before God or merely the instrument through which righteousness is imputed.[13] This in turn would lead to ambiguity about what, in fact, was being imputed, i.e., of what did the righteousness received by the believer consist?

Melanchthon is nearest to Luther in Article IV of the Apology, *De Iustificatione*. Throughout he accuses the opponents of focusing only on the "righteousness of reason" or the "righteousness of the law."[14] Melanchthon willingly maintains that this righteousness is necessary and commanded by God,[15] yet it does not justify. Rather justification is only from the righteousness of faith which receives the forgiveness of sins for Christ's sake.

> [... The opponents] teach the law and think that righteousness is *obedience to the law*. For human reason only focuses on the law and does not understand *any other righteousness* except obedience to the law. [...] But Paul protests loudly and teaches that

10 Lauri Haikola, *Gesetz und Evangelium bei Matthias Flacius Illyricus* (Lund: C.W.K. Gleerup, 1952), 87.

11 WA 56: 226f; LW 25: 211f.

12 See Kolb, "Two Kinds of Righteousness," 457–459.

13 See Mark Seifrid's very helpful comparison of Luther and Melanchthon on this point, "Luther, Melanchthon, and Paul on the Question of Imputation: Recommendations on a Current Debate," in *Justification: What's at Stake in the Current Debates*, ed., Mark Husbands and Daniel J. Trier (Downers Grove, IL: IVP Academic, 2004), 137–152.

14 Ap, 121:7–9.

15 Ap, 124:22–24.

> righteousness is *something different*, namely, obedience to the promise of reconciliation given on account of Christ [...].[16]

Here the two kinds of righteousness are clearly expressed. Like Luther, Melanchthon understands these two kinds of righteousness to be the result of two kinds of relationships, i.e., *coram deo/coram hominibus:* "Faith and hope deal only with God whereas love has an infinite number of outward responsibilities toward others."[17] As in Luther, "forgiveness of sins" embraces the totality of justification in the Apology: "To obtain the forgiveness of sins is to be justified."[18] Likewise, justification "makes us alive"[19] and "reconcile[s] to the Father."[20]

In the Apology, Melanchthon's distinction between the two tables of the law corresponds to the two kinds of righteousness.[21] He accuses the opponents of only focusing on the second table which are directed toward the neighbor and ignoring the foundational demands of the first table.[22] If they truly understood what the first table required, "truly to fear God, truly to love God, truly to call upon God [...] expect help from God in death and all afflictions",[23] they would abandon the foolish notion that justification is through the law. The works of the first table require Christ and the Holy Spirit,[24] in other words, another kind of righteousness than one achieved by human performance.

In other places, however, Melanchthon is not as clear. At times, it seems that "theoretically" the righteousness of the law could justify if kept perfectly.

> The opponents are right in thinking that love is the fulfillment of the law, and that *obedience to the law would be righteousness if we kept the law.* However, up to this point we have shown that the promises have been given precisely because we are unable to keep the law. [...] [the gospel] teaches that we are not regarded as righteous on account of obedience to the law *for we do not live up to the law.*[25]

The reason, then, why the righteousness of the law does not justify is not because justification is based on an entirely different kind of righteousness, that of faith, but because *the law is not kept.* Rather than the righteousness of faith being

16 Ap, 154–155:229 (italics mine).
17 Ap, 154:226; "it is foolish to dream that this love by which we act toward human beings justifies us before God" 154:224.
18 Ap, 133:76; 128:51.
19 Ap, 130:62.
20 Ap, 133:81.
21 Ap, 155:231, "There is no reason to think that Paul has attributed either justification or perfection before God to the works of the second table of the law rather than to the first."
22 Ap, 121:7–9; 125:34; 141:131.
23 Ap, 121:8.
24 Ap, 140:126.
25 Ap, 145:159 (italics mine); cf. 125:31; 126:38; 126:40; 145:157–158; 154:227f; 155:232.

definitive for man's relationship *coram deo*, it only justifies because sin makes fulfillment of the law impossible.

The confusion may lie in that Melanchthon is using "law" here as primarily the first table, which in other places he equates to the righteousness of faith. Or, he may be simply attempting to turn his opponents' line of argumentation upon itself; a tactic certainly used by Luther as well. On the other hand, this kind of "theoretical" fulfillment of the law is symptomatic of the more central position that the law would take on in Melanchthon's theology.[26] Especially in his later writings, Melanchthon would increasingly establish the doctrine of the law on the basis of a more abstract *lex aeterna* – "an eternal and immovable rule of the divine mind."[27] In the later editions of his *Loci communes*, Melanchthon began to speak of the law as the fundamental basis for humanity *coram deo*, namely a relationship defined as one of obedience or disobedience, reward or punishment, rather than Luther's more foundational faith or unbelief.[28]

This understanding of the law was demonstrably influential on Melanchthon's students. When talking about justification, Melanchthon himself stayed rather close to the language of the Apology throughout his life. His students, however, followed their preceptor's logic on the law in order to draw conclusions about justification and the atonement that would change how Lutherans talked about righteousness and imputation.[29] "Forgiveness of sins" was no longer synonymous with "justification" nor was it sufficient for our status before God. Because the law was the immutable "rule of righteousness in God," it was the basis for the divine/human relationship. Further, there was a "double debt" that had to be paid to the law.[30] Christ not only had to bear the punishment for our transgression of the law; he also had to perform perfect obedience to the law in our

26 See Timothy Wengert, *Law and Gospel: Philip Melanchthon's Debate with John Agricola of Eisleben over* Poenitentia (Grand Rapids: Baker Books, 1997), 177–210.

27 CR 21, 685: *"Sed Lex Dei est regula eterna et immota mentis divinae"*; CR 21, 686, 688, 711; cf. also CR 15, 389; 24, 385: *"Lex, quae est regula iustitiae in Deo, ita est immota, ut oporteat ei satisfacere. Obligat autem lex vel ad obedientiam, vel ad poenam."*

28 See Lauri Haikola, *"Melanchthons und Luthers Lehre von der Rechtfertigung, ein Vergleich"* in *Luther and Melanchthon in the History and Theology of the Reformation*, ed., Vilmas Vajta (Philadelphia: Muhlenberg Press, 1961), 89–103.

29 See Robert Kolb, "Not Without the Satisfaction of God's Righteousness: The Atonement and the Generation Gap between and Luther and His Students," in *Archive für Reformationsgeschichte: Sonderband: Die Reformation in Deutschland und Europa, Interpretation und Debatten*, ed., Hans R. Guggisberg and Gottfried G. Krodel (Gütersloh: Gütersloher Verlagshaus, 1993), 136–156.

30 Flacius, *"Und ist nun solche pflichtige gerechtigkeit in zwey stück geteilet. Zum ersten / das wir volkomene straff geben / vor die vorige missethat / Zum andern / das wir Gotte hernachmals volkomlichen gehorsam leisten / wo wir wollen ewiglich leben." Verlegung des Bekentnis Osiandri von der Rechtfertigung der armen sünder durch die wesentliche Gerechtigkeit der Hohen Maiestet Gottes allein.* (Magdeburg, 1552), E_2. Cited in Haikola, *Gesetz und Evangelium*, 207.

place. It is this obedience to the law that is properly called "righteousness," imputed to us through faith. Such "active" and "passive" obedience of Christ thus corresponds to this "double debt" which the law required. In effect, this new formulation of justification establishes obedience to the law as a *Heilsweg*, a path toward salvation. We ourselves cannot tread the path because of sin, so Christ does so for us. Nevertheless, the formulation assumes that there is only one kind of righteousness, the righteousness of the law.

1. Andreas Osiander and the Reframing of Righteousness

This way of talking about righteousness and justification was first most clearly evident in the context of the Osiandric controversy.[31] Andreas Osiander (1498–1552) equated the "righteousness of God" with God's *essential righteousness* which is imparted to us through the indwelling of Christ's divine nature.[32] Justification is literally a "making righteous," rather than a declaration or imputation. For Osiander, the "forgiveness of sins" is not properly part of justification but only a prerequisite for the "righteousness" which we receive by faith.[33] Christ's principal work for our salvation is his incarnation by which he mediates the essential righteousness of God to humanity. The events of his life and death are only "fruits" of his essential righteousness, and therefore have nothing really to do with the righteousness of God with which he justifies us.[34]

Osiander's opponents did not dispute that Christ was essentially righteous according to his divine nature, nor that Christ dwells within the believer. But this essential righteousness was not the righteousness of God with which we are

31 J. Döllinger, *Die Reformation, ihre innere Entwicklund und ihre Wirkungen im Umfange des Lutherischen Bekenntnisses*, Band III, (Regensburg, 1848) 558f. See also G. Thomasius, *Christi Person und Werk*, Band III, (Erlangen: Verlag Bläsing, 1862), 326f; Ibid., *Historia dogmatis de obedientia activa* (Erlangen: 1855); Wilhelm Preger, *Matthias Flacius Illyricus und seine Zeit* (Erlangen: Verlag Bläsing, 1859), 204–297; Franz H. R. Frank, *Die Theologie der Concordienformel*, Band I, (Erlangen: 1858), 5–36.

32 The essential righteousness of God is what the law demands. Love, the fulfillment of the law, is God himself (1 John 4:16). *"Nun fordert das gesetz die liebe [...] Die liebe aber ist Gott selbs [...] Darumb, wer das gesetz mit der liebe erfullen sol, der mus in Gott sein and Got in im [...]"* *Andreas Osiander D. Ä. Gesamtausgabe*, Band 10, ed.,Gerhard Müller and Gottfried Seebaß, (Gütersloh: Gütersloher Verlagshaus Gerd Mohn, 1975), 104.

33 *"Es is aber nit gnug, das uns die sund von Got verzigen und die straff nachgelassen ist, dhwel wir dannocht sunder pleiben. Sonder es muß sich Christus zu uns auch wenden [...] Das thut und vollendet er aber in zwaien wercken: Er bricht und vertilgt die sund in uns und plantzt dagegen die gerechtikait in uns."* Osiander's *"Schlußrede auf dem Religionsgesprach"* (1525) in *Osiander Gesamtausgabe*, Band I, 559–560.

34 *"Das gehorsam Christi mit seinem leiden etc. [ist] nicht die gerechtigkeit, sondern es [sind] der gerechtigkeit früchte; dem die gerechtigkeit [muß] zuvor dasein ehe der gehorsam [folget]."* *Osiander Gesamtausgabe*, Band 9, 615.

justified. Rather, the righteousness of justification is Christ's "total obedience." For example, after attending one of Osiander's lectures, Joachim Mörlin (1514–1571) wrote to Osiander and criticized him for denying the "double righteousness" of Christ, namely: 1.The righteousness which he possesses from eternity as the Son of God; 2. His obedience in the form of a servant.[35] Mörlin asserts that it is the second, Christ's obedience, which is our righteousness in justification. Justification is not what Christ does *in us*, but what Christ does *for us*; it is *extra nos.*

When Osiander set forth his theology in "*Von dem Einigen Mittler*" in October of 1551, it received numerous written responses and critiques.[36] Consistently the "obedience of Christ" was set over against the "indwelling of Christ," and it was this line of argumentation that would eventually be reflected in the language of the Formula of Concord. However, *within* this insistence on the *extra nos* character of justification, the additional distinction of the active and passive obedience of Christ was also introduced. This was the case even though the active/passive distinction as such did not appear to be directly relevant to the controversy with Osiander. There the antithesis was *obedience* versus *indwelling*; the *deeds* of Christ versus the *essence* of Christ. It seems that the further division of Christ's obedience to the law (active) and his obedience to submit to death (passive) was merely occasioned by the conflict with Osiander, while the cause should be attributed to the increasingly nomistic conception of the human being that was developing among many of Melancthon's students.

Some of the most detailed discussions of this distinction come from the pens of Justus Menius (1499–1558) and Matthias Flacius (1520–1575). For Menius, God's essential righteousness is given voice and testimony in the divine law.[37] Therefore human righteousness before God consists of perfect obedience to the divine law. On account of such obedience God gives eternal life and salvation.[38] But since sin prevents us from rendering this obedience, Christ our mediator

35 "*Secundo negas duplicem in Christo iusticiam, quod non ego solus, verum universa asserit scriptura: Certum est emim Christum a iusto Patre ab aeterno iustum Filium natum, etiam ante incarnationem et sine incarnatione. Postea in forma servi omnem vitam eiusdem usque ad mortem crucis fuisse obedientiam Filii erga Patrem. […] Hanc obedientiam Filii esse iusticiam et legis consummationem nemo postest aut debet.*" (April 18, 1551) Osiander *Gesamtausgabe*, Band 9, 620–621.

36 For a more detailed discussion of the initial reactions to Osiander's confession see *Osiander Gesamtausgabe*, Band 10, 64–72.

37 "*[…] die zehen gebot eigendlich nichts anders sei / den eine stimme der wesenlichen gerechtigkeit Gottes […] Das durchs Gesetz / welchs der ewige wesenlichen gerechtigkeit Gottes stimmen un wort ist […]*" *Von der Gerechtigkeit die für Gott gilt: wider die newe Alcumistische Theologiam Andreae Osiandri*, Erffurdt, 1552, L_2, L_3.

38 Ibid. H_2: "*Also ist widerumb der bereitte / willige gehorsam / damit das gesetz vollkömlich erfüllet wird / die wahrhafftige gerechtigkeit / die Gott von allen menschen fordert / vnd vmb irent willen ewiges leben vn seligheit gibt.*"

must obey the law for us. It is on account of this righteousness of the law which Christ has won that we are considered righteous before God.[39]

Flacius' understanding of the law was similar to that of Menius. He also posits a "theoretical" fulfillment of the law suggesting that the law is the principal way of salvation. "The complete obedience to the law of God is the right and true righteousness through which we can enter into eternal life."[40] Because of our sin, we have incurred a "double debt" to the law which Christ must pay by his active and passive obedience.[41] The forgiveness of sins merited through Christ's suffering and death is not sufficient for our justification; Christ must also perform perfect obedience to the law on our behalf.[42] Ironically, both Menius and Flacius are in agreement with Osiander concerning the need for something added to the forgiveness of sins for our justification. They differ only on what that something is: Christ's active obedience or the indwelling of Christ's divine nature.

Melanchthon also responded to Osiander, setting Christ's "obedience" over and against Christ's "indwelling." Melanchthon, however, spoke only of Christ's total obedience that he rendered to Father when he suffered on the cross for humanity. Consistently he described Christ's obedience or his merit in connection with his *passive* obedience, his suffering and sacrifice.[43] There was no

39 Ibid., M_3: *"das er [Christus] mit seinem gehorsam / das gestez der Göttlichen gerechtigkeit / für vns / vnd an vnser stadt / vns zu gut erfüllet / vnd damit eine gerechtigkeit / die für Gott gilt / vnd nicht verworffen / sondern angenommen wird / auffgerichtet vnd erworben hat."*

40 *Kurtze vnd klare erzelung der argument Osiandri. Gedruckt zu Magdeburg* / bey Christian Rödinger. 1552, D_1a, *"Der volkomene gehorsam gegen dem Gesetze Gottes ist die rechte vnd ware gerechtigkeit / Durch welche wir können eingehen in das Ewige leben. [...] Christus aber ist auffs vollkömlischste dem Gesetzt gehorsam worden / hat alles das gethan vnd gelitten / was das gesetze von vns hat erfoddert / das wir thun vnd leiden soten / vnd vns deyselben gehorsam zegerechnet. Darumb ist die selbige gerechtigkeit unsere gerechtigkeit."* Cf. Ibid., A_3b: *"Wir gleuben vnd leren also / das Gesetz oder Gottes wesentliche Gerechtigkeit / oder Gott selbs sagt zu uns mensche / Thut die gebot / so werdet ihr da durch gerecht vñ selig werde / Luce. 10. 18."*; Ibid., B_4a: *"Das Gesetz ist gut / heilig / gerecht / geistlich / zum leben gegeben / ich aber bin fleischlich."*

41 Ibid., A_3b: *"wir könne sie nicht thu / darub sind wir vngerecht vnd verdampt. Da kompt Christus vnd spricht zu vns / Ei seid getrost ich bin komen das ich das gesetze erfülle / die Gerechtigkeit / so das gesetze von euch foddert / euch zu gute thu / vnd alles reichlich für euch bezale. Durch meinem gehorsam vnd leiden oder erfüllung des gesetzes solt ihr gerechtfertigt werden Rom. Viii."* Cf. also Thomasius, *Christi Person u. Werk*, 327–328.

42 *"Derhalben Vergebung der Sünde / ist auch nicht allein ableschung der schuld / das du widders Gesetz gethan hast / sondern auch zurechnung der erfüllung des gesetzes." Verlegung des Bekentnis Osiandri von der Rechtfertigung der armen sünder durch die wesentliche Gerechtigkeit der Hohen Maiestet Gottes allein.* Magdeburg, 1552, A_3. Cited in Haikola, *Gesetz und Evangelium*, 213.

43 *Antwort auff das Buch herrn Andreae Osiandri von der Rechtfertigung des Menschen.* Gedruckt zu Wittenberg / durch Weit Creutzer, 1552, *"[...] durch verdienst seines gehorsams / darin er ein Opfer fur vns worden ist / von welchem gehorsam dise wort rede im XL Pslam [...]"* B_1a, (CR 7, 896); *"Rom. v. Wir sind gerecht worden durch sein blut. Item / durch eines gehorsam werden viel gerecht."* B_2a, (CR 7, 896). Cf. CR 13, 1012: *"Propiciatorium unicum est tota Christi*

"double debt," nor a two-part justification.[44] Christ's obedience was a complete offering of himself focused upon and culminating in his death for our sins. Here Melanchthon is much closer to the language of the Apology than Menius or Flacius. One of Melanchthon's harshest criticisms of Osiander was that he failed to equate "righteousness" with the "forgiveness of sins."[45]

2. Georg Karg and the Controversy over Active Obedience

Many of Melanchthon's students had taken his teaching of the *lex aeterna* to conclusions about justification that seemed to change the definition of human righteousness *coram deo*. Few challenged this new *modus loquendi*.[46] However, in 1567 a controversy arose around a man named Georg Karg (or Parsimonius) who rejected the vicarious significance of Christ's active obedience to the law. The reasons for his objections will be the focus for the remainder of this essay.

Georg Karg was born in 1512. He entered the University of Wittenberg in the winter semester of 1531/2 and received his Masters in 1536. At the invitation of Jacob Schenk, he began to preach in Freiberg without the permission of the

obedientia, hoc unum meretur remissionem peccatorum et reconciliationem hominibus [...] Propiciatorium seu ἱλαστικὸν simpliciter unicum est videlicet tota obedientia Christi, quae sola meretur remissionem peccatorum hominibus;" CR 24, 216 *"Implet legem pro nobis non tantum officiis legalibus et obedientia sua, quae est plena ac perfecta, sed etiam recipiendo in se maledictionem et poenam, quam nos eraamus meriti, ad placandum nobis Patrem et ad nos liberandos a maledictione legis."*

44 CR 24, 18: *"[...] omnis lex obligat vel ad penam, vel ad obedientiam."*

45 *"Nu spricht Osiander offt also / Ich heisse gerechtigkeit dieses / das vns macht recht thun. In diesen worten ist nichts geredt von vergebung der sünden / dagegen sagen wie also / Wir nennen gerechtigkeit / den Herrn Christum / dadurch wir habe vergebung der sünden vnd einen gnedigen Gott."* B_3 (CR 7, 897). Also *"Hie müssen nu auch die heiligen trost haben / vnd wissen wie sie vergebung der sünden vnd gnade haben / das ist / wie sie Gott gefellig sind."* B_1 (CR 7, 895); *"Welches alles mus also verstanden werden / das wir vergebung der sünden haben / vnd angenem sind vor Gott / durch den verdienst Christi [...] Item selig sind die / welchen die sünd gedeckt sind."* B_3a, (CR 7, 897).

46 At the Synod of Eisenach (1556), the first thesis, which suggested that "theoretically" human beings could be saved through perfect obedience to the law, was objected to by Nikolaus von Amsdorf on the grounds that it distorted the two kinds of righteousness. However, Amsdorf still seemed to view the distinction of the active and passive obedience of Christ as significant for justification. See *Auff Osianders Bekentnis ein Unterricht und zeugnis / Das die Gerechtigkeit der menscheit Chreist / darinnen sie entpfangen vnd geboren ist / allen Gleubigen Sündern geschanckt vnd zugerechent wird / vnd für ihr Person hie auff Erden nemmermehr Gerecht vnd heilig werden.* (1552). For more on the Eisenach Synod, see Matthias Richter, *Gesetz und Heil: Eine Untersuchung zur Vorgeschichte und zum Verlauf des sogenannten Zweiten Antinomistischen Streits* (Göttingen: Vandenhoeck & Ruprecht, 1996), 132–167; Robert Kolb, *Nikolaus von Amsdorf (1483–1565): Popular Polemics in the Preservation of Luther's Legacy* (Nieuwkoop: B. De Graaf, 1978), 145f.

Wittenberg faculty. He was, however, reconciled to Luther and Jonas and was ordained in Öttingen, his native home. In 1546, he had to leave because of the Interim, but in 1552 he received a call to Schwabach where he would soon become the general superintendent of Bavaria. He published a catechism in 1564 which was used in the Ansbach congregations until the beginning of the nineteenth century. In 1567, Peter Ketzmann (1521–1570) arrived and began to attack Karg's teaching on justification which he made known from the pulpit, especially regarding Christ's active obedience. This local dispute soon became more widespread with Victorin Strigel (1524–1569),[47] Tileman Heshusius (1527–1588), the Straßbourg, Württemberg, and Wittenberg theologians all taking an active part. Elector August of Saxony demanded a forceful suppression of the "new heresy" in 1569. A delegation of Wittenberg theologians led by Paul Ebers (1511–1569) came at the behest of Margrav Georg Friedrich, but it achieved little. Finally, in the summer of 1570, a verbal hearing was held and on August 10, 1570, Karg was compelled to recant. On October 31, he was reinstated to his office by Jacob Andrea. He died in 1576.[48]

The issue for Karg revolved around the definition of the "righteousness of God" that is imputed to the believer.[49] Confusion over this definition, which he ascribed to the "younger theologians,"[50] was precisely what had led to such distortions in the doctrine of justification as in Osianderism.[51] Karg's definition echoed the language of the Apology: imputed righteousness is the forgiveness of sins on account of Christ's sacrifice. Through this we are reconciled to God and adopted as his children.[52] For Karg, the imputation of Christ's active obedience had no place in this definition and distorted the doctrine of justification. His objections focused on several points: 1. the imputation of obedience is not found in Scripture; 2. the all-sufficiency of the forgiveness of sins; 3. the logical fallacy of the "double debt;" 4. the impossibility of vicarious obedience; and 5. the danger of Antinomianism.

---

47 Cf. K. Schornbaum, *"Aus dem Briefwechsel G. Kargs,"* in *Archiv für Reformationsgeschichte* XVI (1919): 79–83.

48 For more on Karg, see *Realencyklepädie*, 3rd ed., Vol. 10, 70–72; Georg Wilke, *Georg Karg (Parsimonius), sein Katechismus und sein doppelter Lehrstreit* (Dissertation, Universität Erlangen,1904); Döllinger, *Refomation*, Band III, 556f; K. Schornbaum, *"Die brandenburgisch-nürnbergische Norma doctrinae 1573, I" Archiv für Reformationsgeschichte* 19 (1922):161–193; idem., *"Die brandenburgishc-nürnbergische Norma doctrinae 1573, II, III" Archiv für Reformationsgeschichte* 20 (1923): 5–37; 102–126.

49 Primary sources for Karg's dispute are contained in the appendix of Döllinger, *Reformation*, III, 15f.

50 Döllinger, Anhang, 39.

51 Döllinger, Anhang, 16.

52 *"[...] zugerechnete Gerechtigkeit [...] sei Vergebung der Sünd, durch Christi Leiden und Sterben verdient und erworben [...]"* Döllinger, Anhang, 16.

Obedience and Imputation in Scripture. Karg maintained that nowhere in Scripture does it say that Christ's active obedience is imputed to us. Passages such as Rom 8:3–4[53] should be understood as referring to the *renewal* of the Holy Spirit and not to justification, even as Melanchthon interprets it in his Romans commentary.[54] Other passages which talk of Christ's obedience (Rom 5; Phil 2; Heb 10) always point to Christ's obedience rendered to the Father *unto death.*[55] His opponents even seemed to admit that there were no *explicit* passages regarding the imputation of Christ's obedience, but that such a teaching was based on the logical consequences of clear passages of Scripture. Karg argued, however, that such an important doctrine as justification should not be based on extrapolations but on an explicit word of God.[56]

Forgiveness of Sins. On 29 November 1567, Karg published a list of "absurdities," the third of which read

> Justification by faith is not only the remission of sins, accepted with gratitude, but also the imputed righteousness of Christ [...] or that certain obedience and good works according to the law expiate sins, and thus the recompense for sins is not only punishment but also obedience.[57]

Karg rejected that in order to preach the righteousness of faith one must add the imputation of Christ's obedience to the proclamation of forgiveness.[58] When we are justified by faith in the sacrifice of Christ we have peace with God, and there is nothing more that can condemn us.[59] This is the language of the Scriptures and the Confessions. The Württemberg theologians, however, argued that it was absolutely necessary to keep both forgiveness and the imputation of Christ's

53 "For God has done what the law, weakened by the flesh, could not do. By sending his own Son in the likeness of sinful flesh and for sin, he condemned sin in the flesh, in *order that the righteous requirement of the law might be fulfilled in us*, who walk not according to the flesh but according to the Spirit."

54 Döllinger, Anhang, 17.

55 Ibid., 23, *"Dieweil aber die heilige Schrift zeuget, daß uns Christus durch seinen Gehorsam gerecht mache Röm. 5, so ist zu willen, daß sie von dem Gehorsam redet, welchen er seinem himmlischen Vater unserthalben und für uns geleistet hat, nämlich da er seinem Vater gehorsam geworden ist bis in den Tod."*

56 Ibid., 37, *"Nun aber die Rechtfertigung ein hoher Artikel des Glaubens, und dem Menschen viel daran gelegen ist, wer kann gedenken oder glauben, daß er allein auf bloßen Consequenzen stehe, und kein klar ausdrücklich Wort Gottes habe?"*

57 Ibid., 47, *"Iustitam fidei non esse tantum remissionem peccatorum cum acceptatione gratuita, sed etiam iustitiae Christi imputationem [...] aut certe obedientia secundum legem et bonis operibus expiari peccata, et sic stipendium peccati non solum poenam esse, sed etiam obedientiam."*

58 Ibid., 25.

59 Ibid. Cf. also 38, *"Denn ist's weiß, so ist's nicht schwarz; ist's Vergebung der Sünden, welche geglaubt wird, so ist's nichts Anderes, es habe gleich Namen, wie es wolle. Unsere zugerechnete Gerechtigkeit ist Vergebung der Sünd; dieses ist's und kein Anderes."*

righteousness together in justification. For God is not such a judge that he would simply declare someone righteous if no righteousness was present (whether one's own or someone else's)![60] Wittenberg and Straßbourg maintained that the stricken conscience did not receive enough comfort from the forgiveness of sins but needed, in addition, the robe of Christ's imputed righteousness to cover our incomplete obedience.[61] Karg, however, could not fathom how forgiveness could not be all-sufficient for the comforting of consciences.

Double Debt of the Law. Karg's first "absurdity" was "*lege Dei nos obligari et ad obedientiam et ad poenam*" – the law of God obligates us to both obedience and punishment. Despite the logical fallacy which the "double debt" commits, the Straßbourg theologians denied that obedience and punishment are mutually exclusive. Since the human creature can only stand *coram deo* through complete obedience to the law, forgiveness of sins only delivers us from God's wrath and cannot be said to properly fulfill the law.[62] In response, Karg appealed to Melanchthon who taught that the law could only obligate to obedience or to punishment, not to both. Since we failed to obey the law, Christ suffered the punishment in our place. In this the law is "satisfied."[63]

Vicarious Obedience. Karg did not dispute that Christ had a two-fold obedience; he certainly fulfilled the law in a double way: obedience to the law and obedience unto death. This does not mean that both were done *vicariously*, in our place. Karg considered obedience to the law to be highly individualized. The law demands that each person be righteous *according to his vocation.* In other words, what might be an act of obedience for one person may not be so for another. There is no "generic" obedience of the law because the righteousness of the law directs us to individuals encountered in each particular *Stand.* Karg could certainly admit a suffering for another, but one could not be pious for someone else.[64]

---

60 Ibid., 27, "*denn Gott nicht ein solcher Richter ist, der einen gerecht spreche, da gar keine Gerechtigkeit, weder eigene noch fremde, ist, ist auch nicht ein solcher Richter, der den Menschen allerdings laß' bleiben, wie er ihn findet.*"

61 Ibid., 45; Also 43, "*Hie ist nun wahrlich nicht allein dieser Trost nothwendig, daß ein solcher angefochtener Mensch, so er an Christum glaube, von der Straf und Verdammniß durch des Herrn Christi Blut und Tod erleidigt und gefreiet sei, sondern davon auch is ein gründlicher Trost vonnöthen, daß ihm […] die Gerechtigkeit und Unschuld Christi, damit seine Sünd und Schuld als mit einem Kleid und Decke zu verbergen, zugerechnet […].*"

62 Ibid., 28.

63 Ibid., 29, "*Dieß hat Philippus gelehrt und geschrieben und hat's beständlich gelehrt, daß wir durch Gottes Gesetz verpflichtet und verbunden seien entweder zum Gehorsam oder zur Strafe, und das dabei: weil wir den Gehorsam nicht haben geleistet, und derhalben die Straf leiden und tragen sollen, habe der unschuldige Sohn Gottes dieselbe für uns ausgestanden, und das sei eine genugsame Bezahlung für unsere Sünde.*" Cf. CR 24, 18: "*[…] omnis lex obligat vel ad penam, vel ad obedientiam.*"

64 Ibid., 25, "*[…] ein Jeder nach seinem Stand eigene Gerechtigkeit habe, oder aber verdammt*

What then is the significance of Christ's active obedience? It is not for us, but for himself, that is, it is his own. Since he was God he could do no other but be holy. If he had not kept the law then not only would he not be able to save us, but he himself would need a savior.[65] The Straßbourg theologians reacted by asserting that Christ is under no obligation to the law for he is "Lord of the law,"[66] therefore his obedience is freely done for us. Later, Karg seemed to modify his view and admit that Christ has kept the law *for our sakes*, but it does not follow that he has kept the law *in our name* or *in our stead*.[67]

Karg's assertion that Christ did the law for himself received the greatest amount of criticism. The Formula specifically addressed this point at the behest of the theologians in Ansbach who, in their thoughts regarding the Torgau Book of 1576, requested that the teaching of Christ's two-fold obedience be included "for the sake of the young, simple ministers."[68] The inclusion in the Formula reads:

> For since Christ was not only a human being but both God and a human being in one inseparable person, he was thus as little under the law – since he was Lord of the law – as he was obligated to suffer and die for himself. Therefore, his obedience consists not only in his suffering and death but also in the fact that he freely put himself in our place under the law and fulfilled the law with this obedience and reckoned it to us as righteousness. As a result of his total obedience – which he performed on our behalf to God in his deeds and suffering, in life and death – God forgives our sin, considers us upright and righteous, and grants us eternal salvation.[69]

Danger of Antinomianism. Karg argued that a false definition of righteousness not only leads to heresies like that of Osiander, but can also encourage a type of popular Antinomianism ("libertarianism" is probably better). His fear was that the laity would not feel obligated to obey the law if Christ had already done it for them. Apparently, Karg had a real case in mind, having heard a report of a nobleman who on his way to Erfurt boasted, "I don't have to be pious, for my

---

werden soll, daher denn Niemand für Andere fromm seyn kann. Leiden kann man für Andere, und fremde Schuld bezahlen, aber nicht für andere fromm seyn durch des Gesetzes Gerechtigkeit."

65 Ibid., 24, *"Der andere Gehorsam [...] ist und bleibt sein eigen, als der ohne Sünd hat seyn müssen, und nicht ungerecht seyn können, sonst hätte er nicht allein uns nicht können erlösen, sondern hätte auch selbst eines andern Erlösers bedurft."*

66 Ibid., 26, *"Christus, Mensch in seiner göttlichen Gestalt sowohl, als Christus Gott, das gleichviel ist, ist ein Herr des Gesetzes und ihm mit nichten unterwerflich oder etwas schuldig."*

67 Ibid., 44, *"Ich lasse auch gerne zu und gestehe, wie der Sohn Gottes von unsertwegen und uns zu Gutem ist mensch worden und Mirakel gethan, daß er auch also um unsertwillen das Gesetz habe gehalten, und daß wir uns seiner Frömmigkeit mögen trösten, dennoch folget nicht, daß er's in unserm Namen oder an unser statt und für uns gehalten habe."*

68 Döllinger, *Reformation*, III, 572f.

69 FC SD, III, 564:15.

Lord Christ has been pious for me, etc."[70] In fact, when Karg went to Wittenberg in 1570, he maintained that his entire opinion had been aimed against Antinomianism.[71]

Yet Karg's reasons for opposing the imputation of Christ's active obedience appear to have been more complex than the one stated before the Wittenberg faculty in 1570. He found that the "new" definition of the righteousness of God caused logical and theological difficulties. Any talk of Christ's obedience in Luther or Melanchthon were quite insignificant; the tendency was to speak of the cross and the forgiveness of sins. Karg forcefully opposed any definition that would diminish the significance or sufficiency of forgiveness. Whether he saw the new *modus loquendi* as a distortion of the two kinds of righteousness is not clear. More likely, he was a faithful student of Melanchthon and tried to remain closer to his preceptor's words than others.[72]

How is one to evaluate the theology of Luther's disciples? All of them saw the "righteousness of God" as an important part of their theology. The difficulty lay in how they understood what Luther termed "our theology." "Our theology" was a fundamental break from the medieval scholastic way of thinking. The two relationships experienced by every individual – *coram deo* and *coram hominibus* – were of two fundamentally different kinds. Consequently, there were two kinds of righteousness – active and passive – the righteousness of the law and the righteousness of faith. But among the next generations of Lutherans it appears that the law became a controlling category for the understanding of righteousness. Faith in Christ did not constitute the relationship of the human creature to God; faith was only the means by which the righteousness of the law was achieved. Lutherans certainly agreed that we ourselves could not fulfill the law – it was only Christ's obedience, not ours. Yet, in the end, the law still seems to get the last word.

70 Döllinger, Anhang, 34.

71 Ibid., 35, "*Meine ganze Meinung ist fürnehmlich gerichtet wider die Antinomian, auf daß sich die Leut nicht der Lehr von der Zurechnung der Gerechtigkeit und Unschuld Christi mißbrauchen [...].*"

72 Karg was extremely fond of Melanchthon and considered him his principal teacher as is evident from his acclamations, "O, du frommer Philippus, du treuer, werther Mann und Werkzeug Gottes! der lieber getreuer Präceptor!" Ibid., 42.

Guntis Kalme

Exploring Luther's "For Me" Kind of Creed

Once I asked my then *Doktor Vater*, R. Kolb, whether anybody had ever read Luther's explanation of the Apostles' Creed as a unified and self-contained text, namely, as Luther's personal creed? After a brief reflection, he answered "no" and suggested that I explore the avenue. Thus, I propose to read Luther's Small Catechism explanations in one breath as the Reformer might have done:

> I believe that God has created me together with all that exists. God has given me and still preserves my body and soul: eyes, ears, and all limbs and senses; reason and all mental faculties. In addition, God daily and abundantly provides shoes and clothing, food and drink, house and farm, spouse and children, fields, livestock, and all property – along with all the necessities and nourishment for this body and life. God protects me against all danger and shields and preserves me from all evil. And all this is done out of pure, fatherly, and divine goodness and mercy, without any merit or worthiness of mine at all! For all of this I owe it to God to thank and praise, serve and obey him. This is most certainly true (SC II, 2).
>
> I believe that Jesus Christ, true God, begotten of the Father in eternity, and also a true human being, born of the Virgin Mary, is my LORD. He has redeemed me, a lost and condemned human being. He has purchased and freed me from all sins, from death, and from the power of the devil, not with gold or silver but with his holy, precious blood and with his innocent suffering and death. He has done all this in order that I may belong to him, live under him in his kingdom, and serve him in eternal righteousness, innocence, and blessedness, just as he is risen from the dead and lives and rules eternally. This is most certainly true (SC II, 4).
>
> I believe that by my own understanding or strength I cannot believe in Jesus Christ my LORD or come to him, but instead the Holy Spirit has called me through the gospel, enlightened me with his gifts, made me holy and kept me in the true faith, just as he calls, gathers, enlightens, and makes holy the whole Christian church on earth and keeps it with Jesus Christ in the one common, true faith. Daily in this Christian church the Holy Spirit abundantly forgives all sins – mine and those of all believers. On the Last Day the Holy Spirit will raise me and all the dead and will give to me and all believers in Christ eternal life. This is most certainly true (SC II, 6).[1]

1 KW, 354–356.

The center of Luther's Creed here, the one who is speaking it, is God's beloved child using the grammar of faith, namely, the "for me" character of faith. For this reason I propose that we call Luther's explanation his "For Me" Creed. I will touch on some of the main features of the Reformer's confession, emphasizing that all of God's works mentioned in the creed have been done "for me." Then I will explore in some detail each of the articles.

Luther's "for me" confession of Creed gives us more than his personal interpretation of the *Apostolicum.*[2] It gives us insight into the Reformer's thinking on a number of important questions, such as: what information, values, and attitudes need to be taught so that one knows what it means to be Christian? Luther presents the creedal material in very concrete, subjectively significant categories for his people to grasp. He sets forth the basics of what Christian life looks like from the perspective of a gift-giving God. As Charles Arand points out, "The Creed now provides a framework within which the Christian can interpret his or her entire life as a life lived from the gifts of the Triune God from conception to resurrection."[3] Luther worked with the idea that the Catechism both informs the mind by Christian teaching and cultivates a way of life by appealing to the heart. Luther has something important to contribute to both of these aspects of the communication of the faith.

1. The Specific Features of Luther's "For Me" Creed

The text of all three Articles of Luther's "for me" Creed has several interesting features:

Mutuality. There are basically two participants in each Article – me and the respective person of the Trinity.[4] This is a dialogue or conversation between God and the believer. This leads to the next point.

Contrast. Luther contrasts the undeserved love of God with the undeserving human person. And so he contrasts God's giving out of "pure, fatherly, and divine goodness and mercy" and our reception of his gifts "without any merit or worthiness of mine." In the Second Article, "Jesus Christ, true God, begotten of the Father in eternity" is contrasted with a person as "a lost and condemned

2 Luther's other catechetical writings will be referenced here as the contextual material for this particular text. All translations from German, aside from those identified LW, are by the author.

3 Charles Arand, *That I May be His Own: an Overview of Luther's Catechisms* (St. Louis: Concordia Academic Press, 2000), 34.

4 Of course, the Second Article mentions also *devil* and the Third Article speaks of *all believers* but in both cases they mainly play their role in the particular context.

human being." And in the Third Article, he contrasts the Spirit who "has called me through the gospel" with the assertion that I, "by my own understanding or strength I cannot believe in Jesus Christ my LORD or come to him."

A down-to-earth God. Luther's Creed is dominated by the God who enters into a relationship with man and the world. God is actively and deeply involved with them. He is the "God for me" God. He provides for all my needs. He is not afraid of "getting his hands dirty" in order to rescue us. He searches for me and gathers me into fellowship with other believers.

"Gospel monergism." God always takes the initiative. God alone is at the giving end; man is always at the receiving. And so man receives from God: "body and soul, reason and all mental faculties, shoes and clothing, food and drink, spouse and children, property;" along with "eternal righteousness, innocence, and blessedness;" and "enlightenment, forgiveness of sins, resurrection of the body, and eternal life." Thus, God lovingly and actively showers man with the gifts of creation, redemption, and sanctification. We may say that Luther's Creed (implicitly or explicitly) shows forth the Gospel in all three Articles.[5]

Existential character. Luther's Creed is intensely personal as seen in the fact that God creates, recreates, and sanctifies the fundamental realities of human existence - creaturely bodily life, sociality, salvation, new life, and resurrection.

A constantly active God. Luther confesses that God "has created me [...] has given me and still preserves [...] daily and abundantly provides [...] protects me." Jesus "has redeemed me, purchased and freed me from all sins, from death, and from the power of the devil." The Holy Spirit "has called me [...] made me holy and kept me in the true faith." "On the Last Day the Holy Spirit will raise me [...] and will give to me [...] eternal life." For Luther present and future is united in faith as the experience of past and the hope for a God-provided future. This leads to the next point.

5 Overstatement is perhaps possible on account of the First Article. Definitely, it is not about salvation.We Christians, read this Article already as Trinitarian people. We know the Creator also as Christ's Father (Matt 6: 9) who lovingly cares for us. Our God-knowledge makes the Christian understanding of creation different from the heathen understanding although we share the same created order. We inhabit the realm of the First Article as Christians. God's people accept the gifts of the First Article not only for the satisfaction of their bodily needs but also as reminders of the Father who has sent us His Son as well. In addition, as R. Kolb says: "God has worked His re-creative work through selected elements of [the] created order. He did not merely talk about salvation in these elements, but He effects the new creation through specific elements of the material or created order and its visible or audible manifestations," meaning by that the flesh of Christ, and material elements of the sacraments. Robert Kolb, *Speaking the Gospel Today. A Theology for Evangelism* (St. Louis: Concordia Publishing House, 1995), 50.

Luther's Creed is characterized by confidence in God when it comes to both temporal and spiritual matters. God provides, saves, guides me, us – his beloved children. Therefore, each Article ends with the affirmative statement: "This is most certainly true."

For the sake of brevity, we will explore only one of these features. The most important point in the view of this author is that Luther's God is a God "for me," or "for us."

2. The "Gifts Received" Creed

Luther's explanation to the Apostles' Creed provides an anthropological counterpart to the Ecumenical Creeds. The texts of the Ecumenical Creeds concentrate on God while Luther focuses on the human creature.[6] Thus, while the Reformer follows the Trinitarian Creeds, his emphasis is not so much on each person of the Trinity as it is on their particular gifts "for me." Thus, every person of the Trinity is known for his gifts.

Man only *receives* the gifts of the Trinitarian "for us" God. Luther's Creed is a catalogue of God's gifts, with each Article serving as something of a storehouse of the particular gifts. The First Article delivers to man the gifts of creation, the Second the gifts of salvation, the Third the gifts of sanctification.

In the conclusion to the Creed in the Large Catechism, Luther paints an overall picture of the "for us" action of the Trinitarian God.

> For in all three articles God himself has revealed and opened to us the most profound depths of his fatherly heart and his pure, unutterable love. For this very purpose he created us, so that he might redeem us and make us holy, and, moreover, having granted and bestowed upon us everything in heaven and on earth, he has also given us his Son and his Holy Spirit, through whom he brings us to himself. For [...] we could never come to recognize the Father's favor and grace were it not for the LORD Christ, who is a mirror of the Father's heart. Apart from him we see nothing but an angry and terrible judge. But neither could we know anything of Christ, had it not been revealed by the Holy Spirit (LC II, 64–66).[7]

Faith receives all these gifts as a result of the "for us" attitude of God's grace and mercy which drives the Triune God.

---

6 Creeds were written in the midst of controversy over the divinity of Christ, or the person of Christ in general, and also in a time when Gnostic denials of the personal God of the Bible had to be confronted. In Luther's time the focus was on the human creature and whether human creatures could merit salvation, a question of the human relationship to God.

7 Martin Luther, "The Large Catechism," in KW, 439–440.

Faith

Luther begins his explanation of the Creed by exploring the meaning of the word *faith.* In his view, it has two definitions. The one is the faith "about" God (*fides quae*) and everything divine. This pertains mainly to the knowledge of religious facts. It can keep a safe distance from its object. But it remains subsidiary to the second kind of faith, which constitutes human identity by connecting the person with God.

This second kind of faith is personal and existential. It is faith "in" God (*fides qua*): "I put my trust in [God, ...]. I make the venture and take the risk to deal with him, believing beyond doubt that what he will be toward me or do with me will be just as they [the Scriptures] say." Luther continues and claims that only faith as personal trust in God identifies man as a Christian: "this faith, which in life or death dares to believe that God is what He is said to be, is the only faith that makes a man a Christian and obtains from God whatever it will."[8] Thus, the Creed not merely provides the religious facts *about* God but rather "sets forth all that we must expect and receive from God" (LC II, 1).[9]

Faith and Creation

Already in the realm of the First Article, this *fides qua* or *fiducia* is seen as vital for man. The human creature cannot live without it. Therefore, to be a human creature is not merely an ontological construct, but rather the very fact of faith. Kolb says, "[to be] 'human' means trusting God above all else. Being fully human is first of all to recognize that God is the fundamental point of orientation for humanity."[10] As Charles Arand elaborates,

> [A]s a creature of God, a human being is by definition a dependent being. At the most basic level, every person is dependent upon creation (air, water, food, and so forth) for life itself. People are also dependent upon neighbors (parents, spouse, employer, society, and so forth) for community and the sustenance of life. In addition to these needs, human beings ultimately need a foundation for security, meaning, identity, and a framework for making sense of life. All this is to say that life cannot be lived without faith.[11]

---

8 Martin Luther, *Works of Martin Luther with Introduction and Notes;* trans., C.M. Jacobs (Philadelphia: A.J. Holman Company, 1915), 2: 368. WA 7: 215.

9 KW, 431.

10 Robert Kolb, "Luther on the Theology of the Cross," *Lutheran Quarterly* 16 (Winter 2002): 459.

11 Arand, *That I May be His Own,* 154.

In the work of creation and the act of redemption the Triune God comes near to us and is recognized by us.

The created order reflects the continuous primacy of God the Giver and his gifts "for me," and "for us." The human being does not put himself in the middle of the cosmos. He is there as a result of God's created order. Luther says that the First Article, "teaches that you do not have your life of yourself."[12] Albrecht Peters also notes that in Luther's catechetical writings God's *creatio ex nihilo* is put forth as not just the beginning of the cosmos, but is focused upon my existence. Therefore, to believe in God means "to be serious about the fact that God, and no one else, is the Lord of my life and of the entire world in which I live. In this way the Reformer brings the *pro nobis* into the First Article."[13]

3. The First Article of Luther's "For Me" Creed

Luther is eager to point out that "the Father has given to us himself with all creation and has abundantly provided for us in this life" (LC II, 24).[14] In this respect his Creed is a response to both – to the gifts of the "for us" God and also to the Giver himself, whose nature the Reformer goes on to describe: "all this is done out of pure, fatherly, and divine goodness and mercy" (SC II, 2).[15]

This invites the personal relationship of trust and faith with God the Father and his "for us" attitude towards us which in turn establishes man's identity and status before God: "[S]ince I [...] place my trust in him, I am assuredly his child, servant, and eternal heir."[16] Kolb points out, "to recognize trust as the core of our humanity is to perceive the true form of being human as God created his human creature. That means that at the core of human life, our own performance, accomplishment, behavior has no place."[17] Luther, once convinced of his child-Father relationship *coram Deo*, goes further, declaring his unreserved reliance on God's caring, "for us" attitude: "If he is God, he can and wishes to do what is best with me. Since he is Father, he will do all this and do it gladly."[18]

It must be noted that in the First Article of his Creed Luther's emphasis lies on the distinction between the good and merciful Creator and his beloved creature.

12 WA 30.1: 87; LW 51: 163.

13 Albrecht Peters, *Kommentar zu Luthers Katechismen, Der Glaube*, ed., Gottfried Seebass (Göttingen: Vandenhoeck & Ruprecht, 1991), 2: 63. Here including quote from Martin Doerne, "*Praktischer Shöpfungsglaube nach Luther*," in *Luther* 25 (1954): 26.

14 KW, 433.

15 KW, 354.

16 WA 10.2: 391; LW 43: 26.

17 Kolb, "Luther on the Theology of the Cross," 450.

18 WA 10.2: 391; LW 43: 26.

This is clearly expressed in Luther's usage of "me" in the First Article and his enumeration of the particular gifts man receives, expressing the idea that man has been given a lot, in fact, everything he needs and even more. Man is God's special creature in all respects, literally showered with gifts. "God has given everything"[19] for us. We are rich in God.

The First Article of Luther's Creed describes the gifts received in universal ("all that exists," "all danger," "all evil") and down-to-earth ("shoes and clothing, food and drink, house and farm, spouse and children, fields, livestock") categories. The term "all" in Luther's Creed serves as a counterpart of the wording in the Ecumenical Creeds "God the Father almighty, Creator," and thus describes both God's goodness and his power.

The measure of God's love for man as his beloved creature in the First Article of Luther's Creed is that the whole created order is designed especially "for us." It is literally charged with God's love and care toward us, his beloved human creatures. Through it God provides gifts to us on a regular basis. Therefore, the world and all created life is based on the faithfulness of the Creator towards his creatures.[20]

At the same time, man has been given both the abilities and responsibilities to exercise the dominion over the created order. This aspect also should be looked upon as a part of God's care, for human beings are considered to be conscientious participants, not just consumers of this sustenance-care-safety net. Kolb points out, "in exercising [concrete walks of life] we are the hands or feet or mouth of God."[21]

But there is more to it. This overwhelming "for us" gift-relationship with God evokes in man a desire to serve: "if everything is the gift of God, then you owe it to him to serve him with all these things and praise and thank him."[22] Man gives thanks for these gifts by using them for God's purposes.

> Hence, because everything we possess, and everything in heaven and on earth besides, is daily given, sustained, and protected by God, it inevitably follows that we are duty bound to love, praise, and thank him without ceasing, and, in short, to devote all these things to his service (LC II, 19).[23]

It is also important to state that Luther does not believe in God simply because he is showering him with gifts, but just because he is God. There is no other reason to believe in God besides his God-ness. God is caring for, not bribing, man with his

19 WA 30.1: 87; LW 51: 163.
20 Peters, *Kommentar,* 2: 77.
21 Robert Kolb, *Teaching God's Children His Teaching. A Guide for the Study of Luther's Catechism* (Hutchinson, MN: Crown Publishing, 1992), 8–3.
22 WA 30.1: 87; LW 51: 163.
23 KW, 433.

"for us" attitude which sometimes can come to man as a shower of gifts and sometimes as a lack of them. God is God – with or without His gifts. As Luther says, "for this faith of mine must and shall soar above everything that is and everything that is not [...] so that it may remain simply as purely a faith in God."[24]

Thus, Luther's God of the First Article is the One in whom his almightiness, his fatherhood, and his creator character are united in his "for us" attitude. It is the attitude of the Father who establishes man's identity as his own creature and child. The Creator God showers man with creaturely gifts, ordering them in a care-sustenance-safety net for man. Man is not designed to be a consumer but an organic part of God's "for us" commitment to the world.

4. The Second Article of Luther's "For Us" Creed

While the First Article mainly deals with the man as a creature of God, the Second Article focuses on man deprived of God's gifts. Here, like the biblical writers, Luther unfolds the narrative of redemption as a dramatic battle that takes and applies Christ's work "for me." It addresses the central question, "How does Jesus become my Lord?"[25]

The Reformer answers: "He was conceived by the Holy Spirit without any sin whatsoever in order that he might become my Lord [...] he must be so holy that the devil could have no claim upon him."[26] This explains why the first line of the Second Article of Luther's Creed resembles the Nicene Creed. By the phrase, "begotten of the Father in eternity, and also a true human being, born of the Virgin Mary," the Reformer establishes the foundation of the human-divine nature of Christ, from which he concludes that Christ "is my Lord." Only such a Lord is capable of helping man in his disastrous condition.

The knowledge of salvation and particularly of Christ's love "for us" lies beyond human comprehension. The Reformer says: "no human heart can imagine that He should have to do all that for my sake."[27] It is knowledge revealed through the birth, life, and death of Jesus. And thus it comes *extra nos.* Put another way, "No purity or holiness comes from us, but will be found and achieved outside and above us and far from us, indeed, above all our senses, [...] in Christ."[28] Thus, the center of our faith lies not in us but in him, more precisely, in his "for us" attitude, in what this man "has done for us."[29]

24 WA 7: 216. Kolb, *Works of Martin Luther*, 369.
25 Peters, *Kommentar*, 2: 123.
26 WA 30.1: 90. LW 5: 165.
27 WA 37: 45–46.
28 WA 37: 57.
29 WA 37: 48.

In order to explore the "for us" attitude of the Second Article, Luther suggests that we "concentrate on these words, 'in Jesus Christ, our LORD'" (LC II, 26).[30] In the Reformer's mind, the pronoun *our* expresses the "for us" character of faith that permeates the entire Creed. He suggests that we search for God's "for us" commitment throughout the whole Creed and constantly apply it for ourselves as God's great gift. Luther asserts that the central idea of this article is this:

> He is called 'our Lord.' What follows is credited to our account.[31] Therefore, accustom yourself to so look at the words that you always see the word 'Our' being pulled through the rest of the Creed, that everything is credited to us, that I believe on Christ, and [his work] becomes mine against my sin and evil conscience. That is now stated in summary fashion that Christ benefits us.[32]

The Reformer eagerly points out that the "for us" attitude of the Second Article can be found everywhere – either explicitly or implicitly:

> [A]lthough these words [...] 'for us born, suffered, etc.' are not stated there expressly, one must nevertheless take up all others in this piece and apply them here [in the Apostles' Creed] because it shows how Christ is 'ours, mine.'[33]

The phrase "our Lord" is the equivalent of "for us." Albrecht Peter notes the inseparable connection between the confession itself "I believe," and the "*pro me*" which means that Christ's lordship, which I confess, coincides with his mission of being and acting "for me."[34]

The very beginning of the Second Article sets forth Christ's mission for Luther when he speaks of "Our Lord." With that identification we confess that everything which that Man is and does, has happened to us. As Luther states it, "To you He is a Lord, for your benefit born, suffered, died and risen."[35] Luther claims: "I believe only in Jesus Christ; for neither I, nor any man has suffered for me, nor has died."[36] To this end, Luther specifies that Christ's lordship is unique:

> [T]he word 'Lord' here means unlimited mercy. It is a tender, comforting word, namely, that we have such a Man in Him, who can help us and save through forgiveness of sins and resurrection of the dead, [...] in all needs and against all enemies. For He has not done all such things and been so active to redeem us, that He wants to be that kind of a

30 KW, 434.

31 It needs to be mentioned that in the other writings of Luther's *Corpus Catecheticum*, e.g., his Catechisms, the language of forensic justification is not as prominent as it is here in the Torgau sermons.

32 WA 37: 53.

33 WA 37: 49.

34 Peters, *Kommentar*, 2:29.

35 WA 37: 51.

36 WA 37: 48.

> Lord who wrestles with us, as a tyrant, [...] but rather that we should have a friendly, helping master.[37]

There was nothing that Christ would gain for himself. Everything he did was ultimately done to benefit us. As Luther says, Christ "has broken down [the power of death, etc.] by His almighty, divine power, but not for Himself, but rather for us poor, wretched people."[38] Thus, Christ is our Lord because he has fought and won the battle "for us." Therefore, the answer to the question about how Jesus becomes my Lord is a concise one: "by freeing me from death, sin, hell, and all evil."[39]

The true measure of God's love in the Second Article is emphasized by the way in which Christ delivers us not by means of gold or silver but by means of his holy precious blood and innocent suffering and death. Here Luther draws upon 1 Pet 1:18, "For you know that it was not with the perishable things such as silver or gold that you were redeemed [...] but with the precious blood of Christ" (NIV). In doing so, God's gifts of the Second Article go beyond the gifts of the First Article. Thus Christ acquires us as his own. This results in a transfer of human identity, meaning, and security from the reign of sin, death, and devil to the reign of Christ. This again demonstrates God's giving out of "pure, fatherly, and divine goodness and mercy, without any merit or worthiness of mine at all!" (SC II, 2).[40]

Man's destiny is described in Luther's Creed both in terms of spiritual welfare ("freed me from all sins [...] and from the power of the devil") and in terms of eschatological flourishing ("eternal righteousness, innocence, and blessedness"). Luther describes both the "freedom from" and the "freedom for." The former asserts negatively that man must be extracted from "all sins, from death, and from the power of the devil," while the later positively assigns man to his proper place: "that I may belong to him, live under him in his kingdom, and serve him in eternal righteousness, innocence, and blessedness" (SC II, 4).[41] In other words, God's people can be sure that "we through Christ have torn hell apart and destroyed completely the devil's kingdom and power. That is why He died, was buried and descended, that they should no longer harm nor overpower us."[42] The "for us" attitude of Christ led him out of death and hell to his resurrection. Luther says, Christ was not allowed to remain there, since by that we would not finally be helped. He has arisen – that is the end and the best part about it, by which we have everything.[43] His people will also rise from the dead to eternal life. "He has arisen

37 WA 37: 49.
38 WA 37: 67.
39 WA 30.1: 89; LW 51: 164.
40 KW, 354.
41 KW, 355.
42 WA 37: 66.
43 WA 37: 56.

and not for himself, but for our sakes that his resurrection is ours, and we should arise in him and [...] celebrate with him, also bodily, an eternal Easter day."[44] Believers are assured that they will triumph over death in their own resurrection as well. In other words, Christ's resurrection is of the "for us" kind and directly involves our bodies: "we must [...] be reached and touched through his resurrection, and even participate in [his death and resurrection], as having happened for our sake."[45] Christ's resurrection affects also man's life of discipleship:

> I believe that he was resurrected from the dead on the third day to give a new life to me and all believers, thus awakening us with him by his grace and spirit henceforth to sin no more [Rom. 6:4; Gal. 2:20] but to serve him only with every grace and virtue, thus fulfilling God's commandments.[46]

Christ's people possess his "for us" attitude which defines the entirety of their lives.

Luther's emphasis on the Creedal formula "our Lord" highlights the "for us" attitude of Christ. Christ's conception by the Holy Spirit, his birth and life, and redemptive death "for us" were decisive for humanity. Luther argues that the object of the faith is always outside of us, in Christ's "for us" commitment and work.

5. The Third Article of Luther's "For Us" Creed

In Luther's view the Third Article is the place where the gifts "for us" that were acquired in the Second Article are now delivered to us in the present. Without the Holy Spirit, no one can "appropriate any of this [gift] to himself."[47]

Luther labels the Third Article, "Being Made Holy," as the one which directly procures the gifts "for us." He points out that "creation is now behind us, and redemption has also taken place, but the Holy Spirit continues his work without ceasing until the Last Day" (LC II, 61).[48] The sanctifying activity of the Holy Spirit takes place in the here and now. It is not a one moment thing but his continuous work. "[The Holy Spirit] has made us holy and still makes us holy" (LC II, 36).[49]

The Third Article of Luther's Creed again confesses something about the human condition. Instead of the "lost and condemned human being" of the

44 WA 37: 70–1.
45 WA 37: 68.
46 LW 43: 27. WA 10.2: 392.
47 WA 10.2: 393; LW 43: 28.
48 KW, 439.
49 Also: "the third article, therefore, is that I believe in the Holy Spirit, that is, that the Holy Spirit will sanctify me and is sanctifying me." WA 30.1: 93; LW 51: 168.

Second Article, it is the man who by his "own understanding or strength [...] cannot believe in Jesus Christ [his] LORD or come to him." Man is not able on his own to get the gifts which are procured by Christ for him. He needs someone to deliver them on a constant daily basis. This is a job of the Holy Spirit, who does this "for me."

In one breath Luther confesses, "the Holy Spirit has called me through the gospel, enlightened me with his gifts, made me holy and kept me in the true faith," i. e., he re-created, sanctified, and preserved me in trust toward God. His "for me" attitude has enabled me to live a different life, a life "for Christ" (as the opposite of a selfish "for myself" life).

Luther then proceeds to clarify how man is brought into the realm of the Holy Spirit's activity. The Spirit creates the Church "in which all his gifts are to be found."[50] and works through the Church as his instrument: Thus, Luther states, "Through the Christian church, that is, through its ministry [*officium*], you were sanctified; for the Holy Spirit uses its ministry in order to sanctify you. Otherwise you would never know and hear Christ."[51]

With mention of the church, Luther switches from the first person singular to the first person plural. Besides calling, enlightening, and sanctifying me, the Holy Spirit has also led me to the others who have experienced the same. "We" have been guided by the Word to the place where it abides, to the Church and the Sacraments. Here "we" on a daily basis receive the forgiveness of sins. From such a state of personal giftedness and our common ecclesial giftedness (calling, gathering, enlightening, sanctifying and forgiving *us*) my and our eschatological destiny will be revealed. "[O]n the Last Day the Holy Spirit will raise me and all the dead and will give to me and all believers in Christ eternal life" (SC II, 6).[52]

The Church is the mediator of the Holy Spirit to us and "for us" and "through [the Church] He [the Holy Spirit] preaches, calls you and makes Christ known to you."[53] Thus, the Church becomes the main instrument of the Holy Spirit because it is the agency for the means of grace.

Luther argues that without the preaching of Christ, his work, which has happened in the past, would be useless. A. Peters observes,

> [I]f we lose the 'for us' of the proclamation, Christ remains only an executed criminal on the gallows; if He were crucified a thousand times, it would not help us. Without the preaching of the cross we remain under judgment.[54]

50 WA 30.1: 94; LW 51: 168.
51 WA 30.1: 92; LW 51: 167.
52 KW, 356.
53 WA 30.1: 94; LW 51: 168.
54 Peters, *Kommentar*, 2: 197.

The Reformer says, "For where Christ is not preached, there is no Holy Spirit to create, call, and gather the Christian church, apart from which no one can come to the Lord Christ" (LC II, 45).[55] As the world was created through the Word (Gen 1), so is the Church.

The Holy Spirit uses many tools and means, but the end result, the content of the received blessings in the Church, the essence of the preaching of the Word, the fruit of the sacraments are the same – the forgiveness of sins. "[I]n this Christian community we have the forgiveness of sins, which takes place through the holy sacraments and absolution as well as through all the comforting words of the entire gospel" (LC II, 54).

Luther writes extensively about the subject of forgiveness, knowing that the work of the Holy Spirit is continuous "for us" because people are in perpetual need of the forgiveness due to their sinful nature.

> Forgiveness is constantly needed, for although God's grace has been acquired by Christ, and holiness has been wrought by the Holy Spirit through God's Word in the unity of the Christian church, yet we are never without sin because we carry our flesh around our neck" (LC II, 54).[56]

The administration of the power of the keys for forgiveness which brings the Gospel to the people is unique to the Church. Nowhere else are such things available.

> Here there is full forgiveness of sins, both in that God forgives us and that we forgive, bear with, and aid one another. Outside this Christian community, however, where there is no gospel, there is also no forgiveness, and hence there also can be no holiness (LC II, 55–56).[57]

6. The Specifics of Luther's Use of the First Person Singular

The twenty-first century western reader may be tempted to believe that Luther's use of the first person singular foreshadows the individualistic approach of their own period. This is not the case. His Creed focuses on the person of the believer, not on the autonomous individual. Luther emphasizes the creature of God fashioned for a relationship with God his Creator and for relationship to other human creatures and the rest of creation. The self-isolated existentialist or the ideologically brainwashed individual with his crippled self-consciousness is foreign to Luther. Luther's "me" speaks out of the fullness of being gifted with all kinds of God's "for us" gifts. Luther with this approach reaches everybody, for no

55 KW, 436.
56 KW, 438.
57 KW, 438.

one can escape from this God-gifted kind of "me." The whole of humanity is enclosed in this "me" for it is both personal and trans-personal. Everybody is invited to join the fellowship of God's gifts "for us."

7. Summary

Luther's "for us" Creed reflects the Ecumenical Creeds but distinctively focuses on man as the recipient of the Triune God's gifts "for us." Luther describes the gifts in both universal and down-to-earth categories. He places particular emphasis on the distinction between the merciful Father and beloved creature distinction.

The measure of God's love for man in the First Article is the whole created order, which God has organized to exhibit his care "for us." The Second Article deals with man's main predicament, sin, the broken relationship with God, and points out the divine solution, Christ the Lord, who is described in Nicene terms as being the divine-human person who enters human life to win forgiveness through his sacrificial death. The Second Article reveals God's love in a more profound way than the First because of its focus on Christ's sacrifice. Christ provides man with both the *freedom from* all the enemies of the human creature and the *freedom for* living out God's plan for humanity.

The Third Article describes man as being unable to obtain the gifts of the Second Article for himself. Therefore, the Holy Spirit re-creates, sanctifies, and preserves faith in me, enabling me to live a life "for Christ." By shifting from the first person singular to the first person plural Luther exhibits the entrance of the person into the community of the other believers, the Church, which is created and governed by the Holy Spirit using the Word and the Sacraments. Luther's use of the first person singular is not individualistic but rather personal and relational.

8. Conclusion

Taking everything into consideration, this author proposes that Luther's comments on the *Apostolicum* demonstrate that Luther's explanations function as an independent text with desirable liturgical and doxological consequences. What prevents its use as the Creed in the service, e.g., celebrating Luther's birthday?

David Lumpp

Promise, Liberty, and Persecution: Exploring Philip Melanchthon's Contextual Theology[1]

1. Introduction

The year 1520 may be considered the theological "point of no return" for Martin Luther. In 1520 he challenged the Roman sacramental system in *The Babylonian Captivity of the Church* and the hegemony of the Roman magisterium in *To the Christian Nobility of the German Nation.* Only a comprehensive – and implausible – recantation at Worms could have begun to repair Luther's relationship with the church of Rome. However, in the third of his famous treatises of 1520, *The Freedom of a Christian,* which develops the themes of promise and liberty with respect to the Christian life, Luther not only eschews any personal polemics, he also begins with a warm and deferential open letter to Pope Leo X himself. Whatever the intent of this letter,[2] in terms of its all-important content, *On Christian Liberty* constitutes something of an ecumenical proposal. The gospel of Jesus Christ and the freedom it engenders are matters about which there ought to be concord.

Likewise, the same refrains of promise and liberty appear consistently throughout Philip Melanchthon's career, from his early Reformation writings to the last edition of his *Loci communes theologici.* In addition, these themes persist despite nearly constant pressure both from ecclesiastical and imperial foes and from erstwhile colleagues in the expanding Lutheran Reformation.

---

1 I am indebted to Profs. Timothy Wengert, Bo Christian Holm, and Robert Kolb, the esteemed honoree of this volume, for their helpful insights and suggestions at earlier stages of my work on this essay. Indeed, Robert Kolb introduced me to the intricacies of these robust theological debates more than four decades ago, and it is my privilege to participate in this larger celebration of his work. I am grateful as well for the critical reading and comments of Prof. Paul Hinlicky, which he shared with me in seminar sessions of the 11th International Congress for Luther Research in Canoas, Brazil in July 2007. The current essay is an updating and revision of that earlier paper.

2 James Kittelson refers to this letter as Luther's "last attempt at reconciliation" with Rome. See *Luther the Reformer: The Story of the Man and His Career* (Minneapolis: Augsburg Publishing House, 1986), 155.

This essay will explore these themes most particularly in two shorter primary source texts with which Melanchthon is directly associated, specifically, *Instructions for the Visitors of Parish Pastors in Electoral Saxony* of 1528 (hereafter "Instructions"), and the Leipzig Interim (sometimes called the Leipzig Proposal) of 1548. I have chosen these two writings because of Melanchthon's prominent roles in the production of both documents, and because of their intended status for the broader Reformation movement. In other words, in these two instances Philip was working not only as a theologian in his own right, but also as a teacher and reformer quite aware of his public responsibilities. In addition, the issues of doctrine and life converge in these texts, as Melanchthon unfolds for Saxon clergy and people what it is necessary to believe and practice, and what – in the face of unprecedented threats – one might concede and still retain the heart of evangelical faith.

2. Instructions for the Visitors of Parish Pastors in Electoral Saxony (1528)

While not quite the collaborative venture that the Leipzig Interim may have been (see below), Reformation historians have always acknowledged that in these "Instructions" Melanchthon was writing as a spokesperson for the larger Wittenberg Reformation. He was giving voice to Luther's theology as well as to his own, and he was doing so with the endorsement of Elector John of Saxony. Melanchthon's authorial hand and Luther's ongoing role (both in terms of the preface and with respect to subsequent editions) have given the document virtually a dual attribution as witnessed by their inclusion in both the Weimar edition of Luther's works and the *Corpus Reformatorum* materials of Melanchthon.

Because Melanchthon's "Instructions" were intended to help Saxon pastors and their congregations become grounded more responsibly in at least the rudiments of Christian faith and life as taught in Wittenberg, the list of contents in the 1528 edition runs to seventeen topics, ranging from the most central matters of doctrine (e.g., the sacraments, free will, Christian liberty, and so forth) down to very timely practical counsel about how one ought to regard and respond to the threat of the Turks (including some implicit advice about unjust and just wars). Later editions would include as an eighteenth topic some fairly detailed instructions as to how one might organize the curriculum and pedagogy of Christian schools.

Most important, Melanchthon's first topic deals not with doctrine in general, but with "the doctrine," unfolding as his point of departure essentially the words of Jesus in Luke 24:47, "repentance and forgiveness of sins should be preached in [Jesus'] name to all nations." This beginning, both in terms of substance and biblical method, was no historical accident, as it reflected Melanchthon's (and Luther's) position in the initial skirmishes of their protracted dispute with the antinomian Johannes Agricola.

> There neither is forgiveness of sins without repentance nor can forgiveness of sins be understood without repentance. It follows that if we preach the forgiveness of sins without repentance that the people imagine that they have already obtained the forgiveness of sins, becoming thereby secure and without compunction (*fochtlos*) of conscience.[3]

By retaining this "whole gospel (*das Evangelion gantz*)"[4] – repentance and forgiveness of sins, not one without the other and not inverting them – the "common people" can make the necessary distinctions and understand the essence of authentic Christian faith: "the faith in Christ which the apostles call justifying faith, i. e., which makes righteous and takes away sin."[5]

Melanchthon follows this relatively brief introduction, "The Doctrine," with sections on the Ten Commandments, "true Christian prayer," and "tribulation (*Trubsal*)."[6] Here doctrine and life fuse seamlessly in Melanchthon's discussion, for he weaves into these sections the affirmation that "the most important matters of the Christian life"[7] are, sequentially: repentance, faith, good works, and the "knowledge of how one shall meet tribulation."[8] This theological order is most apparent in the discussion of the Ten Commandments:

> These are the two chief elements of Christian life: Repentance or contrition and grief, and faith through which we receive the forgiveness of sins and are righteous before God. Both should grow and increase in us. The third element of the Christian life is the doing of good works.[9]

Melanchthon unfolds the Ten Commandments in such a way that anticipates Luther's much longer treatment in the Large Catechism. In these "Instructions," Melanchthon moves relatively quickly from a short (but nonetheless emphatic) consideration of how the commandments effect contrition[10] to the ways in which the Decalogue now provides concrete instruction to the faithful: "Therefore again

3 "Instructions for the Visitors of Parish Pastors in Electoral Saxony" of 1528 in Conrad Bergendoff, ed. and trans., LW 40: 274. For the German text, WA: 26.
4 LW 40: 275; WA 26: 202.
5 LW 40: 275.
6 LW 40: 287; WA 26: 212.
7 LW 40: 287.
8 LW 40: 287.
9 LW 40: 277.
10 LW 40: 276.

and again the Ten Commandments are to be assiduously taught, for all good works are therein comprehended."[11]

Melanchthon's consideration of "true Christian prayer" affords him the opportunity to discuss both that topic as well as a cluster of other central Reformation themes, among them the atonement of Christ, the proper role of works, ministry, the Christian citizen and his or her appropriate obedience vis-à-vis human governments, the intimation of a theology of the cross (albeit without the label), and the role of the Mosaic law (including Sabbath observance). The condensed summaries of Christ's atonement and the role of works are characteristic of Melanchthon and anticipate the subsequent language of the Augsburg Confession and Apology:

> It is necessary to teach that God forgives our sins without reference to any of our works, on account of Christ. So hostile is God to sin that the work of no creature can make satisfaction for it – only the sacrifice of God's own Son could do this. [...] For the truth is that God gives blessings because of his promise, not because of our works, yet the good works which God has commanded must be done.[12]

Interestingly, the discussion of tribulation, the fourth part of Christian life, affords Melanchthon perhaps his greatest opportunity to integrate doctrine and life. While this section briefly discusses the nature of tribulation as such, Melanchthon's goal is to sketch "the knowledge of how one shall meet tribulation."[13] Tribulation teaches one the sovereignty and sometimes the inscrutability of God;[14] reminds the Christian of his or her weakness and thus elicits repentance; incites one to faithful prayer; and, as God hears and answers prayer, thereby encourages the afflicted that God is the one who delivers the afflicted.[15]

The "Instructions" continue with a discussion of the sacraments, which makes the most sense only in the context of competing Roman and (to a lesser extent) Anabaptist positions. If tribulation is integral to Christian life, Luther's and Melanchthon's doctrine of baptism is one of God's promissory resources to counter it. Children and adults should know that in baptism God claims them as his own ("I will be their God") and extends to them his care and protection.[16] Likewise, "The Sacrament of the Body and Blood of the Lord" (Melanchthon's title; note the accent on the true presence and Melanchthon's pastoral affirmation of communion in both kinds[17]) is intended precisely for those who are

11 LW 40: 277.
12 LW 40: 280.
13 LW 40: 287.
14 LW 40: 280, 287.
15 LW 40: 287.
16 LW 40: 288.
17 LW 40: 288.

"terror-stricken in their consciences,"[18] for whom Christ's words of promise forgive sins, awaken faith, and comfort the heart.[19]

The treatment of "true Christian penance (*Busse*),"[20] "true Christian confession (*Beicht*),"[21] and "true Christian satisfaction (*Genugthuung*) for sin"[22] – the three titles obviously directed at Rome – in some ways returns the discussion full circle to the initial admonition about repentance and the forgiveness of sins. Drawing especially on the biblical example of David, Melanchthon hammers away his earlier point that true faith is impossible apart from "sincere contrition," "sorrow over one's sins," and a "sincere fear of the wrath and judgment of God."[23] Melanchthon does not use the vocabulary of Law and Gospel; instead, he asserts that "through the Word and preaching" God works contrition and faith,[24] and through this faith one receives the promised forgiveness of sins.[25]

Several brief and characteristic paragraphs on confession move Melanchthon into a short but striking summary of atonement theology in his section on satisfaction. As expected, Melanchthon affirms that "Christ alone" makes satisfaction for human sin.[26] But that single "alone" and one later assertion that "no one except Christ the Son of God can make satisfaction for sin" are the lone "exclusive terms" in this section. (He was more explicit in the citation offered above.[27]) An interesting point in this section is the use of the death of Christ to communicate both the wrath of God over sin as well as God's mercy, or, in the language Melanchthon would exploit three years later in the Apology of the Augsburg Confession, both law and promise.[28]

The second major theme of the present essay, Christian liberty, is introduced in the "Instructions" near the end of Melanchthon's consideration of marriage. Based on Gal 5:13, he states the purpose of such freedom as follows: "Christian liberty (*freyheit*) is not given in order that each one might seek or satisfy his own feelings or notions, but that with clear conscience he might live and act as a servant to his neighbor."[29] Before the actual section on "Christian Freedom," Melanchthon inserts roughly a page-long "brief statement," in which he anticipates his distinction between civil and spiritual righteousness in Augustana and

18 LW 40: 292.
19 LW 40: 293.
20 LW 40: 293; WA 26: 217.
21 LW 40: 296; WA 26: 220.
22 LW 40: 297; WA 26: 220.
23 LW 40: 294.
24 LW 40: 295.
25 LW 40: 296.
26 LW 40: 297.
27 LW 40: 280.
28 LW 40: 280.
29 LW 40: 301; WA 26: 225.

Ap XVIII. This necessary interlude, offered at this point to allay confusion, moves quickly into the systematic and practical discussion of Christian freedom.

In unfolding the meaning and implications of Christian freedom in three parts, Melanchthon begins with the all-important gospel point:

> In the first place Christian freedom is the forgiveness of sins through Christ by the Holy Spirit without our merit or aid. [...] Christian freedom [...] means that Christ has promised us the Holy Spirit, to rule over us and protect us against [the] power of the devil.[30]

This gospel point of departure then informs his second and third emphases, namely, that one is neither bound by Moses' ceremonial or civic ordinances and may instead follow the laws of his or her own land; and, that the observance of "human church regulations" does not bring righteousness before God (citing Matt 15:9).[31] The judicial laws of the state are confirmed by God (Rom 13:1; 1 Pet 2:13), provided they are not "against his law or against reason."[32] The spiritual stakes are higher when it comes to church regulations: some rules (e.g., mandatory celibacy) must be avoided because they themselves entail sin (Acts 5:29); others often "encourage the idea" that they are either necessary for grace or that they in fact merit grace.[33] Melanchthon speaks more positively of ordinances such as the fixed days of the church calendar:

> Other ordinances have been made, not in order to earn grace or to make satisfaction for sin, or even because it is necessary to observe them, but because they serve a useful purpose. Such is the observance of Sunday, Easter, Pentecost, and Christmas, which have been fixed in time so that the people may know when to come together to learn the Word of God. Not that it is necessary even to keep these days or that it is sinful to do manual labor on them, but it is well to keep them so that every man may know the time at which to assemble and to learn.[34]

Significantly, when Melanchthon discusses the abuses of Christian liberty in the "Instructions," he devotes the most attention to the kinds of unnecessary and spiritually injurious infringements on freedom outlined above. Christian liberty is destroyed by claims that human traditions (whether civil or religious) are mandatory or express the eternal will of God. Most pernicious of all is the insinuation that observance of these traditions contributes in any way to genuine Christian righteousness.

While the foregoing is clear, it still leaves much unstated. More specifically, Melanchthon here has more to say about how Christian liberty can be truncated

30 LW 40: 303.
31 LW 40: 304.
32 LW 40: 304.
33 LW 40: 305.
34 LW 40: 304.

or abused than he does about how it may be freely exercised. The earlier citation connecting Christ's satisfaction for sin with good works concluded with the largely undeveloped phrase, "the good works which God has commanded must be done."[35] Later, in connection with the Ten Commandments, he asserts:

> They [i. e., the good works 'comprehended,' (verfasset), in the Ten Commandments] are called good works not only because they are done for the welfare of our neighbors, but because God has commanded them, and so they also are well pleasing to God.[36]

Moreover, the afore-cited purpose of Christian liberty was also clear, namely, "that with clear conscience he might live and act as a servant to his neighbor."[37]

In light of Melanchthon's celebrated involvement in such discussions in subsequent writings, he avoids here the specific language of "necessity" in connection with good works (though the idea is obviously expressed in the quote above). Nor is there any systematic discussion of appropriate "uses" for God's law beyond what he says early on in connection with contrition and later with those parts of Moses that can be retained to encourage and facilitate the gathering of Christian people to hear and learn the Word of God.[38]

At the same time, there is movement in these directions, and this movement becomes clearer retrospectively, in the light of Luther's treatment of some of these themes in his two catechisms. If Melanchthon's biggest concern was with the legalistic destruction of Christian freedom, the "Instructions" also show that he was quite aware of the opposite danger of unfettered license:

> For when Christian liberty is abused it is like a herd of swine being invited to the table of a prince. They understand not such an honor, but only ravage what is set before them, even soiling the prince. So when the masses hear of freedom they do not understand the meaning of it. Imagining that they need observe no discipline or proper behavior they even blaspheme God.[39]

Moreover, if the laws given by God to Israel through Moses did not bind the Christians of Saxony as such (nor should they, for the law of Moses is "superseded" [*auffge haben*][40]), they are applicable to the extent that these laws express what "nature itself teaches."[41] A bit more subtly, Melanchthon weaves – without specific theological comment or methodological defense – a consideration of at least the second, third, and fourth commandments into his discussions of the other topics of the "Instructions" (e.g., consideration of the second com-

35 LW 40: 280; WA 26: 204.
36 LW 40: 277.
37 LW 40: 301.
38 LW 40: 279, 297, 298, 304.
39 LW 40: 310.
40 LW 40: 310; WA 26: 233.
41 LW 40: 310.

mandment moves into the discussion of prayer, as does his broad treatment of the third and especially fourth commandments).

These "Instructions" of Melanchthon captured the essence of the Wittenberg Reformation sufficiently to earn Luther's endorsement and near appropriation, as indicated by his revisions to later editions, almost as though the "Instructions" had come from his own hand.[42] The themes of promise and liberty, introduced and treated therein along with others, would receive extensive treatment within several years, both by Melanchthon and Luther, as well as their colleagues in electoral Saxony. This later and more extensive treatment could entail development, refinement, nuancing, and potentially even departure in the next three decades. It is to the specific question of how the dialectic of promise and liberty fares that I now turn my attention.

3. Promise and Liberty in Melanchthon's *Loci Communes:* A Developmental Excursus

Philip Melanchthon, the public leader of the Reformation, was also the *praeceptor Germaniae,* "Teacher of Germany." As Renaissance humanist and university professor, teaching in both the arts and theology faculties, he wrote notable textbooks on Greek grammar and ancient rhetoric as well as theology.

The best known of the theology textbooks were the four (major) editions of the *Loci communes theologici* from 1521, 1535, 1543, and 1555. The first edition was and remains universally acclaimed. It is an extended soteriological treatise reflecting the Pauline accents of Romans, and much of it would appear in reworked form in the Apology of the Augsburg Confession. Its "outline" is the simplest of the four editions; and the themes of Christ's promise and the freedom it confers are unmistakable. As to the former, Melanchthon calls the gospel "the promise of the grace, blessing, and favor of God through Christ."[43] The latter theme, Christian liberty, asserts that one in whom the Holy Spirit dwells "will[s] and desire[s] spontaneously and from the heart what the law demands."[44] He does assert that the Decalogue is observed "by necessity," but, at the same time, it has been "abrogated."[45] Melanchthon explains:

42 See the discussion in the Introduction to the "Instructions," LW 40: 265–267.

43 Philip Melanchthon, *Loci communes theologici,* 1521 in Lowell J. Sartre, trans., with revisions by Wilhelm Pauck, ed., in the Library of Christian Classics, vol. 19 (Philadelphia: Westminster Press, 1969), 73. See also page 119: "The gospel is the promise of grace or the forgiveness of sins through Christ." (Hereafter cited as "1521 *Loci.*")

44 1521 *Loci,* 123.

45 1521 *Loci,* 127.

> We are free [from the Decalogue] first because although we are sinners, it cannot condemn those who are in Christ. Secondly, those who are in Christ are led by the Spirit to do the law and they really act by the Spirit. They love and fear God, devote themselves to the needs of their neighbor, and desire to do those very things which the law demanded. They would do them even if no law had been given. Their will is nothing else than the Spirit, the living law.[46]

The above themes recur and are emphasized in the three later editions of the *Loci*. But in terms of the two primary texts under closest scrutiny in the present essay, matters quickly become more complicated. If the "Instructions" considered above contributed to Melanchthon's status as a leader of the Wittenberg Reformation, the Leipzig Interim (considered shortly) for many challenged that status – and for some, destroyed it entirely. Yet the most controversial passages in the Leipzig Interim did not lack antecedents in Melanchthon's pedagogical writings.

Substantively, for students of the Lutheran Reformation and the history of its confessional writings, the Leipzig Interim is probably best known as the catalyst for the adiaphoristic controversy, which is addressed in Article X of the Formula of Concord. However, as I will observe below, the Interim also provoked conflict in its discussion of good works, for it seemed to compromise Christian freedom in ways that threatened to undermine Luther's (and Melanchthon's own!) promissory understanding of the gospel. As one examines the last three editions of the *Loci* and the Leipzig Interim in more synoptic fashion, one may find plausible antecedents, possible contextual concessions, and clarifications (in that order).

The last three major editions of the *Loci* are all much longer than the first edition, and they have similar but not identical outlines. In many respects, their theological emphases on soteriological topics are every bit as direct and comprehensive as one finds in the 1521 masterpiece. At the same time, there are subtle shifts too; and, as Melanchthon's more vociferous Gnesio-Lutheran critics would doubtless aver, the devil was literally in those details.[47]

One such vitally important detail pertained to new obedience or good works, and, most specifically, to their "necessity." On this point, Philip Melanchthon remained consistent in substance and formulation throughout his major public and private writings: good works are necessary. Good works are the expected response of new obedience offered by the regenerate and empowered by the Holy Spirit, who effects personal renewal. Their character as new *obedience* reflects the

46 1521 *Loci*, 124.

47 For present purposes, I am only dealing with the topics referred to in this essay's title, and not with Melanchthon's controverted positions on such matters as conversion (and any alleged synergism beginning with the 1535 *Loci*) or the Lord's Supper (and any potential softening of or departure from Luther's doctrine of the true presence of the body and blood of Christ).

fact that these works are prescribed in the Decalogue, when the original Ten Commandments (i.e., as given in Exodus and Deuteronomy) reflect the natural law and, in addition, are reaffirmed in the New Testament. Sanctification is incipient and inchoate (both cognates of Melanchthon's own vocabulary), and it is always more or less tainted by residual sin. Nevertheless, these flawed and fledgling good works please God precisely because the person who does them is himself or herself pleasing to God for the sake of Jesus Christ, whose righteousness is "imputed" to the sinner with the gospel's promise of forgiveness and new life.

The above paragraph is a very brief synthesis of the relevant sections of Melanchthon's *Loci* from 1535, 1543, and 1555.[48] The key phrase on which there is dissonance is the one that would cause such consternation when it appears in the Leipzig Interim, namely, whether this "necessity" of good works also means that they are "necessary to eternal life" (1535)[49] or "necessary to salvation" (1543).[50] I will argue shortly that this phrase – however unfortunate and inherently erroneous – is not intended as a subtle abridgement of Christian liberty or as a compromise of the promise when one reads it in the context of the larger document. I would make the same claim here, with respect to the 1535 and 1543 editions of the *Loci*. Not only do both editions go to great length to accent the work of Christ (complete with exclusive particles), they are steadfast in maintaining that new obedience or good works are not themselves meritorious.[51]

48 Of the four major editions of the *Loci*, the 1535 edition is yet untranslated and is here cited from *Corpus Reformatorum. Opera quae supersunt omnia*, ed., C. G. Bretschneider and H. E. Bindweil (Halle: Schwetschke, 1834–1860). The above paragraph in the text is gleaned from CR 21, columns 414–434; also the 1543 *Loci Communes*, trans., Jacob A. O. Preus (St. Louis: Concordia Publishing House, 1992), 97–116; and the 1555 *Loci Communes*, trans. and ed., Clyde L. Manschreck (New York: Oxford University Press, 1965), 175–186. See CR for subsequent references to the *Loci* or to the Leipzig Interim.

49 1535 *Loci*, CR 21, column 429. The context of the offending reference provides characteristic Melanchthonian qualification: "Therefore eternal life is not given because of the dignity of good works, but freely (*gratis*) for the sake of Christ. And still good works are thus necessary to eternal life (*bona opera ita necessaria sunt ad vitam aeternam*) because they ought to follow reconciliation necessarily."

50 1543 *Loci*, CR 21, column 798 (more literally, "we say in those being saved it is necessary (*oportere in salvandis*) to exist repentance, faith, inchoate obedience, or love"); the text above uses the Preus trans., 115. Martin Chemnitz, whose own *Loci Theologici* (published posthumously, beginning in 1591) are lectures on Melanchthon's 1543 *Loci*, has an extended discussion of this phrase. As one might expect from a major author of the Formula of Concord, he clearly rejects the statement; and he does so in terms of the proper distinction between Law and Gospel. Characteristically, Chemnitz does not criticize Melanchthon by name, nor does he refer explicitly to Melanchthon's troublesome passages. See Chemnitz, *Loci Theologici*, vol. II, trans., Jacob A. O. Preus (St. Louis: Concordia Publishing House, 1989), 588–592.

51 See 1535 *Loci*, CR 21, columns 414–434; also 1543 *Loci*, 101, 106, 109, 111, 113, 115.

Before commencing the reading of the Leipzig Interim, it is worth emphasizing that the phrase "to salvation" does not appear in the section on good works in the 1555 *Loci.* While Melanchthon does not compromise the "necessity" of good works in the slightest, there is no longer any insinuation that they are necessary to eternal life.[52]

On a related matter of historical context, Melanchthon's detractors would challenge the Leipzig Interim not only in terms of its general strategy (i. e., retain the gospel, concede on adiaphora, to which Formula of Concord, Article X, would respond), but also in terms of the substantive formulation of justification itself. Matthias Flacius and his allies could not abide the absence of "*sola fide*" in the Interim,[53] even though the Interim's proponents could rightfully point to its otherwise sound positive formulation. Indeed, that Melanchthon and his colleagues intended no different doctrine of justification is evident from the elaboration of that doctrine in the section "How the Human Creature Becomes Righteous before God," considered at greater length below.

Equally important contextually, all four editions of the *Loci* are clear as to the role of faith in their treatment of justification. This is no surprise for the 1521 or even the 1535 edition (in the wake of its pervasive role in Apology IV in 1531). It is just as clear in the 1543 edition:

> The exclusive particle [faith *alone*] does not exclude our virtues from being present, but it does exclude them as being the cause of our reconciliation, and this exclusionary idea does mean that the merit of Christ alone is the cause of our reconciliation.[54]

Perhaps most strikingly, coming after the omission of *sola fide* in the Leipzig Interim, the phrase is explicit and prominent again in the 1555 *Loci:* "Thus the converted man, is justified, for the sake of the Lord Christ, by faith alone, *gratis, sola fide*, not on account of his new virtues."[55]

52 See 1555 *Loci*, 179, 182. Robert Kolb has also helpfully identified three letters of Melanchthon in which he himself disavows the phrase: they are epistle #5718, from 1555, CR 8, columns 411–412; epistle #6425, from 1557, CR 9, columns 405–408; and epistle #6471, from 1558, CR 9, columns 474–475.

53 This was a concession to the Interim's intended political role over against the newly victorious empire, whose representatives would never have considered a document with a *sola fide* clause. See the discussion in Olson, *Matthias Flacius and the Survival of Luther's Reform*, 124–127.

54 1543 *Loci*, 109, responding to the precise Roman objection that "it is impossible to say that a person is righteous by faith alone."

55 1555 *Loci*, 179; see also 182. Both references (i. e., from the 1543 and the 1555 *Loci*) come in the section on good works. This follows the approach of the Augsburg Confession itself, where the first place "faith alone" appears is in Article 6, "New Obedience."

4. The Leipzig Interim

If the "Instructions" were drafted for pastoral and catechetical reasons and the *Loci communes theologici* for pedagogical reasons, the Leipzig Interim was an attempt at damage control. Literally everything had changed since 1528, when Melanchthon had prepared the "Instructions." Twenty years later, it looked very much like the Lutheran movement would not reach mature adulthood; and Melanchthon and his Wittenberg colleagues were trying to negotiate the best possible terms for their survival. Facing persecution and the real possibility of destruction, no one could have imagined that only seven years later their movement would be legalized in the Peace of Augsburg of 1555.[56]

In this context of extreme vulnerability, the Leipzig Interim may be said to address the following hypothetical questions: "What is absolutely essential to our confession of faith and therefore must be retained at all costs, and what may be recast or reinterpreted in a way that would be more amenable (or at least less antagonistic) to our imperial and papal adversaries? Are there formulae that are themselves mutually acceptable but that each side can still interpret (or re-interpret) as it will?" That these kinds of questions were operative may be inferred not only from the contents of the Leipzig Interim itself, but also from its ingratiating opening paragraph:

> Our concern (*Bedenken*) is based upon our desire to be obedient to the Roman Imperial Majesty and to conduct ourselves in such a way that his Majesty realizes that our interest revolves only around tranquility, peace, and unity. This is our counsel, made in good faith; it is what we ourselves want to serve and promote wherever possible. For in contrast to what some say and write about us – without any basis – our concern and our

56 One of the clearest presentations in English of the complex historical background of the Leipzig Interim is offered by Robert Kolb in "Historical Background of the Formula of Concord," in *A Contemporary Look at the Formula of Concord*, ed., Wilbert Rosin and Robert D. Preus (St. Louis: Concordia Publishing House, 1978), 20–23. Here Kolb identifies Prince Georg of Anhalt and Johann Pfeffinger along with Melanchthon as participants in the work leading to the Leipzig Interim. A more recent excellent treatment of this period is offered by Irene Dingel in "The Culture of Conflict in the Controversies Leading to the Formula of Concord (1548–1580)," in *Lutheran Ecclesiastical Culture, 1550-1675*, ed., Robert Kolb (Leiden and Boston: Brill, 2008), 15–64, esp. 21–22. In addition, see Günther Wartenberg, "Interims," in *The Oxford Encyclopedia of the Reformation*, vol. 2, ed., Hans J. Hillerbrand (New York and Oxford: Oxford University Press, 1996), 319–321. Much more detail is offered by Olson, though from the perspective of the Leipzig Interim's most celebrated opponent, in *Matthias Flacius and the Survival of Luther's Reform*, 124–127. Finally, see also the historical introduction to the Leipzig Interim, in *Sources and Contexts of the Book of Concord*, ed., Robert Kolb and James A. Nestingen (Minneapolis: Fortress Press, 2001), 183–184. This introduction and the translation itself were prepared by Robert Kolb, and it is Kolb's translation that is used in this essay (cited below as "LI"). Kolb notes that his translation is taken from CR 7, columns 258–264, "with portions printed in the preceding documents," CR 7, columns 51–64 and columns 217, 219–220.

> intention are always directed not toward causing schism and complications, but rather toward peace and unity. We testify to that in the very presence of God, to whom all human hearts are known. Our actions will demonstrate that.[57]

The foregoing paragraph is followed by the famous section on adiaphora (*Mitteldingen*), which is identified as "our first consideration."[58] Harkening back to the ancient church, these adiaphora are defined as "those things that are neither commanded nor forbidden by God."[59] The Leipzig Interim adds that these adiaphora "may still" (*halten mag*) be understood as adiaphora without violating or compromising Holy Scripture.[60] While this initial temporal indicator is likely an innocent reference to the sixteenth-century church, "still" becomes more problematic in the next sentence: "Even when they [the adiaphora] are *still* in use by the other party, they may continue to be observed."[61] The Interim then takes this point one step further, and implicitly links these conclusions back with the earlier unobjectionable definition: "No one should try to make them a burden (*Beschwerung*) or regard them as such or as something to be avoided, since they may be observed without harming good consciences."[62] As the debate played itself out in the ensuing years, the very real question was whether that second conclusion could be sustained in the new context of persecution.

Proportionately, the overwhelming majority of the Leipzig Interim is devoted to the two topics of justification and good works. The former has the subtitle "How the Human Creature Becomes Righteous before God," and here the promise is unfolded in several places in language reminiscent of Apology IV: "God's Son has been appointed as mediator and Savior by the wondrous, unfathomable counsel of God and [...] for his sake forgiveness of sins, the Holy Spirit, righteousness, and eternal life are given in all certainty (*gewisslich*)."[63] This same note of the certainty of God's intention is picked up again two paragraphs later:

> It is [God's] eternal, unchangeable will, confirmed by his own oath and by the blood of his Son and his resurrection and many miracles, that he in all certainty wants to forgive sins, wants to give his Holy Spirit, and to accept us, renew us, and make us heirs of eternal salvation, for the sake of his Son, not because of our merit or worthiness.[64]

57 LI, 184; CR 7, column 259.
58 LI, 184; CR 7, column 259.
59 LI, 184.
60 LI, 184; CR 7, column 259.
61 LI, 184, emphasis added.
62 LI, 184; CR 7, column 259.
63 LI, 185; CR 7, column 51.
64 LI, 185.

The Leipzig Interim devotes considerable attention to how one receives "this great grace and these great benefits (*hohe grosse Gnade und Wohlthaten*)."[65] These comments are predicated on the Leipzig Interim's observation, made immediately before the treatment of justification, that there was "no dispute" regarding the state and nature of human beings before and after the fall.[66] In this context, the Leipzig Interim does move beyond the language of the Augsburg Confession and Apology in Article XVIII (on the freedom of the will). Specifically, the Leipzig Interim asserts that God draws (*zeucht*) human beings in such a fashion that "their will cooperates."[67] The Leipzig Interim posits the medieval concept of "prevenient grace" (*vorgehende Gnade*), which "moves" the will and heart to fear the wrath of God and to despise sin, since personal security (*sicherheit*) and persistent sinning against conscience preclude conversion (*Bekehrung*) and forgiveness.[68]

The "Word and the Holy Spirit" shatter such human complacency (cf. John 16:8), but only for the greater purpose of convincing the sinner that the promise of God's forgiveness "is conveyed to me and not only to others."[69] From this point on, the Leipzig Interim talks about faith with rhetoric strikingly similar to that of Apology IV.

> True faith accepts (*annimmt*) the promise and its gracious comfort, as Paul clearly testifies, Romans 4[:13]; there he speaks of this faith which accepts the promise, which is not only the knowledge that the devils or human beings who live with a bad conscience have, but this faith believes, together with the other articles of faith, in the forgiveness of sins. It accepts the promise and has in the heart a true trust in God's Son, who bestows trust and the ability to call on God and other virtues.[70]

Nor is there any further reference to a cooperating will, for God or the Holy Spirit is now usually the subject of the pertinent sentences: "[T]he Holy Spirit is given into our hearts [...] so that we may grasp (*fassen*) the divine promise with faith and be comforted and set upright [cf. Gal 3:2, 14]."[71] The Interim then offers the following summary, attributing literally every saving blessing to the work of the triune God.

65 LI, 185; CR 7, column 51.

66 LI, 184.

67 LI, 185; CR 7, column 51.

68 LI, 185; CR 7, column 51.

69 LI, 186. See also, LI, 187: "[I]t is God's serious intention and command in true conversion that we accept his promise and believe that not because of our worthiness but because of the reconciler and mediator God is gracious, wants to forgive us our sin, and to accept us and come to our aid, etc."

70 LI, 186; CR 7, column 54.

71 LI, 186; CR 7, column 53.

> In the heart, the Holy Spirit produces (*wirket*) a steadfast faith, comfort, and life, and arouses (*zundet an*) all necessary virtues, firm faith, the invocation of God, fear of God, love, good intentions, hope, and other virtues. And these are they who have received the forgiveness of sins, and in whom the Holy Spirit has begun faith and trust in God's Son, love, and hope, as heirs of eternal salvation for the sake of the Savior, as Paul says in Romans 6[:23]: 'Eternal life is God's gift through Jesus Christ our Lord.'[72]

Nothing about personal cooperation, in any sense, should lead one to think that the Leipzig Interim is sanguine about the human condition. This observation obtains even for the regenerate. The propensity to "doubt, tremble, and flee from God" is congenital, a by-product of original sin.[73] The only antidote to such manifestations of weakness is the promise itself: "Against [these symptoms], God has given his promise to comfort us and to strengthen us that we may overcome doubt and find refuge in him."[74] Citing Paul in 1 Cor 4:4 ("I am not aware of anything against myself, but I am not thereby acquitted; it is the Lord who judges me") and St. Augustine, the Leipzig Interim asserts what amounts to a confession that the Christian person is *simul iustus et peccator:*

> With these words [Paul] teaches [...] that we may conclude both points: the conscience should stand upright, but there is still much weakness in us, and therefore we should know that we are at the same time righteous, that is, God-pleasing (*Gott gefallig*), for the sake of the Son, and it is correct, as Augustine says, 'The certainty of faith (*totius certitudo fiduciae*) ought to rest in the precious blood of Christ.'[75]

At this point the Leipzig Interim rehearses another theme that is prominent in Apology IV, over against late medieval soteriology (at least in popular perversions thereof). God in Christ does not win and provide an initial merit, to be completed or complemented by human performance. New obedience is precisely that, and nothing more; it is not in any sense meritorious before God. Instead, Christ, and Christ alone, remains the sole mediator between God and sinners. For the Leipzig Interim, new but imperfect obedience, recurrent sin, and genuine repentance were all spiritual realities, all at work and churning within the same person. This conflict would be self-destructive apart from the abiding work of the one who is and speaks the decisive Word of God, Jesus Christ.

> Therefore, although new obedience has been begun, we should not think that the person who has forgiveness of sins, and is therefore pure, has no need for forgiveness of sins and a mediator. The Son of God is and remains at every moment our mediator and stands in the divine secret council and prays for us, that the severe wrath of God against our sin may not be poured out upon us. It is not enough to say that God does not want to credit

72 LI, 186; CR 7, column 53.
73 LI, 187.
74 LI, 187.
75 LI, 187; CR 7, column 56.

> to our account the remaining weakness, that he acts (*dichtet*) as if the person were without sin; this creates a false trust in our own righteousness. Instead, both must be in us, a good conscience and initial obedience, and with them this humility and faith, that we confess that we still have sin and that in us there is serious regret and displeasure over our sin. We confess as well that we have merited punishment, and that in it we submit to God, as Daniel says, 'You, O Lord, are righteous; we are ashamed' [9:7]. Along with that there must exist the necessary comfort, that God most certainly wants to accept this person and be gracious for the sake of his Son.[76]

The Interim pulls these emphases together in one trenchant sentence: "This trust, that looks to the mediator in the face of the divine judgment, must at all times overshadow (*überschatten*) the other virtues in this life of weakness."[77]

The Leipzig Interim's next major section is "On Good Works." Next to the principle regarding adiaphora with which it began, these are its most controversial paragraphs, for they assert again what would become Georg Major's notorious slogan, "Good works are necessary to salvation."[78] The Interim prepared the way for this section near the end of its article on justification, for there it noted that the faith that clings to the promise of Christ also produces "comfort, love, and the ability to call on God" – and it immediately adds that such faith is "not to be found without love."[79] The Interim is quick to emphasize that such incipient righteousness does not confer any worthy standing before God, and in stark language it ties these new positive impulses to the work of Christ: "God wants to take pleasure in this weak, initial obedience in this miserable, vulnerable, impure nature in believers for the sake of his Son."[80]

The Leipzig Interim reflects Melanchthon's long-standing sensitivity to the charge that Lutheran soteriology, most specifically its *sola fide* apprehension of Christ's promise, would inexorably prove destructive of Christian living. Therefore, at the outset of the section on good works, the Leipzig Interim offers this "reliable rule" (*gewisse Regel*): "[W]e declare that those works are good and necessary which God has commanded, according to the Ten Commandments and the explanation of these commandments, which is sufficiently expressed in

76 LI, 188; CR 7, column 57. See also LI, 189: "From all of this it is clear that it is true that in us new obedience must be initiated, and that nonetheless faith and trust in God's Son must continually remain and must hang on to this comfort, that God is gracious to us for the sake of his Son."

77 LI, 188; CR 7, column 58.

78 LI, 190. See also the citations offered in notes 49 and 50 above. For a discussion of Major and the controversy that would bear his name, see Robert Kolb, "Georg Major as Controversialist: Polemics in the Late Reformation," *Church History* 45, no. 4 (December 1976): 455–468. Kolb includes a briefer summary in "Historical Background of the Formula of Concord," 26–29.

79 LI, 189.

80 LI, 189; see also, especially, LI, 190: "God takes pleasure [...] in the virtues and good works of the reconciled because they believe that God accepts a person for Christ's sake and wants to take pleasure in this imperfect obedience."

the writings of the apostles."[81] Since it is a much shorter document than the "Instructions" and is written for an altogether different purpose, the Leipzig Interim does not expound on the Ten Commandments, nor is there any discussion of the functions of the law. While it is a minor point, the "Instructions" did connect at least portions of the Decalogue to the natural law; conversely, the Leipzig Interim observes that the Ten Commandments and their explanation are "sufficiently expressed in the writings of the apostles."[82]

The Leipzig Interim is emphatic that saving faith in Christ could not coexist with persistent sins against conscience. Such sins challenge the authenticity of one's conversion[83] and invite God's wrath, as well as God's eternal and temporal punishment.[84] Moreover, the Leipzig Interim's section on good works is more direct and forceful than it was in its own earlier observation that faith is to be accompanied by love.[85] Now the Leipzig Interim argues not only that good works are necessary because they are commanded by God, but also that those who lack such good works are "discarding God's grace and the Holy Spirit."[86] In fact, the absence of good works indicates that "there is no reception of divine grace."[87] Such sins of omission "merit eternal damnation."[88] The Interim's biblical references tie the presence of good works to the persistence of saving faith: "In these verses [Isa 38: 13, 17; 2 Cor 5:3; Rev 2:10] the two parts are comprehended: first, that in this life the beginning of eternal salvation must take place, and second, that we must not fall away before our end."[89]

The Leipzig Interim's most fateful paragraph follows. The paragraph begins by tying "rebirth and eternal life" to "a new light, fear of God, love, joy in God, and other virtues" on the basis of John 17:3. Then comes the sentence that would provoke such strife in the ensuing years: "Just as this true knowledge must enlighten us, so it is certainly true that these virtues, faith, love, hope, and others, must be in us *and are necessary for salvation* (*und zur Seligkeit seyn*)."[90] It is

81 LI, 189; CR 7, column 60.
82 LI, 189.
83 LI, 189.
84 LI, 190.
85 See above, and LI, 189.
86 LI, 190.
87 LI, 190.
88 LI, 190.
89 LI, 190.
90 LI, 190, emphasis added; CR 7, column 61. Interestingly, in the paragraph immediately before his own rejection of this phrase, Martin Chemnitz discusses its context in the period of the Augsburg and Leipzig Interims: "Many people were pretending that they were supporting this expression so that Epicureanism might not be introduced into the church while at the same time they believed that they were holding to the correct faith in Christ. But insidiously another thing was creeping in, namely that little by little there was too much omission of the word *sola*

followed immediately by qualification and further contextualization, but the damage was done, especially when the last portion of that sentence took on the status of a slogan in the clumsy hands of Georg Major.

This qualification and contextualization, however, is important for understanding the theology of the Leipzig Interim – and of the Wittenberg theologians more generally – in the aftermath of Luther's death, the disastrous Smalkaldic War, and the persecution looming under the new imperial policy. For on the heels of this sentence – better, this phrase or clause – the Leipzig Interim adds that those who fear God seek and experience their comfort "in God,"[91] not in their works. Certainly the "virtues and good works" do please God and merit spiritual, temporal, and even eternal rewards, but they do so "on the basis of (*vermöge*) the divine promise."[92]

If that affirmation is not sufficient, the Leipzig Interim follows it up with two expressions of anti-Roman polemics. First, the monks err to the extent that they maintain that salvation is merited through the worthiness of their works, much less those works that bishops and monks have devised as a "special service of God."[93] Second, the Roman penitential system (though not mentioned by name) is likewise assailed, insofar as it holds that "we can convey our merit to others."[94] These remarks are followed immediately by one of the clearest statements of gospel in the entire document: "[F]aith recognizes our own weakness and takes refuge in God's Son and receives this eternal comfort and his merit and treasure according to his gracious and immeasurably rich promise."[95] Moreover, it is "despair," not the absence of works or even sins against conscience, that is "blasphemy and the greatest sin" precisely because it refuses to believe God's promise of grace, a promise God confirms "with an oath."[96]

Does the Leipzig Interim condition and thereby attenuate God's promise? I would argue that on this particular issue (i. e., putting aside for now the whole adiaphoristic debate), it does not; and, it certainly does not intend to do so. To be sure, Rome's accusations about the alleged disparagement of works stung; and for Melanchthon and his colleagues in 1548 theological and political coexistence with Rome were preferable to annihilation. But in terms of the Leipzig Interim, an editorial deletion of two infelicitous words would have rendered its defense

when they said that 'we are justified by faith' and too little caution about merit." See Chemnitz, *Loci Theologici*, II, 589.

91 LI, 190.

92 LI, 190; CR 7, column 61.

93 LI, 191, again citing Matt 15:9, "in vain do they worship me, teaching as doctrines the precepts of men."

94 LI, 190.

95 LI, 190.

96 LI, 191.

(against this particular charge at least) unnecessary – as Article IV of the Formula of Concord would show.

5. Conclusions

Are the themes of promise and liberty consistently defined and discussed over these two key documents of the Wittenberg Reformation? If their treatment is not totally consistent, is it compatible? If the discussions are divergent in some ways, are they theologically incompatible? On the basis of the foregoing examination of the "Instructions" and the Leipzig Interim, I offer the following tentative and brief conclusions:

(1) On the matter of the promise, the two sources state the promise clearly and are theologically consistent, though they express this promise in different ways. The "Instructions" do not devote as much space to the matter as such, and when Melanchthon states the promise he tends to use language of atonement and satisfaction. The Leipzig Interim explicitly uses the language of justification, and summarizes several of the most important themes of Ap IV.

(2) On the matter of liberty, the two documents are compatible; but their very different historical contexts give rise to two equally different approaches to the topic. Both seek to affirm Christian freedom and reject abuses thereof. The "Instructions" define liberty more explicitly, expound the law evangelically, and assert the necessity of good works. The Leipzig Interim works harder to define the boundaries of liberty rather than the concept itself (cf. the whole discussion of adiaphora), it asserts the Law only in passing, and it is much more intentional about the relationship of justification to good works. Moreover, while I have sought (on the basis of its context amid potential persecution and its own internal qualifications) to defend at least the intent of the Leipzig Interim, its language – and certainly the use to which that language was later put – undeniably engendered sufficient discord to call for subsequent theological clarification and even correction.

Daniel L. Mattson

What Did Luther Know about Islam, and Why Did He Want to Know It?

I am honored to contribute this article to the Kolb festschrift since we have been friends for about 55 of his 76 years. I dare say that I was present at the beginning of his enormous literary output when a small group of friends at Concordia College, St. Paul, as it was then known, began to publish *Keeping in Contact*, to make their first attempts to put their "theological" ideas in writing, to edit one another's work, and to distribute their mimeographed copies (and to learn that there could be consequences).

I have chosen to use the title in this form because it is a characteristic of Kolb's teaching style. His many students will frequently raise the question in the form, "As Dr. Kolb would say, 'Why do you want to know?'" I first heard him use this technique on the first of what would become his many trips as mission teacher, a trip to address Lutheran missionaries in Nigeria in 1980. The relevance of the question was immediately recognized, for in cross-cultural conversations, the *why* questions of the hearer determine to a large extent *what* can be offered and what the outcome of the conversation is likely to be.

That Islam raises important questions in America at the present time is a truism. There are many issues, but perhaps the basic issue determining the shape of American public opinion is the question of whether Islam is a disguised political movement dedicated to harming Christians and destroying their institutions, or is Islam a universal faith, an alternative to Christianity, but nevertheless a universal faith pursuing its own doctrines, rituals, and cultural agenda as Christians have done for nearly twenty centuries. The twenty-first century struggles with these issues largely in terms of social-political issues; the sixteenth century saw these issues largely in terms of social-religious issues. Perhaps by looking at the past, it is possible to gain additional insight into the present.

The intention of this article is to call attention to an aspect of Luther's life and thought that needs further consideration. To answer the second question: why did Luther want to know about Islam? I want to test the idea that in addition to his roles as theologian, teacher, pastor, and religious movement leader – and to a large extent, because of those roles – Luther was one of the leading public intellectuals of the early sixteenth century. In that role, he perceived that he had an obligation to church and state in the midst of the Ottoman crisis to support the war effort by providing a theological basis for opposition to the *Other*, the outside forces of Islam that Europeans believed were intent on destroying a united Christian Europe.

How much did he know? He knew something about Islam, but what he knew was based on books about Islam written decades, if not centuries before. I am not aware that Luther ever claimed to have learned anything from a living Moslem or Islamic teacher. Nevertheless, to accomplish this task, he used the best of the resources available to him, namely, Christian writers from the Middle Ages, who had lived among Islamic people and had some familiarity with Islamic texts, as well as his own research and conclusions about Islam and about the biblical message and the truth of the Christian faith.

For the purposes of this study, I will look in chronological order at the four Luther documents available in English translation in the American Edition of Luther's Works. The fifth document Luther produced in this period, *Muster Sermon against the Turk* will appear in the forthcoming volume 56 of Luther's Works. Each makes a contribution to understanding Luther's assessment of the "Turkish threat." These documents are "On war against the Turk,"[1] "Preface to [George of Hungary,] Book on the Ceremonies and Customs of the Turks Published Seventy Years Ago,"[2] "Appeal for prayer against the Turks,"[3] and "Preface and afterword" to Brother Richard, OP [Riccoldo da Monte di Croce] *Refutation of the Koran*,[4] and his "Preface to the Koran by Martin Luther, Doctor of Theology and Preacher of the Church at Wittenberg [1543]."[5] Reference will be made to other Luther documents as needed.

However, first a note about the nature of the Turkish threat to the German lands of the Holy Roman Empire. The Luther documents are all written within a narrow context of sixteenth-century concerns and fears. While these are certainly understandable, to make an assessment of Luther's contribution, it is helpful to place these documents in a larger context.

On March 19, 1452, Frederick III, great-grandfather of Charles V, became the first Habsburg crowned as emperor of the Holy Roman Empire. He was crowned in Rome (the last Holy Roman Emperor to be crowned there) by Pope Nicholas V.

1 M. Luther, "On War against the Turk [1529]," LW 46: 155–205.

2 M. Luther, "Preface to [George of Hungary,] Book on the Ceremonies and Customs of the Turks, Published Seventy Years Ago [1530]," LW 59: 258–262.

3 M. Luther, "Appeal for Prayer against the Turks [1541]," LW 43: 219–241.

4 M. Luther, "Preface and Afterword to Brother Richard, O.P.[Riccoldo da Monte di Croce]. *Refutation of the Koran* [ca. 1301] [1542]," LW 60: 251–266.

5 M. Luther, "Preface to the Koran by Martin Luther, Doctor of Theology and Preacher of the Church at Wittenberg [1543]," LW 60: 289–294.

As further evidence of the rapidly changing times, it should be noted that Charles V was the last Holy Roman Emperor to be crowned by a pope. By the time of Charles V, the Habsburg territories included areas of eastern, southern, and western Europe. Spanish territories were perhaps most important to him, although his pursuit of the title Holy Roman Emperor, illustrated his continuing commitment to reclaiming the glories of the past, a united Europe as a new Roman Empire.

Charles V was by no means an unchallenged ruler, and his ability to make and enforce decisions was frequently limited by lack of resources, on the one hand, and the need to negotiate with and involve contentious allies. The Habsburg rulers did not have at their disposal sufficient resources to deal with both the outside threat posed by the Ottomans and the Lutheran threat on the inside.[6] This was the situation from the beginning of the Luther matter as illustrated when the Diet of Worms, the same diet that heard and rejected Luther, also heard and rejected an appeal of representatives from Hungary who were trying to prepare for an expected Ottoman attack. The diet decided that no help would be given to Hungary at the moment, but the request could be considered again if the situation became critical.[7] This was the first of many negotiations where the Habsburgs learned that the Luther/Lutheran situation and the Ottoman threat were inextricably joined.[8]

On the Ottoman side, Mehmed II, the great-grandfather of Suleiman the Magnificent, conquered Constantinople, long the capital of the Eastern Roman Empire, on May 29, 1453. After Mehmed's conquest of the city, he took as one of his titles, Caesar of Rome, a title that remained part of Ottoman titles into the twentieth century.[9]

With these developments involving two very different royal families, who, nevertheless, both traced their ancestry back to Noah[10] and both regarded themselves as defenders/restorers of the Roman empire, the scene was set for the century of conflict. The differences between the competing dynasties could be

6 A. Clot, *Suleiman the Magnificent* (New York: New Amsterdam, 1992), 127.

7 S.A. Fischer-Galati, *Ottoman Imperialism and German Protestantism, 1521–1555.* Harvard Historical Monographs, XLIII (New York: Octagon Books, 1972), 19.

8 Fischer-Galati, *Ottoman Imperialism and German Protestantism*, 117: "Almost all major concessions wrested from the Habsburgs since 1526 were connected with Ottoman activities in Eastern and Western Europe, and the all-important Lutheran campaign for legal recognition in Germany exploited the insoluble Habsburg-Ottoman conflict over Hungary. The Recess of Speyer of 1526, the Religious Peace of Nuremberg, the Compact of Cadan, the Frankfurt Anstand, the Declaration of Regensburg, the Recess of Speyer of 1542, the Treaty of Passau, and the Religious Peace of Augsburg – all milestones in the Protestant struggle for recognition and the course of the German Reformation – were deeply influenced by the ebb and flow of Ottoman aggression."

9 A. Wheatcroft, *The Enemy at the Gate* (New York: Basic books, 2009), 7–8.

10 Wheatcroft, *The Enemy*, 7–8.

summarized as Christian Habsburg vs Ottoman Turk; but, as usual, this is inaccurate since a whole host of social, political, economic, cultural, etc. issues were involved.[11]

It is beyond the scope of this article to discuss the religious policies of the Ottomans or the Habsburgs, particularly with reference to tolerance for other religions. New issues are regularly added to the discussion as scholars reread the texts from an Ottoman perspective and raise new questions that add new perspectives to the discussion.[12]

For the purposes of this study, the focus of attention is Suleiman the Magnificent, the sultan whose attacks on Europe provoked Luther's response. He believed himself to hold legitimately the title of Sultan of the Romans and regarded himself as a successor to Alexander the Great in the creation of a universal empire.[13] The Sultan and his court delighted in comparisons of himself with Charles V and the pope.[14] The crown and the scepter, well-known symbols of power and authority in the West but not used in the East, became a part of Suleiman's regalia, for example,[15] not a mere political gesture, but a deliberate goal of the Sultan's foreign policy. Recognition as the successor of the Roman emperors was as important to him as it was to Charles V.

Suleiman recognized, however, that this goal could not be reached if he were required to face a united Europe, and he constantly searched for political solutions that are beyond the scope of this article. The critical difference was that Luther and his followers had destroyed the unity of Roman Catholic Europe and

11 Clot makes this observation about the crusades, but it applies equally to the entire European situation, "there were no more Crusades because the European sovereigns, now that great monarchies had been formed, were primarily concerned with their own political and, more and more, economic interests. There was much talk of religion, but it played only a minor role." Clot, *Suleiman the Magnificent*, 137.

12 Frederique Guerin, "Re-orienting the Reformation? Prolegommena to a History of the Reformation's Connection with the Islamic World," in *The Role of the Arab-Islamic World in the Rise of the West: Implications for Contemporary Trans-cultural Relations*, ed., N.R.F. Al-Rodhan (Houndmills, Basingstoke, Hampshire, New York, NY: Palgrave Macmillan, 2012), 38–60.

13 G. Agoston, "Information, Ideology, and Limits of Imperial Policy: Ottoman Grand Strategy in the Context of Ottoman-Habsburg Rivalry," in *The Early Modern Ottomans: Remapping the Empire*, ed., V.H. Aksan and D. Goffman (Cambridge, UK, New York: Cambridge University Press, 2007), 75–103 (99).

14 D. Goffman, *The Ottoman Empire and Early Modern Europe*. New Approaches to European History, 24 (Cambridge: Cambridge Univ. Press, 2002), 106–107.

15 Goffman, *The Ottoman Empire*, 107–108. Goffman notes as well that since woodcuts illustrating the coronation of Charles V in 1529 were well-known, it is surely a deliberate act that the helmet worn by Suleiman in the invasion of the Balkans in 1530, designed and executed in Venice, combined the designs of the Holy Roman Emperor's crown and the papal crown. Political claims were being made.

as a result raised new possibilities for Ottoman success.[16] A European response to virtually any Ottoman incursion would now have to be negotiated, and the negotiators would have to consider not only the Turkish threat but also the possibility of attack from other European forces: Catholic vs Lutheran and vice versa.[17]

The Ottoman desire to keep Europe divided is reflected in an "intelligence report" that specifically mentions Luther.[18] The report is garbled and impossible to connect with specific events, perhaps not surprisingly since it is a report about the information a Turkish cloth merchant had brought back from his travels in Europe. The report probably dates to July or August, 1530, not long after Suleiman's attack on Hungary and Vienna. The report is of special interest in that the author of the report knew the context into which he was sending his report – its viewpoints and expectations that his account needed to support – as well as the new information about events in Europe. The key section reports,

> A lord from the German borders named Fra Martin Luther created a religion of his own, opposing cursed Spain's [Charles V] false rite. About two months ago, he gathered about thirty thousand soldiers, and met cursed Spain at a place called San Borgo by the German borders at the time of [Muslim] afternoon prayer. They battled until evening. Cursed Spain was routed at evening time.[19]

Luther is correctly described as a German, incorrectly as a lord (Turkish, *bey*). He is identified as Brother Martin Luther, and his key role in articulating the Lutheran faith is described in terms of creating "a religion of his own," an accusation that Luther repeatedly rejected. The important function of this new religion from an Ottoman point of view was that it opposed the Roman Catholic position advocated by the non-Islamic ruler of Spain – not the Holy Roman Empire – Charles V (who is never referred to by name in this document but always as the "cursed Spain"). The document then goes on to describe a force of

16 Dimmock summarizes the importance of this issue to even the humanist scholars of the time: "As the religious and political environment of the 1520s became increasingly fractious following Leo X's bull *Exsurge Domine* against Luther in 1520, the predominantly orthodox [Roman Catholic] humanist community strove to reanimate centuries-old conceptions of the 'common faith' of 'Christendome' in order to highlight the dangers with which this unity was threatened." M. Dimmock, "'*Machomet dyd before as Luther doth nowe*': Islam, the Ottomans, and the English Reformation," *Reformation* 9 (2004): 99–130 (99–100).

17 Iyigun argues that the Ottoman threat actually worked to the advantage of Catholic Europe. Statistically speaking, he notes that fewer intra-European conflicts took place; those conflicts that did occur lasted for shorter periods and resulted in fewer casualties. The Europeans recognized the Ottomans as a superpower (my terminology), calculated the risk, and drew the appropriate conclusions. M. Iyigun, "Luther and Suleyman," *The Quarterly Journal of Economics* 123, no.4 (2008): 1465–1494.

18 C. Isom-Verhaaren, "An Ottoman Report about Martin Luther and the Emperor: New Evidence of the Ottoman Interest in the Protestant Challenge to the Power of Charles V," *Turcica* 28 (1996): 299–317.

19 Isom-Verhaaren, "An Ottoman Report," 305.

30,000 soldiers raised by Martin Luther that fought and won a battle against Charles V. Luther was never a political leader, never raised an army nor fought a battle, but there were princes and cities committed to Luther's views who did. Even though times and places cannot be specifically identified, the report of intra-European conflict based on different religious views is essentially correct.

1. Luther on Islam

From the beginning of the Reformation, Luther had a position on the role of the Turks in God's plans for Christian Europe. There is no specific mention of the Turks in the *Ninety-five Theses*, but already in his *Explanations of the Ninety-five Theses*[20] in 1518, Luther states in his commentary on Thesis 5 that the power of the Keys cannot be used to avert the penalty that God has decided for the unrepentant.[21] In contrast, Luther accuses the Roman Catholic side of holding a position that, based on assessment of military power, would lead to war against the Turk without any recognition of the need for repentance in Europe, a position that God would not bless with success.

> Many, however, even the "big wheels" in the church, now dream of nothing else than war against the Turk. They want to fight, not against iniquities, but against the lash of iniquity and thus they would oppose God who says that through that lash he himself punishes us for our iniquities because we do not punish ourselves for them.[22]

This statement was made in the context of the Ottoman defeat of the Mamluk kingdom in 1516–1517, bringing the Arabian Peninsula and Syria (bringing all five Islamic holy places), and Egypt under Ottoman control. This created an empire that was about the size of the empire of Alexander the Great. The threat to Europe was clearly growing.

Pope Leo X recognized the provocative nature of Luther's statement, and in the papal bull, *Exsurge Domine*, he included in his list of 41 errors requiring Luther's excommunication, "34. To go to war against the Turks is to resist God who punishes our iniquities through them."[23] With this accusation, Luther's emphasis that God required the repentance of his people, not just military might, in dealing with the Turk had been stripped of its meaning for Christian faith and

20 M. Luther, "Explanations of the Ninety-five Theses or Explanations of the Disputation Concerning the Value of Indulgences [1518]," LW 31: 81–252.
21 Luther, "Explanations of the Theses," 91–92.
22 Luther, "Explanations of the Theses," 92.
23 Leo X, "Exsurge Domine: Bull of Leo X Issued June 15, 1520," accessed at www.papalencyclicals.net/Leo10/l10exdom.htm.

changed into a general statement that God was opposed to military resistance to the Turkish threat.

Luther recognized the danger that Pope Leo X was trying to identify him in the public mind as an ally of the Turk.[24] In the following year, in his *Defense and Explanation of All the Articles*[25] Luther affirmed his position that there could be no success in war against the Turk without repentance on the part of God's people. The real problem as Luther saw it was the pope.

> It is a scandal how the pope has all this time led us by the nose with this war against the Turks. He has used it to make off with our money, destroy many Christians, and cause much misery. When will we learn that the pope is the devil's most dangerous tool?[26]

Nevertheless, in spite of the pope's wrong-headed and unfaithful leadership, Christians were not excused from warfare against the Turk.

> But this article does not mean that we are not to fight against the Turk, as that holy manufacturer of heresies, the pope, charges. It means, rather, that we should first mend our ways and cause God to be gracious to us. We should not plunge into war, relying on the pope's indulgence, with which he has deceived Christians in the past and is deceiving them still. The historical books of the Old Testament, especially Josh. 7[:1–26] and Judg. 18 [20:12–48], and many other passages, show clearly what it means to fight against an angry God and against an enemy whom we have deserved.[27]

These opening exchanges reflect what Luther knew about Islam and why he wanted to know it. From the beginning his view was that the Ottoman threat was the tool that God planned to use to punish his people. Even though this was the case, Luther wanted to know about Islam in order to understand the full extent of the Islamic threat in his efforts to prepare the German people.

The Ottoman invasion of Hungarian lands and their decisive victory in 1526 at Mohacs, and the brief capture of Buda made it clear that the Islamic threat to Europe was real, and it was important that Christian Europe produce a united front. In many ways, the Hungarian experience illustrated all that was wrong with Europe in its conflict with the Ottomans. The political leadership was in no way united on who should rule or what should be done. The ruling class, the Hungarian nobles, were virulently anti-Lutheran[28] even as they were totally dedicated

24 That this was an effective tactic is shown by Luther's comments at the end of *Whether soldiers, too, can be saved [1526]*, illustrating that five years later some people still felt that he had Turkish sympathies. M. Luther, "Whether soldiers, too, can be saved [1526]," LW 46: 93–137 (136–137).

25 M. Luther, "Defense and Explanation of All the Articles [1521]," LW 32: 7–99.

26 Luther, "Defense and Explanation All Articles," 89.

27 Luther, "Defense and Explanation All Articles," 90.

28 Fischer-Galati quotes an anti-Protestant enactment of the Hungarian diet from the early 1520s providing that Lutherans should be "routed out of the country and, wheresoever they be found, they shall be seized without restriction not only by the clergy but also by laymen,

to using the system to advance their own interests. There were deep class divisions as well as a revolt by the peasantry that had been violently suppressed in 1514. Divisions on every side for every reason made the defeat at Mohacs virtually inevitable.

It is not important for the purposes of this paper to further detail the continuing conflicts in Hungary between the Habsburgs and the Ottomans and other more local powers. It is sufficient to note that the rivalries continued since the possession of Hungarian lands was economically and politically important to Ferdinand I of the Habsburg family, and all sides were strongly motivated to take what they perceived as defensive action in a fluid, unstable part of the world.

Nor is it possible to deal with the question of whether the people in conquered territories were better off under Ottoman or Habsburg rule.[29] It is important to keep in mind that this was not a time of religious toleration, and for Protestants, discrimination and persecution could be expected from and in Catholic territories. In Ottoman Hungary, Fischer-Galati notes that already by the late 1520s Hungarian students from Ottoman areas were studying with Luther and Melanchthon in Wittenberg. Protestant intellectuals were influential in the state, and the school system was largely in Protestant hands.[30] For the purposes of this paper it is sufficient to note that the European world considered it a realistic threat that Europeans, especially young Europeans, would convert to Islam.

Since Ottoman armies did not move further north or west and the main force returned to Turkey, European fears dropped accordingly. As long as there was no perceived threat to German lands, there was no desire to get involved in conflicts with the Ottomans, and it seemed apparent to the Protestants that assistance to Roman Catholic Habsburgs was only likely to strengthen Catholic opposition to the Protestants in the long run.

Low level conflict continued in Hungary until 1529 when Suleiman decided to end the Habsburg threat, and together with his Hungarian allies bring Habsburg territories, including Vienna, under his control. In May of that year, Ottoman forces began to march. The campaign was long and difficult, not because of military opposition, but because of consistently bad weather that required the

---

and they shall be burned." S. Fischer-Galati, "The Protestant Reformation and Islam," in *The Mutual Effects of the Islamic and Judeo-Christian Worlds: The East European Pattern*. Studies on Society in Change, no. 3, ed., A. Ascher, T. Halasi-Kun and B.K. Király (Brooklyn, NY: Brooklyn College Press; distributed by Columbia University Press, 1979), 60.

29 For a discussion of the ways in which the Ottoman system developed and differed from the European system, see P. Coles, *The Ottoman Impact on Europe* (New York: Harcourt Brace & World, 1968), esp. 45–100 dealing with such subjects as slavery, religious policy and conversion, land management, civil administration, etc. Particularly thought-provoking are his proposals of how sixteenth-century decisions shaped the future of both sides.

30 Fischer-Galati, "The Protestant Reformation," 60.

army to leave its heavy guns stuck in the mud, to deal with soldiers and animals frequently sick, and to solve a host of other supply and logistics problems.

Nevertheless, the Turkish army did reach Vienna, and the siege began in late September. From the viewpoint of both sides, the future of Europe was at stake. Even in Germany, the attack was taken seriously. Catholics and Lutherans together contributed 16,000 men to Ferdinand's cause with the understanding that the aid was temporary and would not be repeated until the religious question had been settled.[31] Protestants and Catholics alike recognized that if Vienna fell, this would be yet another victory in a whole string of Ottoman victories as the Turkish armies came up the Danube River into Central and Eastern Europe. If Vienna could be held, the Ottoman advance, the Islamic advance into the heart of Europe, would be halted.

2. On War Against the Turk

In these chaotic and fearful times, Luther published his first treatment of the Ottoman threat, *On War against the Turk [1529]*[32] to encourage the war effort against the Turk.

Luther regarded this as an exceedingly serious situation, as one of the signs of the end times. As Herod and the Jews had worked together though they hated each other to oppose Christ, so pope and Turk stood together to oppose Christ and his kingdom.[33]

At the same time, Luther had little confidence in the German people or their leadership. He thought that they consistently underestimated the Turkish threat and were in danger of getting themselves into a situation they could escape only if God provided a miracle, a miracle that God was unlikely to provide given the current state of affairs in Germany.[34]

Luther wrote the pamphlet in part to defend himself against Pope Leo's accusation that Luther was against resistance to the Turk since the Turk was the agent of God's punishment. Not so, said Luther. There were circumstances in which the Turk must be fought such as his coming attack on Vienna.[35]

In supporting the war effort, his first concern was that God permitted only defensive wars, and he did not want soldiers to think of themselves as a Christian army fighting an Islamic army. In Luther's view no army can be described as "Christian" because, on the one hand, Christians are required to bear all kinds of

31 Fischer-Galati, *Ottoman Imperialism and German Protestantism*, 34.
32 Luther, "War against Turk."
33 Luther, "War against Turk," 200.
34 Luther, "War against Turk," 184.
35 Luther, "War against Turk," 162.

wrongs and, on the other hand, every army is made up of committed Christians and those who are not. The proper role for Christians as Christians was "to fight against the devil with the word of God and with prayer."[36]

If the war against the Turk were not a kind of Christian crusade against Islam, what was the basis for the war? Luther applies to the Turk the same standard that he has just applied to the Christians. The Turk started the conflict; he does not fight out of necessity or to protect his lands; he is attacking and ravaging lands that have never belonged to him. In all of this he shows that he is a tool of the devil, while at the same time he is the instrument of God's punishment on his people.[37]

In addition to the fact that the Turk was waging an unjust war, Luther has two further reasons for opposition. Some of his concerns are doctrinal, others are concerned with the attractiveness of Turkish life. In his treatment, Luther repeats and does not go beyond what Norman Daniel calls "the substance of the medieval canon."[38] Luther did not invent the allegations about the inadequacy of Quranic teaching about Christ or the allegations about the person and work of Muhammad. These (and many, many more) were standard accusations that had been developed over the preceding centuries, and Luther simply repeats them in his own context.

Somewhat surprisingly, Luther's basic theological arguments are stated in roughly two pages out of an article of approximately 50 pages in English translation. The need for repentance and prayer is Luther's principal concern, and that permeates the document, but the defense of specific articles of the Christian faith occupied little space.

In dealing with the definition of the faith, Luther's first and greatest concern is that the Quran does not do justice to the work of Jesus Christ. Although the Quran respects him as a prophet, he is prophet whose work was finished with the communication of his message from God in his own time and place. The Quran failed to recognize, Luther maintained, that Christ was true God and God's son and the savior of the world.[39] Luther was not the first to raise this article, and he is simply repeating the medieval accusations.

Luther's other concern in this section concerning inadequacies in the Quran is to raise doubts about the person and work Muhammad. Essentially, the argument is that Muhammad derived his message from Jewish, Christian, and heathen beliefs. That was why his message in some respects appears to be acceptable to Christians and other respects not. At base, however, Luther (and his world)

36 Luther, "War against Turk," 165.
37 Luther, "War against Turk," 170.
38 N. Daniel, *Islam and the West: The Making of an Image* (Oxford, UK: Oneworld, 1993), 302ff.
39 Luther, "War against Turk," 176.

regarded Islam as a Christian heresy. A book written by a heretic and the articles of faith drawn from that book could not represent the orthodox Christian faith.[40] And since both the religion of Muhammad and the religion of the papacy were heretical, both could be subjected to the same criticism.[41]

Luther gives attention to other features of Ottoman life that he thought show disregard for the proper way of doing things and ultimately weakened government and public order. Included in his list is the observation that it is said that among themselves Turks are friendly and honest, but it needs to be kept in mind that no one is entirely evil. They boast in battle, "There is no God but God," and since they do not define who God is, they are in fact worshipping the devil, who is also a god; and they are radically iconoclastic in both religion and state.[42]

As far as the administration of government is concerned, Luther lumps the Ottomans together with the followers of Thomas Müntzer as people who kill rulers and tolerate "no gradations of government such as princes, counts, lords, nobles, and others. He [the Turkish ruler] alone is lord over all in his own land, and what he gives out is only pay, never property or rights of rulership."[43] In addition, he notes that the Turks are papists for they are convinced that they will be saved by their works.[44]

Luther says that he has reported all of these weaknesses and failures in order to demonstrate to Christian (the personification of the pious and believing German) the importance of repentance and prayer in order defeat Allah, the Turk's god, who is in fact the devil and to turn aside God's wrath so that he no longer uses the Turks as his rod. Christian is not called to warfare on the battlefield, but his "repentance, tears, and prayer" are his contribution to the battle against the Turk.[45]

There is a person, however, who is to meet the Turk on the battlefield, and Luther specifically identifies him as "Emperor Charles [V] or whoever may be emperor; for the Turk is attacking his subjects and his empire, and it is his duty, as a regular ruler appointed by God, to defend his own."[46] Luther may have had his problems with the empire and with Charles, but it did not change the fact that Charles was the God-appointed head of the empire who had a God-imposed duty to defend his subjects.

40 Luther, "War against Turk," 177.
41 Fischer-Galati, "The Protestant Reformation," 53–54.
42 Luther, "War against Turk," 183.
43 Luther, "War against Turk," 183.
44 Luther, "War against Turk," 183.
45 Luther, "War against Turk," 184.
46 Luther, "War against Turk," 184.

Luther considered the Turkish challenge to be so great that no single kingdom or land would be powerful enough to resist.[47] It was important that they take united action. He urged the Germans to learn from the example of Constantinople and the Greeks, who "quarreled with one another and looked after their own affairs for a long time until the Turk overwhelmed both of them, as he has already come very near doing to us in a similar case."[48] They were to ignore those who urged the emperor to take the role of defender of the faith and to wipe out the Turkish religion. The church had its own defender, namely, God, and state attempts to protect the church regularly led to lamentable results. In Luther's analysis of the situation,

> There are entirely too many Turks, Jews, heathen, and non-Christians among us with open false doctrine and with offensive, shameful lives. Let the Turk believe and live as he will, just as one lets the papacy and other false Christians live. The emperor's sword has nothing to do with the faith; it belongs to physical, worldly things, if God is not to become angry with us.[49]

Luther could clearly see what had to be done. The emperor and the princes were required to fight the Turk. As God had made them rulers, so, whether they held the Christian faith or not, they were required to defend their subjects. "With continual preaching and exhortation" they were to be reminded that

> it is their duty to God not to let their subjects perish so terribly, and that they commit serious sin when they are not mindful of their office and do not use all their power to bring counsel and help to those who should live, with body and goods, under their protection and who are bound to them by oaths of homage.[50]

At the same time, Luther recognized that some argued that the pope was at least as great a threat (Luther had labelled him as the Antichrist) and should also be resisted militarily. Luther agreed that in many ways the Turk and the pope were similar, but there were two critical differences. Most importantly, the Turks were not Christians. They were respectful of the Christian story, but "he believes that his Mohammed is superior to Christ and that Christ is not God."[51] Secondly, the Turks willingly used the sword to spread their faith. Luther had no doubt that the pope would willingly use the sword against Luther and his followers and would try bring the whole world under his control, but so far military force had not been given him.[52]

47 Luther, "War against Turk," 184.
48 Luther, "War against Turk," 200.
49 Luther, "War against Turk," 186.
50 Luther, "War against Turk," 186–187.
51 Luther, "War against Turk," 196–197.
52 Luther, "War against Turk," 198–199.

Luther has one final group of people he wishes to warn, namely, those Germans who might wish to be ruled by the Turks. Luther realized that many people had to submit to Turkish rule because their side was defeated by the Turks, but people who desired to be ruled by the Turk rather than "the emperor or princes" need to be warned "about the danger they are in, the wrong they are doing, and that by holding this opinion they make themselves a party to serious and innumerable sins in God's sight."[53]

Luther specifically lists the major wrongs in desiring Turkish rule. Such people in the first place, break the oath of loyalty and obedience made to the existing government; secondly, share accountability for all of the evil done by their new masters; and finally, it is not likely that they will better themselves, for the Turks regularly move people who appear to be successful to remote lands and make slaves of them.[54]

Summary

In this pamphlet Luther made clear that he was a faithful son of the Habsburg kingdom. He rejected the accusation of the pope that he was opposed to military resistance to the Turk, and he made it clear that he wanted nothing to do with any pastors who might hold this position. He argued that anyone who thought that rule by the Turk might be better than rule by Roman Catholics was seriously misled. He urged Emperor Charles V, not the pope, to mobilize the army and protect the state. This was not to be a religious war to militarily destroy Islam, but it was the emperor's God-given responsibility to wage a defensive, just war to protect the citizens of his kingdom. The Turkish threat was so great that all states within the empire, meaning the German Lutheran territories, needed to take part.

What he knew about Islam he used in support of the war effort. The Turks were worshipers of the devil and engaged in his work. The accusations that had been made against the pope still applied, but the need to resist the Turk overrode all other considerations.

3. Book on the Ceremonies and Customs of the Turks

The Turks were able to besiege Vienna under the personal direction of Suleiman, September 23 to October 15, 1529. In this short period of time, tens of thousands of soldiers and civilians on both sides lost their lives, but perhaps the most

53 Luther, "War against Turk," 193.
54 Luther, "War against Turk," 194–195.

decisive factor was the continuing rainfall and unseasonable snowfall at the end of the siege. The battle was a decisive win for Habsburg forces, and demonstrated that Turks had reached the limits of the territory into which they could project their forces.[55]

The threat of Turkish immediate expansion was past in 1530, but the threat from the Turks in their faith and way of life continued. There were reports about people who had been taken prisoner in the Turkish campaign and sold as slaves. There were stories about Christians who had converted to the Islamic faith, and there were still Germans who questioned whether or not it was better to be ruled by the Turkish state.

Luther's contribution to the whole discussion was his German translation in 1530 of the Latin volume by "George of Hungary" (the author's name was unknown to Luther), *Libellus de ritu et moribus Turcorum*, and Luther's form of the title is translated into English as "Book on the Ceremonies and Customs of the Turks, Published Seventy Years Ago."[56] "Seventy years ago" would place the initial publication of the book about 1460, but modern scholars are convinced that the publication date should be closer to 1480.[57] The book was exceedingly popular in the fifteenth and sixteenth centuries, being printed in many different Latin editions between 1480 and 1550 and in eleven different German translations from 1482/83 to 1531.[58]

George of Hungary was a young man, born in Siebenbuergen region of the Hungarian empire in 1522. In 1538, he was captured by the Turks, taken to Turkish territories, and sold as a slave. He remained a slave for twenty years in spite of eight escape attempts that each led to severe punishment. In 1458 he finally succeeded in his escape and made his way to Rome where he eventually became a member of the Dominican Order.[59]

It is important to remember that Luther probably did not know more about life among the Turks than he could find in George's book. Undoubtedly, there were daily reports and stories on the streets of Wittenberg about Turkish atrocities, about life in Turkish lands, but an authoritative account based on twenty years of experience was a rarity. He very likely read this book with as much fascination as other German academics. Many people wanted to know about the

55 Coles, *Ottoman Impact on Europe*, 103.

56 Luther, "Preface to George of Hungary."

57 J.A.B. Palmer, "Fr. Georgius de Hungaria, OP, and the *Tractatus de moribus condicionibus et necquicia Turcorum*," *Bulletin of the John Rylands Library* 34 (1951/52): 44–68 (44).

58 A. Classen, "The World of the Turks Described by an Eyewitness: Georgius de Hungaria's Dialectical Discourse on the Foreign World of the Ottoman Empire," *Journal of Early Modern History* 7, no.3 (2003): 257–279 (257–258).

59 Palmer, "Fr. Georgius de Hungaria," 45–46.

Turkish way of life, and Luther could expect that a German translation of this work would find a ready audience.

Luther makes it very clear that his interest goes beyond publishing factual information about Turkish life. In his view, the document was useful in opposing Islam.

> I am also publishing this book for another purpose: to forestall the stumbling block of Mohammedanism. Because we now have the Turk and his religion in our vicinity, our people must be warned, lest, moved by the outward appearance of their religion and the façade of their behavior, or taking offense at the lowliness of our faith or the deformity of our behavior, they deny their Christ and follow after Mohammed.[60]

Right from the start of his Preface Luther makes it clear that his purpose in providing this translation is to urge people not to leave the Christian faith and become followers of Islam. He was particularly concerned that an understanding of the Christian faith that emphasized works – his chief dispute with the Roman Catholic Church – would find the Islamic faith attractive.

Luther found George's book valuable because it seemed to him that the book was fair and balanced in its treatment of Islam. He lamented that he had only [Riccoldo of Monte Croce's] *Refutation of the Koran* and Nicholas of Cusa's *Analysis of the Koran* that he could use to study Islam since he was unable to obtain a copy of the Quran. While he appreciated their efforts to help people understand Islam, Luther thought that their criticism of Islam was too one-sided, unfair, and failed to deal with the positive side of Islam. The result was that ordinary people rejected the scare tactics and were more likely to be unconvinced by the arguments against the Islamic faith.[61]

In contrast, Luther found George's book to be better balanced and, therefore, far more believable. By pointing out favorable features of faith and life among the Turks, readers could see that George had been a careful observer whose explanations could be trusted. At the same time, George's believable descriptions of Turkish faith and life was more likely to hold the reader's attention.[62]

Luther then goes on to list at length specific areas of life where he considers Islamic practice to be superior to the practice of the Christians. The modesty and simplicity of the Turks in "food, clothing, buildings and all things" is stressed along with "fasts, prayers, and common assemblies of the people." As Luther extravagantly puts it,

> Our religious are only a shadow compared to them, and our people are simply profane in comparison to theirs. Not even true Christians nor Christ Himself nor the apostles nor the prophets ever presented such a fine appearance. And this is why so many people

60 Luther, "Preface to George of Hungary," 261.
61 Luther, "Preface to George of Hungary," 258.
62 Luther, "Preface to George of Hungary," 258.

> readily abandon faith in Christ for Mohammed and cling to him so stubbornly. To be plain: I believe that no Papist, monk, cleric, or anyone else sharing their faith would remain steadfast in their faith if they lived three days among the Turks.[63]

This is a key paragraph in explaining Luther's use of this document. Since the *Other* is even more legalistic and obedient to its own rules than the Roman Catholics and yet are clearly outside of the kingdom of God, then the Roman Catholics, who cannot even attain the same level of obedience, are clearly outside the kingdom of God and must be rejected. George's reports of the superiority of Islamic practice were a confirmation of the inherent weakness of the Roman Catholic faith.

At the same time, it should also be noted that even while George's account was full of episodes in which George reported a positive reaction to the Turkish way of life or the practice of the Islamic religion, even with comments on the inferiority of the European way of life, he was clear and consistent in his reporting that Islam was a false religion in conflict with the Christian scriptures and a seductively attractive alternative to the Christian faith.[64] Since this was part and parcel of George's work as it came into Luther's hands, the book was ready-made for Luther's use in translation.

Luther may have regarded one other aspect of George's story as particularly useful for his purposes. In about his fifth year of slavery, after thorough observation and consideration of the Islamic faith, George seriously considered giving up the Christian faith and becoming a Moslem himself. At virtually the last moment, he received a gift of grace that enabled him to hold firmly to the Christian faith.[65]

Luther probably has this aspect of George's story in mind when he writes,

> This author, however, should be pardoned if, through the common fault of the age, he did not manage any better, and if what he did manage to do, he shaped according to the customary style of his time. Rather, he should be praised for the distinguished zeal, candor, and diligence with which he faithfully accomplished as much as he could.[66]

Luther does not specifically mention the temptation to apostasy nor the solution that George had found in return to the Roman Catholic faith (and eventual membership in the Dominican Order). In a context where many Germans faced the same temptation to apostasy and where some had gone over to the Islamic side either as prisoners or voluntarily, the lesson could be drawn from George's book that return to Christian faith was possible.

63 Luther, "Preface to George of Hungary," 259.
64 Classen, "World of the Turks," 265–267, 270, 273–275.
65 Palmer, "Fr. Georgius de Hungaria," 58.
66 Luther, "Preface to George of Hungary," 262.

Summary

At a time when victory over the Turk at Vienna was still fresh in people's minds and interest in the Turk was still strong, at a time when some Germans found themselves under Turkish rule in Hungary or even contemplated placing themselves under Turkish rule, Luther translated George of Hungary's description of life in the Turkish realm to make clear what life among the Turks was really like. He did not question that in some ways Turks appeared to be admirable people, but he wanted to make clear that this was only an outward show intended to mislead Christians and draw them away from faith in Christ. Especially those – like his Roman Catholic opponents – who thought God would save them because of their acts of piety needed to be warned that this was not the Christian faith.

4. Appeal for Prayer against the Turks

In 1541, Turkish forces succeeded in taking control of Buda, having defeated the Habsburg armies and set about the task of organizing a Turkish province in Hungarian territories. The possibility that Germany would be drawn into conflict with the Turks and might lose that conflict needed to be taken seriously once again. At the request of Elector John Frederick, Luther's contribution in the new circumstances was his pamphlet, *Appeal for Prayer against the Turks* [1541].[67] Luther produced this document in one draft in September, and that it fit the mood of the times is illustrated by the seven reprints in 1541 and two in 1542.[68]

By this time, Luther was about five years away from his death and about 24 years away from the beginning of the Reformation. It is perhaps not surprising that this pamphlet has little to say about the Turk and quite a lot to say about the sorry state of German Christendom.

In the fifth paragraph of the pamphlet, Luther sets out the context in which he will make his arguments. The context is not about the Turk but about the widespread unfaithfulness of the German people.

> Except for the very few who are faithful and gratefully accept God's word, the majority are ungrateful, stubborn, brash, and live as if God had given us his word because we deserved it, and as if he had freed us from the papacy along with its devilish fetters so that we might do just as we please. So we think we need not serve under God's word to his glory and our salvation, but do so for our own purposes, even though it cost the blood

67 Luther, "Appeal for Prayer against Turks."
68 Luther, "Appeal for Prayer against Turks," 215.

> and death of his dear Son, Jesus Christ, our Lord and Savior, in order that the Word might be proclaimed so abundantly among us.[69]

In Luther's view, people have reached this state of affairs through their refusal to listen to their pastors, whose advice and counsel they disregard.[70] They should realize that these men were no different than the heroes of faith in Old and New Testaments for they announce the same message and worship the same God. As he answered prayer in biblical times, so, "He cannot ignore the church when it earnestly beseeches him. For that reason, it is not impossible for God to accomplish deeds as great or greater through us."[71]

Luther moves immediately to the specific tasks pastors must accomplish, namely, to "boldly reprove and rebuke the people from the pulpit for their sin and wickedness," and lead them in prayer. "These are the two tasks of the preacher: toward the people, to teach them what is right and good; toward God, to pray that we may do right and that we may win a happy victory."[72]

In this section of the pamphlet Luther offers specific examples of the ways in which he has made these emphases in the worship life of the congregation. The clergy are to urge people not to lose heart in their prayers for deliverance from the Turk. On the one hand, no one in Germany had received a command from God, that as Jeremiah was instructed not to pray for Judah, he should no longer pray for Germany's deliverance from the Turk. On the other hand, Luther warned against adopting the fatalism of the Turks with their conviction that God would simply do what he wants, where and when he wants to do it. No, says Luther, "We have to do what we know we ought to do according to God's word and the light he has given us. That which God has decreed will come to pass without our doing."[73] Prayer for deliverance from the Turk must go on even though God would ultimately answer prayer according to his own timetable.

With these observations, Luther felt that he had dealt with the issues that were the responsibility of Christian clergy, but there was still an important portion of German society that had a role to play, namely the political leadership of the country. Their role as Luther saw it was to provide pious and faithful examples to the community.

> Please take this to heart: come and hear God's word and join with us in prayer. See to it that justice prevails in the land. Punish usury and all other wickedness. Curb those vicious, disgraceful sins of drinking, gambling, and extravagant spending. Prepare yourselves for the holy sacrament. Don't act, as some do, as though the sacrament were

69 Luther, "Appeal for prayer against Turks," 220.
70 Luther, "Appeal for Prayer against Turks," 222–223.
71 Luther, "Appeal for Prayer against Turks," 227.
72 Luther, "Appeal for Prayer against Turks," 229.
73 Luther, "Appeal for Prayer against Turks," 236.

poison or a disgraceful subservience for one in your position. If we want to confess God's word, then we surely must partake of the sacrament which has been instituted as a confession, or, as Christ himself says, as a memorial. Certainly, to neglect the sacrament, as those do who have not partaken for many years, will not please God.[74]

For Luther, the faults of the nobility that needed to be corrected to make a difference included social justice issues, a number of personal behavior issues, and the nobility's neglect of the worship and sacramental life of the congregations.

As for the Turk, Luther's concerns are summarized in a long prayer that could be prayed by an individual, acknowledging that the Turks (and the pope) are the tools of God's wrath,

[T]hou knowest, Almighty God and Father, that we have not sinned against the devil, the pope, nor the Turks, and that they have no right nor might to punish us. But thou canst and mayest use them against us as the rod of thy wrath, we who have sinned against thee and deserved all this tribulation.

But reminding God at the same time that the Turks were a totally anti-Christian force dedicated to the destruction of the Christian religion, an attack not only on German Christians but on God himself.

The Turk wants to put his Muhammad in the place of thy dear Son, Jesus Christ, for the Turk blasphemes him and asserts that Christ is no true Son of God and that Muhammad is a greater prophet than he. If it is sin to confess and praise thee, the Father, and thy Son and the Holy Spirit as the one true God, then thou thyself art the sinner, for thou didst create and command this faith in us. Therefore, when the enemy hates and attacks us because of our faith, he hates and attacks thee.[75]

As to the question of what could or should be done by the German people in the face of this threat, Luther acknowledged that the Turk had won many battles, but this was because the Germans had failed to recognize that they were not fighting against flesh and blood only, but were in fact "fighting against a great host of devils, for the army of the Turks is really Satan's army."[76] This kind of army, as was also the case in the conflict with Rome, could only be opposed successfully with God's word.

At the same time, there was no doubt in Luther's mind that the army was engaged in a just war. The conflict was completely defensive and intended only "to establish God's word and his church" especially for the sake of future generations.

74 Luther, "Appeal for Prayer against Turks," 236–237.
75 Luther, "Appeal for Prayer against Turks," 232–233.
76 Luther, "Appeal for Prayer against Turks," 237.

In Luther's mind, there was the possibility that Christian forces might be defeated. In preparation for such an event, children should be taught the catechism so that if they were taken prisoner, they might take their faith with them. In the case of women who were captured, Luther's advice is that pastors should teach that women are not guilty for any behavior that Turkish men may require of them.[77]

Nevertheless, since the conflict was a spiritual one, Luther could see the possibility of direct divine intervention. He thought that if the world continued in its evil ways, it would fall for the Last Time, and God would bring about the last judgment.[78] This meant for Luther that he could imagine that both the Turk and the papacy would suddenly disappear. In his view,

> the two kingdoms, that of the Turk and that of the pope, are the last two plagues of the wrath of God, as the Apocalypse calls them [Rev. 15:1]. They are the 'false prophet' and 'the beast' and both must be bound and cast into the 'lake of fire' [Rev. 19:20].[79]

No matter how deliverance from the Turk came about, ultimately, it was not a matter of the cleverness or strength of the Christians or even the strength of their faith. "Our solace, boldness, self-confidence, security, victory, life, joy, our honor and glory are seated up there in person at the right hand of God the Father Almighty."[80]

Summary

This document is an extended call for repentance on the part of the German people. It continues to maintain that the Turks are the agents of God's wrath, but it urges German clergy to take seriously the need to call people to repentance and prayer. Only if this happens will God provide deliverance from the Turk. There are no favorable statements about Islam or the customs of the Turks in the document.

77 Luther, "Appeal for Prayer against Turks," 239.
78 Luther, "Appeal for Prayer against Turks," 223.
79 Luther, "Appeal for Prayer against Turks," 238–239.
80 Luther, "Appeal for Prayer against Turks," 241.

5. Refutation of the Quran [1301]

In his preface to George of Hungary's *Book on the Ceremonies and Customs of the Turks*, Luther had identified Riccoldo of Monte Croce's *Refutation of the Koran*[81] and Nicholas of Cusa's *A Scrutiny of the Koran*[82] as his sources of information about the faith and customs of Islamic people. These were his sole sources of scholarly information about Islam until he finally obtained a copy of the Quran in February of 1542.

In 1542, Luther translated and published Riccoldo's *Refutation of the Quran.* In choosing this book, Luther selected a book published nearly 250 years before in 1301, one of the most widely used treatments of Islam from the Middle Ages on. Nicholas of Cusa had used it approvingly in his *Scrutiny of the Koran* although his work is substantially different in tone and substance.[83]

Riccoldo (1243–1320) was a Dominican monk, born and raised in Italy. He left Italy in 1288, commissioned to preach in Acre, and travelled through Palestine, eventually reaching Baghdad where he stayed until 1299. He was in Baghdad in 1291 when the Christian city of Acre was overthrown by Saracen forces, and he saw firsthand the treatment of Christian slaves in the slave markets of Baghdad. He knew from personal experience the militancy of the Islamic religion.[84]

At the same he was prepared to treat the Islamic faith and its practitioners with respect. He describes himself as serious in his study of Islam. He learned (and loved) the Arabic language. He studied in Islamic schools and with Islamic masters. He says that he attempted a translation of the Quran but was unable to accomplish the task. He actually met Islamic people and discussed the Islamic faith with them. He observed the actual practice of Islamic adherents and treated it with respect.[85]

---

81 Riccoldo of Monte Croce, OP, *Refutation of the Koran*, trans. L. Ensis; ([Place of publication not identified]: L. Ensis, 2010).

82 Nicholas of Cusa, "*De pace fidei and cribratio alcorani:* Translation and Analysis," in *Complete Philosophical and Theological Treatises of Nicholas of Cusa*, vol. 2, ed., J. Hopkings (Minneapolis: A.J. Banning Press, 2001), 965–1105.

83 R.W. Southern, *Western Views of Islam in the Middle Ages* (Cambridge: Harvard University Press, 1962), 94: "he [Nicholas] abandoned the philosophical ground, and he tried to carry further the plan of discovering in the Koran itself the issues which separated Islam and Christendom, treating it as a document written in good faith, with a character and virtues of its own. In this way he hoped that he had defined and limited the area of dispute. He reduced it essentially to a dispute between Western Christianity and Nestorian Christianity, a heresy which erred in the relatively minor matter of the mode of the union of God with the human nature of Christ."

84 Riccoldo of Monte Croce, OP, *Refutation of the Koran*, Preface iii.

85 R. George-Tvrtković, "Deficient Sacraments or Unifying Rites? Alan of Lille, Nicholas of Cusa, and Ricoldo da Montecroce on Muslim and Jewish Praxis," in *Nicholas of Cusa and Islam: Polemic and Dialogue in the Late Middle Ages*. Studies in Medieval and Reformation

His experiences in the Islamic world led to three books: *The Book of Pilgrimage* (*Liber peregrinationis*), *Letters to the Church Triumphant* (*Epistolae ad ecclesiam triumphantem*), and *Refutation of the Koran* (*Confutatiuo Alcorani* or *Contra legem Saracenorum*), the book which Luther translated into German. Marcia Costigliolo suggests that the work of Riccoldo marks a significant turning point in Christian Europe's assessment of Islam.

> The circulation of texts on the interpretation of the Quran, especially Riccoldo's *Contra legem Saracenorum*, created a slow but growing knowledge about the affinities and the differences between Islam and Christianity, which consequently shaped the formation of a Christian and Western identity in opposition to the 'uncivilized' Turk. A pattern thus emerges: until the thirteenth century Islam was considered a terrifying enemy, however starting in the fourteenth century, apologetic and polemical works turned towards emphasizing the barbarism and ignorance of the Muslims more than the dangers they posed.[86]

With this change, the perception of Islam changed from that of an enemy to be feared, fought, and conquered to an *Other* whom it was necessary for the more civilized and accomplished Christian Europe to understand and convince. New modes of interaction seemed to be becoming possible.

Unfortunately, this shift in the understanding was possible at a time when the threat to Christianity in Europe was lessening; but when the Ottoman armies marched into Central Europe and began their conquest of Hungarian lands, fear of the Turk again became a reality throughout Germany.

In this changed context, Luther could make use of Riccoldo's *Refutation of the Koran*. Although this book took seriously Islamic faith and practice, coming as it did at the very beginning of the fourteenth century, there are strong expressions of fear of Islam and defensiveness about Christianity. The book is extremely aggressive against Islam. In his preface to George of Hungary's work approximately a dozen years before, Luther had criticized Riccoldo's book on the grounds that its purpose was "to scare simple Christians away from Mohammed and to keep them in the Christian faith."[87] He thought that the book was entirely too negative in its approach to Islam. In 1530, the Habsburg armies had prevented the Ottoman armies from entering Vienna; in 1546, the Turkish armies were again on the march.

Luther is very straightforward in stating the purpose for his translation of Riccoldo's book. It is entirely apologetic.

Traditions 183; ed., I.C. Levy, R. George-Tvrtković and D. Duclow (Leiden: Brill, 2014), 105–122.

86 M. Costigliolo, "Perspectives on Islam in Italy and Byzantium in the Middle Ages and Renaissance," in *Nicholas of Cusa*, ed., C. Levy, R. George-Tvrtković, and D. Duclow, 123–144 (124).

87 Luther, "Preface to George of Hungary," 258.

> Therefore, I thought it useful and necessary to translate this little book into German [...] so that we Germans, too, may know what a shameful faith the faith of Mohammed (sic) is, and in order to strengthen us in our Christian faith. For while Mohammed obtains victory, success, power, and honor in the world by the wrath or permission of God, we Christians carry the cross of our Lord and shall be blessed not here upon earth but in the life to come.[88]

Luther could imagine that German Christians might continue to lose, and they would find themselves living in an Islamic state. In those circumstances, they would need a kind of handbook to help them oppose Islam. Luther's translation of Riccoldo's work could serve as that handbook.[89]

At the same time, Luther had to deal with a special issue faced by German Christians. Their experience for centuries had been that Christians always won. There had been struggles, but Christian armies had accomplished their goals, and defeated people had joined the Christian community. In the conflict with Islam, the experience was entirely different:

> [E]ven if we cannot convert the Saracens, and now the Turks, still let us remain firm and strong in our faith, and not let it trouble us that the Saracens and Turks have for so many centuries enjoyed nothing but victory and success against the Christians, while we have had much ill fortune against them, so that now they have become lords of the world, always winning victories with great honor and riches, whereas we lie defeated with great shame and injury. Yet this does not happen because the faith of Mohammed is true and our faith is false, as the blind Turks boast. Rather, this is the manner in which God rules His people.[90]

The Islamic community had won victory after victory and shown itself resistant to the Christian message. For Luther, this did not mean that Islamic armies were proven right because they won. Rather, God was permitting the Turks to oppress his people and punish them for their sins, but ultimately, God is in charge of the lives of his people.

Luther briefly explains the basis for Turkish unbelief as a refusal to accept the testimony of the Scriptures.

> And how could anyone convert them, seeing that they reject all of Holy Scripture, both the New and the Old Testaments, as being now dead and corrupt, and they will not permit anyone to speak or to dispute on the basis of Holy Scripture, shutting fast their ears, eyes, and hearts against the blessed book of Holy Scripture and sticking with their Koran.[91]

88 Luther, "Preface and Afterword, Riccoldo," 254f.
89 Luther, "Preface and Afterword, Riccoldo," 261f.
90 Luther, "Preface and Afterword, Riccoldo," 255.
91 Luther, "Preface and Afterword, Riccoldo," 256.

As is typical of these publications, Luther argues also that Christians were not much better. They were not dedicated to their scriptures alone, but they allowed themselves to be distracted to other writings ("our korans" [sic]), namely, much of Roman Catholic literature of uncertain origin, in Luther's opinion, that misled people away from the gospel. In addition, their behavior of "dividing themselves by heresy and sects with many new doctrines," and by living scandalous lives without repentance clearly demonstrated that God was right in allowing Turkish victories to punish his people.[92]

In both the case of Turks and Germans, the willingness to stop short of full commitment to the scriptures alone was driven by the desire for wealth and power. Thus they knowingly and deliberately despise and persecute what they know and confess to be the truth in order to defend their open and acknowledged idolatry, lies, and injustice.[93]

Luther also emphasizes that the Islamic faith has consequences for the way society is organized and for daily living. He is particularly agitated about marriage and family situations, convinced that "there is no decency or estate of marriage among the Mohammedans, but only a life of free fornication."[94] They may pray much, but so does the adulteress in Proverbs 7, etc.[95]

Luther also attacks Muhammad as the author the Quran. Luther describes him as "a conjurer, with the sort of black art that has always existed and still exists today among the Arabs, his countrymen."[96] While it is true that he has led many people astray, Luther does not regard him as the Antichrist since he attacks the Christian faith as an outsider.[97] No,

> if we are to have success against Mohammed, the external enemy of Christendom, we must first through genuine repentance renounce the internal enemy, the Antichrist, along with his devils, and turn to our Lord and Savior Jesus Christ in real earnest and with sincere hearts, so that we may be able to pray rightly and in truth and thus may be certain of being heard.[98]

The repudiation of the internal Antichrist, the pope, was necessary to accomplish the overthrow of the external Antichrist.

Since Moslems are unable to see the irrefutable logic of the Christian faith, "they are not worthy to be called human beings, as those who, having been robbed of common human reason, have become altogether inhuman, nothing but stocks and stones." Yet some Turks are human, Luther says, because they

92 Luther, "Preface and Afterword, Riccoldo," 255.
93 Luther, "Preface and Afterword, Riccoldo," 259.
94 Luther, "Preface and Afterword, Riccoldo," 262.
95 Luther, "Preface and Afterword, Riccoldo," 263.
96 Luther, "Preface and Afterword, Riccoldo," 258.
97 Luther, "Preface and Afterword, Riccoldo," 264.
98 Luther, "Preface and Afterword, Riccoldo," 265f.

have rejected the Islamic faith or because the Islamic faith did not play an important role in their lives. They were still a part of the Turkish community but confined their researches to philosophy and other non-religious subjects (and taught the West).[99] Clandestine believers within the Islamic community were a possibility for Luther.

Summary

As far as what Luther knew about Islam is concerned – the answer for this preface is that he knew what Riccoldo taught him. What Luther found to be Riccoldo's most useful argument was the evaluation that Islam was a devilish religion and an implacable enemy of Christian faith. Muhammad and his Quran were the outside opponents of Luther and his followers.

But Luther thought that they were not the only opponents, for the Antichrist was also at work on the inside destroying Christian faith and practice. Because of continued lack of commitment to the Christian faith and outright disobedience, God continued to punish the Germans through the victories of the Turks. In this dire situation, when a Turkish state was being formed in Europe, repentance was the required response.

6. Preface to the Koran

On Shrove Tuesday, 1542, Luther had his first opportunity to study a Quran. This was at the same time he was preparing to publish Riccoldo's *Refutation of the Koran.* Perhaps not surprisingly, when Luther read the actual Quran after about a dozen years or more of Riccoldo, he found that the Quran confirmed virtually all of the accusations that Riccoldo had made against Islam, accusations that in some cases Luther had regarded as exaggerated.[100]

Why, then, the publication of the entire Quran? The question had arisen while publication was being considered in Basel. Johannes Oporinus, a printer newly arrived from Strasbourg, had contracted with Theodore Bibliander, a premier authority on all things Arabic, to publish the first translation of the Quran in Latin. While publication was in progress, the Basel city council decided that the book was a danger to the public (it was on the Roman Catholic Index of Prohibited Books at the time) and proceeded to seize all copies as well as arrest

99 Luther, "Preface and Afterword, Riccoldo," 258.
100 Luther, "Preface and Afterword, Riccoldo," 253–255.

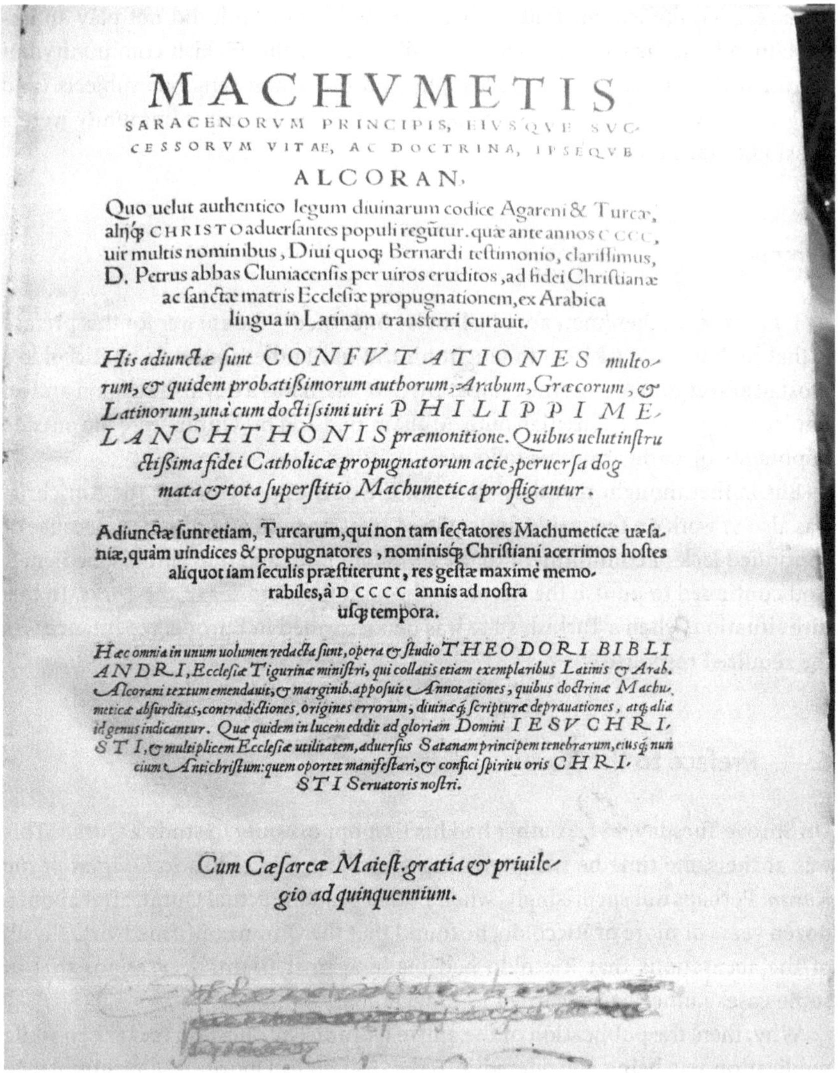

MACHVMETIS
SARACENORVM PRINCIPIS, EIVSQVE SVC-
CESSORVM VITAE, AC DOCTRINA, IPSEQVE
ALCORAN.

Quo uelut authentico legum diuinarum codice Agareni & Turcæ, alijq; CHRISTO aduersantes populi reguntur. quæ ante annos CCCC, uir multis nominibus, Diui quoq; Bernardi testimonio, clarissimus, D. Petrus abbas Cluniacensis per uiros eruditos, ad fidei Christianæ ac sanctæ matris Ecclesiæ propugnationem, ex Arabica lingua in Latinam transferri curauit.

His adiunctæ sunt CONFVTATIONES multorum, & quidem probatissimorum authorum, Arabum, Græcorum, & Latinorum, unà cum doctissimi uiri PHILIPPI MELANCHTHONIS præmonitione. Quibus uelut instructissima fidei Catholicæ propugnatorum acie, peruersa dogmata & tota superstitio Machumetica profligantur.

Adiunctæ sunt etiam, Turcarum, qui non tam sectatores Machumeticæ uæsaniæ, quàm uindices & propugnatores, nominisq; Christiani acerrimos hostes aliquot iam seculis præstiterunt, res gestæ maximè memorabiles, à DCCCC annis ad nostra usq; tempora.

Hæc omnia in unum uolumen redacta sunt, opera & studio THEODORI BIBLIANDRI, Ecclesiæ Tigurinæ ministri, qui collatis etiam exemplaribus Latinis & Arab. Alcorani textum emendauit, & marginib. apposuit Annotationes, quibus doctrinæ Machumeticæ absurditas, contradictiones, origines errorum, diuinæq; scripturæ deprauationes, atq; alia id genus indicantur. Quæ quidem in lucem edidit ad gloriam Domini IESV CHRISTI, & multiplicem Ecclesiæ utilitatem, aduersus Satanam principem tenebrarum, eiusq; nuncium Antichristum: quem oportet manifestari, & confici spiritu oris CHRISTI Seruatoris nostri.

Cum Cæsareæ Maiest. gratia & priuilegio ad quinquennium.

Fig. 2: The title page of the Bibliander edition of the Quran [1543], the first published edition of the Quran translated into a European language. While Philip Melanchthon alone is announced as the author of a preface, Luther is the author of the first preface and Melanchthon is the author of the second. © Photo courtesy of Concordia Seminary Library, St. Louis, MO, USA.

Oporinus. Oporinus's supporters wrote to leading European scholars to ask for their support.

Luther sent a letter, a letter that was probably the most influential in the council's decision to release Oporinus and allow the publication to go forward (although not to be sold in Basel and without Basel being mentioned on the title page). The Bibliander translation appeared in 1543 with the preface by Luther as the lead document with a preface by Melanchthon immediately following, although Melanchthon is the only preface author mentioned on the title page.[101]

Luther saw the value in the translation as providing the opportunity for the Quran to speak for itself and clearly show its unreasonableness and hostility to the Christian faith. Just as contemporary texts and practices of the Jews showed their perversion of the biblical faith, in Luther's opinion, so the publication of the Quran would have the same effect.

In the same way, Luther stated that as he had written against the "idols of the Jews and Papists" he would respond to the "Pernicious opinions of Mohammed" at greater length in the future,[102] a task to which he did not return.

For Luther, the key divisive issue separating Muhammad from Christianity was that he "utterly rejects the prophetic and apostolic writings;" and "that he has invented a new belief that differs from the prophets and apostles."[103]

In addition, "the doctrine of the Church must be perpetual; whereas this book makes it clear that this invention of Mohammed is something new." Since this new faith rejects the authority of the Scriptures, it rejects God's eternal plan of salvation that the Son of God should be a sacrifice and propitiation for the sins of the world and Muhammad also rejects "the doctrine concerning the causes of human weakness, failure, and death—namely, the sin passed down after the fall of our first parents," and for Luther there are many other differences that could be listed as well.[104]

Luther thought that Christian Europe was about to be punished for her ignorance and neglect. Since the Turk, in Luther's view was at the door so that "the punishment is now in sight, it should admonish us to separate ourselves (as I have said) from the Turks, Jews, and heathen, and to invoke the true, eternal God, Creator of all things." Nevertheless, God may use German captives to call Turks out of the darkness of unbelief as he had used Daniel and his companions to call the king of Babylon and many others or as prisoners of the Goths, Vandals, and Franks had called their captors to faith.[105]

In any case, Luther's final observation is that "There can be no thought of leisure, especially for those of us who teach in the church. We must fight everywhere against the armies of the devil,"[106] and to be prepared requires that

101 J.P. Rajashekar and T.J. Wengert, "Martin Luther, Philip Melanchthon, and the Publication of the Qur'an," *Lutheran Quarterly* 16, no.2 (2002): 221–228 (222). This article also contains a complete translation of Melanchthon's preface.
102 Luther, "Preface to Koran," 291.
103 Luther, "Preface to Koran," 291 f.
104 Luther, "Preface to Koran," 293 f.
105 Luther, "Preface to Koran," 293.
106 Luther, "Preface to Koran," 294.

Christian leaders read "the writings of their enemies – so that they may more accurately refute, strike, and overturn those writings, so that they may be able to correct some of them, or at least to fortify our own people with stronger arguments."[107]

Summary

Luther did not claim to have learned anything new as a result of reading the Quran. In fact, he only grew in his conviction that Islam was an anti-Christian religion, and the Turks were the army of the devil.

In this context, the purpose of the translation of the Quran was essentially defensive. If the Quran were allowed to speak for itself, it would show its thoroughly anti-Christian nature. Christians would see this and reject the Islamic faith. At the same time, there was one positive value in that because Christians knew and understood Islamic arguments, they would be better able to formulate their answers to the challenge of Islam.

7. Conclusion

What did Luther know about Islam? He knew as much as he could learn from reading Riccoldo's *Refutation of the Koran* published in 1301. He only grew in his conviction that Riccoldo was correct when he was finally able to read the entire Quran in 1542 and after.

From Riccoldo he had some basic information about Islamic belief and practice. He knew about Islamic monotheism and iconoclasm. He knew something about their piety and their ability to live in peace with one another.

But most clearly, he knew that the Islamic faith was the enemy of Christian teaching, the relentless opponent of Christian doctrine at every point from the doctrine of original sin to the saving work of Jesus Christ, the savior of the world. Moslems preferred their Quran over the Scriptures, and they could never be converted because they could never see the error of Islam and the beautiful logic of the Christian faith. The evidence from daily life that seemed to indicate that people in the Ottoman world were better off, were better organized, were better ruled was only hiding a darker reality. The reality was that the Ottoman armies were the armies of the devil and were intent on destroying the Christian world.

Luther was also convinced that the Christian world was receiving at the hands of the Turk the punishment it deserved because of its lack of repentance and faith,

107 Luther, "Preface to Koran," 294.

and he maintained this from 1518 to his last document in this series in 1542. More was at stake than the strategic and political threat of Turkish victories. Success against the Turk might be possible but only if people abandoned their faithless living and returned to God.

Why did Luther want to know this? Luther recognized his importance as a spiritual leader in a time of crisis, and he wanted to make it clear that Christians had a responsibility to support the state against the Turk. He needed to communicate how wrong the Turk was and how right the European state.

To those who wondered if the Ottoman armies were a genuine threat to Christian Europe, Luther answered that these are the armies of the devil who will surely destroy Christian life and faith. To those who wondered if the conflicts with Roman Catholic political and spiritual leaders made it impossible to join them in the war against the Turk, Luther argued that the size and seriousness of the threat required immediate, united action. To those who thought that Ottoman rule might be better than Roman Catholic, Habsburg rule, Luther replied that the Turks offered a way of life that was deceptive and built on false foundations quite different than the Christian foundations of the European states, and needed to be resisted, not welcomed.

Those influenced by Luther needed to support the state in its just war against the Turk. This was a purely defensive war, fought not to gain wealth and power, but to protect the people of God. This was not to be a kind of religious crusade and was certainly not to be carried out by an army led by the pope; but, Luther said, God called upon Emperor Charles V to do his duty and protect his people.

Nothing could be accomplished without repentance and faith, without repentance and prayer, but the power of God and his ultimate victory could not be doubted.

Richard A. Muller

Lutheran Natural Theology in the Early Modern Era

A Preliminary Glance

Modern discussions of the natural theology in the older Lutheran tradition are scarce and the subject has seldom been addressed in a detail approaching the level of definition found in the early modern sources. Moreover, although the subject has not been debated quite as strenuously among modern Lutherans as it has among modern Reformed or Calvinist theologians, the extant scholarship exhibits a significantly parallel variety of opinion, either posing Luther's understanding of theology radically against the later orthodox or arguing a developing Lutheran theology that adapted to changes in academic, confessional, and polemical contexts without entirely losing sight of the teachings of the early reformers.

Thus, in his survey of Lutheran theology, *From Luther to Kierkegaard*, Jaroslav Pelikan offered a critique of the orthodox Lutheran approach, on the ground that it was too optimistic concerning man's natural ability to demonstrate the existence of God and that it tended to close the gap between the natural knowledge of God available to human reason and the supernatural knowledge afforded by the special revelation in Scripture. In Pelikan's view, the older Lutheranism all too easily held natural knowledge as a proper beginning for the knowledge of God upon which a supernatural superstructure might be built.[1] Similar concern had also been expressed by other scholars, often by way of a distinction between Luther's views and those of Melanchthon and an emphasis on Melanchthon's influence on subsequent Lutheran orthodoxy – and, in the case of Elert's critique, replete with denunciations of the proofs of God's existence and of recourse to metaphysical language of God as *actus purus* or *ens spirituale*. Natural theology, according to Elert, undermined the theology of the original Reformation and set

1 Jaroslav Pelikan, *From Luther to Kierkegaard* (St. Louis: Concordia Publishing House, 1963), 64–66; also note the somewhat more nuanced reading in idem, "Natural Theology in David Hollacz," *Concordia Theological Monthly* 18 (1947): 253–263, where Pelikan concludes, following Hans Emil Weber, that orthodox Lutheran natural theology indicates a certain continuity with later rationalism; and see Hans Emil Weber, *Der Einfluss der protestantischen Schulphilosophie auf die orthodox-lutherische Dogmatik* (Leipzig: Deichert, 1908), 50–65.

Protestant theology on a rationalistic course toward the Enlightenment.[2] These particular lines of critique parallel the Barthian antipathy to natural theology and, in the case of Lutheran scholarship, may evidence a rootage, shared by Barth, in the anti-philosophical, anti-scholastic, and anti-metaphysical concerns of Ritschlian theology.[3]

Robert Preus, who had considerable respect for Elert's understanding of the older orthodoxy and even identifies Elert as offering "a reliable picture of the theology of Lutheran orthodoxy" and characterizes his analysis as "usually appreciative,"[4] nonetheless presents a very different reading of the sources. Whereas Elert offers little reference and much denunciation, Preus more objectively surveys Lutheran sources, notably Johannes Gerhard's *Loci theologici* and Abraham Calov's *Systema locorum theologicum*, indicating that Calov recognizes both the problem of the noetic effects of sin and the genuine presence of a natural revelation, leading him to affirm a limited and often confused natural knowledge of God, insufficient for salvation, but sufficient to the recognition of the existence of God. Preus also has a clear sense of the contextual nature of the older Lutheran approach – namely, opposition to the Socinian denial of the natural knowledge of God.[5] There was clearly a place for natural knowledge and, arguably, a distinct, albeit non-salvific function allowed by natural theology in orthodox Lutheranism.[6] Still, Preus examines only the definitions and discussions of natural theology in the orthodox Lutheran systems of revealed theology; he does not investigate the Lutheran natural theologies themselves.

More recently, Pannenberg has commented on natural theology in the Lutheran tradition, recognizing that a distinction between natural and revealed theology had been made "within the concept of *theologia viatorum*" beginning in

2 Cf. Ernst Troeltsch, *Vernunft und Offenbarung bei Johann Gerhard und Melanchthon* (Göttingen: Vandenhoeck & Ruprecht, 1891); Adolf Sperl, "A Note on Philipp Melanchthon: the Problem of Natural Theology," *Lutheran Theological Journal* 16, no.1 (1982): 46–49; Werner Elert, *The Structure of Lutheranism*, trans., Walter A. Hansen (St. Louis: Concordia Publishing House, 1962), 49–58, 231; also note Roland F. Ziegler, "Natural Knowledge of God and the Trinity," *Concordia Theological Quarterly* 69, no.2 (2005): 133–158, who takes the Barth-Brunner debate as his argumentative point of departure.

3 See Paul Jersild, "Natural Theology and the Doctrine of God in Albrecht Ritschl and Karl Barth," *Lutheran Quarterly* 14, no.3 (1962): 239–257; also note "Judgment of God in Albrecht Ritschl and Karl Barth," *Lutheran Quarterly* 14, no.4 (1962): 328–346; and cf. Richard A. Muller, "Karl Barth and the Path of Theology into the Twentieth Century: Historical Observations," *The Westminster Theological Journal* 51 (1989): 25–50.

4 Robert D. Preus, *The Theology of Post-Reformation Lutheranism*, 2 vols. (St Louis: Concordia Publishing House, 1970–1972), I: 20, 22.

5 Preus, *Theology of Post-Reformation Lutheranism*, I: 173–180.

6 See, e.g., Ralph A. Bohlmann, "Natural Knowledge of God," *Concordia Theological Monthly* 34, no.12 (1963): 721–735.

the "the time of Gerhard."[7] Pannenberg argues that the term "natural" in this older theology did not mean "in accordance with the nature of God" but "in accordance with human nature," and, as a consequence, was a "form of the knowledge of God that is compatible with us."[8] He also claims that "the older Protestant theology did not distinguish between natural knowledge of God and natural theology" or "between natural theology and natural religion."[9] Pannenberg, however, cites no seventeenth-century Lutheran natural theology in proof of his assertions and skips from his reference to Gerhard's time to comments on the natural theology of Leibniz, Buddeus, and Wolff.[10]

Historians of early modern philosophy differ in their assessment, given that they have not participated in the various biases characteristic of the theological commentators – but neither have they provided a consistent picture of early modern natural theology.[11] Pünjer understood a distinction between natural theology and metaphysics, but argued that the Protestant natural theologies lacked genuine "philosophical expositions" and simply duplicated "the corresponding parts of dogmatics."[12] By contrast, Wundt recognized that natural theology was typically viewed as a form of philosophy and, certainly in the case of Johannes Scharff, saw that "*pneumatica*," understood as knowledge or spiritual being, stood somewhat distinct from metaphysics. Wundt also recognized differences over the place of rational discourse concerning God in the metaphysics of the era.[13] In Beck's somewhat negative assessment, Lutheran writers differed little over the contents of metaphysics and "simply" defined pneumatology and

7 Wolfhart Pannenberg, *Systematic Theology*, 3 vols., trans., Geoffrey W. Bromiley (Grand Rapids: Eerdmans, 1992–1994), I:73.

8 Pannenberg, *Systematic Theology*, 81.

9 Pannenberg, *Systematic Theology*, 95.

10 Pannenberg, *Systematic Theology*, 84–85 (Leibniz and Wolff), 96 (Buddeus). In the course of his discussion, e. g., 95–96, 110, Pannenberg cites several of the Lutheran orthodox – Hollaz, Musaeus, Calovius – none of whom produced a natural theology. Abraham Calovius, *Theologia naturalis et revelata secundum tenorem Augustanae Confessionis, quinque libris adserta* (Rostock: Joachim Wildens, 1646), does not actually include a full natural theology, only a single chapter, *De existentia Dei ejusque naturali cognitione*, in which he argues against the views of Falcius, Hofmann, and Vedelius. My thanks to Lyle Buettner, Special Collections Librarian at Concordia Seminary, St. Louis, for his help in surveying the volume.

11 Note the useful survey of issues facing early modern natural theology by Scott Mandelbrote, "Early Modern Natural Theologies," in *The Oxford Handbook of Natural Theology*, ed., Russell Manning (New York: Oxford University Press, 2013), 75–99. Unfortunately, Mandelbrote does not examine Lutheran writers nor, oddly, does he pay much attention to the actual genre of *theologia naturalis* in the early modern era.

12 Bernhard Pünjer, *History of the Christian Philosophy of Religion from the Reformation to Kant*, trans., W. Hastie (Edinburgh: T & T Clark, 1887), 177.

13 Max Wundt, *Die deutsche Schulmetaphysik des 17. Jahrhunderts* (Tübingen: J.C.B. Mohr, 1939), 116. Peter Petersen, *Geschichte der aristotelischen Philosophie im protestantischen Deutschland* (Leipzig: Felix Meiner, 1921), makes no attempt to identify a distinct natural theology.

natural theology "as branches of metaphysics [...] with little content and in no position to challenge the hegemony of speculative and critical metaphysics."[14]

In the following essay, I propose to examine seventeenth-century Lutheran natural theologies, looking at several with attention to definitional detail and relation to other disciplines, to test these several modern descriptions against the sources and to show that the variety of these older theologies precludes both the hasty categorizations and the facile dismissals characteristic of the modern literature on the subject, particularly on the identity of natural theology in relation to sacred theology and metaphysics.

1. Lutheran Natural Theologies: General Characteristics and Varied Definitions

In his groundbreaking *Loci theologici*, Gerhard adopted the distinction between a divine archetypal theology and a divine-given human ectypal theology or *theologia viatorum*. This latter, he recognized, consisted both in supernatural theology bestowed by the light of grace and natural theology given through the light of nature.[15] After Gerhard, various major Lutheran theologians of the era discussed the issues of natural knowledge of God and natural theology in their dogmatic works,[16] but a significant group of thinkers also went beyond this basic issue of definition and wrote natural theologies, among them Valentin Fromme,[17] Stephan Klotz,[18] and Johannes Scharff.[19] There were also natural theologies by

14 Lewis White Beck, *Early German Philosophy* (Cambridge: Harvard University Press, 1969), 126.

15 Preus, *Theology of Post-Reformation Lutheranism*, I: 113.

16 Cf. Preus, *Theology of Post-Reformation Lutheranism*, I: 152–153, 164–166, 173–180.

17 Valentin Fromme, *Isagoge Philosophica: in qua Disciplinae Philosophicae Omnes, Reales & Instrumentales [...] adumbrantur* (Brandenburg: Müllerus, 1665). Fromme (1601–1675), studied in Wittenberg and served as Rektor and Superintendent in Brandenburg; he did not hold an academic post.

18 Stephan Klotz, *Pneumatica sive theologia naturalis* (Rostock: Michael Mederius, 1640). Klotz (1606–1668) was Professor of Theology at Rostock, 1632–36.

19 Johannes Scharff, *Pneumatica, seu Pneumatologia, hoc est Scientia Spirituum Naturalis [....] In ordinem disciplinae redacta, & methodo conveniente denuo edita* Johanne Scharfio (Wittenberg: Balthasar Mevius, 1644), fifth edition with modified title, *Pneumatica, Hoc est: Scientia Spirituum Naturalis: e Principiis Philosoph. extructa. [...] In qua breviter proponitur, I. To GnwstoVn touV Qeou, Theologia Naturalis de Deo uno [...] II. Aggelografiva, seu doctrina de Intelligentiis creatis, & Angelis. III. Doctrina de Anima Rationali, quatenus ea est natura spiritualis & immortalis* (Wittenberg: Balthasar Mevius, 1670), hereinafter citing this "1670 edition;" also idem, *Theoria transcendentalis primae philosophiae, quam vocant metaphysicam* (Wittenberg: Haered. Zacharias Schürer, 1630); idem, *Metaphysica exemplaris: seu prima philosophia* (Wittenberg: Mevius & Schumacher, 1655); and idem, *Methodus philosophiae peripateticae prior, hoc est tabellarum philosophicarum pars prima, in qua*

Heinrich Julius Scheurl,[20] Balthasar Cellarius,[21] Johann Meisner,[22] Kilian Rudrauf,[23] Johann Christoph Hundeshagen,[24] Tobias Pfanner,[25] Ulrich Heinsius,[26] Johann Andreas Schmidt,[27] Christoph Reuchlin,[28] and Johann Paul Hebenstreit.[29]

Abraham Calovius, who did not produce a natural theology, did however write a significant treatise on metaphysics.[30] This list includes professors of theology

ordine & breviter delineatur [...] logica [...] praxis [...] paideia [...] metaphysica [...] pueunatica [...] physica (Leipzig: Gregorius Ritzich, 1631). Scharff (1595–1660) was Professor of Philosophy at Wittenberg, 1627–49 and subsequently Professor of Theology, 1649–1660.

20 Heinrich Julius Scheurl, *Epitome theologiae naturalis* (Wolfenbüttel: Cunrad Bunonis, 1650). Scheurl (1600–1651) was Professor of Moral Philosophy at Helmstedt, 1649–51.

21 Balthasar Cellarius, *Epitome theologiae philosophicae seu naturalis: ex Aristotele & libro de mundo concinnata, scholasticorum doctrina illustrata et cum Scriptura S. collata* (Helmstedt: Henning Müller, 1651). Cellarius (1614–1689) was Professor of Theology at Helmstedt, 1642–1689.

22 Johann Meisner, *Theologia naturalis, tribus disputationibus comprehensa* (Wittenberg: Michael Wendt, 1648). Meisner (1615–1681) was Professor of Theology at Wittenberg, 1650–81.

23 Kilian Rudrauf, *Theologia Naturalis Sive Contemplationum In Primam Philosophiam Duodecas Proposita A M. Kiliano Rudrauff Schott* (Giessen: Joseph Dietrich Hampel, 1657); idem, *Cursus metaphysicus methodicus* (Giessen: Karger, 1664, 1665); idem, *Philosophia theologica, vel Agar Sarae exemplaris, recognita, aucta et emendata* (Giessen: Karger, 1676); and also note idem, *Protheoria Theologica Generalis De Theologia In Genere, Eius Natura Et Constitutione &c. & Specialis De Religione, Symbolis Oecumenicis, Apostolico, Niceno, Athanasiano, Constantinopolitano &c itemque Articulis Fidei, Haeresi Et Haereticis* (Giessen: Karger, 1677). Rudrauf (1627–1690) was Professor of Ethics, Logic, and Metaphysics at Giessen, 1659–75 and Professor of Theology, 1675–90.

24 Johann Christoph Hundeshagen, *Theologia Naturalis* (Jena: Peter Brössel, 1671); also idem, *Metaphysica nova methodo tabulis inclusa* (Jena: Johannes Bielken, 1672); and *Metaphysici commentarii breves de ejusmodi materiis, quae usum insignem in sacrosancta theologia praebent* (Jena: Sengenwald, 1667); also note, idem, *Notitia Dei Naturalis Sive Disputatio Philosophica De Deo, Quatenus Ex Lumine Naturae Cognosci Potest* (Jena: Bauhofer, 1667). Hundeshagen (1635–1681) was Professor of Logic and Metaphysics at Jena.

25 Tobias Pfanner, *Systema theologiae gentilis purioris: qua quam prope ad veram religionem Gentiles accesserint, per cuncta fere eius capita, ex ipsis praecipue illorum scriptis ostenditur* (Basel: Hermann Widerhold, 1679); Pfanner (1641–1716) was a jurist who served in Saalfeld, Weimar, and Gotha.

26 Ulrich Heinsius, *Theologia naturalis a croamatica [...] methodo scientifica pertractata* (Jena: Johannes Meier, 1685). Heinsius (d. 1684) was Professor of Philosophy at Jena.

27 Johann Andreas Schmidt, *Theologia naturalis positiva: ad normam scientiarum practicarum tradita* (Jena: Tobias Öhrlingius, 1689). Schmidt (1652–1726) was Professor of Philosophy and Logic at Jena, 1676–97, after 1695 Professor of Antiquities and Theology at Helmstedt.

28 Christoph Reuchlin, *Erotema Pneumaticvm An detur Theologia naturalis?* (Wittenberg: Henckel, 1684). Reuchlin (1660–ca. 1706) was Professor of Theology at Tübingen after 1692.

29 Johann Paul Hebenstreit, *Theologia naturalis Arminianis imprimis opposita* (Jena: Johann Bielkius, 1696). Hebenstreit (1664–1718) was Professor of Philosophy and, later, Professor of Theology (1710–1718) at Jena.

30 Abraham Calovius, *Scripta Philosophica: I. Gnostologia. II. Noologia, Seu Habitus Intelligentiae. III. Metaphysicae Divinae Pars Generalis. IV. Metaphysicae Divinae Pars Specialis. V. Encyclopaedia Mathematica. VI. Methodologia vel Tractatus De Methodo Docendi Et Disputandi. VII. Ideae Encyclopaedias Disciplinarum Realium, Philosophiam Universam,*

and professors of philosophy, as well as writers – notably Scharff, Rudrauf, and Hebenstreit – who served in both capacities.

If one adopts a chronological perspective on the development of Lutheran philosophical thought, the faculties of Lutheran universities and academies first identified the place of physics in the curriculum (beginning already with Melanchthon),[31] then metaphysics initially in a late sixteenth-century return to commentaries on Aristotle and shortly thereafter in the form of more perspicuously ordered metaphysics following the work of Iavellus, Fonseca, and Suarez,[32] and lastly, in the wake of metaphysics, natural theology.

Arguably, the positive reason for the appearance of distinct natural theologies after the post-Reformation return to a curricular interest in metaphysics was the reconstitution of metaphysics at the hands primarily of Francis Suarez. Suarez's impact on Protestant as well as on Roman thought rested on his detailed synthesis of philosophy and theology in the context of liberating metaphysics from the tradition of commentaries on Aristotle and reorganizing the discipline into a general-special model that discussed first being in general and then specific kinds of being, first God as infinite being and then the being of creatures as finite being. The result of Suarez's method was to deploy natural theology in the second part of metaphysics.[33] Natural theologies that were developed as independent from metaphysics in many cases represent a negative reception of Suarez. There was also a negative or adversative reason for interest in natural theology: the subject itself had been denied by the Socinians and the positive use of philosophy

---

Facultates Superiores, Ut Et Logicam Repraesentantes; Quae partim primum nunc prodeunt, diu multumq[ue] desiderata, Partim revisa & locupletata, ita exhibentur; Ut non minus SS. Theologiae, quam accuratioris Philosophiae cultoribus insigni usui esse queant, simulq[ue] abusum, ac Sophismata varia Socinianorum Calvinianorum & Pontificiorum solide refellant (Rostock: Joachim Wildens, 1651). Calovius (1612–1686) was Professor of Theology at Königsberg (1640–1643), Rector in Danzig (1643–1650); and Professor of Theology at Wittenberg (1650–1686).

31 On which see Sachiko Kusukawa, *The Transformation of Natural Philosophy: The Case of Philip Melanchthon* (Cambridge: Cambridge University Press, 1995).

32 Cf. Karl Eschweiler, "*Die Philosophie der spanischen Spätscholastik auf den deutschen Universitäten des siebzehnten Jahrhunderts*," in *Gesammelte Aufsätze zur Kulturgeschichte Spaniens*, ed., H. Finke (Münster: Aschendorff, 1928), 289–296, 302–309; Ernst Lewalter, *Spanisch-jesuitisch und deutsch-lutherische Metaphysik des 17. Jahrhunderts* (Hamburg, 1935; repr. Darmstadt: Wissenschaftliche Buchgesellschaft, 1967), 21–44. Note Ian Hunter, "The University Philosopher in Early Modern Germany," in *The Philosopher in Early Modern Europe: The Nature of a Contested Identity*, ed., Conal Condren, Stephen Gaukroger, and Ian Hunter (Cambridge: Cambridge University Press, 2006), 35–65, argues the rise of metaphysics in Lutheran circles to have been fueled by an interest in "reconciling natural philosophy and Christological doctrine […] in the service of the Formula of Concord's speculative Christology," 57, even granting that this is a suitable explanation for the rise of metaphysics, it does not explain the development of a distinct pneumatology or natural theology.

33 Cf. José Pereira, *Suárez: Between Scholasticism and Modernity* (Milwaukee: Marquette University Press, 2006), 13–14, 16–17, 28, 53; with Beck, *Early German Philosophy*, 123.

in general had been the subject of a major controversy initiated in the late sixteenth century by Daniel Hofmann, professor of philosophy and later of theology at Helmstedt.[34] Refutations of Hofmann are a common feature of early modern Lutheran natural theologies – indeed, Hofmann's polemics cast a shadow over Lutheran natural theology long into the seventeenth century.

Among Protestant philosophers and theologians, there was both appropriation of and debate over Suarez. Like the Reformed writers of the era, orthodox Lutherans differed over the relationship of natural theology to metaphysics, some following the Suarezian model but others overtly departing from Suarez's model and explicitly constituting natural theology as one branch of "pneumatology," the knowledge or science of spiritual being, not part of metaphysics properly so called.[35] The authors were also generally agreed that referencing natural theology as "theology" rested on Aristotle's usage, but that the discipline rightly understood as a rational exercise was in fact a form of philosophical knowledge.[36] In addition, they shared with Reformed writers very specific apologetic reasons for proposing natural theologies: the proper definition and delimitation of the natural knowledge of God and of natural theology served as a response to the Socinian denial of natural revelation, to the rationalistic tendencies of Arminian or Remonstrant theology, and to the alternative rational theisms often identified as "atheism" in the early modern era.[37]

One approach, echoing Suarez's identification of the disciplines, and following a course previously laid out in the Giessen philosopher, Christoph Scheibler's metaphysics,[38] is quite clear even in the title of Rudrauf's natural theology: it is a contemplative discipline concerned with the specific portion of "first philosophy [*prima philosophia*]" or metaphysics that addresses the

34 On the Hofmann controversy, see Inge Mager, "*Lutherische Theologie und aristotelische Philosophie an der Universität Helmstedt im 16. Jahrhundert. Zur Vorgeschichte des Hofmannischen Streites im Jahre 1598,*" in *Jahrbuch der Gesellschaft für Niedersächsische Kirchengeschichte*, 73 (1975), 83–98; Markus Friedrich, *Die Grenzen der Venunft: Theologie, Philosophie und gelehrte Konflikte am Beispiel des Helmstedter Hofmannstreits und seiner Wirkungen auf das Luthertum um 1600* (Göttingen: Vandenhoeck & Ruprecht, 2004); in the older literature, Ernst Schlee, *Der Streit des Daniel Hofmann ueber das Verhaeltniss der Philosophie zur Theologie: theilweise nach handschriftlichen Quellen* (Marburg: Elwert, 1862); and note Hunter, "University Philosopher," 58–60.

35 Note that there is a similar difference over the content of metaphysics – whether or not God is a proper topic – among Lutheran authors of treatises on metaphysics as well.

36 Cf. Cellarius, *Epitome theologiae philosophicae seu naturalis*, i.5 (5); with Rudrauf, *Theologia Naturalis*, i.3–4 (2); Scheurl, *Epitome theologiae naturalis*, i.1, 4 (3, 4); Fromme, *Isagoge Philosophica*, III (199); Reuchlin, *Erotema Pneumaticum*, art. Iii, fol. B3v; Heinsius, *Theologia naturalis acroamatica*, i.21–22; ii.1 (17–18, 35).

37 Cf. Meisner, *Theologia naturalis*, 7–8, against Socinus and Ostorod; with Hundeshagen, *Theologia naturalis*, i. (6 14), against the atheists.

38 Christoph Scheibler, *Opus metaphysicum, duobus libris universum hujus scientiae systema comprehendens* (Giessen: Chemlinus, 1617); cf. Hunter, "University Philosopher," 62, 63.

knowledge of God and of the divine attributes that is available to human beings by the light of nature – a knowledge confined to "this mortal life," necessarily imperfect, and devoid of the truths of the triune God, the person of Christ, providence, predestination, redemption, and eternal salvation that are accessible only by way of special divine revelation.[39] Further, like Suarez, Rudrauf divides his subject into general and special metaphysics – the former, which occupies the greater part of his work considers being in the abstract, the latter examines specific instances of nonphysical being, namely God, angels, the separable soul, substance and accidents.[40]

This approach is found also in Heinsius's and Schmidt's natural theologies, both of which distinguish between general metaphysics and special metaphysics. Heinsius indicates that the general or first part of metaphysics deals with being in general, whereas the special or second part deals with God, angels, and souls – what is usually identified as metaphysics thus belongs to the first part and natural theology to the second.[41] Schmidt also specifically defined natural theology as an ultimate part of metaphysics,[42] but also (like Gerhard) defined it as a particular form of *theologia viatorum*, resting on the natural light, but by implication a Christian discipline.[43]

Similar assumptions governed Hundeshagen's natural theology despite the absence of any definition of the subject in his *Theologia naturalis*. There he only indicates that natural theology arises from the handiwork of God who produced the "excellent & perfect engine of the world" out of nothing and serves as a preparatory path to revealed theology.[44] In his *Metaphysica*, however, he engages the traditional definitions of the subject, noting that metaphysics can be identified as *philosophia prima* or, as Aristotle indicated, as *theologia*, inasmuch as it considers God, his essence and his attributes, on the basis of principles drawn from nature. The portion of metaphysics concerned with God, however, considers him as a "partial" rather than as an "adequate" object given that it lacks the revelation by which divine mysteries are known.[45]

Another model, running contrary to the Suarezian approach (and contrary to Beck's generalization), found in the works of Scharff, Scheurl, and Fromme, evidences a clear distinction between natural theology and metaphysics. Scharff argues a separate discipline or *scientia* concerning rational spirits, *neumatologia*,

39 Rudrauf, *Theologia Naturalis*, i.4 (2).
40 Rudrauf, *Theologia Naturalis*, i.11–12 (9).
41 Heinsius, *Theologia naturalis acroamatica*, 1–2.
42 Schmidt, *Theologia naturalis positiva*, 2.
43 Schmidt, *Theologia naturalis positiva*, 19.
44 Hundeshagen, *Theologia naturalis*, *Dedicatio* (unpaginated).
45 Hundeshagen, *Metaphysica*, Tabula I (1).

the initial part of which concerns the natural knowledge of God.[46] As to metaphysics properly so called, Scharff defined it as the *universalissimus scientia* which does not, therefore, treat of individual beings, whether specific creatures or God, but rather of the meaning of terms such as *natura, substantia, causa, Unus, Verus*, and *Bonus* that reference being in general and that are applied to God as well as to creatures – which is why, he adds, Aristotle called metaphysics *theologia naturalis.*[47] Scharff, over against Aristotle's definition and contrary to the Suarezian approach, maintained his distinction of the disciplines and did not discuss either the existence or the essence of God in his *Metaphysica*, reserving his own *theologica naturalis* for the initial section of his *Pneumatica* or philosophy of spiritual being.[48] Nor was Scharff alone in separating natural theology from metaphysics. Calovius pointedly restricted the subject of metaphysics to "Being" in its most general sense, defined abstractly and in an undifferentiated manner, or "Being insofar as it is Being" and went on to declare that anyone who included God or immaterial substance in metaphysics to be utterly ignorant and hallucinatory.[49] Fromme also distinguished between *Metaphysica* and *Pneumatica*, while Scheurl defined natural theology as a distinct fourth *scientia*, alongside mathematics, physics, and metaphysics, devoted to the knowledge of "incorporeal substances," namely, God, angels, and the soul.[50]

This careful identification of the nature of the subject was accomplished, moreover, against a backdrop of extensive examination of the philosophical tradition. Aristotle appears as the "Prince of Philosophers" against atheism on the basis of his assumption all things, even brutes, tend toward a goal.[51] Hun-

46 Scharff, *Pneumatica*, 2; cf. Beck, *Early German Philosophy*, 126.

47 Scharff, *Metaphysica exemplaris*, 2–3.

48 Scharff, *Pneumatica*, 2. The clear distinction disciplines can also be seen in Scharff's *Methodus philosophiae peripateticae* (Leipzig: Gregorius Ritzich, 1631), 59–111 (*Metaphysica*); 115–133 (*Pneumatica*), with the *Pneumatica* consisting in 1. *Theologia naturalis*; 2. *Angelographia*; and 3. *Doctrina de animi rationali.* Note the identical understanding of *Pneumatica* in Fromme, *Isagoge Philosophica*, III.ii (209–210).

49 Calovius, *Metaphysica Divina: e principiis primis eruta in abstractione Entis repraesentata, ad SS. Theologiam applicata, monstrans Terminorum, & Conclusionum transcendentium. Usum genuinum abusum haereticum. Pars Generalis* (Rostock: Joachim Wildens, 1650), 951 *[In Scripta Philosophica]: "Hallucinantur proinde, qui vel Deum, vel substantiam immaterialem Objectum Metaphysicae constituunt indolem Sapientiae plane ignorantes. Remove vero omnia Entia determinara, & ad particulares disciplinas dimitte: quid remanebit? Hoc, quod omnibus, quae sunt, commune est; Ens incommuni, sub notione indifferentiae, in abstractione summe, vel quatenus Ens."*

50 Cf. Fromme, *Isagoge Philosophica*, III.i–ii (199–213); Scheurl, *Epitome theologiae naturalis*, i.1 (1). Note that this model also differs from what Hunter, "University Philosopher," 61, describes as "Helmstedt metaphysics [...] as a Zabarellan science of 'being as being'" that included discussion of God's essence and existence – despite Scheurl's presence on the Helmstedt faculty.

51 Hundeshagen, *Theologia naturalis*, 10–11.

deshagen cites Aquinas against the Socinians as arguing that the existence of God is demonstrable *a posteriori* – and as seconded in this by Richard of Middleton, Hervaeus Natalis, Durandus of Sancto Porciano, Johannes Capreolus, Francis de Sylvestris (Ferrariensis), Gregory of Valencia, Luis de Molina, Francis Suarez, Gabriel Vasquez, Thomas di Vio Cardinal Cajetan, Domenico Bañes, Adam Tanner, Alexander Pesantius, "and all Thomists."[52] Thus, in the case of argument against atheists, even Luther's great adversary Cajetan finds a place among the allies. Likewise, in addition to rehearsing ancient philosophical positions and patristic argumentation, Meisner details late medieval and early modern debate over Aquinas' definition of self-evident (*per se nota*) propositions – citing arguments of Duns Scotus, Henry of Ghent, Gregory of Rimini, William of Ockham, Johannes de Rada, and others – before concluding in agreement with Aquinas.[53] Philip de Mornay, a Reformed writer, is cited positively on the issue of the universal consent of humanity to the existence of God,[54] and other Reformed writers, Ludovicus Crocius, Markus Friedrich Wendelin, and Clemens Timpler are identified as in agreement with Flacius Illyricus' *Clavis scripturae* on the point that there is no *notitia Dei innata* but that some knowledge of God can be gained on the basis of natural abilities. Meisner himself advocated a universal, rudimentary innate or engrafted knowledge of God.[55]

In short, Lutheran writers of the early modern era evidence a detailed reception both of the earlier philosophical and theological tradition and of more contemporary works – ranging from the ancients to scholastic theologians of the thirteenth, fourteenth, and fifteenth centuries, to Renaissance philosophers, and to Roman Catholic and Reformed thinkers of the sixteenth and seventeenth centuries, as well as their own Lutheran predecessors and contemporaries. Given, moreover, the shared philosophical foundations and the common apologetic task, the reception was frequently positive.

52 Meisner, *Theologia naturalis*, 8–9.

53 Meisner, *Theologia naturalis*, 9–11.

54 Hundeshagen, *Theologia naturalis*, 7; Meisner, *Theologia naturalis*, 19; Scheurl, *Epitome theologiae naturalis*, i.31 (15).

55 Meisner, *Theologia naturalis*, 12–13, 23–24, 25–25; cf. the comments in Pelikan, "Natural Theology in David Hollaz," 258, who fails to note the distinction between innate knowledge, implanted knowledge, and the ability of fallen human beings to learn something of God by the use of reason.

2. The Natural Theologies: Some Particular Issues

The early modern Lutheran natural theologies, given their differences over the definition of the discipline also evidence a series of significantly different approaches to the content and import of natural theology. We can examine only a sampling here, first looking to the definitions of the subject in the non-Suarezian approaches of Scharff, Scheurl, and Fromme. Of these, Scharf and Fromme specifically identified natural theology as belonging to *pneumatologia* as distinct from *metaphysica.*[56] Their primary concern for doing so appears to be to restrict metaphysics to the discussion of *ens qua ens*, being understood simply as being, indeed, as being in the most general sense.

Johannes Scharff's effort is noteworthy as one of the earliest major Lutheran works on the subject by a thinker who also wrote on sacred and polemical theology, physics and metaphysics. He served first as professor of philosophy at Wittenberg from 1627 to 1649 and as professor of theology from 1649 until his death in 1660. Whereas the larger portion of his theological oeuvre appears to have been devoted to polemics and disputations *pro gradu*, his earlier philosophical efforts beyond the cycle of disputations produced a series of major tomes that served to define the field of study positively. As exemplified in his *Methodus philosophiae peripateticae*, Scharff was intent both on organizing his works using a bifurcatory method that could be drawn up as tables but also, despite the bifurcatory method, on identifying his thought as Peripatetic rather than Ramist.[57]

Contrary to the generalizations found in Pünjer and Beck, Scharff neither identified his natural theology with metaphysics nor assimilated it to the contents of the related dogmatic *loci.* Neither did Scharff work to close the gap between natural and sacred theology by making the former a necessary prologue to the latter - nor, *pace* Pannenberg, did he fail to distinguish between natural knowledge and natural theology! Scharff's two works on metaphysics mention both God and creatures in their discussions of being, and acknowledge that God most eminently possesses the attributes or properties of Being that are discussed in metaphysics - as Aristotle recognized when he identified metaphysics as

56 This definition of discipline is found also in Stephan Klotz's natural theology, a work that I have as yet been unable to obtain. Cellarius' *Epitome theologiae philosophicae* also focuses on spiritual beings, God, angels, and the separable soul, but departs from the typical model by including also a disputation on creation, *De rerum productione, conservatione, ordinaitone et gubernatione* (110–120).

57 Scharff, *Methodus philosophiae*, fol. 2r. On the varieties of Ramism, semi-Ramism, and anti-Ramism among early modern German Reformed and Lutheran writers, see Howard Hotson, *Commonplace Learning: Ramism and its German Ramifications, 1543–1630* (Oxford: Oxford University Press, 2007); also note Joseph S. Freedman, "The Diffusion of the Writings of Ramus in Central Europe, c. 1570–1630," *Renaissance Quarterly* 46, no.1 (1993): 98–152.

theologia naturalis. Still, Scharff focuses his exposition on the contemplation of "Being, insofar as it is Being,"[58] and, accordingly, does not include distinct expositions of either divine or creaturely existences in either of his works on the subject. His fairly standard division of metaphysics into the categories of general and special, qualified as a distinction between *communis* and *propria*, moreover, deals in the former portion with being and its universal attributes, and in the latter with the concepts of genus and species, substance and accidents.[59] This approach to the division of metaphysics stands as an implicit rejection of Suarez's division of the subject into discussions of infinite and finite being, with a philosophical doctrine of God constituting the first division.[60]

The scope of Scharff's natural theology was determined by his primary decision to identify "pneumatology," the philosophy concerned with spiritual beings, as distinct from metaphysics. He begins with an initial "book" on the "nature of spirits in general," and then divides the remainder of his work into three books or sections, his second book dealing with the knowledge, existence, and attributes of God, the third book with the nature of finite spiritual being, specifically of angels, and the fourth and final book with the rational soul. The same division of the subject appears in Scheurl's *Epitome* and Fromme's *Isagoge*. This definition of natural theology as the first part of pneumatology served to restrict the contents of natural theology to the rational doctrine of God, his existence and attributes – eliminating consideration of not only of finite spiritual being but also of creation from natural theology proper.

Whereas Scheurl did not offer any detailed explanation of the anti-Suarezian approach, Scharff and Fromme certainly did, making a pointed distinction between "the thing [or object] considered, and the manner of considering" it.[61] The discussion of God belongs to metaphysics insofar as God is a being and, accordingly, as being, is one true, good, independent, and so forth, but this recognition in no way removes a distinct philosophical *scientia* concerning God as its proper object. Metaphysics does not address specific spiritual beings – that is

58 Scharff, *Metaphysica exemplaris*, 3, citing Aristotle, *Metaphysica*, VI.i.

59 Scharff, *Metaphysica exemplaris*, 5; so also, Daniel Stahl, *Metaphysica In qua Generalissimi non solum, sed etiam Specialissimi termini & distinctiones accurate explicantur, Controversiae dilucide tractantur, Et Metaphysicae usus in diversis disciplinis, praecipue Theologia breviter ostenditur* (Frankfurt: s.n., 1652).

60 Francis Suarez, *Metaphysicarum disputationum, in quibus et universa naturalis theologia ordinate traditur*, 2 vols. (Cologne: Franciscus Helvidius, 1614), II: disp. xxviii–xxx. Note that Suarez's argument depends on his conception of the univocity of being – with which Scharff appears to disagree, on the ground that the *modus* of divine being differs infinitely from the *modus* of finite being: cf. Scharff, *Methodus philosophiae*, 65. The nominally "Scotist" concept of the univocity of being was widely rejected in Protestant circles in the early modern era; cf. Richard A. Muller, "Not Scotist: Understandings of Being, Univocity, and Analogy in Early Modern Reformed Thought," *Reformation and Renaissance Review* 14, no.2 (2012): 125–148.

61 Scharff, *Pneumatica*, 13–15.

the task of Pneumatics – but only addresses God as the "primary analogate" in its discussion of being as such, with the analogy clearly not of proportion but of proportionality. Scharff's referencing God as *analogatum primarium* in discourse on being assumes that being is predicated analogically, not univocally – a point against both the Scotist notion of the univocity of being and the Suarezian division of being into infinite and finite.[62]

Pneumatica, therefore, is a distinct discipline and not a part of metaphysics – and natural theology is a division of *Pneumatica*. Scharff and Fromme offer several reasons for this separation of disciplines: metaphysics rightly treats only of being in general; the Scotist and Suarezian concepts of the univocity of being were to be rejected; and metaphysics cannot, therefore, include discussion of individual spiritual beings.[63] In Fromme's view, moreover, Aristotle's equation of metaphysics with theology was untenable, given the extreme poverty of natural reason in understanding spiritual matters, in particular, truths concerning God.[64]

In discussing the sources of natural theology, neither Scharff, nor Scheurl, nor Fromme argues a distinction between natural and supernatural revelation – rather their distinction is between natural knowledge (*notitia naturalis*) or the light of nature (*lumen naturae*) as the source of natural theology and divine revelation as the basis for revealed theology. Revelation, in other words, is not a category that appears in their natural theologies.[65] Pannenberg's critique, therefore, does not quite apply to these thinkers inasmuch as they do distinguish between natural knowledge as source and natural theology as the discipline or *scientia* based on natural knowledge of God and, by implication, reserve the category of divine revelation for sacred theology. True, this natural knowledge and its theological development is compatible with human nature – but to say that the adjective "natural" references human nature and not the divine nature is also not quite to the point, given that "natural" references primarily the source of the knowledge but the result does argue something of the nature of God.

Neither do these three non-Suarezian writers identify natural theology as a basis for or necessary prologue to sacred theology – rather, as a form of philosophy, it remains ancillary to the task of sacred theology. In Scharff's detailed division of the disciplines, philosophy must be clearly distinguished from "the other higher faculties," standing higher than the instrumental disciplines of

62 Scharff, *Pneumatica*, 14–15; also Fromme, *Isagoge Philosophica*, III.ii (212); cf. the argumentation in Jacob Martini, *Disputationum metaphysicarum decima quarta, de divisione entis in intinitum et finitum* (Wittenberg: Martin Henchel, 1610), q.3, where univocity of being is rejected in favor of a Thomistic understanding of analogy.

63 Scharff, *Pneumatica, proemium*, 3–4.

64 Fromme, *Isagoge Philosophica*, III.ii (211–212).

65 Cf. Scharff, *Pneumatica, proemium* (2), II.i (55–58); with Scheurl, *Epitome theologiae naturalis*, i.11–12, 21, 23, 24 (6, 9, 10–11); and Fromme, *Isagoge Philosophica*, III.ii (210).

grammar, rhetoric, poetics, languages and logic, but lower than revealed theology, jurisprudence, and medicine.[66]

Among these writers who followed the alternative more Suarezian pattern, Kilian Rudrauf's approach is significant both for its scope and for his clear placement of natural theology into a larger theological project that moved on to both sacred and polemical theology. The word *theology* itself, he indicates, is homonymous, having a series of distinct meanings and represented in pairs of distinctions – such as true and false theology, natural and supernatural, archetypal and ectypal, perfect and imperfect, and so forth. Ectypal or finite but true theology also takes on a series of forms – among them catechetical, practical, homiletical, didactic, polemical.[67] Once false theology and partial definitions are ruled out and the fallen human condition is taken into consideration, the right definition of theology can be formulated, albeit in two ways, either *accidentaliter* or *essentialiter*, namely, either as exemplified incidentally in teaching or instruction or as defined for what it is according to the divine intention in and for human beings.[68]

The primary definition, then, is the essential and subjective: theology is a God-given practical habit or disposition of the soul, drawn from the revealed word, instructing sinful human beings concerning things to be believed and things to be done. It is the presentation of true religion for the sake of eternal salvation and the celebration of God's glory – or, more simply, a supernatural disposition of believing in God to the end of life eternal.[69] The secondary definition of theology "systematically and incidentally (*accidentaliter*) considered" is as "*doctrina* drawn out of the word of God."[70] Rudrauf, then, makes a clear distinction between the discipline of theology and the practice of religion as well as indicating their necessary connection.

Although he adopts the Suarezian model of including natural theology in metaphysics or "first philosophy," Rudrauf echoes Scharff's phrasing, rejecting a Suarezian view of the univocity of being and explicitly noting that *ens* is to be understood "equivocally & by analogy" given the different modes of the being of things.[71] Where Rudrauf comes closest the Suarezian approach is his integration of his discussion or as he calls it *contemplatio* of the divine essence and attributes into the broader presentation of metaphysics, as the dividing point between his discussion of "substance in general" and his identification of kinds (*species*) of being or substance, beginning with God as the "most noble" and moving on the

66 Scharff, *Methodus philosophiae*, 3.
67 Rudrauf, *Protheoria theologica*, 2, 3.
68 Rudrauf, *Protheoria theologica*, 5.
69 Rudrauf, *Protheoria theologica*, 4–5.
70 Rudrauf, *Protheoria theologica*, 5.
71 Rudrauf, *Cursus metaphysicus, De ente rationis*, ii, nota 1.

discussion of angels and the separable soul.[72] His inclusion of God in metaphysics comes with a clear distinction of what can be known by way of the natural light and what belongs to revelation alone (and is thereby excluded from metaphysics).[73] The contemplation is quite brief, citing only Suarez and Mendoza and arguing the existence of God by denying infinite regress of causes.[74]

Rudrauf reacts explicitly to the denial of natural theology by the Socinians and the double truth theory of Daniel Hofmann. He insists on the existence of natural theology and denies that, rightly argued, natural theology can contradict supernatural or revealed theology.[75] Taken together the two assertions – first against the Socinians, then against Hofmann – lead to a declaration of the proper place and use of the rational disciplines, in this case, natural theology. Rational efforts are not to be excluded, Rudrauf indicates, but are in fact presupposed as means or instruments. What is excluded is the use of rational principles as the sole and sufficient means of attaining truths.[76]

With Hundeshagen, writing in 1671, we do come to a clear statement that natural theology stands prior to revealed theology and even "prepares a way toward it." There is also, however, the comment that Scripture itself "recommends" natural theology, given the vast number of things found in the books of Moses, Job, Psalms, and even the New Testament, that can draw on natural theology for explanation. Given, moreover, that natural theology rests on the work of God in the created order and arises from the most basic encounter of rational beings with the divine handiwork, it has a certain priority: natural knowledge precedes revelation and revelation presumes its existence. Even so, natural theology indicates both that God exists and that he must be worshiped. Accordingly, natural theology provides a basis for debate with "pagans & profane persons."[77] These latter points provide Hundeshagen with his argument that natural theology prepares the way for revealed theology. He does not indicate that natural theology is necessary to the justification and presentation of sacred or revealed theology.

Despite its differences with Scharff, Scheurl, and Fromme, Hundeshagen's *Theologia naturalis* largely observes their distinction between natural theology and the discussions of finite spiritual beings. Of its twenty chapters, seventeen are concerned with the divine existence and attributes, with the decrees of God standing as a sub-category of the divine will. An eighteenth chapter discusses divine providence and then, in what is rather unique among the natural theol-

72 Rudrauf, *Theologia naturalis*, xiv (189).
73 Rudrauf, *Theologia naturalis*, xiv (189–190).
74 Rudrauf, *Theologia naturalis*, xiv (190).
75 Rudrauf, *Protheoria theologica*, 21.
76 Cf. Rudrauf, *Protheoria theologica*, 25.
77 Hundeshagen, *Theologia naturalis*, *Dedicatio* (unpaginated).

ogies of the era, two final chapters raise the issues of demonic capabilities – foreknowledge and power. There is no definition of natural theology provided and its relationship to metaphysics is left unclear. Hundeshagen refrains from engaging in separate topical discussions of the existence, essence, and attributes of God and specific finite spiritual beings in his metaphysics, even though he indicates briefly that these topics belong to "special metaphysics."[78] On the other hand, the collection of five academic dissertations under various professors collected by Hundeshagen as *Metaphysici commentarii breves* includes two dissertations on God (unity and goodness) and one on the separable soul, with the intention that these philosophical discussions might be useful to sacred theology.[79]

The natural theology published in 1689, while Johann Andreas Schmidt was still serving a professor of Logic and Philosophy at Jena, provides in its initial "apparatus" a significant bibliographical approach to the various traditionary and contemporary philosophical approaches, ranging from the ancients, to the fathers and medievals, to contemporary proponents of the ancient philosophical "sects," to early modern theological and philosophical writers of the major confessional affiliations.[80] Schmidt's work offers some indication of the inroads of rationalism into the theologies of the era in its highly recommendatory approach to the discipline and assumption that natural theology actually teaches that human perfection "consists in the imitation of God & the conformity of our life with the life of God" – even though human beings consistently neglect the means provided to achieve this end, stand guilty before God, and cannot be saved apart from the expiation of their sins.[81]

Schmidt's "positive" presentation of natural theology as a "practical" form of philosophical knowing begins with the assertion that the "universal scope of philosophy" is to inquire concerning the self and God.[82] As to natural theology itself, it is a philosophical discipline related to the disciplines of logic, metaphysics, physics, and mathematics – with logic providing rules for argument and demonstration; metaphysics dealing with God and immaterial substance in its final, special section; physics and mathematics providing the basis for demonstrations of the existence of God. Given these relationships, the "office" of natural

78 Johann Christoph Hundeshagen, *Metaphysica nova methodo tabulis inclusa, quoad parten generalem et specialem cum discursu perpetuo cuilibet tabulae proxime subjecto* (Jena: Johannes Bielken, 1672), 2.

79 Johann Christoph Hundeshagen, *Metaphysici commentarii breves de ejusmodi materiis, quae usum insignem in sacrosancta theologia praebent* (Jena: Sengenwald, 1667).

80 Schmidt, *Theologia naturalis positiva*, apparatus, §iii (4–14).

81 Schmidt, *Theologia naturalis positiva*, pars tertia, §xvii–xviii (143–144).

82 Schmidt, *Theologia naturalis positiva*, introductory address, first leaf.

theology is the explanation, testing, and defense of truths concerning God.[83] Further, it is a practical knowing, available to fallen or "pilgrim" human beings (*homini viatori*), that conduces (as Hundeshagen also stated) to the knowledge and worship of God.[84] Schmidt even goes so far as to argue that, in its three parts, natural theology deals with God in his essence and essential perfections, as the object (*obiectum*) and goal (*finis*) of humanity; with human beings as the subject of the practical effort (*subiectum operationis*) directed toward eternal happiness; and with the means to that end, namely the knowledge and worship of God.[85]

By definition natural theology is an account (*ratio*) or deliverance (*oratio*) concerning divine things, resting on the "light of nature," an acquired form of knowing drawing on natural foundations or *principia*.[86] Schmidt's relatively optimistic assumptions concerning the scope of natural theology and the rational capacities of its human "subjects" leads him to a pointed attack on the Cartesian principle of doubt and its corollary that truth consists in "clear & distinct" knowledge as conducive to ignorance.[87] Over against Descartes, Schmidt declares that God is utterly knowable (*maxime cognoscibilis*) by the light of nature through implanted and acquired knowledge (*notitia insita/acquisita*), as evidenced by the testimony of conscience and the universal consent of mankind.[88] The Cartesian proof of the existence of God, however, is defective and absurd – the presence of an idea in the mind in no way requires the existence of the being in actuality. Rather, reflecting the older largely Peripatetic tradition, the existence of God is to be demonstrated *posteriori* – and that in several ways, such as from ontological "motion," from ontological dependence, from contingency, by way of degrees of perfection, and so forth.[89]

Hebenstreit's natural theology, composed of extended *exercitationes* or discourses in the form of disputations for degrees and published at the close of the seventeenth century, draws out a paradigm for the understanding of theology in dialogue and some dispute with the ground-breaking theological prolegomenon, *De vere theologia*, written by Franciscus Junius of Leiden a century earlier. Like Junius, Hebenstreit allows a distinction between theology *in se*, in itself or as

83 Schmidt, *Theologia naturalis positiva*, apparatus, §i–ii (1–3).

84 Schmidt, *Theologia naturalis positiva*, §iii (19).

85 Schmidt, *Theologia naturalis positiva*, §iv (23); cf. ibid., *Pars prima* (24ff), *Pars secunda* (117ff), and *Pars tertia* (132ff).

86 Schmidt, *Theologia naturalis positiva*, natura & constitutione, §i (17).

87 Schmidt, *Theologia naturalis positiva*, pars prima, §ii (28), citing positively the anti-Cartesian works of two Reformed writers, Paulus Voetius, *Theologia naturalis refomata* (Utrecht: Johannes à Waesberge, 1656) and Petrus van Mastricht, *Novitatum Cartesianum Gangrena, nobiliores plerasque corporis theologici partes arrodens et exedens, seu theologia Cartesiana detecta* (Amsterdam: Jansson, 1677).

88 Schmidt, *Theologia naturalis positiva*, pars prima, §iii–vi (29, 30, 34–35, 36).

89 Schmidt, *Theologia naturalis positiva*, pars prima, §vi (36–51).

such, and theology as argued by human beings, yielding the recognition that natural or philosophical theology in itself is "true and certain."[90] Hebenstreit also continues to reference the double truth theory of Daniel Hofmann and the opposing views of Albert Grawer and Bartholomaeus Keckermann – the former defending philosophy as neither Socinian nor Calvinist, the latter arguing against a theory of double truth.[91]

The scope of Hebenstreit's work reflects the general tendency of Lutheran writers of the early modern era to restrict natural theology to a rational or philosophical doctrine of God, to the exclusion of discourse concerning finite spirits and the created order. After three initial discourses on the nature of natural theology and contents of natural theology, its insufficiency for salvation, and the natural knowledge of God, Hebenstreit examines names of God, proofs of God's existence, and the divine essence. He then turns to a discourse on the foundation of *principium* of natural theology, and from there to discourses on those attributes of God that are capable of rational derivation: infinity, immensity and omnipresence, unity, simplicity, immutability, eternity, knowledge, and wisdom.

Hebenstreit's proofs begin with the assumption that among Christians the existence of God is presupposed rather than proved, but that proofs are necessary given atheistic denials of the existence of God.[92] For Hebenstreit the question of "whether God exists" debated between Lutherans and the atheists of the day extends beyond the simple grammar of the question to ask whether there truly is a noblest and first Being who exists of himself, upon whom the entire universe depends, and by whom it is governed – and whether the existence of this Being can be known and validly proved by the light of nature.[93] Hebenstreit's proofs, like those noted of other Lutheran writers of the era are *a posteriori* and, despite the late date of his work, maintain a noteworthy continuity with the traditionary conversation, including Aristotle, the church fathers, Aquinas, the second scholasticism of the preceding seventeenth century, and various Reformed

90 Hebenstreit, *Theologia naturalis*, i, thesis16 (25); cf. i, thesis 15 (21–25) for the discussion of Junius.

91 Hebenstreit, *Theologia naturalis*, i, theses 18–19 (29–30), referencing Albertus Grawer, *Libellus De Unica Veritate. Addita sunt nonnulla ejusdem Argumenti […] Cornelii Martini […], Duncani Liddelii* (Weimar: Weidner, 1619); and probably Bartholomaeus Keckermann, *Brevis et simplex consideratio controversiae hoc tempore a nonnullis motae, de pugna Philosophiae & Theologiae*, in *Operum omnium quae extant*, 2 vols. (Geneva: Petrus Aubertus, 1614), I, col. 68–74; cf. on Grawer, see Pünjer, *History of the Christian Philosophy of Religion*, 181; on Keckermann, see Richard A. Muller, "*Vera Philosophia cum sacra Theologia nusquam pugnat:* Keckermann on Philosophy, Theology and the Problem of Double Truth," in *Sixteenth Century Journal* 15, no.3 (1984): 341–365.

92 Hebenstreit, *Theologia naturalis*, v, thesis 2 (189–190).

93 Hebenstreit, *Theologia naturalis*, v, thesis 2 (195–196).

writers sometimes negatively (as one would expect) but often in terms of their agreement against the more rationalistic tendencies of the era.[94]

3. Conclusions

As indicated at the outset, this essay has provided only a preliminary glance at early modern Lutheran natural theology. That brief glance not only offers an indication of the significant productivity of Lutheran writers in what they held to be a form of philosophy, it also offers a sense of the detailed, critical reception of the older tradition of natural theology. The Lutheran natural theologies examined in this essay all stood in relation to the older tradition of Christian Peripateticism; all recognized and reckoned with the ancient philosophical heritage in which many rational truths about God were understood; all drew selectively on the medieval and early modern scholastic tradition of language concerning the existence, essence, and attributes of God; and all operated on the assumption that human reason, albeit limited and incapable of delving unaided into doctrines concerning salvation, was nonetheless a gift of God and, as such, capable of yielding correct conclusions concerning the being of God. All also understood natural theology, given its grounding in human reason, to be a form of philosophy. They drew both broadly and deeply on the entire older tradition and resisted the inroads of the new rationalisms – perhaps less in the case of Schmidt than of the other theologians and philosophers noted.

In some contrast with various Reformed natural theologies of the era, in which such topics as creation and the soul were regularly discussed, the Lutheran natural theologies tended for the most part to restrict their discussions to the rational or philosophical doctrine of God, thereby restricting natural theology to the nominally metaphysical topic of infinite spiritual being even when the discipline was clearly distinguished from metaphysics properly so called. This absence of a discussion of creation served to separate Lutheran natural theology from developments in physics or natural philosophy, and, arguably, to maintain its connection to the older tradition of proofs of the existence of God and of philosophical discussion of the divine essence and attributes.

One can, of course, note the rather pronounced discontinuity with Luther simply by the engagement of Lutheran writers in the topic of natural theology, indeed, of metaphysics. What these writers did not do, however, was step outside the boundaries of their confessional orthodoxy, nor did they confuse sacred theology with natural theology. Their work also evidences what can only be called a broad sense of the catholicity of their enterprise, specifically to be noted in their

94 Hebenstreit, *Theologia naturalis*, v, thesis 2 (e.g., 181, 187, 191–194, 199–212).

appropriation of the tradition and their approach to contemporary materials in defense of Christian rationality against what they understood to be the atheistic tendencies and philosophical aberrations of their time. The absence of clear connection between this Lutheran philosophical theology (or theological philosophy) and the new rationalisms of the seventeenth century undercuts the modern claim that this form of natural theology served as a prologue to the Enlightenment.

Paul Robinson

"One Foot Already Out of the Grave": Luther Preaches the Resurrection

Martin Luther stood in the pulpit of St. Mary's, the city church in Wittenberg.[1] It was Sunday afternoon, November 3, 1532, and he was not quite halfway through his series of sermons on 1 Cor 15. He had been speaking for only a few minutes of what was likely a half hour sermon when he said something like this:

> But a Christian has already been thrust into death by the very fact that he became a Christian. Wherever he may be he occupies himself with this hourly [...]. However, he enjoys the advantage of already being out of the grave with his right leg. Moreover, he has a mighty helper who holds out His hand to him, namely, his Lord Christ; He has left the grave entirely a long time ago, and now he takes the Christian by the hand and pulls him more than halfway out of the grave; only the left foot remains in it.[2]

This idea, that the Christian who is looking forward to the resurrection already has one foot out of the grave, memorably captures how Luther understood the resurrection. For him, the resurrection of the believer could not be bound to the future any more than Christ's resurrection could be contained by the past. Instead, both spilled over into the present, forming and informing every aspect of Christian faith and life.

Luther scholars generally agree that the events of 1532 had a profound impact on the Reformer's series of sermons on 1 Cor 15 begun in that year – not only with regard to the content of these sermons but with the choice of the Apostle Paul's great resurrection chapter as the text. Luther himself was quite ill at the time. In fact, illness would keep him from the pulpit in the city church almost entirely for the two years following these sermons. Reading the sermons, one can easily

1 The precise place of preaching is not indicated for each sermon in this series in the critical edition, though Luther's Sunday afternoon preaching was routinely done at St. Mary's. Caspar Cruciger, in his dedication of the published sermons to Elector John Frederick, suggested that some of them were delivered in the Castle Church. WA 36:xxxiii.

2 LW 28:133; WA 36:581b (Note that lowercase letters are used, as in the Weimar online edition, to indicate which text is being cited where more than one is available. I have used the LW translation when available and given the corresponding reference in WA. Where a note references only WA, the translation is my own).

imagine Luther preaching to himself the comforting doctrine of the resurrection of the dead. In addition, Elector John the Steadfast had died on August 16, less than a week after Luther's first sermon in the series. Such a public death and funeral meant that death was on everyone's mind. Moreover, the critical nature of the succession of John's son, John Frederick, in times of trouble with the emperor and the pope added uncertainty and anxiety to the grief elicited by the Elector's passing. So, in response, Luther preached eloquently on the resurrection.

As a result of this meeting of text and occasion, Luther's 1 Cor 15 sermons of 1532–1533 mark a high point in his treatment of the resurrection of the body, specifically the resurrection to eternal life promised to believers in Christ. Yet the themes he expounded in these sermons were by no means new, but had informed his preaching on resurrection, both Christ's and the believer's, in the past and would continue to be present in his future preaching, particularly when he returned to 1 Cor 15 as a text. Similar themes can be found, for example, in Luther's many sermons for the Easter season. They were also present when he preached on 1 Cor 15 again in 1544–1545.[3]

Through an examination of these sermons, this study analyzes key themes in Luther's preaching on the resurrection. Three categories that capture, though certainly do not exhaust, Luther's emphases form the structure for this analysis: faith, the body, and proclamation.

1. Faith

Faith, as might be expected, often stands at the center of Luther's explanation of how resurrection functions in the life of the Christian. Yet many of Luther's sermons on the resurrection began by elaborating the opposite of faith, that is, doubt, or at least insolent and impious questioning. The motif of skepticism concerning the resurrection is suggested by the text of 1 Cor 15:35 itself, since Paul wrote, "But someone will ask, 'How are the dead raised? With what kind of body will they come?'" (ESV) Paul, in his day, had to deal with scoffers and skeptics, and Luther rose to the challenge of identifying their kindred spirits in his own times. He frequently preached on these very words: "But someone will ask, 'How are the dead raised?'"

3 His five sermons on the text from those years, four of which were collected and published much later, seem to have been intended as a serial treatment, even though they were not given on successive Sundays as were most of the sermons of 1532–1533.

It may or may not come as a surprise that Luther frequently identified the pope and cardinals as skeptics of this sort. On the Wednesday after Easter in 1529, Luther had this to say about faith in the resurrection:

> For this reason there is even today a great lacking of faith in this article, so that there are only a few who believe the article of the resurrection of the body. Especially in Italy and among the nobility and big shots it is a ridiculous sermon that there should be a resurrection of the dead, and they mock: 'Do you think that one fellow is hiding in another? Don't you think when you have died that the soul leaves the body like a pea from a pod?'[4]

Here Luther calls out the Italians, though identifying these mockers generically as "nobility and big shots" (*bey dem adel* is the phrase in Rörer's notes) rather than specifically as churchmen.[5] The Italian Platonists, such as Pico della Mirandola, have been named as the possible source of such ideas.[6] Pico was a humanist active in the Platonist revival and, indeed, a likely source of such attitudes among the nobility. Specifically, the Platonist idea of the transmigration of souls is reflected in the phrase *the soul leaves the body like a pea from a pod.* Such ideas were far from uncommon among churchmen interested in philosophy.

Indeed, two years later, Luther specifically accused the pope and the cardinals of mocking the idea of the resurrection. In his 1531 Easter sermon he said,

> This is the article that's the laughing-stock of the whole world. The pope and the cardinals make fun of it because it's foolish according to reason to say that there are other things after this life. They are Plinians. And in our territories, they consider the article to be fool's work and for the same reason hinder it, so that it does not enter into the heart as deeply as necessary.[7]

By calling the pope and cardinals *Plinians*, Luther identified the first-century Roman naturalist Pliny the Elder as the source of their mockery. In his *Natural History* (*Naturalis Historia*), Pliny had called ideas about the immortality of the soul "fictions of childish absurdity." He went on to say, "Similar also is the vanity about preserving men's bodies, and about Democritus's promise of our coming

4 WA 29: 325–326a. Translation from *The 1529 Holy Week and Easter Sermons of Dr. Martin Luther*, trans., Irving L. Sandberg, annotated by Timothy J. Wengert (St. Louis: Concordia Academic Press, 1999), 170.

5 WA 29: 326a.

6 See Timothy Wengert's note in *The 1529 Holy Week and Easter Sermons of Dr. Martin Luther*, 176.

7 *Is articulus est, qui est ludibrio toti mundo. Papa et Cardinales haben ein ludibrium draus, quia rationi stultum dicere, quod post hanc vitam sit alia. Sunt Pliniani. Et in nostris regionibus helt den artikel fur narrenwerck et ipsa ratio wehret, ut non so tieff ein ghe in cor, ut necessarium.* WA 34.1: 273a.

to life again – who did not come to life again himself. Plague take it, what is this mad idea that life is renewed by death?"[8]

With his *Plinian* accusation against the pope and cardinals, Luther may be referring to the relatively recent controversy surrounding Pietro Pomponazzi, a Bolognese professor of philosophy. Pomponazzi defied the 1513 decree of Lateran V by asserting that the authentic teaching of Aristotle was that the human soul was in its essence mortal rather than immortal. Two of Luther's opponents, Cajetan and Sylvester Prierias, were drawn into the ensuing controversy. Cajetan, in fact, had earlier stated the very opinion held by Pomponazzi, demonstrating that even leaders in the church were debating the nature of the soul, and with it the nature of the resurrection, at least within the realm of philosophy.[9]

It is perhaps not surprising that Luther quoted Pliny again in connection to the resurrection in his sermon for Cantate, the Fourth Sunday of Easter, in 1544. In this sermon, he speculated that those mentioned by Paul in 1 Cor as doubters of the resurrection were none other than the Sadducees. To this identification, he added a confirming observation: "As Pliny also says: those who say that people will live again [after death] are genuine rascals."[10] Luther's point seems to be that in the first century, as the Apostle Paul experienced, the resurrection of the body was a hard sell.

Yet in Luther's own day this was hardly the case, notwithstanding his accusations to the contrary. Renaissance humanists, both laymen and clerics, would have known – or at least known of – Pliny's, Pico's, and Pomponazzi's texts, and Luther seems to identify mockery of the resurrection of the dead with certain Platonic or Aristotelian revival schools of Italian humanism. Nevertheless, it is unlikely that more than a few people in the sixteenth century, even in Italy, doubted the idea of life after death as had Pliny.[11] Luther may be referring more to questions concerning the relationship of the soul to the body, and thus questions concerning the resurrection of the body, than to doubts about immortality generally.

His aim, at any rate, was not to reproduce such arguments accurately but to use them as a foil to his presentation of faith in the resurrection. He had begun his 1544 Cantate sermon by reiterating the connection made in the text between

8 *Naturalis Historia* VII, LV. Quotation from Pliny, *Natural History*, Loeb Classics Library (Cambridge: Harvard University Press, 1942), 2:635.

9 See especially Michael Tavuzzi, "Silvestro da Prierio and the Pomponazzi Affair," *Renaissance and Reformation* XIX (1995): 47–61.

10 *[W]ie auch Plinius sagt: Ey es sind ettliche buben, die sagen, es werden die leut lebendig &c.* WA 49: 398a.

11 See for example, Paul Oskar Kristeller, "The Myth of Renaissance Atheism and the French Tradition of Free Thought," *Journal of the History of Philosophy* 6 (1968): 233–243; Lucien Febvre, *The Problem of Unbelief in the Sixteenth Century: The Religion of Rabelais*, trans., Beatrice Gottlieb (Cambridge, MA: Harvard University Press, 1982).

Christ's resurrection and that of all believers. From this he concluded, "If you don't believe your own resurrection, then you can't believe Christ's resurrection."[12]

Luther emphasized the absolute faith Christians should have that they will rise to eternal life over against the medieval understanding that Christians remain lifelong pilgrims, that is, that they are heading toward the goal of eternal life with God but are uncertain about whether they will reach it. For this reason, his preaching on the resurrection often had more to do with faith or with other aspects of the Christian life than it did with heaven or the resurrection itself. The 1532–1533 sermons on 1 Cor 15 are a notable exception to this generalization, because in them Luther engages in an extended treatment – I am tempted to say, wild speculation – about the nature of the risen body.

2. The Body

In his sermon on January 19, 1533, Luther explained what Paul meant when he wrote to the Corinthians that the body was "sown in weakness" but would be "raised in power." As Luther elaborated, he painted the resurrected body in bright colors to contrast strongly with the weakness and corruptibility of bodies in this sinful world.

> We, however, know that later and at the proper time the body, weak and devoid of all strength and power though it may now be when it lies in the grave, will be so strong that with one finger it will be able to carry this church, with one toe it will be able to move a tower and play with a mountain as children play with a ball. And in the twinkling of an eye it will be able to leap to the clouds or traverse a hundred miles. For then the body will be sheer strength, as it is now sheer feebleness and weakness. Nothing that it decided to do will be impossible for it. It will be able to defeat the whole world alone. It will become so light and nimble that it will soar both down here on earth and up above in the heavens in a moment.[13]

This description of the body occurs at a pivotal point in the logic of Luther's sermon series. It serves as a bridge between his portrayal of life in heaven and his detailed explanation of what Paul means by a "spiritual body." The body described above is simply the opposite of the body a person experiences on earth. Yet it is also a reasonable, if somewhat playful, foray into demonstrating what a "spiritual" as opposed to "physical" body might be.

12 *Drumb gleubstu dein aufferstehung nit, so kanstu auch nit gleuben Christi aufferstehung.* WA 49: 396a.

13 Fourteenth sermon, January 19, 1533. LW 28: 188; WA 36: 657b.

Luther's descriptions of the resurrection body extend and expand upon his understanding of life in heaven as being in many ways the opposite of life here on earth rather than any sort of continuation of it. Sometimes his depictions of the differences between earth and heaven have a firm grounding in the inner logic of the distinction between creation and new creation. For example, he distinguished between nature and office in order to explain which aspects of life would remain in eternity and which would prove transient. So the body itself and its members remain but the use to which those members are put does not. Luther explained that everything belonging to temporal life would disappear in the resurrection.

> For a person's position as manservant, maidservant, father, mother, lord, prince, king is not something that was created, but that is a regulation regarding the creature. Therefore, only what was created in man, the different members, will remain, but these will no longer be employed for the bodily needs as they are now. It will no longer be necessary to eat, to drink, to digest, to sweep, to live with husband or with wife, to beget children, to cultivate the fields, to rule home or city. In short, all that pertains to the essence of these temporal goods and is part of temporal life and works will cease to be.[14]

Whether or not one might agree with the particulars of this portrayal, the logic is nevertheless clear. In an earlier sermon in the series, however, Luther had constructed the distinction between heaven and earth based not on the distinction between nature and office but seemingly as a response to human desires.

> Now just consider what you would like to have or what you might wish for. Would you like to have money and goods, and abundance of food and drink, a long life, a healthy body, beautiful clothes, a nice dwelling, eternal joy and delight, furthermore perfect wisdom and a knowledge of all things, dominion, and honor? Just look there; there you will receive enough of everything. God will clothe you more beautifully than any emperor was ever clothed, indeed, more beautifully than the sun and all jewels. If you aspire to be a lord, He will grant you more than you can wish for. If you want to possess acute sight and hearing that reaches farther than a hundred miles, if you want to be able to see through walls and stone, if you wish to be so light as to be in any place of your choice in a moment, down below on earth or up above near the clouds – that will be granted you. And whatever else you might think of and desire for body and soul, you shall have in rich measure when you have God.[15]

Whether or not he realized it, Luther was preaching this on the afternoon of his 49th birthday. What he did realize was that he was old and increasingly ill, and his physical condition may well have shaped some of his language about the body before and after the resurrection.

In the examples quoted so far, Luther's ideas about heaven and the body seem, at least in part, to respond to the conditions of life in the sixteenth century. In a

14 Twelfth sermon, December 8, 1532, Second Sunday in Advent. LW 28: 172; WA 36: 634b.
15 Ninth sermon on the afternoon of November 10, 1532. LW 28: 144; WA 36: 595–596b.

time when life was difficult due to hard work, rampant disease, and what we now euphemistically call "food insecurity," the idea of resting – or playing, as the earlier quote might indicate – eternally in a body that did not experience these things would have proved irresistible. So Luther excludes from heaven even eating, which for us might be considered an enjoyable activity, because for most people in his day it was a chore rather than a pleasure. Acquisition and preparation of food required enormous amounts of labor – and that was when food was readily available.

Absent extensive and specific descriptions of heaven in Scripture, Christians in every age have pictured it in a way that responds to their concerns about this life and the one to come. Two more recent examples will help to demonstrate this point. During the Civil War most families in America experienced the death of a family member or friend. The burning questions became, Will we know these people in heaven? Will we be with them again as family and friends? The desire to answer those questions affirmatively created a picture of heaven that was cozy and domestic – a better version of life at home here on earth.[16] In the United States today, we seem to be preoccupied with the meaning of our work, or at least afraid of boredom, in our questions about heaven. So our descriptions of heaven often include the assurance that we will have things to do. It won't just be sitting around on a cloud all day.[17]

Luther did not, however, base his exposition of 1 Cor 15 only on such foundations. His description of the body is also, and perhaps more importantly, intended to explain what it means that the resurrection body is spiritual. Luther introduced the distinction, based on 1 Cor 15:44, at the end of his January 19 sermon and spent most of the next sermon in the series, delivered on February 1, explaining it. He wanted his hearers to know that the distinction between natural body and spiritual body is not the distinction between body and soul to which they were accustomed.

> Thus you must learn to understand the words 'natural' and 'spiritual' correctly and distinguish in accordance with their usage in Scripture. Here the body is not to be distinguished from the soul, as we customarily do when we hear the words spirit or spiritual. No, we must understand this to mean that the body, too, must become spirit, or live spiritually. We have already begun to do that through Baptism, by virtue of which we live spiritually with regard to the soul and God also views and regards the body as spiritual. It is only that the body must first depart from this temporal life before it becomes completely new and spiritual and lives solely of and by the Spirit.[18]

16 Drew Gilpin Faust, *This Republic of Suffering: Death and the American Civil War* (New York: Vintage Books, 2008), 177–187.

17 See for example Randy Alcorn, *Heaven* (Wheaton, IL: Tyndale House Publishers, Inc., 2004), 395–398.

18 Fifteenth sermon, February 1, 1533. LW 28: 192; WA 36: 665b.

Once again, we find Luther being drawn back into this present life even as he attempts to explain the resurrection and the body that is to come. Here he notes that because of baptism the Christian already has one foot out of the grave.

A final consideration in Luther's treatment of the resurrection body is his obvious joy in Paul's metaphors, particularly that of a seed being sown. In one sermon he exults, "What a precious artist St. Paul becomes here, painting and carving the resurrection into everything that grows on earth!"[19] In fact, much of Luther's language is driven by his commitment to this organic metaphor. So, for example, in the same sermon he used the idea to explain the necessity of death.

> God wants to create a new life for the very purpose that all that is perishable be entirely abolished. Death must serve that purpose. He must approach us and say: 'Stop eating, drinking, digesting, etc. and lie down and decompose so that you may acquire a new, more beautiful form, just as the grain does which sprouts from new soil.'[20]

The role of death in this example is worthy of comment, since Luther always thought of death as the enemy. Here, although death is still the enemy, it is an enemy that had been forced into God's service and now accomplishes God's purpose. In the sermon following this one, Luther equated the power he presumed for the resurrection body with the power even a tiny seed has to break through the soil.[21] Most often, however, he extends that image and pictures a farmer who sows his seed as a way of demonstrating how the Christian should have faith in the resurrection in spite of appearances.

> Well, what does a pious peasant or husbandman do and think when he scatters his seed about like that? It looks like futile labor and loss, and he appears to be a fool who wantonly squanders his grain. But ask him, and he will be quick to tell you: 'Why, my dear man, I am not casting it away to lose it and let it spoil, but I am doing this that it might grow forth again most beautifully and bear and yield far more in return for this handful. Indeed, now it seems lost, scattered into the wind for the birds and worms; but let summer come, and you will see it grow forth. One handful will grow into ten, one bushel will yield six others.' Such are the peasant's thoughts. They do not dwell on the kernels which fall into the ground and rot.[22]

These sermons on 1 Cor 15 from 1532–1533 represent something of an exception to Luther's usual resurrection preaching, since apart from them he did not discuss the resurrection body at length, even in his later sermons on 1 Cor 15. Yet this sort of scene – a farmer sowing seed – does appear in other sermons and figures prominently in a sermon from the later series.

19 Thirteenth sermon, December 22, 1532. LW 28: 175; WA 36 :639b.
20 Thirteenth sermon, December 22, 1532. LW 28: 182; WA 36: 650b.
21 Fourteenth sermon, January 19, 1533. LW 28: 188; WA 36: 658b.
22 Thirteenth sermon, December 22, 1532. LW 28: 176; WA 36: 641b.

Luther's second sermon in that series, originally given on Exaudi Sunday, the Sixth Sunday after Easter, in 1544, consists almost entirely of a dialogue between a dim-witted interlocutor called Hans Pfriem[23] and a peasant farmer and his family.[24] Hans Pfriem, whom Luther describes as "a crude, clumsy ox and uncomprehending fool, who nevertheless wished to be excellently wise and wished to wholly reform God in heaven and master him there,"[25] asks the farmer how he could be throwing perfectly good seed into the ground when it could be used to feed his family. The farmer, Luther says, should have told this fool to go away and leave him in peace, but instead tells him to come back in a half year or so, and he will see that the earth had produced twenty or thirty times the amount of grain that he is sowing. Hans Pfriem remains unconvinced, so the farmer explains in detail, adding that he will also pray God to send sun, rain, and good weather.[26] The good farmer waits for the earth to produce its seed. God, Luther concludes, is a good farmer. Luther says,

> We are clever Hans Pfriems, from good German clumsy, uncomprehending fools. Let us always preach and hear every day that God is the farmer who not only plants us into the earth but also says that He wishes at the right time to give rain and sun, moisture and sap, growth and blessing, richly and extravagantly.[27]

These blessings are spiritual - word and sacrament like the rain and the Holy Spirit like the sun. "This," Luther concludes, "is a strong sermon on the resurrection."[28]

Luther's preaching on the resurrection body demonstrates the varied ways he attempted to bring the text to his hearers. The importance that preaching and the word had in the Reformer's theology is nowhere better demonstrated than in his sermons on the resurrection.

23 Luther appears to be using a name that was common in storytelling. A cobbler named Meister Pfriem figures in a story collected by the Brothers Grimm. Jacob and Wilhelm Grimm, *Kinder- und Hausmärchen. Vollständige Ausgabe.* Nineteenth edition (Dusseldorf and Zurich: Artemis and Winckler, 2002), 726–730.

24 WA 49: 422ff.

25 *Einen groben Toelpel und unverstendigen Narren, der doch trefflich klug sein wil und wol Gott im Himel reformieren und meistern thar.* WA 49: 424b.

26 WA 49: 426b.

27 *Aber wir sind kluge Hans Pfriemen, auff gut Deutsch grobe, unverstendige Narren, Lassen uns jmer predigen und hoeren teglich, Das Gott unser Ackerman sey, Der uns nicht allein in die Erde seet, Sondern auch spricht, Er woelle zu rechter zeit Regen und Sonn, Feuchte und Safft, Gedeien und Segen geben reichlich und uberschwenglich.* WA 49: 427b.

28 *Das ist eine starcke Predigt von der Aufferstehung.* WA 49: 428b.

3. Proclamation

It is fitting, then, that proclamation itself is a prominent element in Luther's Easter and resurrection sermons. This is not surprising, since his theology emphasizes that faith, another prominent element, comes from hearing the word. Preaching, therefore, is how Christ intends his resurrection to be used; his resurrection is meant to bring forgiveness and life, including the promise of the resurrection of the body, to those who trust his saving actions.

Because of this focus on the benefits of resurrection preaching, Luther did not believe the Roman church of his day took Christ's resurrection seriously as something absolutely essential to Christian existence. In sermons for the Easter season, he speaks of church leaders and preachers as being content with the mere story of Christ's resurrection or as not being concerned with the purpose or utility (*usum*) of that resurrection. We find a good example of this approach in a sermon from Quasimodogeniti Sunday, the Sunday after Easter, in 1531. The text, a classic for the theme of faith in Christ's resurrection, is the story of Christ's appearance to Thomas.

> When we have stories and words, we take the words for the most important part. There is a sure rule: whoever wishes to handle the Gospels well, let him look to the words, especially to those that Christ speaks. [...] And there the passion and resurrection of Christ come into use. If it is only so much story, it is a useless resurrection, as it is in the preaching of the papacy, which makes from the story a noisy history that Christ accomplished. In the same way we listen to the stories of Theodoric of Bern[29] and have a good laugh. But they should bring the resurrection into custom and practice.[30]

The reason for this harsh judgment lies in the effect that papal preaching, according to Luther, aimed for in the hearer. This effect, he explained, was precisely the opposite of faith.

> Therefore faith alone justifies; our papal ass doesn't understand that. For they establish forgiveness of sins upon our works. The passion and resurrection of Christ are efficacious when I take them up and have remorse and suffering. They actually preach such shameful blasphemy! Look at it, so that you don't forget what the teaching of the popes

29 A reference to the fantastical poems about Theodoric the Ostrogoth, King of Italy from 493 to 526, who was known in German works of this sort as Dietrich von Bern.

30 *Quando habemus historias et verba, nhemen wir die wort fur das heubstuck. Est certa regula: qui vult bene tractare Euangelia, videat auff die wort, praesertim quae Christus loquitur. [...] Et ibi passio Christi et resurrectio kompt in usum, si tantum esset historia, esset frustranea resurrectio, so weyt est in papatu praedicatum, quod draus gemacht ein lauter geschicht quod, Christus fecit, Sicut alias historias audimus de Theodorico de Berna und haben ein lust. Sed sollen resurrectionem in brauch und ubung bringen.* WA 34.1: 318–319a.

> has been and moreover so that you understand better our teaching and that of the Gospels. Our works belong not to these things but to the mouth of the Apostles.[31]

For Luther the choice between story and word or between the resurrection and its use was the choice between works and faith. Even remorse and suffering were not works proper to the Gospel. The work proper to the Gospel was faith in the risen Christ and trust in the fruits of his resurrection, which is what Luther meant when he said, "Our works belong [...] to the mouth of the Apostles." Luther believed that his proclamation and that of his evangelical colleagues was also that of the apostles and, in addition, that such proclamation was God's very word, powerful to accomplish what it says in and for those who trust in it.

Even when preaching on the resurrection on the Last Day, that is, when the benefits of Christ's resurrection for the believer would be fully experienced, Luther could not resist the pull to the present and to the daily proclamation and use of the word. The final sermon of his 1532–1533 series on 1 Cor 15 provides a fitting and typical example. Preaching on verse 54, "Then shall come to pass the saying that is written: Death is swallowed up in victory," he stated:

> This also applies to Christendom now, when Word, Baptism, and the Sacrament are administered and nothing is proclaimed but that Christ died and rose again. That is the only prescription or *purgatio* for our sin and death. That we must take daily and let it work, in order to drive the poison from our heart and take us from death and hell to eternal life. He promised us that; and He commanded us to proclaim it and believe it.[32]

The focus on proclamation in the present is rarely absent from Luther's preaching on resurrection, whether *resurrection* refers to Christ or to the Christian. Proclamation, indeed, is where those two events come together for him, and why he can say that the Christian already has one foot out of the grave.

Luther had sounded this theme frequently in Easter sermons in the years prior to his sermons on 1 Cor 15. Preaching on the Wednesday after Easter in 1529, Luther expounded these words from Luke 24, "Christ had to suffer and to rise on the third day, and repentance and forgiveness of sins is to be proclaimed in his name." After introducing this text, Luther paraphrased it this way:

> This is certainly a powerful text. With clear words [Christ] emphasizes his suffering, and for this reason we also emphasize its goal and fruit so that repentance and forgiveness of sin is preached. It is as if he were saying: Without this, had I not died and risen, there would be no repentance and forgiveness of sins. Judas and Cain also repented. But what

---

31 *Ideo sola fides iustificat, das wissen unser Babst esel nicht. Nam fundaverunt super nostra opera remissionem p|eccatorum. Christi pas|sio et res|urrectio ist efficax, quando ich anhebe und hab rew et le|id. Solche schend|liche lesterung praedicarunt. Vide, ut non oblivis|caris, quae fuerit doct|rina pap|istarum, tum melius intelliges nostram et Euangelii doctrinam. Nostra opera gehoren nicht zw dem ding, sed Apostolorum mund.* WA 34.1: 328a.

32 LW 28: 206; WA 36: 684.

> was the result? Cain said, 'My sin is greater than what can be forgiven me.' And Judas said, 'I have sinned by betraying innocent blood.'[33]

Luther went on to characterize this as a "gallows repentance, despair, but not repentance."[34] The bulk of the sermon from this point on contrasted the understanding of repentance in the Roman church, on one hand, with its reliance on papal authority and works, which according to Luther lead to despair; and true Christian repentance, on the other hand. He concluded the sermon:

> Judas dealt with his repentance according to reason and did not grasp the statement that repentance and forgiveness of sins should be preached in Christ's name. Our adversaries do not tolerate this teaching. […] [T]rue repentance must be preached throughout the entire world. Thus we have now spoken about the resurrection of Christ and what its purpose is.[35]

Luther preached a similar message two years later in his sermon on Thomas for Quasimodogeniti Sunday. There he stated that Christ had placed into the mouths of the apostles his suffering and resurrection and as a result had also placed in their mouths power over the devil and the law.[36] Christ's resurrection does no good without this proclamation. Moreover, Luther emphasized that such proclamation was the only remedy for sin and that this remedy had been given to the whole church.

> There is no distinction between Muhammed and the Pope, except that he [Muhammed] does not have the word. If you feel that sin lives in you, don't run to St. James, to your works. Go to your pastor. If you are not able to do this, go to your brother neighbor and ask that he speak the word to you in the name of Christ. If you believe this word, you certainly have even Christ and all the rest.[37]

So Luther's message once more returned to faith and works; these are the two religions of mankind. Because both Islam and the papacy preached works, the only difference between them was that the pope actually had the word of God, and so should have known better. Yet despite possessing that word, the papal church had created works that it declared holy as remedies for sin, such as the pilgrimage to Santiago de Compostela, which Luther calls running to St. James. The genuine and apostolic proclamation of Christ's resurrection, however, had nothing to do

33 *The 1529 Holy Week and Easter Sermons*, 160.

34 *The 1529 Holy Week and Easter Sermons*, 161.

35 *The 1529 Holy Week and Easter Sermons*, 166–167.

36 *Christus legt sein leyden et resurrectionem in eorum os et omnem potestatem diaboli, legis und wirffts in eorum mund.* WA 34: 321a.

37 *Non est discrimen inter Mahometh et Papam, nisi quod is verbum non habet. Si sentis peccata in te vivificari, noli currere ad S. Iacobum, ad tua opera, ito ad tuum pfarrer. Si hunc non potes habere, ad proximum fratrem et rogato, ut tibi verbum spreche nomine Christi. Si kanstu gleuben huic verbo, habes tam certe, ac Christus &c.* WA 34: 327–328a.

with works, even those ordained by the church, but only with faith in the word of Christ. Christ gave his word abundantly and freely – it could be spoken by the pastor, to be sure, but also "in the name of Christ" by any believer. This word certainly – Luther emphasized this certainty – brought with it Christ himself and all his benefits, including ultimately resurrection to eternal life.

4. Conclusion

For Luther, the only appropriate response to such good news was to sing and dance. In a 1544 sermon, he pictured an antiphonal song between death and the believer, with death singing of its power to kill. "But on Easter Day," he said, "another song is raised. Then it is sung: Death, where is your victory? Grave, hand over [the dead]. Where is the one whom you killed? There another song is sung: Death is swallowed up in victory."[38] Luther could not stay focused only on the Last Day because he believed the resurrection was already at work. Faith that trusted this should be, he thought, a continuous source of joy for those with ears to hear Christ's word. "We are thick headed," he once preached. "If we understood [the resurrection], we would always be dancing."[39] What could be more appropriate than dancing for those who already have one foot out of the grave?

38 *Ibi canit: Jch hab macht, Sieg, occido omnes &c. Sed am Ostertag hat sich ein ander lied erhebt. Ibi canitur: Mors, ubi victoria? Grab, gib her. Ubi is, quem occidisti? Ibi canticum aliud. Mors absorpta bis in den Sieg.* WA 49: 769a.

39 *Nos habemus dicke ohren. Si intelligeremus, semper saltaremus.* WA 37: 31a.

Timothy Wengert

Justifying the *Variata*: Observations on Melanchthon's 1540 Edition of the Augsburg Confession

As Robert Kolb reminded us in *Confessing the Faith*, one of the neuralgic points in the development of early Lutheranism was the struggle over the authoritative text of the Augsburg Confession in the 1560s and beyond. Leaving aside changes in article X on the Lord's Supper, this essay will examine other changes, especially in articles IV, V, VI and XX, and show how they not only reflected Melanchthon's own developing theology but how they also answered opponents' challenges to Wittenberg's understanding of justification by faith and thus, as the 1580 preface to *The Book of Concord* indicated, provided an important exposition of the Augsburg Confession itself.

1. Variata Controversa

In 1561, decisions at the diet of Naumburg sparked an uproar over which version of the Augsburg Confession was authoritative. In an attempt to placate the Elector of the Palatinate, who with the help of his theologians Caspar Olevianus and Zacharias Ursinus was leading his principality in a decidedly Reformed direction regarding Christ's presence in the Lord's Supper, the *Variata* – the heavily edited version produced by Philip Melanchthon in 1540 – was offered as the official confession of the Evangelical princes and cities because of its broader language on the Lord's Supper in article ten.[1] Johannes Wigand, among others, objected strongly to this shift. Given the raging dispute over Melanchthon's 1559 memorandum on the Lord's Supper to the Palatine Elector, which led to the dismissal of Tilemann Hesshus from his positions in Heidelberg as superintendent and university professor, changes in the wording of AC X (as well as of

1 See Robert Kolb, *Confessing the Faith: Reformers Define the Church, 1530–1580* (St. Louis: Concordia, 1991), 59–62.

AC V on the role of the Holy Spirit in working faith) only besmirched the recently deceased reformer's reputation further.[2]

The repercussions of this uproar even echoed in the publication of Melanchthon's works. While both the original 1560 version of the *Corpus Doctrinae* (which contained the ecumenical creeds, the Apology, and other doctrinal statements written by Melanchthon) and its first reprint in 1561 contained only the text of the *Variata*, a second edition from 1561, printed in a smaller typeface, included both versions interwoven, with the text of each article from the 1540 edition given first and, when there were variations, the 1530 version following.[3] Moreover, the printer gave an explanation for this change in the introduction to these documents.[4] Vögelin complained about the calumnies against his earlier printings of the *Corpus doctrinae* – despite the fact that the original version of the Augsburg Confession was quoted in the Apology – and described how, to prove such critics (labeled sycophants) wrong, he had decided to include both versions, printing the oldest versions (*anitquissima exempla*) and the more recent one together.

Similarly, when Caspar Peucer published the first volume of his father-in-law's *Opera* in 1562, he placed the two versions one after the other, beginning with the complete text of the 1530 edition. In the title of the 1540 *Variata* he identified its original context and claimed that the changes represented fuller explications of the same substance: "The same articles more copiously and more clearly declared at Worms in 1540 on account of the calumnious interpretations and sophistic artifices of the adversaries, with the meaning of the issues unchanged."[5]

In his epistle dedicatory, addressed to Archduke Maximilian II, later Holy Roman Emperor, Peucer went to great lengths not only to describe the origins of the *Variata*, which he claimed was written in 1538 and then distributed at the colloquy in Worms in 1540, but also to defend its authority. According to this

2 Timothy J. Wengert, "Philip Melanchthon's 1557 Lecture on Colossians 3:1–2: Christology as Context for the Controversy over the Lord's Supper," in *Philip Melanchthon: Theologian in Classroom, Confession, and Controversy*, ed., Irene Dingel et al. (Göttingen: Vandenhoeck & Ruprecht, 2012), 209–235.

3 Philip Melanchthon, *Corpus doctrinae christianae: quae est summa orthodoxi et catholici dogmatis [...]* (Leipzig: Vögelin, 1560), 1–56 [VD16: M 2883 (cf. the second printing: M 2884); http://www.mdz-nbn-resolving.de/urn/resolver.pl?urn=urn:nbn:de:bvb:12-bsb10196625-6, accessed on 10 January 2014] compared to *Corpus doctrinae [...]* (Leipzig: Vögelin, 1561), 1–75 [VD16: M 2885; http://www.mdz-nbn-resolving.de/urn/resolver.pl?urn=urn:nbn:de:bvb:12-bsb10175594-3, accessed on 10 January 2014]. VD16 inaccurately lists the latter under M 2883.

4 See B 1 r-v.

5 *Omnium Operum [...] Pars Prima* (Wittenberg: Crato, 1562), 39 [VD16: M 2331]: "*Iidem articuli copiosius et explicatius declarati Wormatiae anno M. D. XXXX. Propter adversariorum calumniosas interpretations & sophisticas elusions, non mutata rerum sententia.*" See Timothy J. Wengert, "The Scope and Contents of Philip Melanchthon's *Opera omnia*, Wittenberg, 1562–1564," *Archive for Reformation History* 88 (1997): 62.

account, although Melanchthon wrote the document, he did so at the command of Luther, who examined and approved the results. Not only that, but Peucer addressed specifically a story about Johann Eck, Melanchthon's chief opponent in the colloquies, who was reported to have said that the new version did not accurately reflect statements in the original. Johannes Wigand and others had used this story to bolster their own case against the *Variata*. Peucer stated on the contrary:

> We remembered that at Worms, when Eck objected to our dissimilar copies of the Augsburg Confession, Philip responded that it was the same meaning of the issues, although some things in the latter edition were somewhat milder and others explained more clearly, to which Eck acquiesced.[6]

Peucer then explained that he included both texts so that one could see that the same defense of the faith was being proposed in both.

2. Augustana IV and Forensic Justification

While most of the furor over the *Variata* revolved around the Lord's Supper and the way in which Melanchthon had edited this article to correspond more completely to his construal of the Wittenberg Concord,[7] Peucer's account helps explain why many of the most important changes in the first twenty-one articles came in articles IV, V, VI and XX, that is, on the doctrines of justification and good works. Although some complaints arose over article V, no one to my knowledge objected after Melanchthon's death to the sweeping changes in articles IV or XX, perhaps because their formulation had been so helpful in refuting Andreas Osiander's view of justification during the 1550s.[8]

AC IV had stated the case for justification by faith quite briefly.[9]

> Likewise, they teach that human beings cannot be justified before God by their own powers, merits, or works. But they are justified as a gift on account of Christ through

6 *Omnium Operum […] Pars Prima*, A 5 r-v.

7 Heinz Scheible, "Melanchthon und Bucer," now in *Melanchthon und die Reformation: Forschungsbeiträge*, ed., Gerhard May & Rolf Decot (Mainz: von Zabern, 1996), 256.

8 See Timothy J. Wengert, *Defending Faith: Lutheran Responses to Andreas Osiander's Doctrine of Justification, 1551–1559* (Tübingen: Mohr Siebeck, 2012), 317–351.

9 Throughout this essay, we will use AC to designate the "unaltered" Augsburg Confession and *Variata* for the 1540 version. The translation of the *Variata* is the author's own. For the Latin text of the *Variata*, see Philip Melanchthon, *Corpus Reformatorum: Philippi Melanthonis opera quae supersunt omnia*, ed. Karl Bretschneider and Heinrich Bindseil, 28 vols. (Halle: A. Schwetschke & Sons, 1834–1860) 26: 351–371. For an English translation, see Henry Eyster Jacobs, ed., *The Book of Concord*, vol. 2: *Historical Introduction, Appendixes and Indexes to the Book of Concord* (Philadelphia: Sherman, 1883), 103–158.

> faith when they believe that they are received into grace and that their sins are forgiven on account of Christ, who by his death made satisfaction for our sins. God reckons this faith as righteousness (Rom. 3 and 4).

This was where the battle royal with Wittenberg's opponents was joined. Whereas the Roman *Confutatio* accepted AC I and III and only complained that in AC II the reformers had confused the actual sins of lacking true fear and faith in God with original sin, it dismissed AC IV out of hand.

Melanchthon's spirited defense of this article in the first edition of the Apology, one that he sharpened in the second edition of September 1531, answered objections from a variety of opponents, including Johannes Cochläus, Nicholas Herborn, and Johann Eck.[10] Some, in turn, wrote refutations of the Apology, which in part he had already been defending in his 1532 *Commentarii in Epistolam Pauli ad Romanos* (Wittenberg: Klug, 1532).[11] Lectures on the *Loci communes* in 1534 and the subsequent printing of a new edition of the *Loci communes theologici* in 1535, respectively, again allowed him to sharpen his arguments. By this time, however, Melanchthon was engaged in the first conversations with the Roman side since the Diet of Augsburg in 1530. It was in light of these discussions that he developed a third use of the law to delineate more clearly the distinction between law and gospel.[12]

At the same time, however, there were certain rumblings from theologians within Wittenberg's orbit. In particular, Johannes Brenz objected to Melanchthon's forensic approach to the doctrine of justification. The reformer of Schwäbisch-Hall argued in line with Augustine that the promise of forgiveness was based upon the future work of the Holy Spirit making a person intrinsically holy. In response, Luther and Melanchthon wrote to Brenz separately but in a single letter, in their own way questioning Brenz's more Augustinian approach.[13] But by 1540 Melanchthon also had become concerned with the theology of John Calvin and his insistence on a form of predestination so strict that it threatened to undermine the certainty of God's promise in Word and sacrament for a believer.

10 For example, Johannes Cochläus, *De libero arbitrio hominis, adversus locos communes Philippi Melanchthonis, libri duo* (Tübingen, 1525); Nicolaus Herborn [Ferber], *Locorum communium adversus huius temporis haereses enchiridion* (Cologne: Quentell, 1528); Johannes Eck, *Loci communes theologici* (Ingolstadt, 1529). Attacks written after 1530 include Georg Witzel, *Pro defensione bonorum operum, adversus novos evangelistas* (Leipzig: Blum, 1532); and Johannes Cochläus, *Philippicae quatuor [...] in Apologiam Philippis Melanchthonis ad Carolum V. Imperatorem Romanorum* (Leipzig: Faber, 1534).

11 *Melanchthons Werke in Auswahl* [*Studienausgabe*], ed., Robert Stupperich, 7 vols. (Gütersloh: Gerd Mohn, 1951–1975) vol. 5. See especially Rolf Schäfer's introduction, 15–24.

12 See Timothy J. Wengert, *Law and Gospel: Philip Melanchthon's Debate with John Agricola of Eisleben over "Poenitentia"* (Grand Rapids: Baker, 1997), 177–210.

13 Timothy J. Wengert, "Luther and Melanchthon – Melanchthon and Luther," *Luther-Jahrbuch* 66 (1999): 55–88.

As a result, he began to emphasize far more strongly the universality and dependability of God's promise, privately nicknaming Calvin "our Zeno," after the founder of Stoicism.[14] At the same time, Luther himself was engaged in a dispute with John Agricola over the nature of the law.

All of these forces flowed into Melanchthon's changes to the AC. A splendid example of how these forces also played out in other parts of the AC can be found already in the second article, where the *Variata* eliminated the offensive references to fear of God and faith in God. Yet, far from denying the substance of the original wording or argument, Melanchthon's new version spoke instead of "a lack of original righteousness and original obedience," language used by the scholastics and cited by Melanchthon in his Apology.[15] As was typical of Melanchthon's method, the reformer sought clarity in language and avoided controversy over words in order to prevent the central issue from becoming obscured by what he viewed as superfluous arguments.

Changes to AC IV were far more wide-ranging and deserve more attention. First, perhaps because he had noticed that it was lacking in the AC, Melanchthon connected article III on the nature and work of Christ more clearly to article IV. For one thing, he restructured the surrounding articles. Article I in the *Variata* began, as had AC I, with: "The churches among us teach with complete unanimity [...]." Articles II and III also began, "Likewise, they teach [...]," and introduced the doctrines of original sin and the person and work of Christ. The next time that the phrase occurred, however, was with article VI, thus subsuming *Variata* IV and V under article III. For another thing, he began the article: "However, so that we may obtain these benefits of Christ – namely, forgiveness of sins, justification and eternal life, Christ gives the Gospel in which these benefits are offered to us." Thus, more clearly than in AC IV, Christ himself and his Gospel became the central movers in justification by faith.

To prove his contention, Melanchthon not only cited Luke 24:47, one of his favorite verses describing the work of law and gospel, but also employed another of his favorite biblical phrases from John 16:8, which spoke of the Holy Spirit exposing (or accusing; the Latin verb is *arguo*) of sin. Whereas the Johannine text referred to the Holy Spirit, Melanchthon tied this verb to the gospel itself: to sinful human beings who cannot fulfill the law, "the gospel accuses of sins and shows us the mediator Christ and thus teaches us about forgiveness of sins."[16] Here, even

---

14 Timothy J. Wengert, "'We Will Feast Together in Heaven Forever': The Epistolary Friendship of John Calvin and Philip Melanchthon," in *Melanchthon in Europe: His Work and Influence Beyond Wittenberg*, ed., Karin Maag (Grand Rapids: Baker, 1999), 19–44.

15 The Ap II, 27–30, in KW, 116. He continued this rewriting in the next paragraph of the *Variata* as well, again along the lines of his defense in the Apology.

16 Throughout his life, Melanchthon sometimes used the term "gospel" to denote both law and gospel. See the FC SD V, 3–5 in KW, 582.

more clearly than in the AC, which only introduces law and gospel in AC XII, Melanchthon set about tying justification to the work of law and gospel. At first glance, however, this approach seems exclusively cognitive, using intellective words like *show* and *teach*. However, in the next paragraph, Melanchthon immediately demonstrated the effect of such accusation:

> When the Gospel accuses us of sins, terrified hearts should come to realize that forgiveness of sins is given to us freely (*gratis*) on account of Christ and that this justification is given to us through faith (*per fidem*), by which we should believe and trust, on account of Christ (*propter Christum*), who was given for us as a sacrifice to placate the Father.

The Latin terms are all in AC IV, and the expansions truly function as further adumbrations on the original. Again, however, Melanchthon added reference to the accusatory function of the law.

In the sentence that followed, Melanchthon then addressed a crucial problem in relation to his opponents: their tendency to make *poenitentia* a prerequisite for the gospel. Instead, Melanchthon underscored the unconditional nature of God's grace.[17]

> Therefore, although the Gospel requires penitence, nevertheless, so that forgiveness of sins may be certain, it teaches that forgiveness is given gratis, that is, it does not depend on the condition of our worthiness, nor is it given on account of any works that precede it nor on account of worthiness of works that follow from it.

Otherwise, forgiveness would become completely uncertain, dependent upon some worth or merit in human beings. Again, obtaining forgiveness by "works, merits or satisfactions" was in AC IV. Here Melanchthon went to greater lengths to explain why such works undermined certainty in God's mercy. Already this connection makes clear that in the earlier references to showing, teaching and realizing, Melanchthon was not thinking of human works at all but rather the work of the Word upon the hearer.

Still reflecting on the work of the law, Melanchthon then mentioned how the conscience "in true tremblings (*pavores*)" finds no work to place against God's wrath except Christ, who was given to us as Propitiator. "This honor of Christ ought not be transferred into our works." Citing Paul in Ephesians, Melanchthon insisted that forgiveness only becomes certain, as Paul teaches, when the promise is firm and thus arises from faith, gratis. Only having proved this point could Melanchthon tie the effect of the law (terror) to the effect of the gospel (comfort). "This is the firm and necessary consolation for godly and terrified minds." What

17 To see how central this was in Luther's thought, see, most recently, Berndt Hamm, "*Gabe ohne Gegengabe – die religionsgeschichtliche Revolution der Reformation*," *Jahrbuch für Biblische Theologie* 27 (2012): 241–276.

was a central theme in AC XX, Ap XII, the *Commentarii* of 1532, and the 1535 *Loci communes*, now was being read back into AC IV itself.

To underscore the catholicity of his point, Melanchthon brought the quote in AC VI of Ambrose [=Ambrosiaster] into the text here and followed it with a discussion originally found in AC XX on the nature of faith. The word *faith*, he wrote,

> signifies not only knowledge of the story of Christ but also [signifies] believing and assenting to this promise, which is peculiar to the Gospel, in which forgiveness of sins, righteousness and eternal life are promised to us on account of Christ.

His proof for this came from the Apostles' Creed, which confesses belief not only in the story of Christ but also in the forgiveness of sins. "For this benefit is the point of the story."[18]

Changes to AC II and IV reveal several important aspects of Melanchthon's revisions. First, he was not averse to removing offending language (AC II: "lack of fear and faith in God") by finding appropriate circumlocutions for the same point but using vocabulary more common in the ancient and medieval church. Second, by bringing material from other articles of the AC into AC IV (specifically the citation of Ambrosiaster and the definition of faith), he found ways to anticipate and defuse objections from his opponents. Third, and most importantly, in article IV of the *Variata*, he far more clearly tied justification and forgiveness to the work of the Word of God as law that terrifies and gospel that consoles. For Melanchthon and the Wittenberg reformers, this connection was central to understanding justification, not as a work earned or merited but as a gift received gratis. Indeed, his final sentence ("For this benefit is the point of the story") underscored this connection – proper theological definition always included its effect. As Melanchthon had already written in 1521 in the first edition of the *Loci communes*, "To know Christ is to know his benefits."

3. Augustana V: Defining the Holy Spirit's Work in the Word

With *Variata* IV linked clearly to Christ's person and work and to the function of the Word as law and gospel, while also defining the nature of faith, article V took on even more the character of a corollary to justification. There were, however, some important changes. The text of AC V stated,

18 This underscores why most so-called narrative preaching in today's church, derived from Reformed theologians' concentration on covenant and salvation history, runs directly contrary to Wittenberg's reformation of preaching as law and gospel.

> So that we may obtain this faith, the ministry of teaching the gospel and administering the sacraments was instituted. For through the Word and the sacraments as through instruments the Holy Spirit is given, who effects faith where and when it pleases God in those who hear the gospel, that is to say, in those who hear that God, not on account of our own merits but on account of Christ, justifies those who believe that they are received into grace on account of Christ. Gal. 3 [:14b]: 'So that we might receive the promise of the Spirit through faith.'
>
> They condemn the Anabaptists and others who think that the Holy Spirit comes to human beings without the external Word through their own preparations and works.[19]

By contrast, the *Variata* simply used "therefore" (Latin: *itaque*) to introduce this article. Nevertheless, even this single word establishes the connection. Melanchthon underscored the Christocentric nature of this article, however, by taking the first sentence out of the passive and identifying the subject: "Therefore Christ instituted the ministry of teaching the Gospel, which preaches repentance and forgiveness of sins." This referred directly back to Luke 24 and Christ's institution of preaching law and gospel.

The very next sentence, however, addressed what for Melanchthon had become an increasingly worrisome aspect of some Evangelical teaching: the emphasis on God's election to such a degree as to destroy the universal character of God's Word. Although his position later led to a confrontation with Matthias Flacius and others, Melanchthon here was not so much challenging those in the Wittenberg camp – by the 1530s even Luther could occasionally emphasize the certainty of God's promises over against divine predestination[20] – as those in Strasbourg and elsewhere, especially John Calvin, whose second edition of the *Institutes* in 1539 later led to a public fight with Albert Pighius and would lead Melanchthon to nickname the future reformer of Geneva "our Zeno" after the founder of Stoicism.[21] Thus, in 1540 the *Variata* insisted:

> Each of the two forms of preaching [repentance and forgiveness] is universal: it exposes the sins of all and promises to all who believe forgiveness of sins so that this may not be an uncertain forgiveness but so that all terrified minds may know that they ought to believe that forgiveness of sins is surely given to them on account of Christ, not on account of their merit or worthiness.

As a result of this insistence, however, Melanchthon then made faith and the reception of the Holy Spirit simultaneous, refusing here to address the question

19 KW, 41.

20 See, for example, WATR 4: 641–642 (no. 5070, from between 11 and 19 June 1540).

21 See the material added in 1539 to the *Institutes* III. xxiii–xxiv. For example, see also John Calvin, *Opera* 1: 879 and the discussion of arguments confirmed *a posteriori.* For Melanchthon on freedom of the will, see Timothy J. Wengert, "Philip Melanchthon and the Origins of the 'Three Causes' (1533–1535): An Examination of the Roots of the Controversy over the Freedom of the Will," in Dingel, *Melanchthon*, 183–208.

of causation in any way that might either smack of fatalism or eliminate the work of the Holy Spirit. Thus, he wrote,

> And when in this way we are consoled by the promise or the Gospel and we encourage ourselves[22] by faith, at the same time (*simul*) the Holy Spirit is given to us. For the Holy Spirit is given and is efficacious through the Word of God and through the Sacraments.

As if realizing that this statement needed further clarification, he added: "When we hear or think about the Gospel or handle the Sacraments and are consoled by faith, at the same time the Holy Spirit is efficacious."

In rewriting AC V, Melanchthon refused to divorce faith from the hearing of God's Word, proving this contention with references to Gal 3:22 (the promise given to those who believe), 2 Cor [paraphrasing 3:6–8: the gospel as ministry of the Spirit][23] and Rom 10:17 (faith from hearing). To underscore this simultaneity, Melanchthon then returned to the subject a third time, again emphasizing the efficacy of the Holy Spirit.

> Therefore, when we are consoled by faith and freed from the terrors of sin through the Holy Spirit, hearts take in (*concipiunt*) other virtues: they truly know God's mercy and take in (*concipiunt*)[24] true love, true fear of God, trust, hope in divine aid, prayer and similar fruits of the Spirit.

As in AC V, what then followed were condemnations, which, as in the AC, covered articles four and five. Melanchthon expanded them in the *Variata* to define more precisely what the Evangelicals were opposing. The first condemnation, borrowed from AC XX, related to the Roman opponents who did not teach that one receives forgiveness by faith and left folks in doubt and dependent on their own worthiness. The second, while mentioning Anabaptists in particular, also listed two ancient heresies: Manichaeans and Enthusiasts.[25] Melanchthon called these people "fanatical spirits, who imagine that the Holy Spirit is given or is efficacious without the Word of God." Without naming names, Melanchthon was clearly also worried about John Calvin's extreme doctrine of predestination, which also "condemned the ministry of the Gospel and Sacraments […] and so led souls away from the Word of God to their own opinions, which is most pernicious." He counseled instead constant condemnation of these ravings (*furors*), "For they abolish true use of the Word of God, imagine falsely that the Holy Spirit is

22 Latin: *erigimus nos*. The reflexive form of this verb means here to encourage, cheer, or possibly, arouse oneself.

23 See also CR 21, 931, a discussion in the third edition of the *Loci communes theologici*.

24 While in cognition this verb can mean "conceive of;" here Melanchthon used it more as "to begin to feel" and, thus, "to take in."

25 Manichaeans insisted that the elect possessed a spark of the divine not in the non-elect; the Enthusiasts referred to a group of monks in the ancient church who abandoned Scripture and the sacraments in favor of their own direct inspiration by the Holy Spirit.

received without the Word of God and, trusting in their own opinions, mix together ungodly dogmas and cause unending dissipation."

Whatever Melanchthon's later position on free will, here what Kolb has called Wittenberg's "broken" doctrine of election was already coming to expression. What the Concordists argued so passionately for in article eleven of the Formula of Concord, namely that no doctrine of predestination dare undercut the efficacy of God's promises, already had molded the language and arguments in the *Variata.*[26] Indeed, however much so-called "Crypto-Calvinists" could employ *Variata* X to defend their teaching about Christ's spiritual presence in the Supper, followers of Calvin could hardly have been very pleased with Melanchthon's insistence in *Variata* IV and V on the work of the Holy Spirit *through* God's Word. Moreover, Melanchthon identified the same weakness in both his Roman opponents and in these "fanatical spirits," namely, a deep desire to undermine the certainty of God's promises to those terrified by the law. If only the law were universal, individuals would never know for certain whether God's promises apply to them or not. Either they were forced to rely on their own worthiness or on some internal working of the Holy Spirit divorced from God's promises. Both, in Melanchthon's view, offered recipes for theological disaster: the disappearance of certainty, faith and consolation.

4. Augustana VI: Putting Good Works in Their Place

Article VI of the *Variata* reflected conversations between Melanchthon and those sometimes called "Reformed Catholics" that began in Leipzig in 1534. The deep concern that Wittenberg theology simply caused gross lawlessness evoked from Melanchthon a highly nuanced response, reflected not only in the protocols of the Leipzig discussions but also in documents prepared for French and English delegations, which met with Melanchthon in Wittenberg at nearly the same time.[27] These responses, along with comments from the second edition of the *Loci communes theologici* of 1535, also came to expression in article VI of the *Variata.*

AC VI was again far more succinct than the text of the *Variata.* There, the worry over works righteousness almost obscured the main point of the article: that believers are to do good works.

26 Not surprisingly, *Variata* XVIII, on free will, underwent similar changes, so that faith and the work of the Holy Spirit were once again made simultaneous.

27 For how these conversations influenced Melanchthon's view of free will, see Wengert, "Origins," 204–205. For how they stimulated formulation of a third use of the law, see Wengert, *Law and Gospel.*

> Likewise, they teach that this faith is bound to yield good fruits and that it ought to do good works commanded by God on account of God's will and not so that we may trust in these works to merit justification before God. For forgiveness of sins and justification are taken hold of by faith, as the saying of Christ also testifies [Luke 17:10]: 'When you have done all [things] [...] say, "We are worthless slaves."' The authors of the ancient church teach the same. For Ambrose says: 'It is established by God that whoever believes in Christ shall be saved without work, by faith alone, receiving the forgiveness of sins as a gift.'

We already noted how Melanchthon moved the quotation by Ambrosiaster into the article on justification, where it more clearly belonged. The main change in the *Variata* came in its vocabulary. Melanchthon spoke immediately of a "righteousness of good works."

> Likewise they teach that when we are reconciled by faith, necessarily the righteousness of good works that God commands for us ought to follow, as Christ also enjoins [Matthew 19:17], 'If you want to walk in life, observe the commandments.'

Despite this positive assessment of the necessity of good works, what Melanchthon then added, while reflecting his own language of good works at the time, actually underscored the impossibility of doing works or having them count toward salvation. He first added a description of human inability in fulfilling the law ("but because such is the weakness of human nature that no one can satisfy the law") and talked about how necessary it was to teach "not only that the law must be obeyed but also how this obedience is pleasing." As in *Variata* IV and V (and already in AC XX), Melanchthon concentrated on the effect of such bad teaching ("lest consciences fall into desperation when they understand that they cannot fulfill the law"). Why is such obedience pleasing? "Not because it satisfies the law but because the person is reconciled to Christ by faith and believes that the remnants of sin are forgiven."[28]

Only after these statements did Melanchthon, as in AC VI, return to justification: this time stated in rigorously forensic terms.

> Therefore, it must always be realized that we obtain forgiveness of sins and that a person is pronounced righteous (that is, accepted gratis on account of Christ) through faith. Only afterwards is the obedience according to the law pleasing, is it reckoned some righteousness and does it merit reward.

Why did Melanchthon insist on this? "For the conscience cannot place its own righteousness or works over against God's judgment." This deep concern for the effect of good and bad teaching on the conscience, also expressed in *Variata* IV

---

28 This way of speaking might also have provided an answer to Brenz's criticism of forensic justification. Even when human beings do righteous things, this righteousness falls far short of what God demands and what a person receives by faith alone.

and V, ran through the heart of Melanchthon's theology of the time and was picked up by his successors in many of the debates after Luther's death.

Melanchthon then heaped up Biblical passages that showed how impossible it was for works to justify: Ps 143:2 ("Do not enter into judgment with your servant [...]"), 1 John 1:8–9 ("If we say we have no sin [...]") and, as in AC VI, Luke 17:10. But, unlike AC VI, Melanchthon did not leave it there but also cited passages that talked about what happens as a result of justification, namely, that a believer's obedience is pleasing and is reckoned some righteousness, referring to 1 John 3:6 ("Everyone who abides in him does not sin") and 2 Cor 1:12 ("Our glory is this: the testimony of our conscience"). These passages proved how one's good works, though impure, were reckoned as pure ("does not sin" and "testimony of our conscience"). These were, of course, thrown against the Evangelicals for their insistence on justification by faith alone. Melanchthon instead used them to indicate that even good works were reckoned good and pleasing gratis, because of Christ through faith.

But Melanchthon needed to address directly the charge of lawlessness, and so he added a paragraph that insisted on the importance of believers fighting against depraved desires, becoming purer through spiritual exercises, "lest we commit something against the conscience." Here, 1 Tim 1:5 ("The sum of the law [Vulgate: end of the command] is love from a pure heart, a good conscience and a genuine faith") fixed the limits of Christian freedom. Melanchthon defined those who "obeyed depraved desires and acted against the conscience" as ones who "were engaged in mortal sins, retaining neither the righteousness of faith nor the righteousness of good works," making reference to 1 Cor 6:9 and those who "do not possess the kingdom of God." Although John Agricola's position scarcely matched what Melanchthon was refuting, this language served as a further defense against the worst of antinomianism circulating in Wittenberg.

5. Augustana XX: Faith and Good Works

While article XX of both versions of the Augustana repeats many themes already struck in articles four through six, the changes wrought by Melanchthon in the *Variata* again demonstrate the complexity of relations between the Roman party and Wittenberg at this critical juncture in the Reformation. For one thing, there is a slight change in tone, so that Melanchthon replaced AC XX's strident "Our people are falsely accused of prohibiting good works" with a milder "That our adversaries accuse us of neglecting the doctrine of good works is a manifest misrepresentation."

Other changes, while small, indicate even more clearly the scope of good works for Wittenberg's theologians. Melanchthon specifically mentioned the recent past's lack of teaching "concerning the exercise of faith and the praise of works in and for the government." As in AC XX, he contrasted these proper works to human works but then added, "In particularly harsh sermons the prophets deplored this calamity in the Church, namely, that when true worship is extinguished human ceremonies and ungodly trust in ceremonies will come to reign in the Church." This reference to the prophets allowed Melanchthon to introduce a host of Old Testament references, from the Psalms, Isaiah, Zechariah, Micah, and Hosea. He also mentioned that before the present age some learned men "had wished for better teaching about the consolation of consciences and the distinction among works."

As in *Variata* VI, Melanchthon insisted that there be proper teaching about "the gospel of faith" to console consciences and also about true good works and worship. Because the opposition did not properly teach the gospel and insisted that people remain uncertain about forgiveness, trust in human works and not in Christ resulted. Without faith in Christ, the Christian's inchoate and imperfect obedience could not be pleasing to God. Furthermore, by calling human works "evangelical perfection," the opposition managed to confuse God's commands with human ones.

Two sections, each introduced with a subtitle, followed: the first labeled "Concerning Faith" and the second "Concerning Good Works." Of course, a similar division may be found in AC XX, except that the section on good works was much briefer. This expansion points again to several important shifts alluded to above. In the section on faith, some of the phrases came directly out of *Variata* IV and V. And again Melanchthon moved directly from citing of Luke 24 to insisting that both the law for repentance and the gospel are universal. Again, he underscored that neither contrition nor any other works preceding or following justification merited anything but only faith in Christ's benefits, bestowed gratis on account of Christ. After concluding (in line with AC XX) that "This position offers firm consolation to terrified minds," Melanchthon then returned to the universality of the promise and made an even more pointed (albeit still indirect) reference to Calvin's theology.

> And it contains nothing absurd, nothing perplexing, nothing sophistic. Nor is there need here for disputes about predestination or similar things. For the promise is universal and does not distract from works but rather arouses a person to faith and true good works.

This specific reference to predestination, front and center in Calvin's 1539 edition of the *Institutes*, separates Wittenberg's position from other Protestant options.[29]

At this point in the argument of AC XX, Melanchthon marshaled three kinds of authorities: Scripture, the church fathers, and experience. In the *Variata*, however, having already commingled experience (of the consoled conscience) with his main arguments, Melanchthon referred first to certain Bible passages before giving voice to several sources in the ancient church. Here, Melanchthon quoted Rom 3:24–25a and 4:5 (mentioned in AC IV) as well as Eph 2:8–9 (cited in AC XX).[30] Unlike in AC XX, however, he not only cited specific texts within those chapters but also offered a brief explanation. "In these and similar verses, Paul eloquently teaches that forgiveness of sins and justification are given to us gratis, not on account of the worthiness of our works." He then discussed Rom 4 as being the chapter where Paul "copiously" argued why we needed such consolation.

> For if the promise depends upon the dignity of our works it becomes uncertain. So that, against the terrors of sin and death, we may have certain and firm consolation and so that faith can stand firm, it is necessary that it lean upon mercy alone and not our worthiness.

Before he turned to the fathers, Melanchthon discussed the nature of faith itself, as he had in AC XX and in *Variata* IV. This is the one place where Melanchthon made clear that faith is not a "virtue" or power, echoing some of the themes in AC V that he otherwise omitted and hearkening back to Luther's *Freedom of a Christian.*

> When therefore we say that we are justified by faith, we do not understand it in this way, namely, that we are righteous on account of the worthiness of its [faith's] very virtue (*virtus*, or "power") but this is the meaning: we obtain forgiveness of sins and the imputation of righteousness through mercy on account of Christ. But this mercy can only be received by faith.

The ambiguity or, to borrow Kolb's term, "brokenness" of Melanchthon's position is clear. He wanted both to avoid turning faith into a virtue (and, hence, a work) and he wanted to link mercy directly to faith (and not indirectly via works or via some unknowable decree of election).

After reiterating that faith was not historical knowledge but rather trust in God's mercy, he then discussed the relation between Paul and James, something

---

29 See Robert Kolb, *Bound Choice, Election, and Wittenberg Theological Method: From Martin Luther to the Formula of Concord* (Grand Rapids: Eerdmans, 2005), 244–270.

30 The specific quotes from Romans may clarify the vague language in AC IV simply to Rom 3 and 4. It would seem that, at least ten years later, Melanchthon meant specifically Rom 3:24f and 4:5.

already addressed in Ap IV, 244–252. Here, Melanchthon noted that James was talking about historical faith while Paul was arguing that faith, or trust, in God's mercy justifies.

> For what can be more pleasing to the conscience that is afflicted and quaking in true sorrows than to hear that this is God's mandate and the voice of Christ the bridegroom so that it may establish with certainty that forgiveness of sins or reconciliation is given not on account of our worthiness but gratis through mercy on account of Christ, in order that the benefit may be certain.

This forgiveness, reconciliation or imputation Melanchthon called "the acceptance of the individual" (*acceptatio personae*), a phrase that would later play a major role in his debate with Andreas Osiander.

Only after this explanation of James 2 did Melanchthon return to the church fathers, quoting directly from *De vocatione gentium* (which he thought was written by Ambrose but was in fact the work of Prosper of Aquitaine) and from Augustine's *On the Spirit and the Letter*, ch. 15 [ix]. But while both fathers were already mentioned in AC XX, in the *Variata* Melanchthon added a third, identified as the Synod of Mileve but actually Augustine's letter to Pope Innocent detailing the decisions of the councils in Carthage and Mileve.[31]

Melanchthon labeled the second section of *Variata* XX "On Good Works." Here, too, one can see the results of a decade of his theological reflections. Unlike AC XX, which devotes only a paragraph to good works and even then returns to emphasize justification by faith alone, *Variata* XX outlines five points about good works themselves. First, as in AC XX, Melanchthon emphasized that teaching about good works is a direct result of the teaching about faith. The gospel, he wrote, "preaches about new life according to [Jer 31], 'I will give my law in their hearts.'" This new life, he went on to say, "is obedience toward God." At the same time, the Gospel also preaches repentance (*poenitentia*). "And faith cannot exist except in those who do penitence, because faith consoles hearts in the contrition and terror of sin." Here, as in AC XX, Melanchthon quoted Rom 5:1 but added Rom 6:6 as well as referring to Isaiah.[32]

Second, he argued that faith itself, understood as the chief worship of God, is the most important good work from which the others arise. Using Rom 10:14 as a

---

31 Epistle CLXXVII.13, in Migne, *Patrologia Latina* 33: 769–770. Melanchthon's text reads as follows (noting omissions or additions from the original): "*Nonne satis ostenditur hoc actum esse per legem ut peccatum cognosceretur [MPL: agnosceretur] [...] et sic aduersus victoriam peccati ad divinam graitam, quae in promissionibus [proposita] est, confugeretur [...] ut ad liberationem quaerantur promissiones Dei, hoc est, gratia Dei, et incipiat esse in homine iusticia, non sua, sed Dei [...].*"

32 The Isaiah reference is not accurate: "*Et Esaias inquit, 'Ubi habitabit Dominus? In Spiritu contrito et humiliato etc.'*" Melanchthon may have been referring to the "Song of the Three Young Men" (v. 16).

jumping off point, Melanchthon wrote, "But when we acknowledge [God's] mercy by faith, then we flee to God, love, pray to, hope in, expect help from and obey him, because now we know that we are children and that our sacrifice, our afflictions, please God." As in AC XX, Melanchthon insisted that the reformers' opponents, while seeming to praise good works neglected this one work, faith, and its fruits, despite how necessary such teaching about these interior works and fruits of the Spirit is for the church.

Third, Melanchthon again introduced the notion that "by this faith, which consoles hearts in penitence, we receive the Holy Spirit, who is given to govern and help us" against the devil and human weakness. This simultaneity of faith and Holy Spirit, while differing from Luther's teaching about the Holy Spirit as the one who "calls me through the gospel," nevertheless served for Melanchthon the same end, namely, to keep the cause of the believer's holiness in God's hands.

Fourth, again reiterating arguments from *Variata* IV–VI, Melanchthon described how exactly this inchoate obedience pleased God. Given that the saints cannot satisfy the law, Melanchthon insisted, on the basis of Rom 8:1, that any good works were righteous in God's sight only because the person who was doing them was already "reconciled and righteous on account of Christ." As much as the first three points were true,

> nevertheless this consolation about the person must be held on to first [...] – that by faith gratis we have forgiveness of sins and the person is righteous, that is, reconciled, and an heir of eternal life on account of Christ – and then afterwards obedience pleases [God], according to this verse [Rom 6:14], 'You are not under the law but under grace.'[33]

Those who opposed this teaching were robbing consciences of consolation and imagining that they could indeed satisfy God's law and that "the monks were perfect."

On the basis of this teaching, Melanchthon continued, the Evangelical churches were also teaching those who committed mortal sins that they were not righteous because God requires obedience. Such people possessed neither the Holy Spirit nor faith since they were sinning against their own consciences. Here it would seem that he was not only responding to the opposition's charge that justification by faith led to lawlessness but perhaps also to John Agricola, who at the time was locked into a bitter dispute with Martin Luther over the role of the law, the so-called antinomian controversy. These two opponents – the legalist and the antinomian – were dismissed by means of this teaching.[34]

Fifth, Melanchthon addressed the problem of how people actually do such good works. While admitting that human beings could externally perform good

---

33 He then referred to a series of passages from John 6, Rom 5 and Augustine on Ps 30.

34 One finds similar concerns expressed in the FC SD IV, 22–34, in KW, 578–580, where material attributable to Chemnitz emphasizes the first opponent and that from Chytraeus the second.

works, "nevertheless without faith human beings are in the power of the devil, who drives them to manifest baseness and fills their minds with ungodly and blasphemous opinions." Added to this, human nature itself is weak and can do nothing without God's help. These two enemies of good works had already been mentioned in AC XX, 31–34. Melanchthon went on to say that "true virtues, without a doubt, are gifts of God." Not only had Paul stated this in Rom 12:6 regarding different gifts given by God's grace, but Augustine, in Melanchthon's view had made the same argument by saying that love merits an increase of love.[35] This allowed Melanchthon to argue that, because the church was subject in this life to the cross and physical death, it could hope in reward through mercy on account of Christ but also as compensation for good works. Here, clearly, the conversations of 1534 with the Roman side had forced him to take seriously the biblical passages about rewards (Matt 5:12).

6. A Final Word

In the closing paragraph of *Variata* XX, Melanchthon not only summarized his argument but also revealed what he considered the heart of Wittenberg's teaching about justification by faith and good works.

> From these things it is evident enough that the teaching of good works is taught in our churches with God's blessing in a godly and correct manner. Good minds know well enough how great the darkness, how great the confusion of teaching concerning good works once existed. No one warned about distinguishing human traditions from divine law. No one taught how good works were pleasing in our great weakness. Finally, there was absolute silence about faith, which is necessary for the forgiveness of sins. But now, with these things being clearly explained, godly consciences hold this consolation and certain hope of salvation and understand true worship and know how such worship pleases God and how it is meritorious.

This highly charged conclusion makes clear just what Melanchthon thought he was doing as he edited this and other articles on justification and good works. The *Variata* still addressed the fundamental difference between the two sides. But it also tried to answer some of the perceived weaknesses in the Evangelicals' argument, especially in *Variata* XX touching on the nature of faith in James 2 and the question of reward. One can also see faint glimmers of the "double righteousness" briefly agreed to at Regensburg in 1541 by both sides.

35 This citation of Augustine remains unidentified. See *Supplementa Melanchthoniana*, 4 vols. (Leipzig: Rudolf Haupt, 1910–1926), V/1: 110, n. 1 and its reference to Migne, *Patrologia Latina* 37: 1563, Augustine's sermon on Psalm 119, sermon 22, par. 2.

Perhaps most important, Melanchthon took the brief remarks about comfort found in AC XX and spread them throughout *Variata* IV, V and XX. This theological move toward consolation, which also undergirded Wittenberg's law/gospel hermeneutic, preserved for the next generation, who had been schooled in Melanchthon's methods and raised with the text of the *Variata*, a way through later Lutheran controversies to concord.

In the end, then, this brief foray into the *Variata* underscores why the authors of the Preface to the *Book of Concord* could write,

> Therefore, we have desired hereby to attest and demonstrate publicly that, then as now, it was never our will or intention to gloss over, cover up, or confirm as consonant with Evangelical teaching any false or impure teaching that might be concealed therein [in the *Variata*], inasmuch as we never understood nor accepted the second edition as conflicting with the first Augsburg Confession [...].[36]

Although this comment was directed specifically at those who used *Variata* X to defend an aberrant view of Christ's presence in the Lord's Supper, nevertheless it shows just how unwilling the Concordists were to reject the *Variata* – an unwillingness underscored by the very language and arguments of the Formula itself.

Finally, this close analysis of the *Variata* on justification may also provide a counterpoint to the rather skewed view of Frederick Bente, whose historical introduction to the *Triglot Concordia* of 1921 still lurks all over the internet.[37] Calling the changes made to the AC "an act of presumption" and claiming that the *Variata* was "disowned by [the] Lutheran church," misconstrues not only the original presentation of the Augustana but also the historical reasons for the publication of the *Variata* in 1540. Dismissing this edition as "an incomprehensible trait of Melanchthon's character" (quoting the nineteenth-century Reformation scholar, Paul Tschakert) not only is bad historiography but also misses the point of how early Lutherans understood the document.[38]

Of course, Bente, like many of his contemporaries in The Lutheran Church—Missouri Synod, was worried about unionism. Thus, he writes,

> True, in making all these changes, Melanchthon did not introduce any direct heresy into the *Variata*. He did, however, in the interest of his irenic and unionistic policy and dogmatic vacillations, render ambiguous and weaken the clear sense of the Augustana.[39]

36 Preface, 17 in KW, 11.

37 Frederick Bente, "Historical Introductions to the Symbolical Books," in *Triglot Concordia: The Symbolical Books of the Ev. Lutheran Church, German – Latin – English* (St. Louis: Concordia, 1921), especially 23–28.

38 Bente also cited a criticism of Melanchthon's editing of AC as if it were Elector John Frederick's opinion, when it now seems certainly to have been Gregor Brück's. See Bente, "Introductions," 25 (quoting CR 3, 367) and WABr 8: 80–82.

39 Bente, "Introductions," 26.

A more balanced look at the *Variata* reveals instead Melanchthon's single-minded focus on justification by faith as comfort to the terrified conscience in the face of opponents who undermined the certainty of God's promises in Christ either by mixing works into salvation as the "Romanists" did or by using the logic of double predestination against the means of grace as Calvin seemed to or by minimizing the law and the role of good works in the Christian life as Agricola had. True, a later generation of Lutheran theologians, no longer facing the immediate threats to the gospel as Melanchthon had perceived them in 1540, was forced by their circumstances to reevaluate the *Variata* and place it squarely under the authority of the AC. However, by so doing they managed to preserve Melanchthon's original intent: not so much to create a new or competing confession of faith but to allow the Augustana to speak to a new set of theological issues – something that is also a central part of the legacy of Robert Kolb himself.

To the World

Charles P. Arand

"I Am God's Creature!" Luther's Confession of the First Article of the Creed

Dr. Robert Kolb is well known as a scholar's scholar when it comes to his careful attention to texts and their historical contexts as well as to the various schools of interpretation regarding those texts. But I would also argue that one of Dr. Kolb's greatest assets as scholar lies in his conviction that what he studies is of more than historical interest. It is a way to learn how the church has conveyed the Gospel in the past in order that we might do so today. In that regard, Bob's scholarship for the church often takes on a catechetical hue. And in many respects, Bob is unique in his ability to translate the theology of the Reformation into a contemporary idiom. We can see this in his writings for other scholars, as well as his works intended for a wider audience. It is in that spirit that I offer this essay regarding one of Luther's most foundational and far-reaching statements in the Large Catechism: "I am God's creature."

1. The Language of Creatureliness

Luther's well-known question, "How can I find a gracious God?" marked an anthropological turn in the sixteenth century as a central theological concern for the church. Whereas the creeds of the early church focused on issues related to the Trinity (how the three persons relate to one another) and Christology (how the divine and human natures relate to one another), the Reformation turned its attention to the way in which those decisions impacted human salvation (how God relates to us). Such questions loom large throughout the Augsburg Confession and Apology as is evident from the topics with which they deal: original sin, free will, faith, good works, the church, and Christians in society.[1]

Such questions went to the heart of the different anthropologies of the medieval church and the reformers that served as paradigms within which com-

1 Jaroslav Pelikan, "Doctrine of Man in Lutheran Confessions," *Lutheran Quarterly* 2 (1950): 34–44.

monly used terms such as sin, grace, justification, and faith were interpreted. The medieval church worked with a modular view of anthropology in which the human person was divided into the higher faculties (reason and will) and the lower faculties (passions and bodily locomotion). They focused on how these components functioned relative to each other along with the way in which sin and stabilizing grace affected their functioning. By contrast Luther and Melanchthon worked with a more holistic and relational anthropology that cared less about the way in which the individual components related to each other and more about how the entire person was related to God and to the world.[2]

As heirs of the Reformation, Lutherans continue to address questions like, "Who am I?" and "What am I?" within the context of justification. When we do, usually, the first word out of our mouths is, "I am a sinner." And this is certainly understandable, given Martin Luther's well-known statement that the proper subject of theology is "man the sinner" and "God the justifier."[3] This emphasis on man the sinner is then often developed in connection with two corollary topics.

The first focuses on how humans were made in the image of God (defined as original righteousness). This served to highlight the unique fellowship that God had with humans and to explain why we were accountable to God. More recently, it has been used to downplay our commonality with animals against Darwinism and animal-rights advocates. The second theme shifted the focus to our loss of God's image with the Fall into sin. This often led to an extended treatment of original or inherited sin and the extent to which it has permeated our entire being. These statements traditionally go to the core of Lutheran anthropological concerns.

For those not raised within the church's culture, such theological statements ("I am a sinner" or "I by nature am sinful and unclean") can easily be heard in a Flacian manner in which there seems to be no difference between being a human and being a sinner. They are simply one and the same. Thus it seems that the Christian story begins on a negative note (the Fall) and ends on a down note (the cross). And so it appears to some, that the church does not offer a positive vision of what God envisioned for us and for this world either with its teaching on

2 Kolb has done much to develop the two kinds of righteousness served as a way of addressing anthropological issues in the context of our two relationships: *coram deo* and *coram mundo*. See "God and His Human Creatures in Luther's Sermons on Genesis: The Reformer's Early Use of His Distinction of Two Kinds of Righteousness," *Concordia Journal* 33, no. 2 (2007): 166–184 and "Luther on the Two Kinds of Righteousness: Reflections on His Two-Dimensional Definition of Humanity at the Heart of His Theology," *Lutheran Quarterly* 13 (1999): 449–466.

3 LW 12: 311. Here Luther is commenting on Psalm 51.

creation or redemption.[4] By itself, focus on the image of God and the Fall into sin does not paint a full biblical picture of who we are and what we are.

In addition, it doesn't address some of the other questions that are raised today. For example, the central issue of environmental ethics and environmental philosophy centers on the question, "How do we see ourselves and our relationship to the world in which we live?" These two questions are closely connected. If I see myself as a divine spark trapped within a physical body, then I might see this world as the dungeon from which I need to escape. If I see myself primarily as a consumer, then I might well see this world as my shopping mall. Other questions that have arisen include, what does it mean to have a physical body? Is the real me my "soul" and is my body little more than a "container" for my soul? For that matter, what is a soul?[5] And why did God give us our senses? What is the importance of emotions for human identity?

I will argue that we would do well to recapture Luther's language of creatureliness and to habituate ourselves and our people in the regular use of the language "Creator," "creature," and "creation." There are good reasons for doing so.

First, the language of creatureliness can help us to speak about God, the human person, and our world so as to make the connection between them more obvious. The word *God* today is little more than a placeholder for whatever one thinks about God. And when we speak of the "world," do we primarily use the language of culture and nature?[6] And what about ourselves? We usually speak of the human person as a human "being." Such language is more philosophical than theological. It neither implies nor requires any particular relationship to God or to the world. If I am a creature, it suggests that I belong to my Creator and that I am part of a larger creation.

Second, the language of creatureliness can help us to ground our thinking more firmly in the doctrine of creation in a way that can also shape how we talk about redemption. Even as the church has sought to remain faithful to the Reformation's insights on justification, the language and theology of creation has often receded into the background of the church's thinking.[7] The debate over creation and evolution over the past century as part of the culture wars has had

4 Gabe Lyons, *The Next Christians: How a New Generation Is Restoring the Faith* (New York: Doubleday, 2010).

5 See Malcolm Jeeves, *Minds, Brains, Souls and Gods: A Conversation on Faith, Psychology and Neuroscience* (Downers Grove, IL: IVP Academic, 2013).

6 Robert Quam, "Creation or Nature: A Manner of Speaking," *Word & World* 11, no. 2 (1991): 131–136.

7 See Gustaf Wingren, "The Doctrine of Creation: Not an Appendix but the First Article," *Word & World* 4, no. 4 (1984): 353–371. Arnold D. Studtmann, "The First Article – The Neglected Article," *Concordia Journal* 12, no. 3 (1986): 130–134; See also Mark P. Surburg, "Good Stuff! The Material Creation and the Christian Faith," *Concordia Journal* 36, no. 3 (2010): 245–262.

the unintentional consequence of losing sight of one of main points of the doctrine of creation, namely the character of the world. William Weinrich points out that the confession of God creating *ex nihilo* is first and foremost a statement about the nature of God and how he relates to the world at all times and in all places.[8]

Along similar lines, Norman Wirzba summarizes the value of using creatureliness as Christian grammar for speaking about the world in which we live.

Creatureliness is the overarching metaphysical framework in terms of which human life and action receive their significance and value. "My fundamental presupposition is that creatureliness goes to the heart of human identity and vocation, illuminating both who we are and what we are to do."[9]

2. I Am a Creature of God within His Creation

In the Small Catechism, Luther translates the words of the Apostles' Creed, "I believe in God the Father, maker of heaven and earth" into a more personal idiom, "I believe that God made me together with all creatures." Luther reinforces the point that God is responsible for the totality of existence by stressing the little particle "all" nine times.[10] With this confession, the church speaks of a distinction between Creator and creation that is more fundamental than any other distinction that can be made whether it be between body and soul, between humans and angels, or matter and spirit.

The distinction between the Creator and his creation leads us to see ourselves in two sets of relationships. First, there is the relationship between the Creator and all creatures. The distinction establishes the relation between God as absolute giver and the human person as total receiver. Second, there is the relationship between me and other creatures within God's creation. We live in mutual dependence upon one another. Put another way, "creatureliness is inescapably marked by need and by dependence on fellow creatures and a creator."[11] Thus the doctrine of creation provides the basis for the distinction of the two kinds of righteousness as a framework for understanding what life as a human creature looks like.[12]

8 William Weinrich, "*Creatio ex nihilo*," unpublished paper.

9 Norman Wirzba, *From Nature to Creation (The Church and Postmodern Culture): A Christian Vision for Understanding and Loving Our World* (Grand Rapids: Baker Academic, 2015). Chapter 4 "The Human Art of Creaturely Life," 96.

10 See Charles P. Arand, "Luther on the Creed," *Lutheran Quarterly* 20 (Spring 2006): 1–25.

11 Wirzba, "The Human Art of Creaturely Life," 99.

12 See Robert Kolb, "God and His Human Creatures in Luther's Sermons on Genesis: The

I Am a Creature of God

So what does it mean to confess that God is the maker of heaven and earth? In some ways, we've already answered that. It means that "God created all that exists,"[13] One might expect Luther to describe all the various things that God has made along the lines of Genesis 1. But he does not. Instead, he answers in the Large Catechism (LC II, 13) by proclaiming, "I am God's creature"![14] As such, I am "his handiwork" and "his workmanship."[15] Luther takes great delight in being a creature. In fact, "if you know this, you will be a greater doctor than all the doctors of the university!"[16]

Why is seeing ourselves as God's creatures so important for Luther? First and foremost, I cannot appreciate who or what I am apart from my relationship to my Creator. Such knowledge tells me where I come from, what I am, and perhaps most importantly, to whom I belong.[17] I belong to him and I am dependent upon him. To be a creature is to be dependent and my life contingent. As his creature, God is the source of my life. Another way of expressing this is to say that God gives me life; I receive life from God.

To say that God made me is to say not only that God has given me life but that he continues to give me life. And so immediately after his statement that God made me, Luther goes on to expound what it is to say that God provides all that I need to support this body and life. For Luther, this is not just about supporting or preserving my life, it is actually giving me life. In the Small Catechism, Luther proceeds to enumerate all of these gifts. He begins at the center (me) and moves outward into the world in a series of expanding concentric circles. He begins with my body and soul, expands to the basic necessities of life (food and drink, clothing and shoes, spouse and child, house and home) and then finally out into the wider world (earth, good weather, and stable government). God has done all of this "for me."

At this point, Luther's exposition might seem very anthropocentric to contemporary ears as if God is not concerned about the nonhuman creation. But such is not necessarily the case. It is true that Luther does not explicitly deal with God's provision for nonhuman creatures. Clough rightly points out, however,

---

Reformer's Early Use of His Distinction of Two Kinds of Righteousness," *Concordia Journal* 33, no. 2 (2007): 166–184.

13 KW, 354.

14 KW, 432. See Heinrich Holze, "Luther's Concept of Creation. Five Remarks on His Interpretation of the First Article in the Large Catechism (1529)," in *Concern for Creation: Voices on the Theology of Creation* (Uppsala: Svenska kyrkans forskningsgrad, 1995), 50.

15 LW 43: 210.

16 WA 30.I: 88, 22ff [*Katechismuspredigten* 1528].

17 WA 45: 12, Z16f.

that Luther was seeking to assure his audience of God's care for them. But that does not mean nonhuman creatures are excluded.[18] As the catechism suggests, this would be a good place for such exploration. I see that God does not do this only for me; he does it for all of creation.

Herein lies Luther's goal for helping people see themselves as creatures: so that they will look to God for all that they need. And so to live as the creature God intended, is for me to entrust my life to God and look to him for all good things. One might say that Luther's goal is to enable people to pray the evening prayer where the believer confidently says, "into your hands I commend myself, my body and soul and all things."

The confession that I am God's creature becomes the presupposition for everything else in the catechism. It is, for example, the starting point and assumption with which Luther works in his timeless exposition of the first commandment in the Large Catechism. As a creature, I need to look somewhere for life. The only question becomes, where do I look? To my Creator or to his creation? Similarly, the Creed shows me all the gifts of God from the beginning of creation all the way to the new creation. And so to be justified *coram deo* by faith alone is to be restored as creatures and to life as creatures. For faith in the promises of the Gospel is nothing other than to entrust ourselves and our future to God's care and faithfulness. This is what God first created us to be and to do.

I Am a Creature among Fellow Creatures

As a creature, I am not alone. As I confess that God made "me together with all creatures" I look around and I see that I am part of a much larger creation that fills me with wonder and delight.[19] I see a world of beauty and diversity, of landscapes and seascapes, of cranes and hummingbirds, of dragonflies and butterflies, of whales and dolphins, and of elephants and lions. I am part of this world with its amazing array of creatures. It is little wonder that the Psalmist exclaims, "O Lord, how manifold are your works! [...] the earth is full of your creatures [...] the sea, great and wide, which teems with creatures innumerable, living things both small and great" (Ps 104:24–25). About this Psalm, Luther comments that the psalmist "sings and takes great delight in God's creatures, so

18 David Clough, "The Anxiety of the Human Animal: Martin Luther on Non-Human Animals and Human Animality," in *Creaturely Theology* (London: SCM Pr., 2009), 21.

19 Oswald Bayer, *Martin Luther's Theology: A Contemporary Interpretation*, trans., Thomas H. Trapp (Grand Rapids: Eerdmans, 2008), 140.

wondrously fashioned and so beautifully coordinated. But who pays any heed to this and views them as such? Only faith and the Spirit."[20]

Luther's language of "creatures" helps us to see the creation rightly. These are all my fellow creatures! Like me, they were also created by God. As such, they belong to him.[21] They were created for God's purposes – purposes that may not always evident to me. This is one of the messages of the book of Job. God takes Job on a tour of the universe away from human civilization. He takes Job to "where the wild things are," so to speak. Most of these have nothing to do with me. And so God shows Job wild weather, wild geology, and wild animals. Most of don't care anything about me. Many seem dangerous. Yet, as God's creatures they are the personal expression of God's love. God delights in them.

Not only are they God's creatures, but they are my fellow creatures. How I view them and talk about them affects the way I treat them. If I see them as vermin or pests, I will treat them one way. If I see them as resources, I will deal with them another way. And if I see them as fellow creatures, it will hopefully deal with them another way. This is not to say that they are of equal value as humans. But as God's creatures they have value. And as a creature among fellow creatures, I encounter limits in dealing with them. As the expression of God, other creatures remain mysteries to me. As fellow creatures they are "endowed with the integrity and possibility that is uniquely theirs."[22] For me to impose my agenda on them or to make them what I want them, I distort and harm them. We sin when we "see them in terms of the agendas that please us."[23]

The third thing to note is that we live in mutually dependent relationships with our fellow creatures. "There simply is no such thing as freedom from our entanglement in the lives of others."[24] For me to live as a creature is to live by receiving and giving. This is what it means to be a creature. As members of creation, "giving and receiving are not optional matters. The question is not if but how we are going to go about receiving and giving."[25] We can illustrate this with inhaling and exhaling. I receive from my parents and give to my children. Even here the ritual of thanking people becomes important. Conversely, as Jonathan Wilson, points out, "The word for taking and keeping is death. When we refuse

20 Luther, "The Summaries of the Psalms, 1531," in *Reading the Psalms with Luther* (St. Louis: Concordia Publishing House, 2007), 245.

21 Elijah Judah Schochet argues that the primary argument for an environmental ethic in the Old Testament is not one of "ethical consideration for fauna" but the fact that all belong to him. So man must not interfere with "the creations of God's world." He is "bidden to preserve the authenticity and purity of all species of life." *Animal Life in Jewish Tradition: Attitudes and Relationships* (New York: Ktav Publishing Co., 1984), 65.

22 Wirzba, "Is Creation a Gift?" *From Nature to Creation*, 143.

23 Wirzba, "Drawing on the Iconographic Tradition." *From Nature to Creation*, 83.

24 Wirzba, "Is Creation a Gift?" *From Nature to Creation*, 145.

25 Wirzba, "Is Creation a Gift?" *From Nature to Creation*, 145.

the process of giving and receiving that is life, then we short-circuit the process of life so that all that remains is death."[26]

The ramifications continue into the realm of redemption. I am a creature, but I am a rebellious creature not content to live as a creature in dependence upon him.[27] We wanted to be like God and take charge. Wirzba notes that the heart of idolatry lies not in "the worship of things but the worship of ourselves."[28] This idolatry,

> is born out of a deep distrust in God's power, wisdom, and provision. People embark on an idolatrous path when they believe that God's gifts are not sufficient or God's care misdirected. We begin to think that we must take hold of the world for ourselves.[29]

The entire history of humankind can be described in these terms. In the process, I misused God's good creatures in the worst way (Heidelberg Disputation Thesis 24).

The great irony in all this is that, even as we sought to become like God, the Creator entered his creation in a special way by becoming as a creature. That is to say, the Creator became a creature, a human creature, a male human creature! And to what end? To restore us as creatures! As James Nestingen has noted, "to be restored as a creature [...] that is salvation!"[30]

3. I Am a Breath-Enlivened Body

One of the hallmarks of Christian thought has been the affirmation of the goodness of creation and with it the goodness of the body. Strikingly, God creates a universe that in its basic nature is quite different from God. While God is spirit (John 4:24), he creates a universe of physical matter and brings it to life! The Creator becomes incarnate and dies a bodily death. He rises bodily from the grave and ascends bodily to the right hand of God. This confession of the goodness of creation was – and remains – countercultural. It poses a challenge to all dualistic systems that would separate the spiritual from the material and elevate the former over the latter. It is a "deeply counter-intuitive claim given the tension that

26 Jonathan Wilson, *God's Good World: Reclaiming the Doctrine of Creation* (Grand Rapids: Baker Academic, 2013), 109.

27 Bonhoeffer picks up on this thought nicely. "It [humanity] now lives out of its own resources, creates its own life, is its own Creator [...] Adam is no longer a creature. Adam has torn himself away from his creatureliness." Dietrich Bonhoefer, *Creation and Fall: A Theological Exposition of Genesis 1–3*, ed., John W. De Gruchy (Minneapolis: Fortress Press, 1997), 120.

28 Wirzba, "Making Sense of Idolatry," *From Nature to Creation*, 46.

29 Wirzba, "The End of Idolatry," *From Nature to Creation*, 58.

30 James Arne Nestingen, "Preaching the Catechism," *Word & World* 10 (1990): 39.

we as humans experience between the grandeur and the misery of our existence."[31]

God Made Me an Earth Creature

Greek philosophical dualism has not only shaped our Western conception of the world for several millennia, but has also shaped the way we view ourselves as comprised of an immaterial aspect and a material aspect. This duality exists in tension (and at times in conflict).[32] The soul is viewed as immortal and the body as mortal, or the soul is incorruptible and the body is corruptible, or the soul connects us to the divine whereas our body only connects to the world, or the soul desires higher and more noble things while the body only seeks physical pleasures of the flesh, or the soul returns to God whereas the body returns to the earth at death. The Christian tradition has not been immune from such patterns of thought and speech. Christians often speak in such a way that my soul is the real me and my body is merely the vessel for soul.

The creation of Adam in Genesis 2 does not require or support such a dualistic understanding of ourselves. Verse 7 begins, "then the Lord God formed the man of dust from the ground." It portrays a more holistic and unified picture of the human creature. It describes God almost as getting on his hands and knees to scoop up some earth and form a human body from it. He forms the head, the torso, the arms and legs, and etches out the eyes and nostrils. Verse 7 then continues, "and breathed into his nostrils the breath of life, and the man became *a living creature*" [italics added] (*nephesh chayyah*). The King James rendered this as "living soul," which could be fine if soul refers to the whole embodied person. But it could just as easily be read in a dualistic manner in which God places an [immortal] soul into the body.

The body, however, is the object of the narrative. God forms man out of the dust of the ground. But it is still a lifeless body. Then God breathes into his nostrils the breath of life and he becomes a living creature (*nephesh chayyah*).[33] As a general rule in the Old Testament, to be alive or living is to move (think of how we talk about *lifeless*). That which is alive moves across space. God breathes

31 Ernst M. Conradie, "What on Earth Did God Create? Overtures to an Ecumenical Theology of Creation," *The Ecumenical Review* 4 (2014): 438.

32 Mark Edmundson lays out these tensions in "Body and Soul," *Hedgehog Review* 17, no. 2 (2015). Accessed at http://iasc-culture.org/THR/THR_article_2015_Summer_Edmundson.php.

33 Horace Hummel suggests that "'Nephesh' implies the mystery of life imbuing the 'whole person'; what all that 'life' encompasses must be determined from the total Scriptural context!" in "The Image of God," *Concordia Journal* 10 (1984): 87.

into the body and Adam begins to inhale and exhale. The blood begins pumping through his veins. His mind becomes active and he becomes a conscious and thinking body. He gets up and begins to move around. God's breath created movement. Similarly, death is seen as the breath leaving the body at which point the body ceases to move (Ps 104:29–30). This narrative suggests that it is not so much the case that I have a body as I am a body. God's breath animates the body. I am a moving body, feeling body, and thinking body, imagining body, and creating body. I am a breath-enlivened body.

In light of this, Luther's language of body and soul can be understood holistically. Luther does this when he states that God has given *me* my body and soul. But these are not to be pitted one against another. As Luther notes, "He does not love the head and hate the foot, nor favor the soul and hate the body."[34] Together, body and soul constitute my *self*. Body here then speaks to the outer activity of my *self* as I interact with the world through "eyes, ears, and all my members." Soul speaks to the inner activity of my *self* as I perceive the world with "reason and all my senses" (along with emotions and imagination).[35] So although Luther uses the traditional language of body and soul, he presents a more holistic and unified view of the "self" that reflects the biblical account. I am not a body without a soul; I am not a soul without a body.

God relates to me then not only as a creature, but as a breath-enlivened bodily creature. And so Luther urges that parents should teach their children that God has made them (Ps 139:13–14; Job 10:11) and that everything they have, their eyes, hands, and all their members are gifts from God.[36] Thus, I relate to God with my entire being. My ears hear his word. My brain processes his words. I see the words on the printed page. I feel the water upon my body and I taste the grain and grapes of the Lord's supper. I kneel and fold my hands in prayer. I relate to God as an entire breath-enlivened body. This is what it means to be spiritual.

Because I am a breath-enlivened embodied person, God encounters me and I encounter God in specific places and times within creation. For just as I am not a person without a body, so I am not a body without a place. God created an extravagant park as a place for Adam and Eve to make their home. And it also becomes the place where God chooses to dwell. We find God meeting Adam and Eve at a place in the garden during the cool of the day – perhaps early morning (to discuss the upcoming day's events) or late afternoon (to reflect on the day's accomplishments) – for conversation and fellowship. God continues to meet us within this world.

34 LW 32: 228.

35 Similarly, the Athanasian Creed speaks of Christ as "a perfect human being, composed of a rational soul and human flesh." KW, 24–25.

36 WA 29: 472. 34–473. 1–3.

God encounters us here on earth, not as one who is standing behind the curtain of creation but as one who is working from within creation.[37] Luther has a profound sense of God's presence within the world that could rival any mystic. He can speak of Christ's presence within creation without personifying the world as the mystics do yet without removing God from the world as the deists do. And so even though "I can say of all creatures, 'There is God, or God is in it,' I cannot say 'This is God himself.'"[38] God is powerfully and actively present within creation, but God is also concealed or hidden within creation with the result that no one can discern his person or will "merely from his presence."[39]

But not only do I encounter God in the world, I encounter him *for me*. That is to say, he sustains me or makes me new every day. Luther wants children to perceive that God comes to us clothed in masks, that creatures and creation are the instrument of his blessing for us.

Consider how this picture of embodiedness can inform our understanding of redemption. In pastoral care, how often does one hear, "Lord, free me from this frail body" instead of, "Lord, free my body from the pain, sin and death"? This does not mean that there is some kind of separation that tears us apart at death (soul in heaven and body in grave). But I do think it might be better to speak in such a way that when I die, I am with Jesus, and Jesus will raise me from the grave on the last day.

I Am a Bodily Creature among Other Bodily Creatures

In the last several centuries, we have encountered another kind of dualism. It is not so much a Platonic spirit/body dualism with regard to God, as an Enlightenment mind/body dualism with regard to the world. The real me is now defined in terms of my mind or consciousness. One only has to recall Descartes' famous saying, "I think therefore I am." This dualism of mind/body establishes a hierarchy between mind and body in which the mind is elevated over the body. In this way, human creatures can pursue the "absurd desire of humans to become self-creators."[40] It manifests itself in two ways.

37 Niels Henrik Gregersen, "Grace in Nature and History: Luther's Doctrine of Creation Revisited," *Dialog: A Journal of Theology* 44, no. 1 (Spring 2005): 25.

38 LW 37: 62.

39 Steven L. Churchill, "'This Lovely Music of Nature': Grounding an Ecological Ethic in Martin Luther's Creation Mysticism," *Currents in Theology and Mission* 26, no. 3 (1999): 188.

40 Oswald Bayer, "Self-Creation? On the Dignity of Human Beings," *Modern Theology* 20 (April 2004): 275–290.

First, our bodies have become little more than shipping containers for getting our minds from home to work[41] as society has moved from an agrarian and manufacturing economy dependent upon manual labor to an informational and knowledge economy dependent upon our minds. But our bodies are not the most durable containers. People like Elon Musk insist that we must evolve by exchanging organic parts for machine parts. Other techno-optimists like Ray Kurzweil[42] look forward to the day when we can download our consciousness into a holographic image thus replacing our frail bodies with something more sturdy and lasting.[43]

Second, our bodies have come to be seen as straitjacket for the mind. Paige Bradley, an artist, created a sculpture of a woman in a sitting yoga position entitled *Expansion.* The body is cracking apart with rays of light coming forth from it. Bradley says,

> From the moment we are born, the world tends to have a container already built for us to fit inside: a social security number, a gender, a race, a profession or an IQ. I ponder if we are more defined by the container we are in, rather than what we are inside. Would we recognize ourselves if we could expand beyond our bodies?[44]

Here we might alter Descartes' saying, from "I think therefore I am," to "I am what I think I am." Or "I am what I choose to be."

Both approaches reject the idea that as breath-enlivened bodies, there is a certain "givenness" to our life that we receive as a gift. From my parents, I have inherited a set of bodily characteristics that to a large extent define me in both my outer and inner life. I receive from them a DNA code that gives me a medical history, a particular appearance, a budding personality, and various skills and traits – all of which affect the way in which my life unfolds within this world. My body thus links me back not only to my parents, but to grandparents, great grandparents, and distant ancestors. It connects me to siblings and cousins as well as friends and community. My ancestry also brings a cultural identity and with it a sense of belonging (there's a reason people look up their family trees).

Just as I am not a person without a body, so also, I am not a body without a place in which I move and live. I find myself in a place that was an "accident" of my birth. And it is in those places that I am dependent upon others to sustain and

41 Wendell Berry, "The Body and the Earth," in *The Unsettling of America: Culture and Agriculture* (San Francisco: Sierra Club Books, 1977), 108.

42 Ray Kurzweil, *The Singularity Is Near: When Humans Transcend Biology* (New York: Viking, 2005).

43 For an excellent discussion of these issues, see Joel P. Okamoto, "Science, Technology, and the American Mind," in *The American Mind Meets the Mind of Christ,* ed., Robert Kolb (St. Louis: Concordia Seminary Press, 2010), 96–111.

44 Paige Bradley, http://paigebradley.com/sculpture/metamorphosis/expansion/ a Modern Met blog accessed on May 18, 2017.

protect my life. That begins with parents and family, but also includes my extended family, and for that matter, friends, neighbors, and community. I am dependent upon them socially, psychologically, and physically. A Swahili proverb gets it exactly right: "a person is a people." And I am most fully me when I interact with body and all my senses with someone else in a shared space. Cyberspace communities would free our minds from the confines of our bodies so that we can be "everywhere yet nowhere." But it is one thing to speak by telephone with a child on the other side of the country, it is another thing entirely to be there to give that person a hug.

Perhaps most important, God has created us as specific kinds of breath-enlivened bodies. He made us male bodies and female bodies. We are different and yet complementary to one another. And this is so not only with respect to procreative processes. Being an embodied male or female affects the way in which I relate emotionally, intuitively, and socially to other people as well. For example, Deborah Tannen has argued that men communicate to exchange information while women communicate to build relationships.[45] By creating us similar yet different, God made us complementary to each other with regard to our dominion in the world.[46] Being male or female is not incidental to my identity.

Second, my body not only connects me to other people, but to other creatures and to the earth itself. Augustine was quite right when he noted that our "bodies are the earth we carry." My body is comprised of the elements of the earth's crust. When I am born, I am nearly 90 % water. As an adult, I am 70 % water. God has not only made me (together with all creatures) from the earth but for life on the earth. That is to say, our bodies are suited for life on earth. Our bone density is suited for the earth's gravity along with the muscle mass needed to carry it. Our breath and circulatory system enable us to stand up and resist the pull of gravity. When we travel into outer space, we need to take elements of the earth with us.

And it is through our bodies that we interact with the world in an ongoing mutual activity of receiving and giving. At the most basic level, the permeable membrane of every cell lets things in and lets things out. We inhale the air that circulates around the world. We drink the water and perspire the water that evaporates from oceans and falls to the earth as rain. We consume the energy of

---

45 Deborah Tannen, *You Just Don't Understand! Women and Men in Conversation* (New York: William Morrow Paperbacks; first edition, 2007).

46 Hummel, "The Image of God," 86. He sees it as a "duality in unity." "Suitable helper." "Man and woman belong together in a qualitatively different way over against all other creatures," 87. "Their very difference witnesses also the underlying unity," 86. "The suitable partner is to cooperate in the common task of [...] presumably 'ruling' over creation, as in Genesis 1, and in the immediate context, more specifically of raising a family," 88. See also Oswald, "Being in the Image of God," *Lutheran Quarterly* 27 (Spring 2013): 76–88. For a more comprehensive work, see Andreas J. Köstenberger and Margaret E. Köstenberger, *God's Design for Man and Woman: A Biblical-Theological Survey* (Wheaton, IL: Crossway: 2014).

the sun through the food that we eat from the earth and expel it out. It is only through my eyes that I receive the light that enables me to see. It is through the reception of sound waves and vibrations on the ear drums that I am able to hear. We receive aromas through the nose. With my mind and imagination, I perceive the beauty of the world around me, hear music and rhythms, write a book of poetry.

My body not only tethers me to the earth, it also connects me to specific places on the earth. We occupy these spaces within time. Life thus becomes all that happens to me in these places over time. Again, to draw on Wendell Berry, life is all that happens to us in place over time.[47] We move through these places and live in them. In them we experience the seasons of creation, the rhythms of daily life, and the passage of years. It is here, that we live with our mates, have young ones, feed them, and make our homes. Life is a "storied residence."[48] The same applies for people whether they are raised in Wisconsin or Missouri.[49] These places define the uniqueness of individual creatures.

4. I Am a *Human* Creature

Thus far, we have seen how God's act of creating out of nothing establishes the relationship of Creator and creature, as well as the value of bodily life. Now we turn our attention to the way in which God organized the household of his creation.[50] Here God not only welcomes us into his life, he invites us to share in his own creative activity by making the heads of his household. And this is not just for creation, but extends to redemption as well. In Christ, we are being renewed in his image and have been made his coheirs and co-rulers with him (2 Tim 2:12; Rev 5:10). But we rarely ask what is it that we inherit and over what will we reign? The

47 Wendell Berry, *Life is a Miracle: An Essay Against Modern Superstition* (Washington, D.C.: Counterpoint, 2000), 40. See also, Berry, "Is Life a Miracle?" in *Citizenship Papers* (Berkeley: Counterpoint, 2003), 184–186.

48 Holmes Rolston III, "Down to Earth: Persons in Place in Natural History," in *Philosophy and Geography III: Philosophies of Place*, ed., Andrew Light and Jonathan M. Smith (Lanham, MD: Rowman and Littlefield Publishers, 1998), 285–296. See also, "The Human Standing in Nature: Storied Fitness in the Moral Overseer," in *Values and Moral Standing. Bowling Green Studies in Applied Philosophy*, ed., Wayne Sumner et al. (Bowling Green, OH: The Applied Philosophy Program, 1986), 8: 90–101.

49 See Craig G. Bartholomew, *Where Mortals Dwell: A Christian View of Place for Today* (Grand Rapids: Baker, 2011) and *J. Inge, A Christian Theology of Place* (Aldershot, UK: Ashgate, 2003).

50 This is a common image used by church fathers from Gregory of Nyssa to Martin Luther to describe God's creation. Conradie summarizes it nicely when he observes that this world, God's beloved creation, "is nothing but the household (*oikos*) of the triune God," Conradie, "What on Earth Did God Create?" 441.

answer is the new heavens and the new earth that will appear when Christ returns (Matt 5:5; Rom 8:21).

The Image of God Makes Us Human

As Luther noted above, not only am I a creature, but I am a special creature made by God having been made in his image (Gen 1:26). The image of God is one of the more difficult concepts to define with much precision on the basis of Scripture. Nevertheless, the importance of it in those few places where Scripture makes reference to it have given birth to many dissertations on the topic. Does it refer to our outward (even physical) appearance? Does it refer to specific traits (such as rationality and free will)? Does it refer to relationality within the community of the Trinity? Does it mean that we are the image of God only together as male and female?[51]

The tradition that we have inherited from the Reformation usually links the image of God to original righteousness (Ap II, 18).[52] Righteousness conforming to a standard or meeting one's design specification. In this case, being righteous involves being the human creature that God envisioned us to be – both in our relationship to God and in our relationship to the world. And given the Lutheran emphasis on original sin and the bound will, they insisted that we lost original righteousness before God – and hence the image of God – completely in the Fall only to have it restored in Jesus Christ. But the Lutheran tradition also acknowledges that in some way humans retain the image of God even after the Fall (Gen 9:6).

The one thing that can be said with certainty is that whatever the specific characteristics of the image of God may be, the image of God is what makes us distinctively human. Humans are given the privilege of relating to God in a way that no other creature does. Even though angels share an immaterial nature like God, it is we earth-embodied, breath-enlivened creatures that are given the privilege of representing God and reflecting God's dominion to his entire physical creation. Thus, this relationship comes with unique responsibilities. Luther captures this nicely in the Small Catechism when he writes, "For all this I owe it to God to thank and praise, serve and obey him" (SC II, 2).[53] In the Large Catechism he elaborates, "it inevitably follows that we are in duty bound to love, praise, and thank without ceasing, and, in short, to devote all these things to his

51 For a good article on the overview of the questions and the biblical data, see Hummel, "The Image of God," 83–93.

52 KW, 114.

53 KW, 355.

service, as he has required and enjoined in the Ten Commandments" (LC II, 23).[54] By means of our thanks and praise, we distinguish God from his creation. He is our Creator; we are his creatures. This distinction comes to the foreground in the first commandment ("you are to have no other gods") and Luther's explanation ("we are to fear, love, and trust God above all things) (SC I, 1).[55] This distinction is the presupposition of everything else that the catechism has to say about God and our relationship with him. He alone is the Creator and giver of life to all. Thanks and praise shows that we are dependent upon God, but that we wish to continue in a relationship with him where we trust and rely upon him for all that we need even in the midst of our experiences to the contrary as God's will for us. "We would not swagger about and boast and brag as if we had life, riches, power, honor, and such things of ourselves" (LC II, 23).[56] We would instead see that, "Creatures are the hands, channels, instruments through which God bestows all blessings" that all we receive we receive from him through creatures" (LC I, 26).[57]

When we see in these things the fatherly heart of God "our hearts will be warmed and kindled with gratitude to God and a desire to use all these blessings to his glory" (LC II, 23).[58] Wingren picks up on these thoughts,

> Only he who is secure in faith has the ability to obey God's commands without ulterior motives. Such a faith [...] is belief not only in the forgiveness of sins, but also in God's providence, protection, and direction in material matters.[59]

As Luther puts it,

> [God] makes no greater demand on us than a heartfelt trust in him for every good thing, so that we walk straight ahead on the right path, using all of God's gifts exactly as a shoemaker uses a needle, awl, and thread for his work and afterward puts them aside, or as a traveler makes use of an inn, food, and lodging, but only for his physical needs. (LC I, 47).[60]

Only when we regard God as the giver of all good things are we free to use his gifts properly by not imposing our agenda on them as our idols (LC I, 47).[61]

54 KW, 433.
55 KW, 351.
56 KW, 433.
57 KW, 389.
58 KW, 433.
59 Gustaf Wingren, *Creation and Law* (Edinburgh: Oliver and Boyd, 1961), 71.
60 KW, 392. Theodosius Harnack interprets Luther's words to mean, "I shall honor (*ehren*), love (*lieben*), trust (*vertrauen*) him as father, also regard myself as his child, so that I do not misuse his gifts, but use them according to his will," in *Erklärung des Kleinen Katechismus Dr. Martin Luther's* (Erlangen: A. Deichert, 1882), 189.
61 KW, 392.

Our failure to thank and praise God ignores our creatureliness and the giftedness of our existence.[62] That in turn results in the misuse of God's blessings and gifts for one's "pride, greed, pleasure, and enjoyment" never thanking God or acknowledging him as Lord or Creator (LC II, 21).[63] And how do we misuse those gifts? We force them to carry a burden they were not meant to carry, namely, burden of divinity.[64] In his Heidelberg theses, Luther notes that without the perspective brought on by the cross, we will use the best things in the worst way, i. e., we will ascribe divinity to them.[65]We either treat creaturely gifts as the source of our life – the loss of which would mean the end of our life – or we act as though everything exists for us in which case we use them solely for our own purposes.

Finally, God holds us responsible for how we live within the world as his representatives for God has given us the keys to the house of creation. For this reason, Luther suggests that if we truly believed this article, it would "humble and terrify all of us" for we continually misuse his gifts. The well-being of creation depends upon how we live within it and how we deal with it. Thus when Adam and Eve fell into sin and dragged down the creation with them, God punished them by cursing the earth. The earth must now perform an alien work, a work for which it was not created to do. For it has now become an instrument of death. Luther makes it clear that this was our fault, not creation's fault. Creation did not mess up. Animals did not sin. Trees did not sin. As Luther puts it, "The earth indeed is innocent and would gladly produce the best products, but it is prevented by the curse which was placed upon man because of sin." (discussing Gen 3:19).[66]

62 Johannes Schwanke, "Luther's Theology of Creation," in *The Oxford Handbook of Martin Luther's Theology*, ed., Robert Kolb, Irene Dingel, L'ubomir Batka (Oxford: Oxford University Press, 2014), 201–211. See LW 1: 39; 6: 24–25.

63 KW, 433.

64 Wirzba puts it this way, "An idolatrous impulse compels us to place expectations on things that they simply cannot bear." "Making Sense of Idolatry," *From Nature to Creation*, 49.

65 See Heidelberg Disputation, thesis 24: "Yet that wisdom is not of itself evil, nor is the law to be evaded; but without the theology of the cross man misuses the best things in the worst way." In his proofs for thesis 24, Luther writes, "Indeed the law is holy" [Rom. 7:12], "every gift of God good [1 Tim. 4:4] and everything that is created exceedingly good," as in Gen 1[:31]. "But, as stated above, he who has not been brought low, reduced to nothing through the cross and suffering, takes credit for works and wisdom and does not give credit to God. That person thus misuses and defiles the gifts of God." "The Heidelberg Disputation," in *The Annotated Luther. Volume 1: The Roots of Reform*, ed., Timothy J. Wengert (Minneapolis: Fortress Press, 2015), 85, 84, 101.

66 LW 1: 205.

Human Creatures and Benevolent Dominion

What makes us human creatures is not only that we are made in the image of God but that God commissions us to look after his creation. In Gen 1:26–27, one follows the other.

> Then God said, "Let us make man in our image, after our likeness. And let them have dominion over the fish of the sea and over the birds of the heavens and over the livestock and over all the earth and over every creeping thing that creeps on the earth." So God created man in his own image, in the image of God he created him; male and female he created them.

So, God made us together, male and female[67]– in his image, in order to exercise dominion. At the very least, as God's image bearer, I reflect God's dominion to the world. What kind of a dominion is it?

While in pagan religions, humans are often created to be slaves for the gods, the Bible portrays God as one who rules by looking after the well-being of his creation. In other words, he loves his creation and lavishes his love upon it without measure. And he attends to the specific needs of his creation (Gen 1, Ps 72, or especially Ps 104). God's gracious ruling and lavish love for creation provides the context for considering the well-known verbs with which human oversight of creation is described in Gen 1:26–28 (*radah* and *kabash*) and Gen 2:15 (*avad* and *shamar*). So being in the image of God means that we reflect God's own care outward into the world.

At the same time that we reflect God's own love for creation, we rule over fellow creatures. One might ask, why are we given dominion and not the angels? Ultimately, we cannot answer that question as it lies hidden in God's free and gracious choice. But Richard Bauckham has suggested that it is at least consistent with God's *modus operandi.* He points out that God made it clear to Israel that they should choose a brother from among themselves – and not a foreigner – to rule as their king. Why? A foreigner might well rule as a tyrant. But a brother would be ruling over brothers and sisters and thus hopefully not rule as a tyrant.[68]

In an analogous way, God chosen us to rule over his other creatures because we are fellow creatures of the earth. We see this in several ways. First, we together with all creatures are made from the earth and given the breath of life (Gen 2:7,19). Second, we together with all creatures thus share the same needs for

---

67 This is, in part, where Hummel ends up as the one thing we can say with some certainty as it is "the most immediate result of man's creation in God's image." Hummel, "The Image of God," 86.

68 Richard Bauckham, "Stewardship and Relationship," in *Care of Creation: Focusing Concern and Action,* ed., R. J. Berry (Downers Grove, IL: Inter-Varsity Press, 2000), 105.

space, shelter, food, and water. We have similar needs. Third, we share with all other earth creatures God's blessing to be fruitful and multiply.

God has not only given us many similar characteristics as our fellow non-human creatures, but he has also equipped us with what are arguably distinctive characteristics in order to carry out our responsibility. While it is tricky to pin down the image of God to certain human attributes, it is not too far afield to say that some traits or characteristics come with that image. For example, God has given us the ability of voluntary self-restraint so that we can limit ourselves for the sake of others, the capacity for empathy with other creatures (while our dogs may have a concern for their owners, it is doubtful that they would have such a concern for the entire human race), and the capacity for creativity with regard to the development of culture.[69]

Have we lost this dominion in the Fall? The answer is yes and no. Luther suggests that we did lose it with regard to the way we were intended to exercise it. But we retain a semblance in that we exercise by "industry and skill" and "cunning and deceit."[70] Moreover, even after the Fall into sin, people continue to function as God's instruments for the good of creation, even if they do so unwittingly. Farmers, carpenters, all who handle creation's wares, carry God's gifts to their neighbors, even if their purpose is not always to serve.[71] Even the non-human creation continues to bear forth its bounty in spite of the ecological destruction we inflict (Acts 14).

5. Conclusion

At its heart, the Lutheran Reformation was about the God who justifies the sinner by grace on account of Christ and the sinner who is justified by faith in Christ. But this confession was not offered in isolation from the wider narrative of God and his creation. It was offered within the context of the creedal confession that God is "the maker of heaven and earth." Today, language of creation and creatureliness can help us see better the connection between creation and redemption. We need to confess simultaneously that I am God's good creature and that I am sinful to

69 Robert Rosin notes, "Broadly put, culture is anything not naturally biological, anything people create as they freely interact with their natural environment and each other." Again, high culture is "something not natural or biological but developed out of reflection, used in shaping a view of life and transmitted to subsequent generations who maintained it because it proved useful." See Robert Rosin, "Christians and Culture: Finding Place in Clio's Mansions," in *Christ and Culture: The Church in Post-Christian(?) America* (St. Louis: Concordia Seminary, 1996), 57–96.

70 Luther, "Lectures on Genesis," LW 1: 67.

71 Luther remarks that at times, the godless "fulfill the second table of the decalogue so brilliantly that they 'indeed at times appear holier than Christians.'" LW 41: 167.

the core. So yes, "I am a poor, miserable sinner." But it might be more helpful to say, "I am a fallen or rebellious creature who does not deserve God's love." God made us to be creatures, but we were not content to be creatures. But the cosmic irony is that while we sought to become like the Creator and transcend this creation, the Creator entered his creation, became a human creature, and died and rose in order that we, as human creatures, might be restored as creatures to our Creator and to his creation.

Irene Dingel

Reformation and Confessional Identity As a Two-Phase Model?

The Process of Differentiation in the Development of Lutheranism[1]

In the past decades, research in the early modern period has placed a strong emphasis on its consideration of the late sixteenth and early seventeenth century from the perspective of confessionalization.[2] The question of what is meant by a "*Confessio*" or a confession is often neglected, as is the question of the processes of confessional or denominational formation. From the theological and theological-historical perspective, therefore, it has always been rightly pointed out that confessionalization, which takes place at the ecclesiastical, social, cultural, and political level, and the formation of distinct confessions as a basis for such confessionalization, are closely connected to one another. The processes and phases of confessionalization cannot be described without an eye toward the formation of "Confessions" and their contents.[3]

However, this approach is based on a specific understanding of "*Confessio*" or "Confession." Confessions in these contexts are not so much those that appear in the context of the individual and his faithful worship, nor as the momentary creed of a group, but rather as theological expressions of identity which, with their clear formulations of doctrine – usually in the form of *positiva* and *negativa* – proved to be the basis for the Christian denominations that formed in the late sixteenth century.[4]

1 Translation from the German original by Alec Fisher and the editors.

2 The pioneers for this development were three large congresses on Reformation history, which were documented in the following volumes: *Die reformierte Konfessionalisierung in Deutschland – Das Problem der "Zweiten Reformation,"* ed., Heinz Schilling, SVRG 195 (Gütersloh: Mohn, 1986); *Die lutherische Konfessionalisierung in Deutschland*, ed., Hans-Christoph Rublack, SVRG 197 (Gütersloh: Mohn, 1992); *Die katholische Konfessionalisierung*, ed., Wolfgang Reinhard and Heinz Schilling, SVRG 198 (Gütersloh: Gütersloher Verlagshaus, 1995); Cf. also Heinz Schilling, *Die Konfessionalisierung im Reich. Religiöser und gesellschaftlicher Wandel in Deutschland zwischen 1555 und 1620*, in HZ 246 (1988): 1–45.

3 Cf. also Irene Dingel, *"Bekenntnisbildung und Konfessionalisierung – Strukturen und Verlaufsformen,"* in *Orthodoxa Confessio*, ed., Mihai Grigore and Florian Kührer-Wielach. Forthcoming.

4 Cf. also Irene Dingel, *"Bekenntnis und Geschichte. Funktion und Entwicklung des re-*

According to the thesis underlying this essay, "confessional identity" is thus not conceivable beyond or apart from a distinct "*Confessio,*" at least not from a historical perspective; however, "reformation identity" – provided that one can, in fact, speak of a reformation identity and describe it – is quite conceivable.

However, before these reflections concerning *confessional identity*, or any *reformation identity* are continued, an understanding of the concept of identity is necessary. The term itself originates from psychology. Thus identity is the result of the combination of a variety of characteristics that distinguish a group or an individual from others (a). The individual identity of a person or that of a group can appear or be characterized on the basis of features which are essential for the self-understanding of a person or a group (b). A crucial component for both the identity of the group, as well as the individual identity, is that it is constituted by disassociation and exclusion, that is, concerning a reflection on what the person or group does not accept and with which it cannot or does not want to identify (c).[5] Whether this three-part definition is practical for reflection on reformational or confessional identity will be shown in the following considerations.

However, what cannot be considered in the scope of this essay's question, is the question about the reformation – or confessional – identity of an individual person, how it expresses itself in self-ascriptions or personal testimonies, and actually can be raised only by such sources. Rather, the perspective followed here is to consider the emergence of a community's identity of a reformatory or confessional type, by referring back to key individual events and constellations of events.

1. The Pre-confessional Phase of the Reformation

Reformation and confessional identity as a two-phase model? – Even if we leave the question mark, a thesis is already assumed, lying beneath the question. This thesis runs as follows: in the Reformation emanating from Wittenberg, there is a long, pre-confessional phase that can be distinguished from a phase of gradual and confessional consolidation.

This pre-confessional period of the early Wittenberg Reformation is characterized by the fact that there was not yet any need to draw fixed, delimiting

formatorischen Bekenntnisses im 16. Jahrhundert," in *Dona Melanchthoniana. Festgabe für Heinz Scheible zum 70. Geburtstag*, ed., Johanna Loehr (Stuttgart-Bad Cannstatt: Frommann-Holzboog, 2005), 75–81.

5 Cf. the discussions concerning the concept of identity and its definition in the volume by Aleida Assmann and Heidrun Friese, ed., *Identitäten. Erinnerung, Geschichte Identität* 3 (Frankfurt/M.: Suhrkamp, 1999), esp. 11–23.

boundaries according to Confessions, as there was later when the interplay of political, social, and theological developments led to the establishment of a confessional Lutheranism, Calvinism, and Catholicism. In terms of intra-reformational developments, various factors can be identified:

1. The Reformation, which began in Wittenberg, was not, in the narrow sense, "Lutheran." It was not the work of an individual, but rather the work of a network of reformers,[6] in which Martin Luther and his particular theology undoubtedly took a prominent position. To describe it as a "Lutheran Reformation," and thus already determine it confessionally in a certain way, obfuscates the fact that even in the middle of the sixteenth century a variety of theological positions could exist side by side without one definitively isolating itself from the other. Each member of this network of reformers offered their own particular contribution toward a theological vision of the Reformation and to its extension beyond the boundaries of the city and Electoral Saxony.

As one reviews this group of reformers, it is clear that next to Luther, Philip Melanchthon held an important position that had enormous significance for the distinctive doctrinal and confessional features of the Wittenberg Reformation and its influence throughout Europe.

Next was Johannes Bugenhagen, an outstanding figure. He was not only a confidant and pastor to Luther, but made his greatest impact as an organizer of churches.[7] His church orders, by which he translated the theology of the Reformation into church practice, became the model for many other ordinances, adapted to each region.

Other members of this network included Nikolaus von Amsdorf, who – as Lutheran as Luther himself! – sharpened the Reformation doctrine of justification in the controversy with Melanchthon's student, Georg Major, with the thesis that good works could be detrimental for salvation. In addition, there is Justus Jonas, whose translations of Luther's and Melanchthon's Latin writings into German often turned out to be theologically very pointed, as is shown by his translation of "*De servo arbitrio.*" Then there is Johann Agricola who, having made a distinction between Luther and Melanchthon over the question of law and gospel and the Reformation understanding of the law, did so without affecting Luther's friendship and respect in his lifetime.[8] However, the controversy sharpened the contours of the Wittenberg Reformation theology with respect to

6 This also applies, in modified form, to Zurich, Strasbourg, and Geneva.

7 Cf. *Der späte Bugenhagen*, ed., Irene Dingel and Stefan Rhein, *Schriften der Stiftung Luthergedenkstätten in Sachsen-Anhalt* 13 (Leipzig: Evangelische Verlagsanstalt, 2011).

8 Melanchthon, with whom Agricola fell into dispute, in 1527, still wrote to him as his "*amicus summus,*" his most intimate friend. Cf. Melanchthon to Agricola, Feb. 1535, in MBW Regesten Nr. 1538, MBW Texte Bd. 6. *Eine zeitgenössische Übersetzung* in: *Caspar Peucer, Historischer Bericht* (Basel: 1597), 78–80, num. VI.

the preaching of the gospel and the law as well as the *tertius usus legis*, yet not in a way that produced exclusion.

Also belonging to this circle were Casper Cruciger, Georg Rörer, Georg Major, and certainly not least, the artist Lucas Cranach the Elder. They all contributed in their own ways to the development of the Wittenberg Reformation and its characteristic features.[9]

They did so as Luther's assistants in the translation of the Bible, as editors of his works, as members of consistories, as preachers, teachers or schoolmasters, as recorders of his table talks and sermons, as well as through artistic representation of Reformation themes. The fact that they also developed their own independent theological accents and introduced them into the Wittenberg Reformation, goes without saying.

2. This group of reformers, which operated together in a tight network, was able to tolerate inner-theological diversity for a very long time without definitively or confessionally distinguishing themselves from one another. One was able to bear and overcome controversy, as for example, in the Antinomian Controversy of Melanchthon and Luther with Agricola in 1527 and 1537/1538.[10]

On the other hand, not all of the controversies of the early Reformation were like this. The best example is the decisive separation of the Wittenberg reformers from those, whom Luther called "enthusiasts" or "enthusiasts of the Sacrament."[11] In their theology, Luther saw a danger for the doctrine of the gospel, which he and his like-minded colleagues in Wittenberg claimed to represent.

Andreas Bodenstein von Karlstadt belonged to this second group, as did Huldrich Zwingli, the Anabaptists, and the spiritualists. Nevertheless, the definitive, confessional separation from the Swiss only happened later, for which the *Consensus Tigurinus* and the consequent dispute between Joachim Westphal and John Calvin over the understanding of the Lord's Supper gave, as it were, its

9 The early year meetings for the Wittenberg Reformation, which began in the year 2000 with a session covering Georg Major and successively treat the members of the Reformation network in the regularly appearing conference proceedings, devote themselves to this perspective. Cf. Dingel / Wartenberg, (ed.), *Georg Major*, 2005, and the others in the series: *Leucorea-Studien zur Geschichte der Reformation und der Lutherischen Orthodoxie* (LStRLO) with published volumes on Nikolaus von Amsdorf, Justus Jonas, Philipp Melanchthon, and Georg Rörer.

10 For the Antinomian Controversy see the overview in the historical introduction to *Controversia et Confessio* 4: *"Der Antinomistische Streit,"* ed., Irene Dingel (Göttingen: Vandenhoeck & Ruprecht, 2016), 3–15.

11 The designation *enthusiasts* or *enthusiasts of the sacrament*, even *sacramentarian* is used by Luther and his followers for all of those, who did not advocate, as they did, the teaching of the true and essential presence of the body and blood of Christ under the elements, bread and wine, in the Lord's Supper and granted a higher significance to spiritual performances than to the bodily, experiential, sacramental action, respectively.

initial spark.[12] Even so, there were indications already early on that the doctrine of the Lord's Supper was relevant for the emerging formation of confessional identity.

3. Later, elements emerged that were definitive for dividing the Wittenberg Reformation for the long term – namely, the enduring separation of Lutheran doctrine from the Melanchthonian approach and the further developments of Melanchthon's theology, as well as the Calvinist and confessionally Calvinistic positions.

Yet it is characteristic of the pre-confessional period that even these elements were already present, part of the entire impulse of the Reformation. This is why it is difficult to maintain the persistent view – whether from the Catholic or the Protestant side – that "the confessionalization of Western Christianity [...] [had already begun] in the 1520s" and that "Luther could not remain hidden forever," even if he referred to himself and his colleagues as "we Lutherans."[13] This statement, in which "Lutheran" is equated with the "Wittenbergers," suggests that Luther did not perceive that the theological diversity that existed or was developing in his circle was a divisive one.

In general, one called all of those in Europe who were reformation-minded, "*Lutherani*," even if the hallmarks of confessional Lutheran identity were not evident among them. Moreover, throughout all of Europe, no *Confessio* can be found in the 1520's which effected or could have effected such a confessional identity and its consequent community boundaries and demarcations. Even the *Confessio Augustana* of 1530 took on such a role relatively late.

A striking example of this is the Religious Peace of Augsburg of 1555, which granted the so-called "subscribers of the Augsburg Confession" – as it says in the treaty – imperial toleration. In no way does this assume an existing Lutheran denomination, for the treaty did not specify to which version of the *Confessio Augustana* it referred.[14] This point remained unanswered for a long time, because the *Confessio Augustana variata* – which Melanachthon had reworked in 1536 after the Wittenberg Concord with Martin Bucer and others from upper Germany

12 Cf. also Irene Dingel, "*Calvin im Spannungsfeld der Konsolidierung des Luthertums*," in *Calvinus clarissimus theologus. Papers of the Tenth International Congress of Calvin Research*, ed., Herman J. Selderhuis, Reformed Historical Theology, 18 (Göttingen: Vandenhoeck & Ruprecht, 2012), esp.123–129. The essay also appears in English in "Calvin in the Context of Lutheran Consolidation," *Reformation & Renaissance Review. Journal of the Society for Reformation Studies* 12 (2010): 155–187.

13 Albrecht Beutel, "*'Wir Lutherischen.' Zur Ausbildung eines konfessionellen Identitätsbewusstseins bei Martin Luther,*" in *Zeitschrift für Theologie und Kirche* 110 (2013): 158.

14 Cf. also Irene Dingel, "*Augsburger Religionsfrieden und 'Augsburger Konfessionsverwandtschaft' – Konfessionelle Lesarten,*" in *Der Augsburger Religionsfrieden 1555*, ed., Heinz Schilling and Heribert Smolinsky, *Schriften des Vereins für Reformationsgeschichte* 206 (Gütersloh: Gütersloher Verlagshaus, 2007), 157–176.

for the negotiations at the religious colloquies of Worms and Regensburg – was used regularly in churches and schools, and remained unchallenged from 1540 until the beginning of the 1560's and 70's.[15]

This mainly pertained to the article concerning the Lord's Supper, AC X, so that here the genuine Lutheran notion of the real presence – the identity-forming hallmark of later confessional Lutheranism *par excellence* – was no longer explicitly formulated.[16]

Elector Friedrich III of the Palatinate, leaning toward Calvinism himself, who, in 1563, had introduced the Heidelberg Catechism into his own territory, still appealed to the *Confessio Augustana* at the Diet of Augsburg of 1560 in view of his imminent exclusion from the Religious Peace.[17] This may have been done out of political shrewdness, but that is not the only reason. In order to prove his conformity with the Augsburg Confession, he referred to the *Confessio Helvetica posterior*, written by Heinrich Bullinger and printed in Heidelberg, which seemed to him to be a perfectly fine confession of consensus. Theologically, he was wrong. But this at least shows that the confessional situation at the time was still so open, that such a suggestion did not seem absurd to him.

Initially, in the years that followed, the *Confessio Helvetica posterior* developed into a confessionally theological statement of identity.[18] In addition to this, it happened that the Lutheran confessional formation – which had begun gradually at that time, and after various preliminary stages, found its *telos* in the Formula of Concord in 1577 – discovered anew the unaltered *Confessio Augustana* of 1530 and, with help from the Formula of Concord, made it a prominent document of Lutheran confessional identity, even though the original was already lost.

This development became supported through a now nascent confessional history, which definitively linked the unaltered version of the *Confessio Augustana* to Luther and his theology, and in this manner tried to revise the doctrinal direction developed by the work of Melanchthon.[19]

---

15 A printout of the *Confessio Augustana variata* of 1540 is found in *Der Neuedition der Bekenntnisschriften der Evangelisch-Lutherischen Kirche* [= BSELK], Quellen und Materialien I [= QuM I], 119–167.

16 Cf. BSELK, QuM I, 127.

17 For this connection see Walter Hollweg, *Der Augsburger Reichstag von 1566 und seine Bedeutung für die Entstehung der Reformierten Kirche und ihres Bekenntnisses, Beiträge zur Geschichte und Lehre der reformierten Kirche* 17 (Neukirchen-Vluyn: Neukirchener Verlag, 1964), esp. 81 ff and 241 ff.

18 There is an edition of the *Confessio Helvetica posterior* in *Reformierte Bekenntnisschriften*, ed., Heiner Faulenbach et al., vol. 2, 2: 1562–1569 (Neukirchen-Vluyn: Neukirchener, 2009), 243–345.

19 Cf. [David Chytraeus], *HISTORIA Der Augspurgischen Confession: Wie sie erstlich berathschlagt / verfasset / vnd Keiser Carolo V. vbergeben ist / sampt andern Religions handlungen / so sich dabey auff dem Reichstag zu Augspurg / Anno M.D.XXX. zugetragen: Durch D. DAVIDEM CHYTRAEVM erstlich zusamen geordnet / vnd newlich vermehret.* Rostock Zum andern mal

4. This had been preceded by an intense struggle for the preservation and recovery of unity, both in terms of the intra-reformation church and the older church catholic.

Attempts to overcome the disagreements in the doctrine of the Lord's Supper had occurred by the religious colloquy of Marburg in 1529 and later by the Wittenberg Concord of 1536. The discussions about the free will, as they took place between Luther and Erasmus, were the subject of great religious debate throughout the empire, as was the doctrine of justification and the doctrine of the Lord's Supper. The failure of the efforts toward consensus and the definitions of the different theological positions established the basis for a long-term formation of confessional identity.[20]

2. Reformation Identity – An Initial Orientation

While this development toward a gradual differentiation of various confessional identities seems plausible, it needs to be clarified whether the actors of the pre-confessional phase of the Reformation were united through a single Reformation identity. In light of the pre-confessional, theological pluralism, this unity cannot emerge from the confessional boundaries within the Reformation, but rather, only as that which contrasts to the old Catholic identity markers.

For this, too, there are, undoubtedly, arguments and examples, e.g., the challenge to the ruling authorities by the Reformation. Already in the Leipzig Disputation of 1519, Luther (and with him all of the reformers) called the authority of the Pope, the episcopate, and councils into question, in order to set them in opposition to Holy Scripture.[21] Secondly, the insistence upon the au-

---

gedruckt / durch Jacobum Lucium / Anno M.D.LXXVI. – [Georg Coelestin], *HISTORIA COMITIORVM ANNO M.D.XXX. AVGVSTAE CELEBRATORVM, REPVRGATAE DOCTRINAE OCCAsionem, praecipuas de religione deliberationes, Consilia, Postulata, Responsa, pacis ac concordiae media, Pompas, Epistolas, & tàm Pontificiorum quàm Euangelicorum scripta pleraque complectens. PER ANNOS MULTOS, MAGNIS SVMPTIBVS ET PERICVlosis peregrinationibus collecta, et quatuor Tomos distributa, Per Georgium Coelestinum, S. Theol: Doct: & Ecclesiae Coloniensis in Marchia Praepositum. Cum Gratia & Priuilegio Imp: Francofordiae cis Viadrum, imprimebat IOHANNES EI-CHORN, M.D.LXXVII.* Cf. also Irene Dingel, "*Augsburger Religionsfrieden und 'Augsburger Konfessionsverwandtschaft,'*" 169–174, and "*Das Bild Luthers und Melanchthons in der Historiographie zur Confessio Augustana,*" in *Memoria – theologische Synthese – Autoritätenkonflikt*, ed., Irene Dingel (Tübingen: Mohr Siebeck, 2016), 113–126, esp. 113–117.

20 Cf. also Irene Dingel, "*Von der Wittenberger Reformation zum Luthertum. Konfessionelle Transformationen,*" in *Luther: Katholizität und Reform. Wurzeln–Wege–Wirkungen*, ed., Wolfgang Thönissen and Josef Freitag (Leipzig und Paderborn: Evangelische Verlaganstalt, 2017).

21 Cf. WA 2: 160f and also WA 9: 207–212.

thority of the Holy Scripture and the subsequent portrayal of the doctrine of justification as *iustificatio sola gratia*, as well as the question of the definition of and number of the sacraments. Third, as a result of the evangelical doctrine of justification, the antithesis between the (superior) status of the clergy and that of the laity was eliminated. And finally, fourth, the sacramental understanding of the office and the church as the *successio apostolica*[22] was replaced by the Wittenberg Reformation with a relational definition of the church, the contours of which should be defined by the preaching of the gospel and the right administration of the sacraments (AC VII; Leuenberg Agreement).[23]

Any talk of a Reformation identity must likewise ask about a "platform of demarcation," to determine such identity-defining characteristics. How far this would be possible in detail, would need to be discussed further.

3. The Formation of Confessional Identity

But when – one may ask when taking into account these considerations –did that phase begin, in which the Reformation identity became replaced by confessional identity?

There are two factors to be mentioned here. Paradoxically, this phase is introduced by precisely those politico-religious measures which were intended to prevent the threat of confessional division: namely, the imperial religious diets and colloquies between the reformers and those loyal to the old church.[24] At the same time, the failure of the colloquies sharpened the awareness of those theological questions which separated Protestantism and Catholicism from one another for the long term. After the negotiations in Worms and Regensburg in 1540/1541, such were the doctrine of the Lord's Supper and the understanding of the Mass, as well as the doctrine of justification. They would be taken up again in the decrees of the Council of Trent, repudiations forming lines of demarcation.[25]

22 For Luther's theology according to topic, see Bernhard Lohse, *Luthers Theologie in ihrer historischen Entwicklung und in ihrem systematischen Zusammenhang* (Göttingen: Vandenhoeck & Ruprecht, 1995) and Bernhard Lohse, *Martin Luther's Theology: Its Historical and Systematic Development*, trans. and ed., Roy A. Harrisville (Minneapolis: Augsburg Fortress Publishers, 1999). Also Robert Kolb et al., *The Oxford Handbook of Martin Luther's Theology* (Oxford: Oxford University Press, 2014).

23 Cf. AC VII, in BSELK, 102f. *"Die Leuenberger Konkordie"* in *Evangelische Bekenntnisse. Bekenntnisschriften der Reformation und neuere Theologische Erklärungen*, ed., Rudolf Mau, Teilbd. 2 (Bielefeld: Luther-Verlag, 1997), 289–297, esp. § 2, 289.

24 Those to be mentioned here are the Colloquies of Hagenau, Worms, and Regensburg, in 1540/1541, the Regensburg Colloquy in 1546, and the Worms Colloquy of 1557.

25 Cf. Heinrich Denzinger, *Enchiridion symbolorum definitionum et declarationum de rebus fidei et morum, verbessert, erweitert, ins Deutsche übertragen und [...]*, ed., Peter Hünermann

Also, within the Reformation itself, religious colloquies could be seen as milestones for confessional demarcation and the formation of identity. The Maulbronn Colloquy of 1564, conducted between Lutheran and Calvinist theologians, and, especially, the subsequent accounts published by both sides concerning those negotiations, clearly demonstrated the existing contrast in the doctrine of the Lord's Supper and its rationale in a distinct biblical hermeneutic, as well as in the distinct differences in the Christological doctrine of the two natures.

The Colloquy of Mömpelgard (Montbéliard) in 1586 added the doctrine of predestination, which was, for the first time, officially on the agenda as an element for further confessional distinction. To be sure, already in 1563, the controversy between Johannes Marbach, the Lutheran-minded president of the Strassburg Church Convocation, and Hieronymus Zanchi, the reformed professor at the Academy of Strassburg,[26] showed the first signs that the doctrine of predestination would determine the long-term confessional identity of the Reformed or Calvinists. However, up until the discussion in Mömpelgard in 1586, it was not an issue between the forming confessional camps themselves.

Something for further research is the religious discussion with the Anabaptists (for example, in Pfeddersheim and Frankenthal) in order to examine the course of their confessional identity.[27]

So, it was not until the middle of the sixteenth century that this extensive process of differentiation began, not only into the development of the great Christian denominations, with their specific marks of confessional identity,[28] but also in the different theological positions of the network of reformers in Wittenberg who began to distinguish themselves from each other. One even began to distinguish the theological positions of Luther and Melanchthon from one another, even though during their lifetimes, both had always stressed their agreement and their mutual understanding. Minor disagreements, which had always and repeatedly been there, are of little importance, given the essential agreement stressed by both during their lifetimes.[29] It was this process of differentiation,

---

[= DH], (Freiburg i.Br./Basel/Rom/Wien: Verlag Herder, 2017 [1854]), 498–526 [= Nr. 1500–1516, 1520–1583, 1600–1630].

26 Cf. also Gottfried Adam, *Der Streit um die Prädestination im ausgehenden 16. Jahrhundert*, BGLRK 30 (Neukirchen-Vluyn, Neukirchener Verlag, 1970), and James M. Kittelson, "Marbach vs. Zanchi. The Resolution of Controversy in Late Reformation Strasbourg," *Sixteenth Century Journal* 8 (1977): 31–44.

27 An overview of the various colloquies are found in Irene Dingel, "*Art. Religionsgespräche IV. Altgläubig – protestantisch und innerprotestantisch,*" TRE 28 (1997): 654–681.

28 Alongside Catholicism, Lutheranism, and Calvinism, Anglicanism is also to be mentioned.

29 Cf. also Irene Dingel, "*Philipp Melanchthon – Freunde und Feinde,*" *Theologische Literaturzeitung* 135 (2010): esp. 782–786. Heinz Scheible, *Melanchthon. Vermittler der Reformation* (München: C.H. Beck Verlag, 2016), esp. 70–73.

especially within the Wittenberg theology, which was of critical importance for the development of a confessional Lutheran identity.

But what were the triggering factors? The need for confessional uniformity and clarity was the starting point for the expanding Lutheranism at that moment in which its existence, politically, was called into question. It was the imperial Interim of Augsburg in 1548, which was designed to restore the conditions of the old religion, that seriously threatened the Reformation. The Interim was in existence in the empire for roughly thirty years.[30]

In the historical-theological judgment of many contemporaries, this was the work of Satan in the last days, which, experienced as a crisis and extreme situation, raised the question of whether it was legitimate to compromise in rites and ceremonies – not in doctrine! – in order to secure the survival of the evangelical truth. Those in favor of such a compromise were in line with Melanchthon and the Wittenberg theologians, while the so-called Genesio Lutherans, who gathered themselves in Magdeburg and later also in Jena, strove for a clear and unequivocal confession in the face of what was believed to be a decisive moment at the end of salvation history.[31]

In this context, they increasingly questioned the approach and theology represented by Melanchthon and his students.[32] With the protest against Melanchthon and his chosen path, the question arose as to how and in what theological direction one ought to go if one wished to preserve the Wittenberg theological legacy and make it "sustainable." The numerous controversies starting in this context show that a dramatic process of differentiation began, which not only distinguished the theology of Luther from that of Melanchthon but also advanced the demarcations that set into motion processes of identity formation. All attempts to hold together the teachings of both Reformation authorities, Luther and Melanchthon, and to preserve them as a unity, failed in

30 For the Interim see Horst Rabe, *Reichsbund und Interim. Die Verfassungs- und Religionspolitik Karls V. und der Reichstag von Augsburg 1547/1548* (Köln/Wien: Böhlau Verlag, 1971).

31 Melanchthon had assisted with the creation of an alternative, for the Electorate of Saxony, to the imperial, religious law, referred to as the "Augsburg Interim," of 1548. While the Augsburg Interim existed with an extensive reintroduction of old Catholic doctrine and rites, the plan, denounced by Melanchthon's opponents as the "Leipzig Interim," allowed for a combination of evangelical doctrine and Catholic ceremonies, which one deemed as *adiaphora*. This earned Melanchthon great enmity among the strict advocates of Martin Luther's theology, among whom Matthias Flacius Illyricus, a former student of Melanchthon, was one of the spokesmen. Cf. also Irene Dingel, "The Culture of Conflict in the Controversies leading to the Formula of Concord (1548–1580)," in *Lutheran Ecclesiastical Culture, 1550–1675*, ed., Robert Kolb (Leiden/Boston: Brill, 2008), 15–64.

32 Cf. "*Quellen: Reaktionen auf das Augsburger Interim. Der Interimistische Streit* (1548–1549)," in *Controversia et Confessio* 1 and 2, ed., Irene Dingel (Göttingen: Vandenhoeck & Ruprecht, 2010) with the introduction, 3–34; also: "*Der Adiaphoristische Streit* (1548–1560)," in *Controversia et Confessio* 2, ed., Irene Dingel (Göttingen: Vandenhoeck & Ruprecht, 2012).

the long run, especially as some of the students of Melanchthon drew nearer to the teachings of Calvin as they further developed their teacher's theology.[33]

The clarification processes associated with the controversies thus paved the way for the formation of confessional identity, i. e., towards a confessional Lutheranism and a confessional Calvinism, which, for its part, "imbibed" many Melanchthonian (or rather Philippist) positions. For the Lutheran confessional identity, the significance of the theological clarification process and associated demarcations triggered by the controversies cannot be overestimated. In the second half of the sixteenth century, Catholicism also developed a similar path toward the formation of confessional identity, but it did not fully take effect until the seventeenth century.[34]

Of special significance for this complex process is the second Lord's Supper controversy, which was nearly parallel to the controversies triggered by the Interim. The dispute between John Calvin and the Hamburg pastor, Joachim Westphal, can be regarded as the first crucial break in the relationship of the Wittenberg and the Geneva Reformations.[35] For it epitomized the distinctive and differentiating mark of identity between the later Lutheranism and emerging Calvinism: the understanding of the Lord's Supper.

The stumbling block was the *Consensus Tigurinus*, the agreement between the disciple of Zwingli, Zurich's Heinrich Bullinger, and the Genevan, John Calvin, in the year 1549.[36] It was not until two or three years after the agreement that the first editions of the *Consensus Tigurinus* appeared, for example, in Zurich[37] and in

33 Cf. also the edited "*Quellen: Die Debatte um die Wittenberger Abendmahlslehre und Christologie* (1570–1574)," in *Controversia et Confessio* 8, ed., Irene Dingel (Göttingen: Vandenhoeck & Ruprecht, 2008).

34 Cf. Andreas Holzem, "*Katholische Konfessionalisierung – ein Epochenphänomen der Frühneuzeit zwischen Spätmittelalter und Aufklärung*," in *Die Frühe Neuzeit als Epoche*, ed., Helmut Neuhaus, Historische Zeitschrift Beihefte, NF 49 (München: Oldenbourg, 2009), 251–289.

35 Cf. Wilhelm H. Neuser, "*Dogma und Bekenntnis in der Reformation: Von Zwingli und Calvin bis zur Synode von Westminster*," in *Handbuch der Dogmen- und Theologiegeschichte*, ed., Carl Andresen, Bd. 2 (Göttingen: Vandenhoeck & Ruprecht, 1998), 272–285, and Paul Tschackert, *Die Entstehung der lutherischen und der reformierten Kirchenlehre samt ihren innerprotestantischen Gegensätzen* (Göttingen: 1910, reprint. 1979), 531–537.

36 Cf. the edition of the *Consensus Tigurinus* with annotated sources, ed., Emidio Campi and Ruedi Reich, *Consensus Tigurinus (1549). Die Einigung zwischen Heinrich Bullinger und Johannes Calvin über das Abendmahl. Werden – Wertung – Bedeutung* (Zürich: Theologischer Verlag, 2009), 125–142 (Lat.), 143–158 (Ger.), 159–170 (French).

37 Cf. *Consensio Mvtva in Re Sacramentaria Ministrorum Tigurinae ecclesiae, & Ioannis Caluini ministri Geneuensis ecclesiae / iam nunc ab ipsis authoribus edita, s.l.: s.n. [circa 1551; Tigvri: Vuissenbachius]. – Einhälligkeit Der Dienern der Kilchen zu Zürich vnd herren Joannis Caluinj dieners der Kilchen zu Genff / deren sy sich im[m] handel der heyligen Sacramenten gägen andern erklärt und vereinbared habend [...]*, Zürich: Wyssenbach, 1551.

Geneva.[38] It was also circulated as an appendix to the *Brevis et dilucida Tractatio de Sacramentis ecclesiae Christi* by the Polish religious refugee, Johannes a Lasco.[39]

From the perspective of the Lutherans, this represented a doctrinal agreement that sharply separated itself from the theology of Luther. From then on, one saw the theology of Geneva through Zwinglian lenses. Calvin and the representatives of his theology were now denounced in all polemics as "Zwinglians." The attacks were all the more severe given that until that time – during the pre-confessional phase of the Reformation – Calvin was seen less as a theological enemy and more as a distant ally, someone with whom a doctrinal agreement was not as hopeless as with Zwingli and those in Zurich, who made their theological separation clear with their rejection of the Wittenberg Concord of 1536.[40] At the great Diets of Hagenau, Worms, and Regensburg in 1540/41, Calvin had actually signed the *Confessio Augustana variata*, which, from the Wittenberg side, had been presented as basis for discussion and as a confessional document for all evangelicals.[41]

Because of the open formulation in the article on the Lord's Supper (AC X), which avoided any mention of the real presence of Christ's human nature under the elements of the Lord's Supper,[42] Melanchthon had created the possibility that all of those who were associated with the Genevan Reformation at that time could see their position represented by this confession. Calvin, on the other hand, had formulated his doctrine of the Lord's Supper in *Petit Traité de la Sainte Cène* of 1541 in a manner which indicated that his position was not all that far removed from that of the Wittenbergers. The small tractate adopted a middle way between the positions of Luther and Zwingli.

---

38 *L'Accord Passe Et Conclvd Tovchant La Matière Des Sacremens, entre les Ministres de l'Eglise de Zurich, & Maistre Iehan Caluin Ministre de l'Eglise de Geneue [...]* A Genève: Crespin, 1551.

39 *CONSENSIO MVTVA IN RE Sacramentaria Ministrorum Tigurinae Ecclesiae, et D. Ioannis Caluini ministri Geneuensis Ecclesiae, iam nunc ab ipsis authoribus edita [...], in BREVIS ET DILVCIDA DE SACRAmentis Ecclesiae Christi tractatio, in qua et fons ipse, et ratio, totius Sacramentariae nostri temporis co[n]trouersiae paucis exponitur: naturaque ac uis Sacramentorum compendio et perspicue explicatur, per Ioannem a Lasco, Baronem Poloniae, superintendentem Ecclesiae peregrinorum Londini. [...] Londini per Stephanum Myerdmannum. An. 1552, S. V6a–X7a* [= fol. 1a–11a].

40 Through the drawing up of the *Confessio Helvetica prior*, as well as the decision of the Swiss not to send a delegation to Wittenberg to the concordant negotiations; Cf. *Martin Bucers Deutsche Schriften*, Bd. 6.1: *Wittenberger Konkordie (1536), Schriften zur Wittenberger Konkordie (1534–1537)*, ed., Robert Stupperich et al., *Martini Buceri Opera Omnia*. Series I (Gütersloh: Gütersloher Verlagshaus, 1978–), 29f.

41 Cf. Irene Dingel, *"Art. Religionsgespräche IV. Altgläubig – protestantisch und innerprotestantisch," Theologische Realenzyklopädie* 28 (1997): 659.

42 *"De Coena Domini docent, quod cum pane et vino vere exhibeantur corpus et sanguis Christi vescentibus in Coena Domini"* = AC X (1540), in BSELK QuM 1, 127.

The later Reformed history of Rudolph Hospinians emphasized that it would have been welcomed and appreciated by Luther as a contribution toward resolving the conflict over the Lord's Supper.[43] Also, the correspondance of Melanchthon with Calvin was not intense but quite approachable, yet knowing full well that the Genevan Reformation, both theologically and structurally, contained features that differed from the Wittenberg Reformation that he had so decisively shaped.[44]

This initial, open theological situation, which also influenced Calvin's perspective, began to shut down with the second controversy over the Lord's Supper. If it had previously been thought that Calvin was more inclined to the theology of Wittenberg, the *Tigurinus Consensus* set forth the opposite before the eyes of all. To all those who were in the sphere of Wittenberg's theological influence, to the friends and students of Luther and Melanchthon, this document was the product of a perfidious fraud.

The Lutheran-minded Hamburg pastor, Joachim Westphal, expressed that in his polemical pamphlet *Farrago*, i.e., a "mishmash," the confused and contradictory views of the Lord's Supper by the Sacramentarians. Westphal tries to make clear that Calvin, in reality, against all earlier accounts, should belong to the number of heretics that Luther had already branded as Sacramentarians.[45] Writing from the perspective of one who had been deceived by the *Consensus Tigurinus*, he retrospectively tried to demonstrate the treachery and doctrinal unreliability of Calvin by comparing statements in the *Petit Traité*, with the altered position adopted by Calvin subsequently, in order to expose the Sacramentarian tendencies hidden in Calvin's earlier writings. Westphal then endeavored to warn against the corrupt doctrine of the Sacramentarians, and to demonstrate they lacked any support of the Holy Scriptures.[46]

---

43 The *Petit Traité de la Sainte Cène* with a German translation is printed in *Calvin-Studienausgabe* (Göttingen: Vandenhoeck & Ruprecht, 1994); ed., Eberhard Busch et al., Bd. 1: *Reformatorische Anfänge (1533–1541),* vol. 1.2 (Neukirchen-Vluyn: 1994), 431–493. Busch shows this connection to Rudolph Hospinian, *Historiae Sacramentariae, pars prior, Zürich 1598–1602*; cf. *Calvin-Studienausgabe*, vol. 1.2, 439, note 51.

44 Thus Melanchthon appears to be very cautious towards Calvin's doctrine of Predestination. Cf. *Melanchthon an Calvin*, 11.5.1543, MBW 3245, also *Melanchthon an Calvin*, 12.7.1543, MBW 3273.

45 Cf. *Farrago SenTENTIARVM CONSENTIENTIVM IN VERA ET CAtholica doctrina, de Coena Domini, quam firma assensione, & uno spiritu, iuxta diuinam uocem, Ecclesiae Augustanae confessionis amplexae sunt, sonant & profitentur: Ex Apostolicis scriptis: Praeterea ex Orthodoxorum tam ueterum, quàm recentium perspicuis testimonijs, contra Sacramentariorum dissidentes inter se opiniones, diligenter & bona fide collecta. PER IOANNEM TIMANNVM Amsterodamum, Pastorem Bremensem, in Ecclesia Martiniana.* [...] FRANCOFORTI EXCVDEBAT PETRVS BRVBACHIVS, ANNO M.D.LV.

46 Thus, Westphal in his preface: "*De his causis* [namely, because the Sacramentarians do not cease to lead people into error with their doctrine of men] *collegi, et nunc in publicum emitto*

4. Conclusion

This set the course for a clear distinction from the Calvinist doctrine on the Lord's Supper, which from then on developed into the defining hallmark of the Protestant Confessions. The path toward the formation of confessional identity was definitively taken. This development towards confessionalism in Lutheranism generally concludes with the Formula of Concord and the Book of Concord of 1577/1580. For Calvinism, one references – and justifiably so – the *Confessio Helvetica posterior* of 1566 as the decisive milestone and the Synod of Dordt as the end of this process. The *Confessio Helvetica posterior* became the touchstone confession of the Reformed churches in Europe, even as they retained their own particular confessions, e.g., the Gallican Confession, the Belgic Confession, or the *Confessio Hungarica.* Catholicism, on the other hand, consolidated itself under the *Professio fidei Tridenta* of 1563, and developed, with the decrees of the Council of Trent, an authoritative force for confessional formation and lasting confessional identity.

uiolentas, difformes, inter ße dißidentes, seque inuicem collidentes opiniones de uerbis Domini, Hoc est corpus meu[m], ut leguntur in libris sacramentariorum prelo diuulgatis, […]." Westphal, *Farrago*, A8a.

Werner Klän

God's Word Is the Place Where God Dwells[1]

Impetuses for a Confessional-Lutheran Conversation about Ways to Read Holy Scripture

"Where God's Word is, there is truly God's footstool, home, resting place, and altar," Martin Luther writes in his interpretation of Ps 132:7; God signals his presence through his Word.[2] This is why, for Luther, God cannot be recognized or approached, God cannot even "be known or thought of except through his Word."[3] For it is this very divine Word that calls faith into being as a holy relationship with God: "The Word is the means through which faith enters the heart, and without it, no one can believe."[4] But whoever has been touched by God's Word is certain of his salvation: "In Christ is eternal comfort, joy, peace and desire. This is given to me in the Word as a gift, I have received it in faith, and I place my confidence in it."[5] When the Word is a synonym for God's – in the Gospel: saving – presence, it is effective and powerful against all powers of doom: "Where God's Word is, there is God's kingdom, the heavenly kingdom, the kingdom of life that defeats death, sin and all evil."[6]

Luther has absolutely no doubt that the Holy Scripture is God's Word: "If you hear people who are so completely blinded and hardened that they deny that this is God's Word or are in doubt about it, just keep silent, do not say a word to them."[7] For just as God's Word is his dwelling place, Scripture is the place where Christ is found: "Outside of the Holy Spirit's book, the Holy Bible, Christ cannot

1 Original title: *Gottes Wort ist der Ort, wo Gott wohnt: Anstöße für ein konkordienlutherisches Gespräch über Lesarten der Heiligen Schrift* in *Lutherische Theologie und Kirche* 1, no. 1 (2016): 46–80. Translation by Michelle R. Hoehn.

2 Martin Luther, *Auslegungen über die fünfzehn Lieder im höhern Chor*, W² 4, 2091; WA 40 III: 403, 32ff.

3 Martin Luther, *Commentary on Deuteronomy*, 1525, LW 9: 131.

4 Martin Luther, *Auslegung des siebenzehnten Capitels des Evangelisten St. Johannis, von dem Gebete Christi* (1528/29), W² 8, 830f.; WA 28: 181, 26f.

5 Martin Luther, *Predigt am zweiten Sonntags nach Trinitatis, Hauspostille*, W² 13, 2153; W² 13, 2153.

6 Martin Luther, *Auslegungen über die fünfzehn Lieder* 1894; WA 40 III: 407, 28ff.

7 Martin Luther, *Interpretation of First Epistle of Peter* (1522/23), LW 30: 107.

be found."[8] Stimulating thoughts about this relationship, that is, the relationship between God's Word and Holy Scripture and its application, is the goal of the following ideas.

1. Hermeneutic Considerations Following Luther

That God remains God, whether man can stand before God, what kind of fellowship with God is possible? These are all questions which the Reformation tried to answer – and did. The Reformation found the key to life's vital questions in the witness of God's Word, and it found testimony to these answers in the faithful witness of all Christianity.

Martin Luther relied on the original message of Holy Scripture to be certain of his faith and salvation in the face of the fundamental crisis of his existence. The Reformer took up the confession of Jesus Christ's church to explain the new insights the Bible opened to him about God's honor, man's salvation, and fellowship between God and man.[9] Luther interpreted his life and man's life in general within the horizon of the Bible's meta-narrative, in which God is understood as God through his relationship to human creation, a relationship which, in agreement with biblical findings, unfolds within God's stories, which play out in space and time, in history, even human history.[10]

As a learned theologian of the New Testament and as a church and dogma historian, Hermann Sasse repeatedly posed questions about the relationship between inspiration and historicity in the Bible, particularly when looking at Martin Luther's scriptural teachings. "For Luther, the Holy Bible is [...] the place '*ubi Christus Christum purissime docet.*'"[11] This is the Bible's uniqueness and, at the same time, singularity among all the other books in the world. Scripture as God's gift to mankind, especially to the church, points to Christ as the savior of the world. Accordingly, Luther's scriptural teachings are Christocentric, as is his entire theology. Christ is for Luther the main word, the main point, the main person in Scripture, the content, "the actual theme."[12] Christ himself, or the witness about him can therefore be a criterion in questions about canon and

8 Martin Luther, *Auslegung vieler schöner Sprüche heiliger Schrift, welche Luther etlichen in ihre Bibeln geschrieben*, W² 9, 1775; WA 48: 44, 1.

9 *Vom Abendmahl Christi. Bekenntnis*, WA 26: 499–509; LW 37: 360–372.

10 Robert Kolb, *Luther and the Stories of God: Biblical Narratives as a Foundation for Christian Living*, (Grand Rapids, MI: Baker Academic, 2012), 2.

11 Hermann Sasse, *Letters to Lutheran Pastors*, vol. I, trans. and ed., Matthew C. Harrison (St. Louis: Concordia Publishing House, 2013), 256.

12 Sasse, *Letters*, 256.

authority, as Luther explained in his introduction to the Epistles of St. James and Jude in 1522.[13]

Christ is undoubtedly Lord of the Bible, which is also "the Holy Spirit's book," because it speaks of Christ. For this reason, Luther considers the Bible divine revelation through the Spirit; the Spirit is the *autor huius libri*, for it is his office to witness Christ. In this sense, the "human" authors "received what they should say,"[14] according to Christ's promise through God the Holy Spirit. And he points to Christ, preaches him, proclaims him.

This is also why Luther cannot imagine bringing "Christ and the Scripture into contradiction,"[15] in spite of competing and opposing ideas and explanations of Scripture that can and do arise. For Luther, Jesus Christ as *dominus scripturae* is the highest authority,[16] and as such, can even take a position against understandings of Scripture that try to ignore Christ as "the living Lord, the content, the soul, the Lord of the Scripture [...], without whom Scripture cannot be understood at all, the Lamb of God, who taketh away the sin of the world."[17] It is sufficiently well-known that Luther's Christocentric stand on Holy Scripture cannot be (mis)understood as antinomian. For "as God's written word [it reflects] God's inmost heart" that speaks to us in Law and Gospel; both are inseparable, yet distinct.[18]

Scripture's unity in Law and Gospel[19] is similar to, but not the same as Scripture's unity as God's Word and man's word. Thus, God's proclaimed Word, spoken by man at God's command, becomes Holy Scripture's written Word, again becoming word proclaimed by man, so that one can and must speak of an interpenetration (*Ineinander*) between God's and man's word.[20] The Word's "externalness" applies to its written form as well as its oral form, according to Luther. Within the horizon of Lutheran theology on the means of grace, the (external) Word and God's Spirit are attached inseparably to the "lettered" word,[21] as God the Holy Spirit binds himself to this word. There's more: Luther explains the Spirit and the Word's co-existence and interrelationship as a parallel to the Early Church's teaching on the dual nature of Christ: "The Holy Scripture is

13 Sasse, *Letters*, 258.
14 Sasse, *Letters*, 257.
15 Sasse, *Letters*, 259.
16 Sasse, *Letters*, 259.
17 Sasse, *Letters*, 259.
18 Hermann Sasse, *Luther and the Word of God, in Accents in Luther's Theology. Essays in Commemoration of the 450th Anniversary of the Reformation*, ed., Heino O. Kadai (St. Louis: Concordia Publishing House, 1967), 63.
19 See discussion below, "Martin Luther's Distinction between Law and Gospel."
20 Sasse, *Letters*, 263.
21 Sasse, *Luther and the Word of God*, 77.

God's Word, written and (so to say) spelled out and pictured in alphabetic letters, just as Christ is the eternal God's Word, veiled in humanity."[22]

This parallel, connected with the undeniable Christocentric focus of his approach, combines *sola scriptura* with *sola fide* in Luther's theology:[23] *"Tolle Christum e scipturis, quid amplius in illis invenies?"* Even when the Holy Bible as a collection of writings by human authors shares the "characteristics" and "destiny of such books,"[24] the Christian faith's *assertion* – Christ, the savior of the world – remains. And this conviction holds true for the entire Holy Bible, not least for the Old Testament, which was the "Bible proper of the church."[25] Luther's point of view on this with its implications for the question of canonicity deserves particular attention, because it grants Scripture priority over the church.[26]

Luther apparently "took over the traditional doctrine of Scripture as having been given by inspiration of the Holy Spirit."[27] Admittedly, Holy Scripture does not "inform us about the process of inspiration."[28] Accordingly, the rank of the spoken word over the written word must be attended to, as the proclaimed Word is (again) the same Word of God.[29] Luther emphasizes the Word's enactment, however – and this is the difference between Luther's teachings and theological tradition – the written Word also shares in its inspiration.[30] Of course, first the Gospel is proclaimed, which is "basically always the same,"[31] certainly, in Christianity, bound to Holy Scripture[32] as a written record of the prophets' and apostles' proclamations, men who were "called by a special degree of God's will, equipped with the Holy Spirit to a higher degree than other believers; by virtue of this possession of the Spirit, the infallible teachers of the faith, they proclaim the Gospel."[33]

Holy Scripture's human history of origin also has a part in the figure of the cross as divine revelation.[34] This includes the "inadequacy of historical data,"[35] as well as the "differences in the Easter narratives" and in the "Passion history."[36] Luther does not consider the "Gospel as a whole [...] to be affected" by such

22 Quoted in Sasse, *Letters*, 264.
23 Sasse, *Luther and the Word of God*, 59ff.
24 Sasse, *Luther and the Word of God*, 68.
25 Sasse, *Luther and the Word of God*, 70–71.
26 Sasse, *Luther and the Word of God*, 72.
27 Sasse, *Luther and the Word of God*, 84; 89.
28 Sasse, *Luther and the Word of God*, 89.
29 Sasse, *Letters*, 340–341.
30 Sasse, *Letters*, 267–268.
31 Sasse, *Letters*, 344.
32 Sasse, *Letters*, 346.
33 Sasse, *Letters*, 346.
34 Sasse, *Letters*, 356.
35 Sasse, *Letters*, 356
36 Sasse, *Letters*, 357.

uncertainties in details or the Gospel stories.[37] The "Bible's servant figure" allows him to perceive the "dissimilarities and variations [...], inadequacies," to perceive a "scribal error" here and there, but never to speak of "contradictions" or "mistakes."[38]

Within Luther's reformation views, the conviction of Scripture's divine inspiration is certainly the result, not the prerequisite for faith in Christ, who "truly is the theme of the whole Bible."[39] Accordingly, he is also the "*norma* above the *norma normans* of Scripture."[40] This is why "the Lutheran Christian [...] believes in the Bible [:] because he first believes in Christ."[41]

With this in mind, Oswald Bayer spells out Luther's "three rules" for the study of theology: *oratio, meditatio, tentatio.* They cannot be played out against each other, separated one from another, nor belatedly connected to each other.[42] Luther identifies the book of Scripture, or at least its effects, with the "Word of the Cross."[43] This leads to the concept of Scripture's two-fold clarity. Human understanding cannot perceive eternal life, nor is it able to recognize God or itself.[44] Under these conditions, every attempt towards nearing God via reason falls under the verdict of "speculation." Theological insight, that is, Scripture-led and Scripture-based insight, will only be found when it recognizes and accepts (or is moved to do so) God's patronage and humility, the result of God humbling himself and revealing himself in Christ. Humans can only experience or suffer this reality of God's revelation: "It is not part of man's self-accomplishment or self-ownership."[45]

This is why *meditatio,* at least in Luther's understanding, does not mean experiencing God in the bottom of my heart or my soul, but rather, experiencing him in the "external, lettered Word." This *verbum externum* is just what defines Luther's entire understanding of *meditatio.*[46] Therefore, his foundational rule for interpreting the Holy Bible should be taken to heart, "that you do not grow weary or think that you have done enough when you have read, heard, and spoken them once or twice, and that you then have complete understanding."[47] Knowledge of grammar, rhetoric, style, philology and history, including hermeneutical re-

37 Sasse, Letters, 357.
38 Sasse, Letters, 358–359.
39 Sasse, *Letters*, 358–359.
40 Sasse, *Letters*, 354.
41 Sasse, *Luther and the Word of God*, 82.
42 Oswald Bayer, *Theologie* (HAST 1) (Gütersloh: Gütersloher Verlagshaus, 1994), 71.
43 Bayer, *Theologie*, 72.
44 Bayer, *Theologie*, 74.
45 Bayer, *Theologie*, 81.
46 Bayer, *Theologie*, 87.
47 Martin Luther, WA 50: 659, 22–35; LW 34: 286.

flection, are important parts of this process, and necessarily so.[48] The result is an *externa claritas*, the

> most individual, because [it is] in its greatest depths the individualising experience of myself as a being that denies God (Ps 14:1), yet through him, the Holy Spirit, I am taught a different and better way, and the external, universalness of this spirit cannot be separated from each other.[49]

In the end, *tentatio* (*Anfechtung*) will be "the touchstone which teaches you not only to know and understand, but also to experience how right, how true, how sweet, how lovely, how mighty, how comforting God's Word is, wisdom beyond all wisdom."[50] My existence being interpreted in God's Word leads to suffering for God's Word – Luther is deeply convinced of this. Luther aims for a "passive" understanding of "experience"[51]: I experience Scripture and God's Word, through which I am interpreted and which also "provides for its own interpretation, which is its own interpretation »*sui ipsius interpres*«".[52] This corresponds with reality in Luther's line of thought: the Holy Spirit has bound himself to "oral speech and lettered words in Scripture."[53]

2. Hermeneutic Considerations Following Georg Hamann

In his profound study on Johann Georg Hamann, Oswald Bayer presented how a "radical enlightener" can simultaneously position himself independently from the enlightened mainstream of theology.[54] Hamann (1730–1788) was a contemporary of the many philosophers, poets, and theologians of the Enlightenment and the *Sturm und Drang* ("Storm and Stress") phase of German literary history. Johann Wolfgang (von) Goethe called him "the brightest mind in his day." Characteristically for Hamann, after his conversion, he became a decided opponent of any and every rationalistic type of philosophy.

Bayer describes Hamann's profile as equal to that of Kant and Hegel, although he was apparently "not a recognized authority."[55] Bayer values Hamann's "in-

48 Bayer, *Theologie*, 91.
49 Bayer, *Theologie*, 92.
50 Luther, WA 50: 660, 1–4; LW 34: 286–287.
51 Bayer, *Theologie*, 101.
52 Bayer, *Theologie*, 102.
53 Bayer, *Theologie*, 94.
54 Oswald Bayer, *A Contemporary in Dissent. Johann Georg Hamann as a radical Enlightener*, trans., Roy A. Harrisville and Mark Mattes (Grand Rapids and Cambridge, UK: Wm.B. Eerdmans, 2012). Quotes taken from a book review by Werner Klän.
55 Bayer, *Contemporary in Dissent*, XII.

dependence and freedom."[56] He bases this on the "irrevocable life-change"[57] Hamann experienced in London. His conversion led him to a "metacriticism of modernity" that can be viewed simultaneously as "postmodern" and "premodern."[58] This "metacriticism" is founded in God and his revelation in Holy Scripture, which functions as his concrete *a priori* and is in this respect parallel to Luther's view of the Bible as a "divine Aeneid."[59] What makes Hamann a contemporary of his time – and what may make him so important for our generation – is his manner of combining poetry, history and philosophy[60] in a manner that made it possible to maintain a critical distance from the Enlightenment and its solutions, ideas we still encounter today.

Hamann belongs, as Bayer shows, to the "midwives" of the modern term "history."[61] In opposition to the distinction, or better said, separation, of "truths and reason" and "truths of history" that Gotthold Ephraim Lessing made, who claimed that the latter are random and therefore "necessary truths of reason could not be proven," Hamann insisted that such truths of reason are significantly abstract and, in the end, "empty."[62] In this context, the distinction between "natural and positive" religion has its place; by exercising Spinoza's separation of the historical and the metaphysical, Hermann Samuel Reimarus had played off Jesus against Paul – a strategy pursued in New Testament exegesis, in mainstream theology, and beyond, up to our day.[63]

Lessing considered positive religion(s), like Christianity, merely a pre-form of submission on the road to the goal of "true religion," namely, "love," which is manifested in the "proof of deed."[64] Hamann contradicted all these designs by defining "truth as a daughter of time."[65] In his view, "the reasonable and the empirical, reason and history, the contingent and the necessary, the *a priori* and the *a posteriori*," cannot, under any circumstances, be separated from each other. The Enlightenment philosophers' natural religion was merely, as Hamann saw it, an "artificial abstraction."[66] He saw the solution to the problem in the "one history of Jesus Christ;"[67] in him "the eternal truth is temporal and thus

56 Bayer, *Contemporary in Dissent*, XII.
57 Bayer, *Contemporary in Dissent*, XV.
58 Bayer, Contemporary in Dissent, XVI.
59 Bayer, *Contemporary in Dissent*, XVI.
60 Bayer, *Contemporary in Dissent*, XVII, XIX.
61 Bayer, *Contemporary in Dissent*, chapter 8, 128–155.
62 Bayer, *Contemporary in Dissent*, 142.
63 Bayer, *Contemporary in Dissent*, 136.
64 Bayer, *Contemporary in Dissent*, 140.
65 Bayer, *Contemporary in Dissent*, 141–143.
66 Bayer, *Contemporary in Dissent*, 143.
67 Bayer, *Contemporary in Dissent*, 143.

history."[68] In its reliance on the "certain prophetic word" (2 Pet 1:19, NIV), Christianity can be called a religion of revelation: "Faith, trust, confidence, firm and childlike reliance on divine pledges and promises."[69]

Hamann clearly based this thesis on biblical narratives, especially from the Old Testament, which he held in high esteem.[70] He considered the Old Testament effective "as the historical *a priori* of knowledge."[71] It is the feature that Judaism and Christianity have in common, based on God's promises, the climax of which is the story of Jesus Christ, which constituted his understanding of history.[72] When Holy Scripture is experienced as the "Book of God" in its "liberating authority," the exposition and application of the Bible become greater than history can ever be or that the "spirit of observation" could ever achieve.[73] In the end, it is God the Holy Spirit who is at work through meditating on God's Word, not in an immediacy as supposed by Lessing.[74]

Bayer therefore emphasizes that Hamann was particularly influenced by the Lutheran "perception of the world [...] including the moral, the physical, and [...] the aesthetic" and was, like Luther, defined by the Old Testament.[75] Bayer especially affirms this when he shows how Hamann, "like Luther, emphasized [...] that the human differs from all other creatures through speech;" in language "lies the peculiarity of the human itself."[76]

Bayer further supports these viewpoints when he explains Hamann's understanding of history as "the history of self-interpreting Holy Scripture as God's history."[77] This creates an "open space" caused by "the insatiable fullness of Scripture," but is neither "blind nor lacking in experience"[78] for that reason. Interpretation of Scripture can also function as a criticism of reason in this context.[79]

68 Bayer, *Contemporary in Dissent*, 144.
69 Bayer, *Contemporary in Dissent*, quoted from Hamann, 145.
70 Bayer, *Contemporary in Dissent*, 147–151.
71 Bayer, *Contemporary in Dissent*, 147.
72 Bayer, *Contemporary in Dissent*, 148.
73 Bayer, *Contemporary in Dissent*, 149f.
74 Bayer, *Contemporary in Dissent*, 152.
75 Bayer, *Contemporary in Dissent*, 65.
76 Bayer, *Contemporary in Dissent*, 88.
77 Bayer, *Theologie*, 66.
78 Bayer, *Theologie*, 67.
79 Oswald Bayer, *"Schriftautorität und Vernunft—ein ekklesiologisches Problem,"* in VLAR 10 (Erlangen: 1987), 69–87, here 82.

3. Martin Luther's Distinction between Law and Gospel

God's divine words in Law and Gospel are constant factors in the entire Bible, according to Luther, and their distinction therefore must refer to the interpretation of all of Scripture. Due to the Gospel's – not only – soteriological rank as God's *opus proprium* and, accordingly, the *proprium officium* of *Sacra Scriptura* ahead of God's – or *Sacrae Scripturae* – *opus alienum*, one must avoid speaking of a "dialectic" or "polarity" of Law and Gospel. Even so, in its preference for the Gospel – or, in Scripture's definite trajectory towards the Gospel, which is the same – the unity and oneness of Scripture is guaranteed.

For the Luther of the early reformation, who characterized faith as the "one work," which admittedly has no features of a "work," faith in God and Christ is always a gift of God, granted in the words of promise, in the promise the Gospel brings into being. This corresponds with the basic structure of Lutheran theology: "*promissio ac fides sunt correlativa* / that promise and faith are joined together."[80] In other words, "*sine verbo promittentis ac fide suscipientis nihil possit nobis esse cum Deo negotii* / without the word of him who promised and without faith in the one who accepts, we cannot have anything to do with God."[81] Faith as "the first work," which is not a work, is characterized in the *Sermon on Good Works (1520)* as follows:

> The first, highest, and most precious of all good works is faith in Christ. [...] For in this work all good works exist, and from faith these works receive a borrowed goodness [...] In this faith all works become equal [...]. Faith, therefore, does not originate in works; neither do works create faith, but faith must spring up and flow from the blood and wounds and death of Christ.[82]

Indeed, Luther sees a categorical difference between Law and Gospel already laid down in the Old Testament, for "there cannot be another word beyond the word of Moses, unless it is the Gospel / *aliud verbum ultra verbus Mosi esse not potest nisi Euangelion*,"[83] for the Law was already presented in its entirety through Moses. The difference is categorical, because Moses, as Luther understands him, "demands, but he does not give what he demands / *Exigit, sed non dat, quod exigit*."[84] Accordingly, Moses is a "minister of the Law, sin, death / *minister legis, peccati, mortis*"[85] or even a "teacher of sin, wrath and death / *Doctor peccati, irae*

80 Luther, *The Misuse of the Mass*, LW 36: 169.
81 Luther, WA Br 1: Nr. 231, 23f., an Spalatin, 18.12.1519/LD 10, 69.
82 Luther, LW 44: 23–24, 26, 38.
83 Luther, LW 9: 176.
84 Luther, LW 9: 178.
85 Luther, LW 9: 178.

et mortis,"[86] but Jesus is much more: a "teacher of life, grace and righteousness / *Doctor[em] vitae, gratiae et iuticiae.*"[87]

God's Word is equally Law and Gospel, and not qualitatively different, but they can be differentiated in their effect, as they exist "completely opposed to each other / *impares ac plane contrarii.*"[88] This is the root of Luther's view of Law and Gospel, and that which the Lutheran Church follows in its confession.[89]

When viewed in the light of the ecclesiastical conditions of Luther's time, the theology and church of the late middle ages seemed to be, considering the manner in which the adherents to the old faith and opponents of the Reformation appeared, a category within which the teachers were "even pestilential [...] who trouble[d] consciences with laws and works, when this prophecy [see Deut 18:19] concerning Christ totally [wiped] out and [did] away with that ministry / *prorsus alieni, imo pestilentes illi magistri in novo testamento, qui legibus et operibus conscientias vexant, cum id ministerium prorsus evacuet et tollat haec prophetia de Christo.*"[90] Moses, on the other hand, is and remains, especially and particularly compared to this erroneous interpretation of Law and Gospel, "a perfect lawgiver."[91] But with Christ, the Law ceases, namely, in such a manner that "Moses' office" ceases, because it "no longer increases sins by the Ten Commandments [...]. For through Christ, sin is forgiven, God is reconciled."[92] But for this, "another testament had to come which would not become obsolete, which would not stand upon our deeds either, but upon God's words and works, so that it might endure forever."[93]

The biblical-theological subject matter indicated with the signal words "Law and Gospel" are for Luther and the Lutheran Reformation the characteristically different manners and characteristically interrelated ways through which God speaks – and *acts.*[94] This distinction – coming from Luther and confirmed in the

86 Luther, LW 9: 178.

87 Luther, LW 9: 178.

88 Luther, LW 9: 178.

89 Werner Klän, "*Gesetz – Evangelium – Freiheit. Eine Blütenlese aus dem Bekenntnis der evangelisch-lutherischen Kirche,*" in *Das Maß der Freiheit. Betrachtungen über die Bedeutung der Ansage von Gesetz und Evangelium für kirchliche Verkündigung und christliches Leben in einer nach-christlichen Welt* (OUH 47), ed., Werner Klän and Jeffrey Silcock (Oberursel: Lutherische Theol. Hochschule, 2007), 43–62.

90 Luther, LW 9: 178.

91 Luther, LW 35: 238.

92 Luther, LW 35: 244.

93 LW 35: 246. This is also true for Jesus' Sermon on the Mount: The first beatitude is for Luther a "fine, sweet, friendly beginning of his instruction and preaching. He (Jesus) does not come like Moses or a teacher of the law, with demands, threats, and terrors, but in a very friendly way, with enticements, allurements, and pleasant promises." LW 21:10. See Luther's interpretation of the fifth, sixth and seventh chapters of St. Matthew [1532] in LW 21.

94 "For these are the two chief works of God in human beings, to terrify and to justify the

Lutheran confessions[95] – comes from the Holy Bible itself, as Melanchthon sets down in the Apology to the Augsburg Confession and, in agreement with Luther, retains.[96]

Most important for Luther and the confession formed in his wake was how God's intention worked through these individually unique manners of acting and speaking, for

> From the beginning of the world these two proclamations have been set forth alongside each other in the church of God with the proper distinction between them. [...] That means that both teachings must be alongside each other and must be taught together, but in a proper order and with the appropriate distinction.[97]

"Law" and "Gospel" are not, however, merely formal means that can simply be applied analytically to texts. The existential relationship between two such different proclamations of God's Word must be considered if the Word is to be understood. This is true for a theology of justification as well as for a theology of confession.

Such an existential relationship particularly comes into being in confession and penitence.[98] The prerequisite is God's "self-less" action, in which he shows the conscience how much it forgets God, how far away it is from God, how estranged and how godless the sinner's existence is, and therefore how fallen to

---

terrified or make them alive. The entire Scripture is divided into these two works. One part is the law, which reveals, denounces, and condemns sin. The second part is the gospel, that is, the promise of grace given in Christ. This promise is constantly repeated throughout the entire Scripture" Ap XII, 53f, KW, 195. See the pointed and appropriate title of the chapter in Timothy Wengert's congregational-related interpretation of the Formula of Concord, here in FC V: "What God's Word Does to You: Death (Law) and Resurrection (Gospel)," in Timothy Wengert, *A Formula for Parish Practice. Using the Formula of Concord in Congregations* (Grand Rapids, MI/Cambridge, England: Eerdmans, 2006), here 77; Volker Stolle, on the other hand, put forward the criticism that "Lutheran Law and Gospel cannot be 'located' in Paul"; see Volker Stolle, *Luther und Paulus. Die exegetischen und hermeneutischen Grundlagen der lutherische Rechtfertigungslehre im Paulinismus Luthers* (Leipzig: Evangelische Verlagsanstalt, 2002), 429–433, here 432; Oswald Bayer writes differently: "*Das paulinische Erbe bei Luther*," in *Paulus und Luther. Ein Widerspruch?*, ed., Hans-Christian Kammler and Rainer Rausch (Hannover: Lutherisches Verlagshaus, 2013), 61–76.

95 "But where the law exercises such an office alone, without the addition of the gospel, there is death and hell, and the human creature must despair [...] Moreover, the gospel does not give consolation and forgiveness in only one way – but rather through the Word, sacraments, and the like." Asm III 3, KW, 313.

96 "All Scripture should be divided into these two main topics: the law and the promises. In some places, it communicates the law. In other places it communicates the promise concerning Christ, either when it promises that Christ will come and on account of him offers the forgiveness of sins, justification, and eternal life, or when in the gospel itself, Christ, after he appeared, promises the forgiveness of sins, justification, and eternal life." Ap IV 5f, KW, 121.

97 FC SD V 23, BSELK 585; FC SD V 15, ibid., 584.

98 See Albrecht Peters, "*Beichte, Haustafel, Traubüchlein, Taufbüchlein*," in *Kommentar zu Luthers Katechismen* (Göttingen: Vandenhoeck & Ruprecht, 1994), Bd. 5: 51–53.

wrath and threatened with death.[99] But this threat is not the purpose; much more than that, it serves God's "proper" deeds that grant life and speak comfort;[100] the threat of God's wrath, as real as it is, only fulfills the purpose of creating space for God's manner of granting comfort and life.[101]

4. From the Reformation's Principle of Scripture to the Methodology of the Enlightenment – a Sketch

Lutheran theology and the Lutheran church, whenever and wherever it considers itself confession-bound, begins with Holy Scripture as God's infallible Word. But this basis of understanding merely states the task at hand.

How to understand Holy Scripture, how to interpret it, which methods of approach can justifiably be used – these questions have always been disputed in Judaism and Christianity. In the history of the Western church, the Reformation marks an important turning point with its fundamental principle, *sola scriptura*. One cannot ignore the fact that the Wittenberg Reformation established a pattern of norms[102] for determining everything that was valid in the life and teaching of the Church and the Christian. Of course, the Holy Bible was considered "the one true guiding principle, according to which all teachers and teaching should be judged and evaluated."[103] But there were and are subordinate authorities – like the confessional writings in the Book of Concord – the validity of which must be measured based on their agreement with Holy Scripture.

Compared to the pattern of norms that the Roman Catholic Church established at the Council of Trent,[104] the Lutheran theologians of the second and third generation insisted on the "infallibility" of Holy Scripture. This was not simply a claim of mathematical perfection: it supported the "aspect of certainty" in faith, since *infallible* in the language of the seventeenth century had a meaning close to "unmistakable, true, firm, secure, binding, reliable, unbreakable, certain."[105] In

99 See Ap XII 51, KW, 195.

100 *"Alienum est opus eius, ut operetur opus suum. Alienum opus Dei vocat, cum terret, quia Dei proprium opus est vivificare et consolari,"* BSELK 450–453.

101 *"Verum ideo terret, inquit, ut sit locus consolationi et vivificationi,"* BSELK 450–453.

102 See Robert Kolb, *Confessing the Faith. Reformers Define the Church 1530–1580* (St. Louis: Concordia Publishing House, 1991).

103 FC SD, Binding Summary, KW, 527; cf. Charles P. Arand, Robert Kolb, James A. Nestingen, *The Lutheran Confessions. History and Theology of the Book of Concord* (Minneapolis: Fortress Press, 2012), 1–11.

104 For a confessions-specific and ecumenical referral on the themes touched upon here, see Hubert Kirchner, *Wort Gottes, Schrift und Tradition*, (BenshH 89), (Göttingen: Vandenhoeck & Ruprecht, 1998), 14–55.

105 Bengt Hägglund, *"Die Theologie des Wortes bei Johann Gerhard,"* KuD 29 (1983), 272–283;

the debate about a historical-critical interpretation of Holy Scripture, as it came to be used during the Enlightenment, the term "infallibility" narrowed to "inerrancy."

The methods that were developed following Johann Salomo Semler and Hermann Samuel Reimarus' objectives[106] viewed the Bible principally as a collection of documents in the history of religion and literature. A break was assumed within the uniform context of life and its problems, between the biblical context and "one's own experiences in life and faith," so that a "terrible trench" (Lessing) opened up[107] between biblical witness and contemporary experience. A consistent historical view was intended to help bridge this trench.

Exemplary of the changes that accompanied the Enlightenment is the reference to the "scandal" prompted[108] by the *Wertheimer Bibel* published by Johann Lorenz Schmidt in the years after 1735. In this rationalistic new translation of the Bible, Schmidt confessed himself loyal to the "true knowledge of God and the defense of revealed truths," but in pursuit of the "duty to state reasons [...] with which the radical enlightenment had burdened theology," it was necessary to pay tribute to the "current philosophical standards" and use "terminology that people understand today."[109] Early critics noticed that Schmidt's hermeneutics no longer adhered to the reformational foundation of *sacra scriptura sui ipsius interpres*, but rather were determined by principles of the Wolffian philosophy.[110] August Hermann Francke and his Pietist allies in Halle had already drawn the front lines against these principles personally and at the university (initially, not permanently),[111] claiming the result turned "Religion [... into] a mere societal substructure alongside another."[112] Accordingly, such criticism, whether from late-orthodox or from pietist circles, became little more than *one* contribution

Ernst Koch, *Das konfessionelle Zeitalter - Katholizismus, Luthertum, Calvinismus (1563–1675). Kirchengeschichte in Einzeldarstellungen*, Band II/08 (Leipzig: Evangelische Verlagsanstalt, 2000), 236–238; also in *"Die Lehre von der Heiligen Schrift in der lutherischen Orthodoxie,"* LKW 51 (2004): 31–41.

106 Dirk Fleischer, *"Lebendige Geschichte. Hermann Samuel Reimarus und Johann Salomo Semler auf der Suche nach der biblischen Wahrheit,"* in *Aufgeklärtes Christentum. Beiträge zur Kirchen- und Theologiegeschichte des 18. Jahrhunderts*, ed., Albrecht Beutel, Volker Leppin, Udo Sträter, Markus Wriedt (Leipzig: Evangelische Verlagsanstalt, 2010), 75–92; Jörg Lauster, *Die Verzauberung der Welt. Eine Kulturgeschichte des Christentums* (Berlin: C.H. Beck, 2014, ²2015), 420–429.

107 Hubert Kirchner, *Wort Gottes, Schrift und Tradition* (Göttingen: Vandenhoeck & Ruprecht, 1998), 48.

108 Lauster, *Verzauberung*, 426; see also Steffen Martus, *Aufklärung. Das deutsche 18. Jahrhundert. Ein Epochenbild* (Berlin: Rowohlt Berlin Verlag, 2015), 416–424.

109 Martus, *Aufklärung*, 418.

110 Martus, *Aufklärung*, 420.

111 Martus, *Aufklärung*, 283.

112 Martus, *Aufklärung*, 283.

within "the space of that which could be said, discussed and questioned," space which established itself as (enlightened) "public" space.[113]

Observations from the studies of middle-high German and from classical philology may serve to reflect on a critical approach – which is certainly not limited to theology:

> The thorough going scepticism […] is (was) apparently a phenomenon related to the times. It is not only characteristic for Wolfram's and Neidhardt's philology, or for the exegesis in middle-high German literature, it apparently crosses (crossed) borders. In the Vergil biography by the French classical philologist Pierre Grimal, I find some comments that I emphasize with pleasure: 'The hyper-critical spirits romp in this field as in others because they trust their own powers of judgement more than the statements on record and because they were happy that they, with their sharp senses, if not able to solve all the problems, were at least able to devise a line of argument that could cause all certainty' to waver. […] The process consists of systematically doubting the veracity of the statements contained in the record.

Dieter Kühn's critical comment[114] can obviously be applied without difficulty to historical-critical research on biblical texts.

5. Lutheran-confessional Ways of Reading the Bible in the Nineteenth Century – a Sketch

When the "old Lutheran" church and theology of the nineteenth century took hold, Johann Gottfried Scheibel emphasized the "compatibility of unprejudiced historical criticism and deep Biblical faith," basically making "grammatical-historical research" on the Bible a necessity.[115] One generation later, Karl Friedrich August Kahnis, who sided with the Prussian confessional Lutherans, presented a teaching about scripture in which he placed a traditional assumption of inspiration in question; at one and the same time, he favored a concept of inspiration that understood the Bible as a "historical document," one that required a "historical method of interpretation," thus creating a categorical difference between Holy Scripture and God's Word.[116] Scriptural teaching was, ultimately,

113 Martus, *Aufklärung*, 423.

114 Dieter Kühn, *Neidhart und das Reuental. Eine Lebensreise* (Frankfurt/M: Fischer Taschenbuch, 1996), 530.

115 Volker Stolle, "*J.G. Scheibels Schriftauslegung und Schriftverständnis*," in *Gerettete Kirche. Studien zum Anliegen des Breslauer Lutheraners Johann Gottfried Scheibel (1783–1843)*, ed., Peter Hauptmann, (KiO.M 20), (Göttingen: Vandenhoeck & Ruprecht, 1987), 30–45.

116 Volker Stolle, *Festhalten und Fortschreiten. Karl Friedrich August Kahnis (1814–1888) als lutherischer Theologe, Kontexte. Neue Beiträge zur historischen und systematischen Theologie* 43, (Göttingen: Vandenhoeck & Ruprecht, 2011), 221–230.

one of the debates that led to schisms in confessional Lutheranism far beyond the borders of Germany.[117]

But this development was not unique to Lutheranism, nor to all of Lutheranism. Admittedly, the theological father of the Lutheran Church—Missouri Synod (LCMS), C.F.W. Walther, vehemently supported the idea of inspiration and inerrancy of Scripture,[118] a position the LCMS has upheld several times, as in the documents *Brief Statement of the Doctrinal Position of the Missouri Synod* from 1932[119] and *A Statement of Scriptural and Confessional Principles* from 1973.[120] On the other hand, the conviction of the Holy Bible's "absolute inerrancy" is shared with a number of groups and theologians found within the area of Christian fundamentalism, but who are clearly *not* oriented towards confessional Lutheranism.[121] The question as to the relationship between confessional identity and confessional difference in view of understanding Scripture is obvious. At the same time, interpreters from confessional Lutheran theology cannot avoid the historical question. The question of the Bible's *sensus literalis* had already presented itself in the Reformation and has been closely bound to questions about the authority of interpretation ever since.[122]

In confessional Lutheranism, according to Hermann Sasse's expositions from the year 1950, "the doctrine concerning Holy Scripture" was "being debated like

117 See for example, Gottfried Herrmann, *Lutherische Freikirche in Sachsen. Geschichte und Gegenwart einer lutherischen Bekenntniskirche* (Berlin: Evangelische Verlagsanstalt, 1985), 138–142; 175–190; 204f.

118 August R. Suelflow, *Servant of the Word. The Life and Ministry of C.F.W. Walther* (St. Louis: Concordia Publishing House, 2001), 173–183; Christoph Barnbrock, *Die Predigten C.F.W. Walthers im Kontext deutsche Auswanderergemeinden in den USA. Hintergründe – Analysen – Perspektiven* (Hamburg: Verlag Dr. Kovač, 2003).

119 *A Brief Statement of the Doctrinal Position of the Missouri Synod (Adopted 1932), http://www.lcms.org/doctrine/doctrinalposition, accessed 16.02.2016.*

120 *A Statement of Scriptural and Confessional Principles (Adopted 1973),* http://www.lcms.org/doctrine/scripturalprinciples, *accessed 16.02.2016.*

121 See: *Die Chicago-Erklärungen des Internationalen Rat für biblische Irrtumslosigkeit* (International Council on Biblical Inerrancy); Thomas Schirrmacher (ed.), *Bibeltreue in der Offensive. Die drei Chicago-Erklärungen zur biblischen Irrtumslosigkeit, Hermeneutik und Anwendung.* (*Biblia et Symbiotica* Vol. 2) (Bonn: Verlag für Kultur und Wissenschaft, 1993); Stephan Holthaus/Karl-Heinz Vanheiden (ed.), *Die Unfehlbarkeit und Irrtumslosigkeit der Bibel. Edition Bibelbund,* (Hammerbrücke: 2002).

122 See Friedrich Beißer, *Claritas Scripturae bei Martin Luther* (FKDG 18) (Göttingen: Vandenhoeck & Ruprecht, 1966); Oswald Bayer, *Promissio. Geschichte der reformatorischen Wende in Luthers Theologie* (Göttingen:Vandenhoeck & Ruprecht, 1971); Karl-Hermann Kandler (ed.), *Die Autorität der Heiligen Schrift für Lehre und Verkündigung der Kirche* (*mit Beiträgen von* Oswald Bayer, Joachim Ringleben, Notger Slenczka), (Neuendettelsau: Freimund-Verlag, 2000); Robert Kolb, *"Die Konkordienformel. Eine Einführung in ihre Geschichte und Theologie,"* (*Oberurseler Hefte [...] Ergänzungsbände* 8) (Göttingen: Edition Ruprecht, 2011), 57–65.

no other."[123] Probably nothing has changed in this regard, particularly in view of worldwide Lutheranism at the beginning of the twenty-first century: "the theology of the Lutheran church" still "knows [...] no more burning problem than the doctrine concerning the Holy Scripture."[124]

6. Recent Hermeneutic Reflections on Concord-Lutheran Provenance – a Sketch

Hermann Sasse's reception of Luther has been continued and in some ways corrected by Jeff Kloha. First of all, Kloha shows how, in Sasse's phase of life in Australia, a gradual narrowing occurred towards the concept of "*inerrantia*": Sasse expressly revised his openly critical comments regarding orthodox teaching on Scripture's[125] inerrancy.[126] Kloha's conclusion emphasizes "the importance [of viewing] God's Word in its entirety as equally inspired and authoritative;" but Sasse did not hold a fundamentalist attitude, nor did he simply repeat the old-orthodox position.[127] In fact, ten years later, Sasse defined inspiration "as God's action, the Holy Spirit's action, through which he caused chosen men to write his word in the form of human writing."[128] Therefore, the Bible is the collection of "writings in which God the Holy Spirit witnesses for the Son."[129] Without denying or ignoring questions that human reason may pose in the light of certain conflicts in biblical findings, Sasse holds fast (1960) to the idea that, "Christian theology can never allow one thing: the presence of errors in the sense of incorrect narratives in Holy Scripture."[130] He hopes that "the time [will] come when Chalcedonian Christology will be a model for the solution of teaching Holy Scripture and her inspiration."[131]

---

123 Sasse, *Letters to German Pastors,* Vol. I, 240.

124 Sasse, ibid., 243.

125 Sasse, ibid., 240–284.

126 Jeffrey Kloha, "Hermann Sasse Confesses the Doctrine *De Scriptura Sacra,*" in *Scripture and the Church: Selected Essays of Hermann Sasse,* ed., Jeffrey Kloha and Ronald Feuerhahn (St. Louis: Concordia Seminary Press, 1995), 337–423, here 418.

127 "[T]he importance to see all of God's Word as equally inspired and authoritative," Kloha, *Sasse Confesses,* 422; Sasse's "Comments on the Report of the Commission on Theology and Church Relations, A Study Document on Revelation, Inspiration, Inerrancy" (1964) support this, in *Scripture and the Church,* 318–336, here 335f. in nearly word-for-word agreement with his writing in Hermann Sasse, *"Inspiration und Irrtumslosigkeit der Heiligen Schrift. Einführende Überlegungen,"* in *Sacra Scriptura,* 275–289.

128 See Sasse, *"Inspiration und Irrtumslosigkeit,"* 281.

129 Sasse, *"Inspiration und Irrtumslosigkeit,"* 285.

130 Sasse, *"Inspiration und Irrtumslosigkeit,"* 288.

131 Sasse, *"Inspiration und Irrtumslosigkeit,"* 289.

Kloha takes Sasse's idea of the Chalcedonian Two-Nature Christology for the teaching of Holy Scripture and expands upon it with a sacramental dimension.[132] The Christologic analogy allows the human side of Scripture to be taken seriously without turning it into a form of apotheosis. At the same time, exaltation Christology can never suppress the fact that the Risen One is and remains the Crucified One; while in the crucified Christ, the reality of the Risen One is hidden. God's Word has a performative character, as can be agreed upon. Martin Luther developed this idea from the promise of forgiveness in confession, which was understood to be effective.

Kloha picks up a reception-aesthetic approach like that which James Voelz has presented;[133] undeniably, this has revealed a wealth of increasing pluralism in ways of understanding God's Word or the Bible. This can occur through the assumptions made for the framework of understanding, each of which must be labelled, made clear and be conclusive. Clearly, one must consider that, when the understanding of Scripture or the Word of God is settled within the framework of a church's fellowship of interpretation, the church must not be granted too much leverage. As implied in the *Constitution Dei Verbum* of the Second Vatican Council, this could lead to replacing the determining function of God's Word instead of accepting and carrying out the church's position and task as *creatura verbi.*[134] On the other hand, human understanding is such that it naturally considers each context important for understanding. Nevertheless, one must ensure that the direction God's Word takes in calling forth faith and the church is not reversed. In any case, Kloha's statement regarding the analysis of concepts in narrative theology can be agreed to without reservation: Christ is the subject in the performing act of speaking, "which he himself performs in us."[135]

Translation processes of lingual, cultural, and historical natures occur in the process of understanding; an idea Kloha justifiably adapted from Hans-Georg Gadamer.[136] This includes the expectation that the struggle for an appropriate translation of biblical statements within a new context of understanding can never occur entirely without conflict.[137]

132 Jeffrey Kloha, "Theological hermeneutics after meaning," *Lutheran Theological Journal* 46 (2012): 4–16.
133 James Voelz, *What does this mean? Principles of Biblical Interpretation in the Post-Modern World* (St. Louis: Concordia Publishing House, 2003).
134 See LthK² (*Lexikon für theologie und Kirche*) 13, 497–583 for the German and Latin wording.
135 Kloha, "Theological hermeneutics," 14.
136 Kloha, "Theological hermeneutics," 6–8.
137 The formulation of the Trinitarian and Christological Dogmas from Nicaea (325) until Chalcedon (451) may serve as an example of this. The non-biblical term ὁμοούσιος (homooúsios) appropriately describes what Holy Scripture says about Jesus from Nazareth and his relationship to God the Father. All the same, the fathers of the Old Church held endless debates about the meaning and the correct understanding of this term, until the congenial

In his examination of the concept of biblical interpretation as a "performance," Kloha correctly emphasises the text's authority.[138] For this reason, he favors a "canonical-textual approach," even in the face of difficult texts in the New Testament;[139] he assumes and applies a hermeneutic of scriptural authority, based upon nothing other than Jesus Christ's work, particularly his death and resurrection.[140] The transfer of biblical statements and issues into new contexts, at least as the history of formulating Christian dogmas teaches us, must also prove to be appropriate, understandable, and convincing.

According to Robert Kolb, Luther would be a good conversational partner for twenty-first century Christians with his manner of reading Holy Scripture, not least amidst signs of crisis-like developments.[141] The emphasis on translation works over a distance of centuries and across cultural barriers,[142] and that neither Luther (and Melanchthon) nor we can do this without fulfilling some presuppositions is (almost) obvious.[143] Two basic understandings apply: First of all, that God shapes human existence in a double manner, and second of all, that God works through his Word in many ways and forms. The first anthropological presupposition means that humans are truly human, that is, truly God's creatures, and live solely due to God's grace and goodness; at the same time, that such humanness is proven by acts of love in relating to other creatures. The second, (word-) theological presupposition anticipates that God's Word is applied in oral, written, and sacramental forms,[144] that it does not merely "inform us" of heavenly subjects, but that God speaks through his Word made flesh, Jesus Christ, who creates and grants true and effective new life. According to Robert Kolb, Luther's (and Melanchthon's) approaches to questions about man's humanness and the

differentiation within classic-philologic terminology of οὐσια (ousía) and ὑπόςτασις (hypóstasis) suggested by the three great Cappadocians at the Council in Constantinople (381) created an appropriate, transparent and plausible draft of the Trinitarian dogma. Two generations later, by clarifying the terms ὑπόστασις (hypóstasis) and φύσις (phýsis) at the Council in Chalcedon, a concise, understandable and appropriate (based on Scriptural findings) draft of Christian dogma was made possible. See Wolf-Dieter Hauschild, *Lehrbuch der Kirchen und Dogmengeschichte, Bd. 1: Alte Kirche und Mittelalter* (Gütersloh: Gütersloher Verlagshaus, 1995), 41–52; 135–185.

138 Kloha, "Theological hermeneutics," 12–14.

139 Kloha, "Theological hermeneutics," 14–15.

140 Kloha, "Theological hermeneutics."

141 Kloha, "Theological Hermeneutics," 10–11; see Werner Klän, "*'Echten Glauben und rechtes Leben fördern'* – Laudatio for Prof. Dr Robert Kolb," in LuThK 38 (2014): 3–20.

142 Robert Kolb, *Speaking the Gospel Today. A Theology for Evangelism* (St. Louis: Concordia Publishing House, 1984, 1995), 13–14; Robert Kolb and Charles P. Arand, *The Genius of Luther's Theology. A Wittenberg Way of Thinking for the Contemporary Church* (Grand Rapids: Baker, 2008), 19.

143 Kolb/Arand, *The Genius of Luther's Theology*, 12.

144 Kolb/Arand, *The Genius of Luther's Theology*, 12.

question of God revealing himself build bridges into our time and to our questions.[145]

Luther understands God as being God in relation to his human creatures. In accordance with biblical findings, he sees an unfolding of God's story in this relationship, a story that plays out in space and time, in other words, in history, even human life.[146] Here we find the connection to today's understanding and interpretation. For if God's revelation comes to completion in history, as it is portrayed in the Bible from creation to Christ's return for judgment, then human history is also included there.[147] Luther knows he is dependent on the Bible and he points his listeners and readers to it because God himself is found in the Holy Bible as God's Word. In this respect, the Bible is not so much a "book" as it is a product of a writing process; even more, "it is an event of God's care for his people on earth."[148] His is a communication process.[149] This corresponds with the communicative reality of God himself, a reality found compacted in God's Word made flesh, Jesus Christ: He restores the relationship that human rebellion has destroyed; only then can all of God's other forms of revelation find their place and rank.[150]

In addition, Luther is convinced that the Bible's basic story repeats itself in the daily lives of God's people;[151] this is also why God's Word does not miss its target among its addressees. When it establishes itself among its listeners and readers, recreating them so that they are led in faith to the true destiny of their humanness in fearing, loving and trusting God above all things,[152] this new creation cannot and will not remain without consequence. This is especially true in light of the fact that God's chosen people constantly were, are, and remain helpless faced with the powers hostile to God and detrimental to man throughout history and in the course of a person's life:[153] The history of the world is also the battlefield in God's fight against the devil's attempts to hollow out God's majesty, and the life of God's people is no less so. Suffering is therefore an inevitable part of a Christian's daily life.[154] This eschatological tension grants Luther's theology its depth.[155] But it does not prevent the life of the faithful from finding and fash-

145 Kolb/Arand, *The Genius of Luther's Theology*, 20.
146 Kolb, *Luther and the Stories of God*, 2.
147 Kolb, *Luther and the Stories of God*, 6–7.
148 Kolb, *Luther and the Stories of God*, 13.
149 Kolb, *Luther and the Stories of God*, 13, 15.
150 Kolb/Arand, *The Genius of Luther's Theology*, 166.
151 Kolb, *Luther and the Stories of God*, 9.
152 Kolb, *Luther and the Stories of God*, 65–97.
153 Kolb, *Luther and the Stories of God*, 99–123.
154 Kolb, *Luther and the Stories of God*, 117–122.
155 Robert Kolb, *Martin Luther as Prophet, Teacher, and Hero. Images of the Reformer 1520–1620* (Grand Rapids, MI, Carlisle, Cumbria: Baker Books, 1999), 162–171.

ioning itself in worship, praise and prayer – the latter being already an expression of generous love.

Christians certainly participate in life's phases and events and in the customs of their cultural surroundings, while at the same time bringing their values into societal life.[156] The manner in which this interaction occurs between the different partners is certainly very complicated, and therefore a differentiated judgment of their effects must be allowed.[157] But this cannot be played out against the observation that Luther's new way of defining basic realities in man's life has continued to work over generations and cultures.

7. Word and Spirit – Spirit and Word

Christian faith, in any case, finds its content in Scripture and bases its fundamental criterion for the categorical difference between God's Word and man's word in Scripture. Scripture has been given to the church to interpret and must be considered sufficient for man's salvation. The unity of the Old and New Testaments must be held to in spite of inner differences. Scripture's self-interpretation and self-implementation, even its self-authentication, is considered certain among orthodox Lutheran theologians. The doctrine of justification doubtlessly functions as a vanishing point among scriptural words and as a condensed explanation of Scripture as a whole.

Behind this process is the idea that the Bible is the organ of God the Holy Spirit's speech. The Bible's inspiration aims towards certifying divine speech to and through people; it is based upon the Word and related to the Word. One can therefore speak of a *perichoresi*, a reciprocal penetration of Word and Spirit: God the Holy Spirit uses human language, in which God communicates his will, his salvation, his self-revelation, so that the Bible is his Word; in this sense, spirit-filled Word and word-bound Spirit belong inseparably together.

The interpretation of God's Word in the Bible occurs according to rules of philology, grammar, and history, but these rules still will not completely reveal the meaning of divine speech. The central content of the Word of God, subjects like God becoming man in Christ, his work of salvation on Good Friday and Easter, in a word: the Gospel, must be the standard for teaching and for life in Christianity – if necessary, even as truth beyond all exegetical reason. Lutheran theology and the Lutheran church are against expanding the Bible's witness with human "tradition" as "God's unwritten word," in spite of recognizing a set of

156 Robert Kolb, *The Christian Faith. A Lutheran Exposition* (St. Louis: Concordia Publishing House, 1993), 272.

157 Cf. Robert Kolb (ed.), *Lutheran Ecclesiastical Culture, 1550–1675* (Brill: Leiden, 2008), 6.

norms in which legitimate human tradition finds its place.[158] This place must always be subordinate to the Bible and only be granted when proven that a tradition is in line with scriptural teaching; in this way, the church preserves itself from a spiritualistic emptying of Scripture's witness that thinks it can look away from the "lettered" Word.

Likewise, given the priority of the Gospel made known in Scripture, or in Scripture's gradient towards the Gospel, the Bible's unity is preserved. For "as God's written Word [it reflects] God's inmost heart" that speaks to us in Law and Gospel; it kills and resurrects; both are therefore inseparable, yet differentiable. But without the Spirit, God's Word remains merely an exterior; combined with the Spirit, it is God's communicative self-fulfillment. The relationship between Spirit and Word can only be determined "dialectically": the Word brings the Spirit, which uses the Word to convey itself. One could speak here of a "sacramental" (that is, means of grace) characteristic of the Word and Gospel.[159]

8. On the Priority of God's Word in Scripture

Lutheran hermeneutics must, therefore, begin by placing uncompromising priority on God's Word over and above all human endeavors, over and above all theological research.[160] This does not devalue research and attempts at understanding, but it does appoint them to a position – with theological intentions – that makes them subordinate to God's Word in Scripture. We must remember that God's Word, in the form of the biblical canon, is the first and last court of instance for the church's teaching and for her life.[161] This does not deny that the biblical texts must be read for themselves,[162] or that certain inner-biblical poly-

158 This applies, for example, to Luther's authority in the sixteenth century, which was certainly superseded by the confessions; at the same time, Luther entered the row of authorities as the "foremost teacher of the Augsburger Confession"; see Kolb, *Luther;* also Werner Klän, "*Was machen wir aus Luther?*" in *Das Bekenntnis der Kirche zu Fragen von Ehe und Kirche* (Lutherisch Glauben 6), ed., Karl-Hermann Kandler (Erlangen: Gesellschaft für Mission, 2011), 90–117.

159 See Achim Behrens, *Theologische Reflexionsgeschichte des Alten Testaments. Exegetische Studien im Kontext evangelisch-lutherischer Theologie* (Oberurseler Hefte 15), (Göttingen: Edition Ruprecht, 2015), 243–245.

160 Achim Behrens seems to confirm this: see Behrens, *Theologische Reflexionsgeschichte*, 164.

161 This is the *particula veri* of the "canonical approach," which Behrens unfortunately rejects too abruptly, see Behrens, *Theologische Reflexionsgeschichte*, 41–42.

162 Behrens, *Theologische Reflexionsgeschichte*, 73, 76, 265.

valences and new interpretations of a text become apparent.[163] The motive of an inter-biblical "theological history of reflection" seems helpful to me.[164]

It is not the Church or church interpretation that legitimizes Scripture, Scripture legitimizes the Church and everything that is valid in the Church for her teaching and for the life of a Christian. For the Holy Bible contains everything that humans need to know for salvation. This is the foremost reason why Christian statements of faith, particularly their creeds, measure themselves based on Scripture.[165] The Lutheran confession always considers itself a proper interpretation, fitting for the times, of Holy Scripture, the judgment of which it is subject to;[166] that faith relies on a confession as early as Old Testament times can be shown exegetically.[167]

Scripture and confession are therefore reliant upon each other in a structure of authority. One must consider here[168] that the authors of the Lutheran confessional writings regarded Luther as an authoritative hermeneutic reference for a proper understanding, particularly for the Augsburg Confession.[169] They expressly followed Luther in determining the relationship between God's Word in the Holy Bible and the subordinate confessions of the Early Church and the Lutheran Reformation when they wrote that Holy Scripture "is the one true guiding principle, according to which all teachers and teaching are to be judged and evaluated."[170] Canon, therefore, exclusively applies to and is reserved for Holy Scripture, which acts as a witness to the confessions,[171] but lays claim to the truth.[172] It is assumed that the theologians on one's own side are capable of error.[173]

163 Behrens, *Theologische Reflextionsgeschichte*, 53, 59, 158; he even speaks of "a reflected change in the theological content of Old Testament texts;" see ibid., 61. Clarity would be needed to determine what the term "change" means; whether or not the idea should be formulated that Paul "had no scrupels (sic) about an historic ascertainable meaning of a quoted text," seems questionable to me; see Behrens, 109; his judgment in ibid., 179 is somewhat softened and even affirmative on church styles of reading in ibid., 193–195.

164 Behrens, *Theologische Reflexionsgeschichte*, 144; 152–153; 165; see the passage on Is 7, ibid. 155–165.

165 See Friedrich Beißer, "*Wort Gottes und Heilige Schrift bei Luther,*" in *Schrift und Schriftauslegung* (VLAR 10), (Erlangen: Luther-Akademie Ratzeburg, 1987), 15–29.

166 Behrens, *Theologische Reflextionsgeschichte*, 89–99.

167 Behrens, *Theologische Reflexionsgeschichte*, 199–220, especially 202; 219–220; see 223; 242.

168 See Werner Klän, "*Was machen wir aus Luther?*" in *Das Bekenntnis der Kirche zu Fragen von Ehe und Kirche. Die Vorträge der lutherischen Tage 2009 und 2010*, ed., Karl-Hermann Kandler (Lutherisch glauben 6) (Neuendettelsau: Gesellschaft für Mission, 2011), 90–117, especially 113–117.

169 FC SD VII 41, BSLK, 985; see KW, 600.

170 FC SD, *Von dem summarischen Begriff* 3, KW, 527.

171 FC SD, *Von dem summarischen Begriff* 12, KW, 529.

172 FC SD, *Von dem summarischen Begriff* 13, KW, 529.

173 FC SD, *Von streitigen Artikeln* 19, KW, 530f.

9. God's Word and Human Existence

Oswald Bayer has determined, starting with Luther, that the "content of theology" is "constitutively lingual,"[174] but understanding could only take shape "when theological thought [...] acknowledges three occurrences that are neither related to each other nor are subject to a common title – such as God's self-revelation."[175] He defines them more closely as follows:

> a) the Law's contradiction aimed against me that hands me over to sin, holds court against me and sentences me to death, b) the promise of the Gospel in which God himself speaks for me through Jesus Christ, and even takes my place, and c) the onslaught of the suppressingly incomprehensible secrecy of God that cannot merely be understood as the work of the Law and as radically contradictory to the Gospel.[176]

While the first two occurrences reflect the reference tending towards the Gospel in "Law and Gospel" – very Lutheran –, Bayer bemoans the burdening experience that "God [...] mostly remains anonymous" in the third, that he "is almost always clothed in the passive, is not a lover of life, but accuses and denies it, and who contradicts God's revealed will and the Gospel."[177]

The result of such experiences as befall man is "the deepest affliction [*Anfechtung*];" that God, as Luther says in *De servo arbitrio*, "does not condemn and do away with death, rather causes life, death, and all in all," yet this is the same God who "introduces [himself] in the promise of life and eternal fellowship."[178] Here, "God [stands] against God." In light of and against such "irresolvable differences," all that can help is the lament, which certainly does not create a godly experience as the internal essence of theology; instead, it points an accusational finger at its own disparity.[179] Bayer places and sees the Gospel in Lutheran understanding strictly as a "categorical gift" for which "a human disposition does not" exist. "Gospel means: God speaks on my behalf in the fragmentedness of the times and the destruction of identity."[180] Spelled Christocentrically, this means that only "through the power of Jesus Christ becoming man I [am granted] a new identity;" this identity is "a constant stranger." Bayer sees a fundamental contradiction arising between this and "an early

174 Bayer, *Theologie*, 412.
175 Bayer, *Theologie*, 413.
176 Bayer, *Theologie*, 413.
177 Bayer, *Theologie*, 415–416.
178 Bayer, *Theologie*, 416, see WA 18: 685, 21–23.
179 Bayer, *Theologie*, 416f.
180 Oswald Bayer, "*Mit Luther in der Gegenwart. Die diagnostische Kraft reformatorischer Theologie*," in *Luthers Erben. Studien zu Rezeptionsgeschichte der reformatorischen Theologie Luthers. Festschrift für Jörg Baur zum 75. Geburtstag*, ed., Notger Slenczka and Walter Sparn (Tübingen: Mohr Siebeck, 2005), 297–310, here 307.

modern times metaphysics of substance and a modern metaphysics of subject;" he identifies as the "deciding point of contention in the conflict between reformation theology and modern and post-modern thought."[181] A helpful and healing attitude would be that of "faith that is based on the reliable word of the Gospel […] [to] receive a new – excentric – identity."[182]

With this background, Robert Kolb is convinced that even in the twenty-first century, when the world seems to threaten life and rob us of our humanity in light of "new technologies, new economic powers, new political constellations, and new social structures, while still combined with age-old human sinfulness," the Lutheran message of a God-given new identity for man and a resulting creation of true human life, not only retains its validity, but also gains new importance. "Luther's theology of the cross makes the biblical message of God, his being, and the character of his creation clear for every age – independent of superficial changes in history and culture."[183] Lutheran theology and its confession, clinging as they do to the "one true Gospel,"[184] and the associated hope for one's existence can prove to be and are a vital, leading contribution the Lutheran churches have in the ecumenical debates of our days.[185]

This message is relayed in Christianity and through the Church, which is created as God's reign spreads through his creating Word and thus calls the Church into existence. The Church in her entirety and the individual believers respond to this creating occurrence in worship services in the congregations, then beyond these boundaries in service to one's neighbors.[186] Beyond this, however, Christians build a community of witnesses in the congregation and the Church[187] and are granted the right to do so by God himself commissioning his people to speak for him.[188] They carry the Word of the Gospel, which has brought them from death to new life, to those the Word has not yet reached.[189]

181 Bayer, *"Mit Luther in der Gegenwart,"* 308.

182 Bayer, *"Mit Luther in der Gegenwart,"* 309.

183 Robert Kolb, "*Deus revelatus – Homo revelatus. Luthers theologia crucis für das 21. Jahrhundert,*" in *Gottes Wort vom Kreuz*, ed., Robert Kolb and Christian Neddens, (OUH 40), (Oberursel: Lutherische Theol. Hochschule, 2001), 15; it is "truly a paradigm for every age, perhaps especially for the beginning of the 21st Century." See also 23 and 34.

184 Kolb, *Confessing the Faith*, 135–137.

185 "In the midst of societies around the world, in which new technologies, new economic forces, new political constellations, and new social structures join with the age-old sinfulness of individuals to unsettle life and deprive human beings of their humanity, Lutheran churches need to witness to Christ using the distinction of identity and performance, the distinction of passive and active righteousness," cf. Robert Kolb, "Luther on the Two Kinds of Righteousness; Reflections on His Two-dimensional Definition of Humanity at the Heart of His Theology," *Lutheran Quarterly* XIII (1999): 464–465; see Kolb, *Confessing the Faith*, 137–138.

186 Kolb, *Christian Faith*, 261–263.

187 Kolb, *Christian Faith*, 263.

188 Kolb, *Speaking the Gospel Today*, 12.

10. Closing Remarks–for Now

A basic separation between Christian and theological existence, between academic theology and worship, as has been found in vast areas of Western theology since the Enlightenment, is not allowed for confession-bound Lutheran theology.[190] This also applies to the relationship between faith and reason, whose relationship is certainly "composed asymmetrically," particularly in post-enlightened contexts.[191] On the one hand, "faith carries [with itself] a reflective consciousness of itself in its own un-naturalness."[192] This subject matter, related to the concept of reason, means – at least, according to Luther – "reason in theology in the shape of a logical form," a "confusing integration of reason's recognizing justification in theology," and finally, an "active reasoning [that] can endanger faith and theology as it measures faith with an inappropriate mass. The act of reason and its objects are part of man's sinful world, if he has not allowed himself to be made a fool in Christ."[193] Only the theological claim remains: "Reason [...] cannot offer the framework of understanding that the Gospel of God's grace offers sinners."[194] For reason means, "in terms of recognizing God, denying all one's own competencies."[195]

He who postulates "historical-critical exegesis" without reserve and as the natural standard for theological interpretation of scripture[196] should not forget that just these separations were posited by Johann Salomo Semler at the beginning of historical criticism.[197] He must explain what it means when historical-

189 Kolb, *Christian Faith*, 264.
190 As stated by the faculty of the Lutheran Theological Seminary, Oberursel in a position paper from the year 2010, see Werner Klän, "Nachwort," in Behrens, *Theologische Reflexionsgeschichte*, 315–321.
191 Miriam Rose, *"Glaube und Vernunft in lutherischer Perspektive,"* in *Glaube und Vernunft. Wie vernünftig ist die Vernunft. Dokumentationen der Luther-Akademie* 1, ed., Rainer Rausch (Hannover: Lutherisches Verlagshaus, 2014), 27–53, here 52.
192 Rose, *"Glaube und Vernunft,"* 49.
193 See Theodor Dieter, *"Widersprüchliche Vernunft? Beobachtungen zu Luthers Umgang mit 'der' Vernunft,"* in *Glaube und Vernunft Wie vernünftig ist die Vernunft. Dokumentationen der Luther-Akademie* 11 (Hannover: Lutherisches Verlagshaus, 2014), 73–97, here 96.
194 Mark Mattes, *"Glaube und Vernunft bei Luther im gegenwärtigen Diskurs,"* in *Glaube und Vernunft. Wie vernünftig ist die Vernunft. Dokumentationen der Luther-Akademie* 11 (Hannover: Lutherisches Verlagshaus, 2014), 99–132, here 131.
195 Johannes von Lüpke, *"'Heilig, gerecht und gut' – Theologische Kritik der Vernunft im Horizont der Aufklärung,"* in *Glaube und Vernunft*, 149–166, here 165.
196 Behrens, *Theologische Reflexionsgeschichte*, 156.
197 See Andreas Lüder, *Historie und Dogmatik. Ein Beitrag zur Genese und Entfaltung von Johann Salomo Semlers Verständnis des Alten Testaments. Beihefte zur Zeitschrift für die alttestamentliche Wissenschaft* 233 (Berlin/New York: W.de Gruyter, 1995); Gottfried Hornig, *Johann Salomo Semler. Studien zu Leben und Werk des Hallenser Aufklärungstheologen. Hallesche Beiträge zur europäischen Aufklärung* 2. (Tübingen: Niemeyer,

critical research methodically and methodologically excludes all "transempirical elements" of faith as "strictly immanent."[198] At the least, the issue must be raised as to whether or not an "atheist historical concept of history is being defined as 'more natural' than a theist concept."[199] A principle of "separating historical and dogmatic truth"[200] means digging a new "terrible trench" that separates different "religious cultures." We will certainly hardly be able to avoid[201] respecting the "factual non-universality of both large cultures of the West: the culture of Christian faith and the culture of secular reason."[202]

How to relate both areas to each other properly is an issue that remains to be resolved for post-enlightened theology, particularly that of Confessional Lutheran emphasis. The necessary "critical work" in researching and interpreting Scripture remains, but it "certainly does not mean" that "the exegete can raise himself to be lord over the text."[203] For interpreting biblical – particularly Old Testament – texts, this can mean "that we […] pose a wide variety of questions about the Old Testament texts and, in this manner, that we take up varying impulses and insights to understand the Old Testament."[204] Jorg-Christian Salzmann approaches and expounds upon the problems of hermeneutics that merely see the Old Testament as "a witness of past relationships to God," or "as documentation of various religous-historical pre-stages of Christianity," or that define the relationship between the Old and New Testaments along the lines of "the story of salvation" or "promise and fulfilment." He brings "typology" and "allegory" into the discussion, as well as strategies for direct application of Old Testament statements. He suggests ways of reading that retain God's identity in both Testaments or that begin with "Christ as the center of Scripture," if they do

1996); Dirk Fleischer, *"Lebendige Geschichte: Hermann Samuel Reimarus und Johann Salomo Semler auf der Suche nach der biblischen Wahrheit,"* in *Aufgeklärtes Christentum. Beiträge zur Kirchen- und Theologiegeschichte des 18. Jahrhunderts*, ed., Albrecht Beutel, Volker Leppin, Udo Sträter, Markus Wriedt (Leipzig: Evangelische Verlagsanstalt, 2010), 75–92.

198 Ronald Deines, *"Der 'historische' und der 'wirkliche' Jesus. Die Herausforderung der Bibelwissenschaften durch Papst Benedikt XVI. und die dadurch hervorgerufenen Reaktionen,"* in *"Mitarbeiter der Wahrheit": Christuszeugnis und Relativismuskritik bei Joseph Ratzinger /Benedikt XVI. aus evangelischer Sicht*, ed., Christoph Raeder (Gießen-Basel: Brunnen-Verlag; Göttingen: Edition Ruprecht, 2013), 20–66, here 53.

199 Deines, *"Der 'historische' und der 'wirkliche' Jesus,"* 55.

200 Deines, *"Der 'historische' und der 'wirkliche' Jesus,"* 56.

201 Deines, *"Der 'historische' und der 'wirkliche' Jesus,"* 61.

202 Deines, *"Der 'historische' und der 'wirkliche' Jesus,"* 61.

203 Edvin Larsson, *"Notwendigkeit und Grenze der historisch-kritischen Methode,"* in VLAR 10 (Erlangen: 1987), 113–127, here 124.

204 Jorg-Christian Salzmann, *Das Alte Testament als Bibel der Christen* (OUH 53), (Oberursel: Lutherische Theol. Hochschule, 2014), 39; see also Behrens on this issue, in *Verstehen des Glaubens. Eine Einführung in die Fragestellung evangelischer Hermeneutik* (Neukirchen-Vluyn: Neukirchener, 2005), 95–116; 138–157.

not get side-tracked in "selective perception." Salzmann also briefly treats the topics of "Canonical Approach" and the "aesthetics of reception" as well as accessing the Bible via the pair of terms "Law and Gospel." He correctly challenges a simplistic manner of making Law and Old Testament as well as Gospel and New Testament synonymous.[205] Salzmann's conclusion can be agreed with: "Theologically, our task remains understanding not only the New Testament, but also the Old Testament as God's Word and God's revelation, even in light of diverse approaches to them."[206]

This approach must be carried out according to the hierarchy that the Binding Summary in the Book of Concord presents regarding Scripture, confession and interpretation, and the priority allocated to the Bible.[207] Once again, we must emphasize: God's Word has priority over all human attempts to understand it. This may not be put up for discussion in Confessional Lutheran theology. For a Christian-theological manner of reading the Bible, the assumption "that not only people, but God himself is heard in the writings of the Bible" is a prerequisite. This confession, however, is rooted in faith.[208]

The Christian's testimony is therefore a process of responding and of witnessing to others; but above all, it is located in the life changing power of God's Word itself, which desires to reach all people.[209] Such a witness is inviting as it completes the bridge-building process between God's Word in Scripture and the situations and cultures in which God expects our testimony.[210] In this, the witnesses will not forget that the true promises the Lord of the Church are made for them as the "little flock" (Luke 12:32).[211] But this will not prevent them from proclaiming God's great deeds among the people of the earth.[212] For the Gospel desires to be told and to be delivered directly to the listeners, yet in a manner appropriate for the hearers.[213] In its power to re-create, the Gospel still brings life-giving proclamation and promise at the same time;[214] the Gospel still obtains its depth in its end-times perspective and its eschatological responsibility.[215]

God's goal here is to allow what he has to say to come to those who hear his Word effectively. A translation of Luther's *theologia crucis*[216] says,

205 Jorg-Christian Salzmann, *Das Alte Testament als Bibel der Christen.*
206 Jorg-Christian Salzmann, *Das Alte Testament als Bibel der Christen*, 40.
207 BSELK, 1216–1219; 1308–1319.
208 Behrens, *Verstehen des Glaubens*, 132.
209 Kolb, *Luther and the Stories of God*, 132–133.
210 Kolb, *Christian Faith*, 272.
211 Kolb, *Christian Faith*, 274.
212 Kolb, *Christian Faith*, 298.
213 Kolb, *Speaking the Gospel Today*, 9–12.
214 Kolb/Arand, *The Genius of Luther's Theology*, 211, 223.
215 Kolb, *Speaking the Gospel Today*, 208; Kolb, *Confessing the Faith*, 140.
216 See Kolb, *Christian Faith*, 220–229.

> In a time of deepest doubts in God's existence and love, the cross shows us how he reveals himself in the midst of the evil that threatens our lives. In Christ, the cross shows us who God is. In a time of deepest doubt in humanity and its worth, the theology of the cross defines human life from the perspective of God's presence and his love for his creatures, mankind. In Christ, the cross reveals God's divinity and our humanness.[217]

For this reason, interacting with God's Word in Scripture is not just about understanding what we read and interpreting it historically.[218] It is also primarily about a "listening hearing,"[219] for in light of the fact that "Holy Scripture […] has always been there,"[220] the "oral nature of God's Word"[221] is a feature of God's own way of communicating himself.

217 Kolb, *Deus revelatus – Homo revelatus*, 34.
218 See Alexander Deeg, "*Vom Lesen der Heiligen Schrift,*" in LuThK 39 (2015): 105–128.
219 Christoph Barnbrock,"*Vom Hören der Heiligen Schrift,*" in LuThK 39 (2015): 129–152, here 132.
220 Barnbrock, "*Vom Hören der Heiligen Schrift,*" 133.
221 Barnbrock, "*Vom Hören der Heiligen Schrift,*" 135.

Mark Mattes

Luther's Theological Aesthetics

Luther is not seen as a "go-to" theologian for aesthetics. In general, it is assumed that Protestant theology offers little for a theory of beauty or theological aesthetics because it gives prominence to the word and not the image. Likewise, Luther's retrieval of the Pauline reality that human participation in Christ entails dying and rising with Christ – discontinuity and not continuity with respect to human life – violates or undermines desire as the agent which moves pilgrims through their itinerary of union with Beauty as such. Unfortunately, some Protestant perspectives indeed feed this misperception that Protestant thinking is a wasteland when it comes to the question of beauty.

That sentiment, for instance, is echoed with a vengeance in the theology of Rudolf Bultmann for whom "the idea of the beautiful is of no significance in forming the life of Christian faith, which sees in the beautiful the temptation of a false transfiguration of the world which distracts the gaze from 'beyond'." For Bultmann, the attempt to find a depth dimension of beauty in reality is an attempt to avoid suffering, which in contrast to beauty gives the genuine entre to Christian faith.[1] But Bultmann here is no disciple of Luther. He ignores the deeply paradoxical nature of Luther's thinking. Truer to Luther is Miikka E. Anttila:

> In the cross of Christ there is supreme beauty concealed beneath the most abominable ugliness. Yet there is no ugliness in God. The ugliness of the cross belongs to us, whereas the beauty is God's. God is most beautiful not only when compared to us. He proves to be most beautiful when he makes us beautiful, that is, gives his beauty to us. This is an aesthetic variation of the doctrine of justification.[2]

Reservations about Luther's ability to deliver a vibrant theological aesthetic are, however, understandable. After all, how can a thinker who struggled so much with God, who distinguished a "hidden" or an "absconded" deity from a revealed

1 *Glauben und Verstehen: Gesammelte Aufsätze*, 4 vols. (Tübingen: J. C. B. Mohr, 1975), 2:137, cited in David Bentley Hart, *The Beauty of the Infinite* (Grand Rapids: Eerdmans, 2003), 23.
2 Miikka E. Anttila, "Music," in *Engaging Luther: A (New) Theological Assessment*, ed., Olli-Pekka Vainio (Eugene, OR: Cascade, 2010), 218.

God, or differentiated a "theology of the cross" from that of "glory" possibly have anything to contribute to a theology of beauty? Beauty conveys a tranquility that hardly seems to square with the Reformer's spirituality marked so often by chronic conflict with God, which he actually understood as assault (*tentatio*) from God.

Among all the major reformers, Luther would seem the least likely source for finding anything of significance for beauty. Indeed, *prima facie* we might think of Luther as the enemy of beauty. After all, the medieval catholic system was apt to see union with beauty itself in the beatific vision as a reward for cultivating the habits of faith, hope, and love, provided that grace initiated this cultivation. In his quest to challenge and abolish the tradition of interpreting grace through the lens of merit, it would seem that Luther is the great foe of beauty.

This essay indicates otherwise. In many respects, the gospel as Luther understood it opens a horizon which gives sinners access to beauty and gives a message which is itself so beautiful that desperate, repentant sinners crave it. The God who is like the waiting father in the Parable of the Prodigal Son (Luke 15:11–32) is exactly the one whom sinners can identify as beauty as such because nothing is quite as wondrous or joyful as the full and free forgiveness given through Jesus Christ, and the renewal of human senses[3] which it imparts.

Perhaps the possibility of discerning Luther's theological aesthetic is due to the fact that increasingly Luther scholars have not been satisfied with a "thin" description of Luther which reduces the Reformer's teachings to the doctrine of justification interpreted in existentialist terms. Instead, they have brought to the fore a "thick" description[4] which shows how the doctrine articulates a social dimension such as the "three estates" (the church, the household, and the civil government),[5] as well as an acknowledgement of the word as embodied, administered in the sacraments, or orally. This latter teaching – the embodiment of the word – is rich in significance for theological aesthetics since it acknowledges that faith at its core is markedly aesthetic[6] – awakening the senses, opening receptivity, and evoking gratitude and joy. Such an aesthetic core to the faith is expressed in worship that is sensitive not only to ecstatic delight but also to

---

3 *Lectures on Galatians* (1535), LW 27: 140 (WA 40.2: 178).

4 Admittedly I am playing loose with Clifford Geertz's categories of thick and thin description since for Geertz thick description acknowledges that all description comes with interpretation; there is no neutral objectivity per se. But the parallel between my use here and Geertz's is that adequate interpretation is not reductionist. See *The Interpretation of Cultures* (New York: Basic Books, 1973), 5–6, 9–10.

5 See Oswald Bayer, *Martin Luther's Theology: A Contemporary Interpretation*, trans., Thomas Trapp (Grand Rapids: Eerdmans, 2008), 120–153.

6 Miikka E. Anttila, "Music," in *Engaging Luther: A (New) Theological Assessment*, 219.

complaint or accusation against God when life seems terribly unfair, seen for instance, in the laments in the Psalter.

Luther lived in a time of transition within aesthetic sensibilities in which Europeans increasingly looked away from the tradition stemming from Augustine which tended to intellectualize beauty, seeing it as a way to ascend beyond the senses, toward sense experience itself as pleasing the senses and the mind acknowledging such with appreciation. Luther himself contributed to this trend.

Likewise, Luther shared important convictions of the German Humanists which also shaped his aesthetics. Concerned with educating civil servants, early Italian Renaissance Humanists perceived the medieval model of learning (the *trivium* and the *quadrivium*) as inadequate to prepare courtiers and diplomats. As an alternative, they focused on the *ars dictaminis* (elegant writing), Latin grammar, and classical Greek to cultivate persuasive leaders.[7] This milieu influenced Northern Europe and provided a context for Erasmus to develop his critical edition of the New Testament (1516), a move crucial for Luther's translation of the New Testament (1521).

The early Luther was fond of associating his work with the likes of Lorenzo Valla and Giovanni Pico della Mirandola.[8] Renaissance Humanism, emphasizing formal Latin rhetoric and elegance in style by means of mastering linguistic skills and textual criticism, and critiquing scholastic method, impacted Luther's approach to composing treatises, devotional literature, letters, and his translation of the Bible. Humanists employed learning and ornament in their writings precisely in order to evoke an affective and ethical response in readers. This was not beauty for its own sake, but instead attractiveness as a means to persuade. It is noteworthy that Renaissance Humanists, like their medieval predecessors, did not associate beauty with the arts per se but instead based their views of beauty on ancient or classical models.[9]

But in order to properly situate Luther, it is valuable to understand the continuities and discontinuities between Luther and the previous medieval tradition on beauty which, as represented by Thomas Aquinas (1225–1274), who included proportion, clarity, and integrity as criteria for beauty. As we shall see, Luther's understanding of the gospel significantly altered that tradition. Theorizing about beauty, important for the philosophical school of Realism, seen for example in Aquinas, was not a part of the research program of the Nominalists, nor was theorizing about beauty of great concern to late medieval mystics.[10] Hence, two of

7 Paul Oskar Kristeller, *Renaissance Thought II: Papers on Humanism and the Arts* (New York: Harper & Row, 1965), 4–5.
8 Erika Rummel, *Biblical Humanism and Scholasticism in the Age of Erasmus* (Leiden: Brill, 2008), 4.
9 Kristeller, 186.
10 Though beauty was important for monastic spirituality, seen in the bridal mysticism of

the most important streams influencing Luther's thinking, Nominalism and mysticism, did not explicitly think about the nature of beauty.

Even so, we find in Luther important reflection on beauty as he deals with the implications of the doctrine of justification by grace alone through faith alone. For the Reformer, sinners are clothed in an alien righteousness, Christ's, who adorns them with his own spiritual beauty, even though before the world he was "without form or comeliness." No doubt, God's alien work of divesting sinners of smug self-security is not beautiful but terrifying. But its result, freeing sinners of their various defense structures, and fortifying the new creation in Christ through God's proper work, indicates God's beauty, expressed in the gospel which reassures humans that they are indeed "at home" in the world,[11] allowing them to delight in God's ways, and evoking wonder at the goodness latent in all things.

Luther's own great artistic achievement, even more than his beautiful hymns, was his translation of both the New and Old Testaments into German.[12] His translation had a profound and lasting impact on the German language, providing not only a standard language in contrast to the many dialects, but also turns of phrase which enrich the German language even today. Through such verbal artistry, Luther also has shaped almost a half millennium of German spirituality, not only in Protestant churches, but among Roman Catholics as well. This achievement, in turn, has influenced musicians, artists, poets, and architects of all backgrounds, not only in Germany, but throughout the world.

1. Beauty as Metaphysics

Unlike medieval thinkers, modern people tend to associate beauty with self-expressive creativity or an appreciation of nature. However, in the Middle Ages, beauty was not understood through the lens of what we call aesthetics, the study of how humans appreciate the world or the arts by means of their senses. As a discipline, aesthetics was not established until the mid-eighteenth century. Instead, for medieval theologians, the arts were a form of craftsmanship and beauty was understood "intellectually," that is, metaphysically. For medieval thinkers,

---

Bernard of Clairvaux (1090–1153), where the soul is attracted to Christ because he is beautiful, and Christ as bridegroom nurtures the soul. Such spirituality would, of course, have directly influenced Luther though, in contrast to his forebears, he tends to draw out the forensic consequences for the soul in its marriage to Christ.

11 With reservations about both the Platonism and Kantianism in Roger Scruton's work, I find his metaphor of "at home" as a way to describe the benefit that beauty gives us. See his *Beauty* (Oxford: Oxford University Press, 2009), 174–175.

12 See Birgit Stolt, "Luther's Translation of the Bible," *Lutheran Quarterly* 27 (2014), 373–400.

beauty was a trait or attribute of God. All things share in God's beauty insofar as they "participate," are instances of the divine.

In short, medieval theologians saw the world *pancalistically*, that is, to one degree or another, all creatures are beautiful since they are either vestiges (nonhuman creatures) or images (human creatures) of God who is beauty itself. In various ways, medieval thinkers built on the legacy of Plato and Neoplatonism as they developed *pancalism*, the conviction that everything is somehow an expression of beauty itself.[13] However, the legacies of later Scholastics, such as Duns Scotus (1265–1308) and William of Ockham (1288–1347), whose teachings guided Luther's philosophy professors at Erfurt, Jodocus Trutvetter (c. 1460–1519) and Bartholomäus Arnoldi von Usingen (1465–1532), did not focus their attention on beauty, and this may be one reason that Luther seldom deals with beauty at length in his treatises or later disputations.[14]

Where the theme of beauty comes to the fore in Luther's corpus is in his exegetical works, primarily in commentaries on the Psalms, such as Psalm 45, both early in his career (*Dictata super Psalterium*, 1513–1515) and later in his career.[15] Luther's discussion of beauty is tied to his exegesis. But such exegesis would shape his entire polemical and doctrinal theology.

While beauty is not a major theme in Luther's work, it is a crucial theme. It shapes the question of who God is, who Christ is, and who we are in Christ. Luther's views on beauty share common features with some medieval views, but also depart from them in important ways. Medieval thinkers listed proportion, color (brightness), and integrity as valid indicators of beauty while Luther is apt to see such matters, at least *coram deo*, as hidden. God's beauty, Christ's beauty, and human beauty in Christ are not transparent but instead are concealed to human eyes and grasped only by faith.

Many medieval thinkers asserted that beauty was a transcendental, that is, like being (*ens*), oneness (*unitas*), truth (*veritas*), and goodness (*bonitas*), it applies to the structure of all reality. For Luther, the chief problem in this way of thinking is that matters like divine goodness and beauty cannot be established on purely metaphysical grounds, independently of scripture, because outside of Christ they are not certain. Luther at times appropriated the results of metaphysical enquiry,

---

13 These medieval thinkers included Robert Grosseteste (c. 1175–1253), Bonaventure (1221–1274), and Thomas Aquinas (1225–1274); they reworked the legacy of Plato (427–347 BC), Aristotle (384–322 BC), Plotinus (205–270), Augustine (354–430), and the Pseudo-Dionysius the Areopagite (Fifth and sixth centuries).

14 See Umberto Eco, *Art and Beauty in the Middle Ages*, trans., Hugh Bredin (New Haven: Yale University Press, 1986), 90.

15 For the *Dictata*, see LW 10 and 11 (WA 3 and 4); for his later work, see "Commentary on Psalm 45" (1532) in LW 12: 197–300 (WA 40: 472–610).

but he consistently rejected the method of such research – seeing it as a "work of man" in contrast to the work of God or as uncertain speculation.[16]

Medieval thinkers viewed the world not first of all as raw material for human economic interests or consumption but instead as symbolic, as testifying to God's reality and goodness. While the analogy of being is hardly operative in any definitive sense in Luther's thinking, Luther's alternative is that all creatures participate in God, specifically as masks or instruments[17] through which God speaks to humans and through which God orders human life through the three estates (*ecclesia, oeconomia, politia*).

2. The Early Luther on Beauty

The early Luther was more concerned about the question of beauty, how God, Christ, and humans are beautiful, than what most commentators realize. For instance, many have sought to interpret the significance of Luther's theology of the cross in his *Heidelberg Disputation* (1518), but few have drawn out the implications of those theses for beauty. But the import for a theological aesthetics is present in this disputation. Consider the upshot of thesis 28, "the love of God does not find, but creates, that which is pleasing (*diligibile*) to it. The love of man comes into being through that which is pleasing to it."[18] Something is pleasing to someone because it is beautiful. Thesis 28 shows how humans and God have entirely different approaches to beauty. God does not find sinful humans to be beautiful but instead makes them to be beautiful, due solely to his generous self-giving love, whereas humans cannot love unless they first find the object of their love attractive. Luther sees the second sentence of the thesis as condemning of Aristotle: "thus it is also demonstrated that Aristotle's philosophy is contrary to theology since in all things it seeks those things which are its own and receives rather than gives something good."[19] Seeking one's own self-fulfillment and egocentrically receiving rather than altruistically giving good are expressions of desire or *eros* as embedded in the influential tradition stemming from Plato, especially Diotima's instruction given to the young Socrates, teaching him that *eros* leads one from the love of bodies to the contemplation of truth.

16 See "Heidelberg Disputation" (1518), theses 2, 3, 5, 8, 19, and especially 22 in LW 31:39–40 (WA 1: 353–355).

17 "Creatures are only the hands, channels, and means through which God bestows all blessings. For example, he gives to the mother breasts and milk for her infant or gives grain and all sorts of fruits from the earth for sustenance – things that no creature could produce by itself." See "The Large Catechism, I, 26" in KW, 389; (BSELK 566:26).

18 LW 31: 57 (WA 1: 354, 35).

19 LW 31: 57 (WA 1: 365, 5–7).

Rooted in this early work, Luther's mature theology will reject an egocentric *eros* which uses the beloved for one's own delight precisely in order to affirm an original or renewed *eros* which delights in the beloved's beatitude. The clincher is the first sentence which Luther explains:

> the love of God which lives in man loves sinners, evil persons, fools, and weaklings in order to make them righteous, good, wise, and strong. Rather than seeking its own good, the love of God flows forth and bestows good. Therefore sinners are *attractive* (*pulchri*) because they are loved (*diliguntur*); they are not loved because they are attractive.[20]

For Luther, God is sheer, one-sidedly *overflowing love* (a favorite divine name for Luther) and goodness – reaching out to those reduced to nothing, embracing them, and regenerating them. God finds nothing inherently attractive in the object of his love. But as reduced to nothing, having no obligatory claim over against God, this nonobject can be the recipient of God's mercy. God *regards* (forensic justification) that which is nothing as the raw material on which he can build (effective justification). Unlike human desire, God's love does not need to receive anything in order to generate or sustain it. God loves the unlovely, regards the ugly as beautiful, and the sinner as just, all of which human love is not wired for. Luther rejects the view of egocentric *eros* as a definitive way to understand God's love.

Already within his first series of lectures on the Psalter, the *Dictata super Psalterium*, Luther was developing thoughts about beauty which would lead him to make a distinction between human love as wholly egocentric and the love of God as wholly self-giving. In the *Dictata* we see the young professor as a highly energetic and creative mind constantly bringing to the fore ideas from scholastic theology and mysticism and critically evaluating their ability to assist him in his quest properly to understand God's righteousness. The question which guides Luther in the *Dictata* is this: how do we render God his due? We see the young Luther as a man constantly struggling with God: have sinners any claim or merit before God – some spirituality, goodness, or intelligence – by which God would be obliged to justify us? And, our young exegete demolishes everything offered as a possibility for such an exchange of human merit for God's approval.

This early stage of the Reformer's career has been called a "theology of humility" because for Luther humans are closest to God when they humble themselves before him or when God humbles them through crosses and trials. Increasingly in the *Dictata* and his *Lectures on Romans* Luther moves toward a passive role for humanity in the presence of God and an active role of God as accuser or granter of mercy. Building on work in the *Dictata* and *Romans*, Luther

20 LW 31: 57 (WA 1: 365, 8–12). Italics mine.

in his *Lectures on Hebrews*[21] (1517) and several early sermons[22] articulated an alien work (*opus alienum*) of God which reduces the sinner to nothing and a proper work (*opus proprium*) which re-establishes the sinner through forgiveness. In spite of the differences between the *Dictata*'s theology of humility and Luther's mature stance of *solus Christus* and *sola fide*, we can see in Luther's early theology the seeds which germinate and blossom into his mature theology, such as the rudiments of the theology of the cross, the distinction between law and gospel, and God's alien and proper works.

At the core of this theology of humility is the conviction that humans justify God in his judgment against human pride, specifically the assumption that we can offer something to God and by which he would be obliged to us, when humans agree with God's judgment that they truly have nothing of their own to offer. At their core, humans both as created and as deformed by sin are nothing, not only in relation to God but ontologically, at the core of their being, because human existence is wholly sustained by God.

But this theology of humility has wide reaching implications for a theology of beauty. Paradoxically, whoever is most ugly, that is, most self-accusatory and thus humble, making no claims before God but in fact accusing oneself in agreement with God, is in fact the most beautiful – because such sinners are able to admit their sins due to God's illumination. Commenting on Ps 51:4, Luther noted:

> Whoever is most beautiful (*pulcherrimus*) in the sight of God is the most ugly (*deformissimus*), and, vice versa, whoever is the ugliest is the most beautiful. [...] Therefore the one who is most attractive in the sight of God (*speciosissimus coram deo*) is not the one who seems most humble to himself, but the one who sees himself as most filthy and depraved. The reason is that he would never see his own filthiness, unless he had been enlightened in his inmost being with a holy light (*lumine sancto*). But when he has such a light, he is attractive (*speciosus*), and the brighter the light, the more attractive he is. And the more brightly he has the light, the more he sees himself as ugly (*deformem*) and unworthy (*indignum*). Therefore it is true: The one who is most depraved in his own eyes is the most handsome (*formosissimus*) before God and, on the contrary, the one who sees himself as handsome is thoroughly ugly before God, because he lacks the light with which to see himself.[23]

Clearly beauty here is influenced by an aesthetics of light (brightness or clarity) due to the enlightenment of God. But the corollary is that the more glory sinners claim for themselves the more they have lost beauty before God:

---

21 LW 29: 135 (WA 57: 128, 14).

22 See "Sermon on St. Thomas' Day" on Ps 19:1 (Dec. 21, 1516), LW 51: 18–19 (WA 1: 111–112).

23 LW 10: 239 (WA 3: 290, 23–291, 3).

> But if you are beautiful (*pulcher*), righteous, strong, and good to yourself, this will already be a denial and vileness in you in the presence of God. For as long as you have removed confession, beauty refused to remain. For you have bent glory in on yourself, and therefore you have also lost beauty. Therefore give glory and confession to God, and this very glory will be your adornment, and the confession to God will be your beauty. But affirmation of yourself will be abasement of God, as far as you are concerned.[24]

Said pithily, "whoever makes himself beautiful (*pulchrum*), is made ugly (*fedatur*). On the contrary, he who makes himself ugly, is made beautiful."[25] Such paradoxical convictions about finding ugliness in human "beauty," and beauty in human ugliness is not without precedent in the tradition. In spite of Luther's implicit critique of *caritas*, we must take note of Augustine's Christological approach to aesthetics: "Let that fairest one [Christ] alone, who loved the foul to make them fair (*qui et foedos dilexit, ut pulchros faceret*), be all our desire."[26] Whether or not this Augustinian aesthetic had a direct bearing on Luther, a Christological approach to aesthetics eventually took shape in Luther's hands as a two-fold approach to divine hiddenness. God is not only hidden as the *deus absconditus*, God's backside (*posteriora dei*) to those seeking complete transparency between his nature which utterly transcends human thought or will, but God is also hidden as mercy in the ministry of and preaching of Jesus Christ.[27]

In his own way, the early Luther affirms *pancalism*, but not on the basis of metaphysically defending the theological conviction that beauty is the same as goodness and that creatures are beautiful to one degree or another since they participate in beauty itself. That approach Luther would find in the *Heidelberg Disputation* as a presumptuous "theology of glory." To the point: even metaphysicians must be exposed to and expose their own inherent ugliness due to sin. To claim any divine trait or attribute for oneself, such as goodness, beauty, or freedom, is to take from God what is God's. The upshot: Christ alone is beauty – and the beauty of anything must find its place not in itself, which as such is nothing, but only as sustained by God.[28]

More than anything, for the early Luther, it is our humanity, our status as *creatures* in opposition to self-deifying pride, which is at stake.

> When you call God good, you must deny that you are good and confess that you are altogether evil. He will not suffer Himself and you to be called good together at the same

24 LW 11: 262 (WA 4: 110, 21–26).
25 LW 11: 263 (WA 4: 111, 7, 15).
26 *On the Gospel of St. John*, tractate 10:13.
27 See Brian Gerrish, "'To the Unknown God': Luther and Calvin on the Hiddenness of God" in *The Old Protestantism and the New: Essays on the Reformation Heritage* (Edinburgh: T & T Clark, 1982), 131–149.
28 LW 11: 387 (WA 4: 252, 10–14).

time, for He wants to be regarded as God, but He wants you to be regarded as a *creature.*[29]

3. Beauty and the New Creation

Already in Luther's early theology of humility we see the beginnings of what would be his unique approach to theology: God must kill us as sinners before he makes us alive as new creatures,[30] ones with clean hearts. God forensically regards those who are nothing on the basis of their own merit as the raw material of his new creation.

Luther's whole approach in the theology of humility is one increasingly governed by a forensic approach to the human relationship with God. That is, what counts in the human relationship with God is how God evaluates us. As we admit our nothingness, so are we embraced by God. Through his study of specific mystics, such as Johannes Tauler (c. 1300–1361), Luther claimed that the core Christian identity before God – as all human identity – is one which is wholly passive.[31] New creations are active with respect to their fellow creatures, their neighbors, serving others in their need, but before God they know that they are entirely receivers.

Hence, the humility of the earliest phase of Luther's theological career is transformed over time into a theology of the cross. Through various "trials and sufferings,"[32] and the accusing voice of the law, God is crucifying the old Adam or Eve so that humans lose confidence in the old being's claims for its own self-deification and ability to control life. Thereby, sinners put their trust in God's goodness – *and beauty* – granted in Jesus Christ. But, such beauty is hidden. It is grasped by the eyes of faith alone. Rid of self-justifying ego-centricism as definitive of the core of their being, humans can live extrinsically, outside themselves, in Christ in whom their confidence is centered, and also in their neighbor in whose ethical service they now become "Christs,"[33] but also in aesthetic appreciation of God's good gifts present throughout creation.

We should note that with his focus on God's forensic regard of sinners Luther reinterpreted "bridal mysticism" with its implicit affirmation of beauty, that

29 LW 11: 411 (WA 4: 278, 37–279, 2). Italics mine.

30 For more on this theme, see Robert Kolb, "God Kills to Make Alive: Romans 6 and Luther's Understanding of Justification (1535)," *Lutheran Quarterly* 12 (1998): 33–56.

31 Oswald Bayer, *Martin Luther's Theology: A Contemporary Interpretation*, trans., Thomas Trapp (Grand Rapids: Eerdmans, 2008), 43.

32 *Lectures on Hebrews*, LW 29: 130.

33 "I will therefore give myself as a Christ to my neighbor, just as Christ offered himself to me [...]," *The Freedom of a Christian*, LW 31: 367 (WA 7: 66, 3–5).

Christ is beautiful and desirous to the soul and the soul is beautiful to Christ. It continues the forensic character established from the young Luther's earliest work appropriating beauty. That is, the bride comes into the relationship with debts and liabilities, "sins, death, and damnation."[34] But Christ as a bridegroom "must take upon himself the things which are his bride's and bestow upon her the things that are his. If he gives her his body and very self, how shall he not give her all that is his?"[35] Hence, Luther said that "here we have a most pleasing vision (*dulcissimum spectaculum*) not only of communion but of a blessed struggle and victory and salvation and redemption."[36] Christ absorbs these debts of his "wicked harlot."[37] She has a *right to* and *can claim* his status and properties even as he absorbs her debts. Once again, we have a kind of "forensic beauty" established. The "divine bridegroom Christ marries the poor, wicked harlot, redeems her from all her evil, and adorns (*ornans*) her [beautifies her] with all his goodness (*omnibus suis bonis*)."[38]

4. The One and Only Beauty

These themes about beauty are solidified and heightened in the mature Luther. Based on lectures given in 1532, Luther's commentary on Psalm 45 clarifies that Christ's beauty is not to be looked for in his physical but instead in his spiritual traits. If beauty is a spiritual trait, God's faithfulness even to sinners, then beauty is no longer found in an Aristotelian golden mean but instead in God's own self-giving and in trust in God's promise. The Reformer repeats his conviction originally forged in the early theology of humility that sinners who claim beauty for themselves ignore their own ugliness *coram deo*. Again, the appearance of beauty, with its boastful attempt to claim merit before God, results in an ugliness before God and is ever at work in sinners' lives. Sinful humans are blind to such ugliness, but even worse, are blind to the beauty of Christ. Elsewhere, Luther noted that sinners can only see their nothingness *coram deo* through the Holy Spirit's enlightenment. It is Christ alone who is truly beautiful.

> It could perhaps be that some were fairer in form than Christ, for we do not read that the Jews especially admired His form. We are not concerned here with His natural and essential form, but with His spiritual form. That is such that He is simply the fairest in form among the sons of men, so that finally He alone is finely formed (*solus formosus*) and beautiful. All the rest are disfigured, defiled, and corrupted by an evil will, by

34 LW 31: 351 (WA 7: 55, 1).
35 LW 31: 351 (WA 7: 55, 5–6).
36 LW 31: 351 (WA 7: 55, 7–8).
37 LW 31: 352 (WA 7: 55, 26).
38 LW 31: 352 (WA 7: 55, 26–27).

> weakness in their resistance to sin, and by other vices that cling to us by nature. This ugliness of man (*turpitudines*) is not apparent to the eyes; it makes no impression on the eyes, just as spiritual beauty makes no visual impression. Since we are flesh and blood, we are moved only by the substantial form and beauty that the eyes see. If we had spiritual eyes, we could see what a great disgrace it is that man's will should be turned from God [...].[39]

But, what makes for Christ's beauty? Is it that unlike sinners he is truly righteous on the basis of the law? The Reformer does not indicate this. On the contrary, he claims that Christ's beauty is his identifying and becoming one with sinners, all for the sake of helping and saving them.

> [Christ] did not keep company with the holy, powerful, and wise, but with despicable and miserable sinners, with those ruined by misfortune, with men weighed down by painful and incurable diseases; these He healed, comforted, raised up, helped. And at last he even died for sinners.[40]

So, what makes Christ beautiful simply violates the standard medieval criteria of proportion, clarity, and perfection. In aligning himself with sinners of all sorts, Christ associates with the disproportionate, the shady, and the imperfect, and he himself becomes all this ugliness. Hence, Christ's beauty is one which is "hidden under the opposite appearance (*sub contraria specie*)."[41]

Instead of the three standard criteria of beauty as applying to Christ, Luther's new criterion for beauty is Christ's compassionate, self-originating love which reaches out to the lost and outcast, those who do not register as important, mighty, or valuable on the scale of law. Indeed, those in power, those with proportion, clarity, and perfection, threatened by such compassion, can only reject Christ and deem him ugly. It would seem then that the medieval criteria for beauty are constituted by law, not gospel. Luther's quest then is to re-situate beauty as gospel, if any beauty is to be had *coram deo*.[42] Speaking of the righteous upholders of the law, the Pharisees, and their rejection of Christ, Luther noted:

> [The Pharisees and priests] were so inflamed with hatred for Christ that they could not even bear to look at Him. While He was present and speaking among them, there still proceeded from His mouth rays – in fact, suns – of wisdom, and from His hands beams of divine power, and from his entire body suns of love and every virtue. But whatever of His beauty (*pulchritudinum*) He showed them was nauseating and an abomination to them, not through Christ's fault but through their own.[43]

---

39 "Commentary on Psalm 45" in LW 12: 207 (WA 40.II: 485, 5–11).
40 "Commentary on Psalm 45" in LW 12: 208 (WA 40.II: 486, 11–12).
41 "Commentary on Psalm 45" in LW 12: 208 (WA 40.II: 487, 26).
42 As *the* artist of resituating beauty as gospel, the Lutheran Johann Sebastian Bach, see James R. Gaines, *Evening in the Palace of Reason: Bach Meets Frederick the Great in the age of Enlightenment* (New York: Harper Perennial, 2006).
43 "Commentary on Psalm 45" in LW 12: 208 (WA 40.II: 487, 15–20).

In Jesus Christ, God gives his beauty as compassion and his compassion as beauty to those oppressed by law, but such a gift threatens the power structures sustaining human self-righteousness. "That is the manner and nature of the world; it judges this King to be shameful beyond all the sons of men, and it holds His most beautiful gifts and virtues to be diabolical villainy and malice. We encounter the same thing today."[44]

Hence, for Luther, a paradoxical approach to beauty is unavoidable: those who claim their own beauty are in fact ugly before God, while those who are ugly before other humans are in fact endeared to God. Jesus Christ, who is God's beauty, is ugly to sinners and put to death by them because he is a threat to their ways of maintaining power and their own defense structures. For that reason, sinners are condemned and in need of mercy. In summary, Luther writes,

> [T]his King is hidden under the opposite appearance: in spirit He is more beautiful (*pulcher*) than the sons of men; but in the flesh all the sons of men are more beautiful than He, and only this King is ugly, as He is described in Isaiah 53:2, 3 [...]. Therefore we see that delightful and pleasant things are stated of this King in the Psalm, but they are enveloped and overshadowed by the external form of the cross. The world does not possess or admire these gifts; rather it persecutes them because it does not believe. These things are spoken to us, however, to let us know that we have such a king. All men are damned. Their beauty (*pulchritudinem*) is nothing in God's eyes. Their righteousness is sin. Their strength is nothing either. All we do, think, and say by ourselves is damnable and deserving of eternal death. We must be conformed to the image of this King.[45]

If humans are to have a beauty *coram deo*, they must receive it forensically and externally as a gift from God. Since the fall, only as other than nature can grace permit nature to be nature. "Then you are beautiful (*decora*) not by your own beauty, but by the beauty of the King, who has adorned (*ornavit*) you with His Word, who has granted you His righteousness, His holiness, truth, strength, and all gifts of the Holy Spirit."[46] In other words, for the Reformer, beauty *coram deo* is another way of saying righteousness *coram deo* and it is quite consistent to say that God's righteousness is likewise beauty. Justification by faith alone is God imparting his beauty to sinners, clothing them in his beauty. To be justified by faith is to be made beautiful. In Christ humans are made both "lovely" and "acceptable to God."

> Our beauty (*pulchritudinem*) does not consist in our own virtues nor even in the gifts we have received from God, by which we exercise our virtues and do everything that pertains to the life of the Law. It consists in this, that if we apprehend Christ (*Christum apprehendamus*) and believe in Him, we are truly lovely (*vere formosi*), and Christ looks

44 "Commentary on Psalm 45" in LW 12: 208 (WA 40.II: 487, 22–25).
45 "Commentary on Psalm 45" in LW 12: 208–209 (WA 40.II: 487, 26–39).
46 "Commentary on Psalm 45" in LW 12: 278 (WA 40.II: 580, 28–30).

> at that beauty (*decorum*) alone and at nothing besides. Therefore it is nothing to teach that we should try to be beautiful by our own chosen religiousness and our own righteousness. To be sure, among men and at the courts of the wise these things are brilliant, but in God's courts we must have another beauty (*aliam pulchritudinem*). There this is the one and only beauty (*sola pulchritudo*) – to believe in the Lord Jesus Christ.[47]

Defined not by law but by Christ, sinners are deemed beautiful. Perhaps to be consistent, we must say, they are simultaneously beautiful and ugly, just as they are *simul iustus et peccator.*

5. Creational Beauty

Luther's commentary on the creation of humans and their "original righteousness" (*iusticiae originalis*) has extensive references to beauty. While his paradoxical understanding of Christ who appears ugly before God but is in truth beautiful and of people who appear beautiful to themselves but are in fact ugly undermines the medieval criteria for beauty as proportion, clarity, and completeness, these criteria excluded *coram deo* find a place *coram mundo* as Luther presents the fitness of human ability to care for creation as it originally comes directly from God's hand.

For this reason, we can draw a distinction between beauty associated with the gospel from that of beauty associated with the law as a "creation beauty." The former is not apparent to reason or the senses. Instead, it is claimed only on the basis of God's imputing Christ's righteousness to sinners. The latter has a place for these three medieval criteria. If anything, for Luther, when we deal with the creation of Adam, the problem with the medieval criteria *coram mundo* is that they say far too little. Indeed, the Reformer's overall perspective on Adam's qualities is similar to Albert the Great's (c. 1193–1280) view of beauty as "resplendence of form":

> Just as corporeal beauty requires a due proportion of its members and splendid colours [...] so it is the nature of universal beauty to demand that there be mutual proportions among all things and their elements and principles, and that they should be resplendent with the clarity of form.[48]

Again, it is hard not to view Luther's portrait of the pre-lapsarian Adam's physical and mental traits as hyperbolic. Speaking of the image of God in Adam,

47 "Commentary on Psalm 45" in LW 12: 280 (WA 40.II: 583, 19–27).
48 Umberto Eco, *Art and Beauty in the Middle Ages*, 25.

and using the Augustinian trio of memory, intellect, and will as a venue by which to speak of God's image in humanity, Luther notes:

> Both his inner and his outer sensations were all of the purest kind. His intellect was the clearest, his memory was the best, and his will was the most straightforward – all in the most beautiful tranquility of mind (*pulcherrima securitate*), without any fear of death and without any anxiety. To these inner qualities came also those most beautiful and superb (*pulcherrima et excellentissima*) qualities of body and of all the limbs, qualities in which he surpassed all the remaining living creatures.[49]

No doubt Luther accentuated the sufficiency of Adam's physical and mental prowess to serve as a just lord over the other creatures in Eden. Likewise, Luther heightened the contrast between humanity in a state of integrity and fallen humanity. Pivotal to this contrast is the peace of mind and security which the pre-lapsarian Adam experienced, unlike the post-lapsarian Adam who fears death. The pre-lapsarian Adam wholly living in fear, love, and trust, and thus in right relationship with God, has nothing to fear of death, or anything else for that matter. Hence, "Before sin Adam had the clearest eyes, the most delicate and delightful odor, and a body very well suited and obedient for procreation. But how our limbs today lack that vigor!"[50] Even stronger, the Reformer notes that through the fall, humans have lost

> a most beautifully enlightened reason (*pulcherrime illuminatam rationem*) and a will in agreement with the Word and will of God. We have also lost the glory of our bodies, so that now it is a matter of the utmost disgrace to be seen naked, whereas at that time it was something most beautiful and the unique prerogative (*pulcherrimum et singularis praerogativa*) of the human race over all the other animals. The most serious loss consists in this, that not only were those benefits lost, but man's will turned away from God.[51]

In fact, for Luther, due to the pervasiveness and perversion of sin, we are not able to comprehend the nature of the *imago dei*, the image of God in humans. For Augustine and the Scholastics, the image of God consisted of (1) memory which should blossom in hope in God, (2) intellect which should lead to faith in God, and (3) will which should exercise itself in loving God. Indeed, God's image would be perfected by means of humans exercising the gracious gifts of hope, faith, and love.[52] For Luther, the definitive traits ascribed to the image of God, memory, intellect, and will are presently "utterly leprous and unclean,"[53] due to sin. However, such convictions serve not just to chastise human disobedience but

49 "Lectures on Genesis" in LW 1: 62 (WA 42: 46, 18–27).
50 "Lectures on Genesis" in LW 1: 100 (WA 42: 76, 15–18).
51 "Lectures on Genesis" in LW 1: 141 (WA 42: 106, 12–17).
52 "Lectures on Genesis" in LW 1: 60 (WA 42: 45, 11–17).
53 "Lectures on Genesis" in LW 1: 61 (WA 42: 46, 7).

to accentuate the beauty and power of humans in their state of original righteousness. It is clear that the proportions of Adam's members were commensurate for his needs and to take care of Eden, "a garden of delight and joy (*deliciarum et voluptatis*),"[54] and thus his sight stood superior to that of eagles or lynxes while his strength was greater than that of lions and bears. Luther makes it clear that in Eden, Adam and the other animals were not competitors for food or, least of all, planning to make a meal out of one another. Instead, Adam and the beasts ate from a "common table," and would have lived on rye, wheat, and other products of nature, had there been no sin.[55]

The affirmation of proportion (at least *coram mundo*) is likewise reinforced in the *Lectures on Genesis* as Luther agrees with Peter Lombard that humans were "created for a better life in the future than this physical life would have been, even if our nature had remained unimpaired." Repeatedly the Reformer states that humans "at a predetermined time, after the number of saints had become full, these physical activities would have come to an end; and Adam, together with his descendant, would have been translated to the eternal and spiritual life."[56] Indebted at this point to Augustine and the Pythagorian tradition in which Augustine stood, which so highly valued mathematics as the key to unlocking the meaning of reality, the cosmos, human nature, as well as the criterion of beauty itself, Luther writes,

> With the support of the mathematical disciplines – which no one can deny were divinely revealed – the human being, in his mind, soars high above the earth; and leaving behind those things that are on the earth, he concerns himself with heavenly things and explores them [...]. Therefore man is a creature created to inhabit the celestial regions (*terra coelestia*) and to live an eternal life when, after a while, he has left the earth.[57]

For Luther, the human ability to do mathematics, which as harmony and rhythm of course includes music, indicates human destiny which is more than physical, indeed is properly spiritual.

Finally, the beauty of Adam's and Eve's original righteousness indicates that nature and grace were not external to each other, as they are since the fall, but instead interpenetrated with one another.

> Let us rather maintain that righteousness was not a gift which came from without, separate from man's nature, but that it was truly part of his nature, so that it was Adam's nature to love God, to believe God, to know God, etc. These things were just as natural for Adam as it is natural for the eyes to receive light. But because you may correctly say

54 "[T]he world was most beautiful (*pulcherrimus*) from the beginning; Eden was truly a garden of delight and joy." See "Lectures on Genesis" in LW 1: 90 (WA 42: 68, 35–36).
55 "Lectures on Genesis" in LW 1: 38 (WA 42: 29, 4).
56 "Lectures on Genesis" in LW 1: 56 (WA 42: 42, 24–27).
57 "Lectures on Genesis" in LW 1: 46 (WA 42: 34, 37–35, 7).

> that nature has been damaged if you render an eye defective by inflicting a wound, so, after man has fallen from righteousness into sin, it is correct and truthful to say that our natural endowments are not perfect but are corrupted by sin (*non integra sed corrupta*). For just as it is the nature of the eye to see, so it was the nature of reason and will in Adam to know God, to trust God, and to fear God. Since it is a fact that this has now been lost, who is so foolish as to say that our natural endowments are still perfect?[58]

Certainly such a characterization of the relation between nature and grace indicates the depth of beauty, the resplendence of form, with which Adam and Eve were created. Adam's nature as such was graced so that he lived in harmony with God, his wife, Eve, and his fellow creatures. It was *natural* for him to love God. Indeed, similar to a metaphor of Augustine's,[59] Luther's Adam was "intoxicated with rejoicing toward God […]"[60] It is such a state that God's people and the world are being renewed. In his commentary on 1 Cor 15 Luther repeatedly indicates that the resurrection body will be beautiful.[61] And, recalling his description of the happy exchange in the *Freedom of a Christian* (1520), we find the same metaphor of intoxication to describe the properties of Christ shared by the Christian.[62]

Comparing this conviction with that of the Genesis passage immediately above, it is clear that grace restores human nature to its original righteousness. The promise of God is able to intoxicate the soul, making it to love God, in a way that is reminiscent of original righteousness. In other words, nature does not need perfection but liberation, ultimately for its divine-wrought perfection and fulfillment "in the future life." Healing the wounds of sin inflicted on the intellect and will and elevating them by means of a super-added gift of the Holy Spirit is insufficient for human need in light of sin. Instead, God remakes believers to be new creations. The upshot is: "In this life we lay hold of this goal [the likeness of God] in ever so weak a manner; but in the future life we shall attain it fully."[63] In other words, as our salvation, God is leading his people towards beauty.

Far from a theology devoid of aesthetics, Luther's is one that seeks delight in the senses and not as a stepping stone to a higher spiritual reality. Instead, for the

58 "Lectures on Genesis" in LW 1: 165 (WA 42:124, 4–13).

59 "[…] inebriate the heart," *Confessions*, I, v.

60 "Lectures on Genesis" in LW 1: 94 (WA 42: 71, 31).

61 Luther writes of the resurrection life, "You will always be strong and vigorous, healthy and happy, also brighter and more beautiful than sun and moon, so that all the garments and the gold bedecking a king or emperor will be sheer dirt in comparison with us when we are illumined by but a divine glance" (LW 38: 142; WA 36: 593, 34–38) and he notes, "This will make the whole body so beautiful, vigorous, and healthy, indeed, so light and agile, that we will soar along like a little spark, yes, just like the sun which runs its course in the heavens." See "Commentary on 1 Corinthians 15" in LW 28: 143 (WA 36: 494, 40–495, 1).

62 *Freedom of a Christian* (1520) in LW 31: 349 (WA 7: 53, 15–20).

63 "Lectures on Genesis" in LW 1: 131 (WA 42: 98, 22–24).

Reformer beauty is given in the gospel which clothes and adorns sinners with the righteousness of Christ. But this forensic justification carries a powerful effective dimension: sinners are renewed in heart, mind, and even body, their senses are opened so that they can honor creation as gift, as we see when Luther preached on Jesus' command "Ephphatha, Be opened!"[64] and so give God glory for his goodness. God's alien work is not beautiful, but it exists for his proper work of giving favor to repentant sinners, which indeed is beautiful and shows us that God is beauty itself. The gospel restores desire such that it is no longer unnaturally self-serving but instead allows us to desire "what God desires."[65]

As his work in the theology of music indicated, believers can find an "innocent delight" in the appreciation of music, which itself is written into the fabric of creation. Luther's reformation was not iconoclastic because the gospel comes tangibly, in, with, and under visible signs, such as we see in the Lord's Supper: there is no "kernel" (promise) without the physical "shell."[66]Indeed, God only ever presents himself to humans as "covered," and so all physical things present God – albeit not always clearly or mercifully. Hence, the accusation that Luther's theology leads to a disenchantment, as Charles Taylor claims,[67] with the world, found at the core of secularity, is to be contested.[68] The office of Jesus Christ is to make God known with certainty.[69] Gospel beauty – paradoxically granted in the ugliness of Jesus Christ, who bears human sin, so re-orders humans as creatures to God through faith. As re-ordered to God through faith, believers not only live as Christs in the world for the sake of their neighbors, but also enjoy the beauty which God has built into creation. In all artistic endeavors humans "cooperate" with God, as part of the fabric of God's ever creative activity.

64 Oswald Bayer, *Martin Luther's Theology*, 108.

65 LW 1: 337 (WA 42: 248, 12–13). In *de servo arbritrio* (1525), Luther notes how the Holy Spirit in the gospel works to re-situate the human will: "[...] when God works in us, the will is changed under the sweet influence of the Spirit of God. Once more it desires and acts, not of compulsion, but of its own desire and spontaneous inclination. Its bent still cannot be altered by any opposition; it cannot be mastered or prevailed upon even by the gates of hell; but it goes on willing, desiring and loving good, just as once it willed, desired and loved evil." See *The Bondage of the Will*, trans., J. I. Packer and O. R. Johnston (New York: Revell, 1957), 103; (WA 18: 634, 37–635, 2).

66 "Confession Concerning Christ's Supper" (1528) in LW 37: 219 (WA 26: 333, 17).

67 See Charles Taylor, *A Secular Age* (Cambridge: Belknap, 2007), 25–27, 29–43, and other places.

68 Ronald Thiemann, "Sacramental Realism: Martin Luther at the Dawn of Modernity," in *Lutherrenaissance Past and Present*, ed., Christine Helmer and Bo Kristian Holm (Göttingen: Vandenhoeck & Ruprecht, 2015), 165–173.

69 Oswald Bayer, *Theology the Lutheran Way*, trans., Jeffrey Silcock and Mark Mattes (Grand Rapids: Eerdmans, 2007), 103.

Robert Rosin

Looking Around with New Eyes: A Certain Modesty As a Way to See

In his "Theses on the Philosophy of History," philosopher and cultural critic Walter Benjamin begins with this scenario:

> The story is told of an automaton constructed in such a way that it could play a winning game of chess, answering each move of an opponent with a countermove. A puppet in Turkish attire and with a hookah in its mouth sat before a chessboard placed on a large table. A system of mirrors created the illusion that this table was transparent from all sides. Actually, a little hunchback who was an expert chess player sat inside and guided the puppet's hand by means of strings. One can imagine a philosophical counterpart to this device. The puppet called "historical materialism" is to win all the time. It can easily be a match for anyone if it enlists the services of theology, which today, as we know, is wizened and has to keep out of sight.[1]

As a supporter of the Frankfurt School that arose between the two World Wars, Walter Benjamin championed Critical Theory, an approach that rejected the usual explanations and traditional analysis of how history and culture arose, and instead sought to deconstruct life's social, historical, and ideological components, looking behind the ostensible causes in order to find out what actually makes things tick and then how to bring change.

Is it really possible to decipher the past, make sense of the present, and see a clear path into the future? The proponents of Critical Theory were convinced the key lay in socio-economics both to explain and then to shape life. Religion, on the other hand, was now thought to have no real place or little use, despite having a long and prominent history and despite its long-accepted claim that it was how one ultimately made sense of this life and the life to come. But now its time was past. Its stories about how things came to be, about what should be valued, and about what was to come, were worn out and needed to be set aside for what it deemed to be a modern and realistic explanation. If religion had a role at all, it was minimal, useful only as rhetorical cover for economic forces that were really

1 Walter Benjamin, *Illuminations: Essays and Reflections* (New York: Schocken Books, 1969), 253.

at work, window dressing to make those forces more palatable as the hard truth of socio-economic relationships made the world go around. Historical materialism did not finally need religion, but it might still use it if it helped make straight the path and the rough places plain for what really counted and was even now coming in.

Benjamin and his Frankfurt School colleagues were convinced that historical materialism ultimately wins. But note: Benjamin put "historical materialism" in quotation marks. He had faith in the ideal, but could it be that he thought the version on display in the Europe at his time was just as empty as theology had become? The cruel reality in Stalin's era brought soaring hopes back down to earth. Theory ran up against oppressive practice that betrayed the cause. It seemed enough to have given Benjamin pause for a moment. He wrote his "Theses" shortly before his death in 1940. Things would only get worse.

Fast-forward a couple of generations, and the picture of the automaton and the hunchback surfaces again but now with a twist. In *The Puppet and the Dwarf*, Slavoj Žižek, also a philosopher and cultural critic, writes:

> Today, when the historical materialist analysis is receding, practiced as it were undercover, rarely called by its proper name, while the theological dimension is given a new lease on life in the guise of the "postsecular" Messianic turn of deconstruction, the time has come to reverse Walter Benjamin's first thesis on the philosophy of history: 'The puppet called 'theology' is to win all the time. It can easily be a match for anyone if it enlists the service of historical materialism, which today, as we know, is wizened and has to keep out of sight.' One possible definition of modernity is: the social order in which religion is no longer fully integrated into and identified with a particular cultural life-form, but acquires autonomy, so that it can survive as the same religion in different cultures.[2]

Historical materialism is weighed in the balance and found wanting, unable to shake the shadow of the Soviet experiment along with other later "me too" regimes that betrayed hopes and dashed expectations. Religion, on the other hand, has made a comeback. At times (suggests the quotation) it might don shopworn materialist rhetoric to help gain an audience, especially among the old guard missing the bygone era, but religion just as well could stand on its own. Why? Because it turns out that religion is able to fill a need and serve a purpose. It does so especially, writes Žižek, when religion "is no longer fully integrated into and identified with a particular cultural life-form, but acquires autonomy, so that it can survive as the same religion in different cultures." In other words, religion succeeds when it no longer is carried by and identified with a single culture and when it no longer expects those on the receiving end to also accept that outside

2 Slavoj Žižek, *The Puppet and the Dwarf: The Perverse Core of Christianity* (Cambridge, MA: MIT, 2003), 3.

culture as well, as if the culture were necessary for the religion. Instead religion succeeds when it has learned to adapt – same message but in different cultures.[3]

But be careful and keep several things in mind. While Žižek turns the table on Benjamin and is critical of historical materialism while speaking up for religion,[4] Žižek has his own notion of what is important about religion, about its role, and about the world in which it works. By putting "postsecular" in quotations marks, is Žižek in effect telling the reader that the secular is not really gone? Then there is the mirroring of Benjamin by putting "theology" also in quotation marks suggesting a different, nontraditional understanding.

In fact, for Žižek religion that matters has nothing to do with the substance of Christian teaching. Dogma about sin and salvation, for example, or any other locus is beside the point. Beliefs drawn from texts and voiced in creeds are not the focus. Instead religion serves a utilitarian role as it helps people learn how to live now and live anew by influencing culture. Christianity is worth defending, because its radical nature – take Luke 14:26, for example – turns things topsy-turvy and then sweeps clean, opening possibilities for new relationships, as people live in hope and anticipation of whatever may come into their lives.[5]

Traditional Christianity obviously thinks it has more to offer with eternal importance beyond the here and now, and so it is not about to abandon the message. Žižek has a different use. Still, his comment at the end of the passage quoted is worth noting: as religion reaches out and engages the world whenever and wherever, the exhortation ought not to be wrapped up part and parcel with

3 The comment here reminds one of St. Paul's remark in 1 Cor 3:2 that "I have become all things to all people, that by all means I might save some." The irony is that the targets of the remarks in both cases are not hostile critics outside in the world but some within the family who ought to know better.

4 Žižek would side with Benjamin on historical materialism in principle or in the ideal, but the added decades since Benjamin have provided an even more sobering view of historic failures. Žižek does not want to defend and is not about to long for something with such a miserable record. Elements of the theory might be tried another way. Here religion could help to demonstrate the need not to tinker around the edges but to make a radical change with total commitment.

5 Slavoj Žižek, *The Fragile Absolute: Or, Why Is the Christian Legacy Worth Fighting For?* The Essential Žižek, second edition (London: Verso Press, 2009). It is a complex book with much to discuss and debate. In the end, however, that which is praised in Christianity seems to pale before what the traditional understanding has to offer. Sacrificing what one loves in order to clear out what-ever is old and broken and hinders so that new can come does not quite measure up to the idea of the Father sacrificing his Son – but then that sort of theological worth by default simply isn't there for Žižek. Still, finding support of sorts is interesting and stirs the pot for another look at Christianity's value. What bubbles up is the kind of revisiting of Christianity seen, for example, in David Bentley Hart, "Christ's Rabble: The First Christians Were Not Like Us," *Commonweal* (online; posted September 27, 2016); Source URL: https://www.commonwealmagazine.org/christs-rabble. Hart's is a stinging criticism of present Christian socio-economics that makes one wonder, as he noted, if Kierkegaard were not right that Christianity no longer really exists.

simply one culture, but rather the same religion learns to mesh with different cultures. Here is support from a surprising quarter – an ally at least for the moment on this point (and a position worth revisiting later).[6]

Both Benjamin and Žižek in their own ways are trying to make sense of the world, trying to figure out what drives it and what can be done about better orchestrating life as it unfolds. They are hardly alone in this. Looking back at history, taking stock of the present, and gazing ahead toward the future are all difficult if not impossible tasks that defy crystal clear vision. Yet throughout history, people have sought to understand how we got to the present, what makes life tick, and then what is next and can we do anything about it. The irony in the case of Benjamin and Žižek is that while they disagree on the nature of religion, they agree in the decision to eliminate religion when seeking ultimately to make sense of things. For Benjamin, the flow of history has reduced theology to a nonfactor. (It always was, but it had not been so obvious.) For Žižek religion is important, but only when religion is recast as a tool to prepare the way, not as an end or especially as a body of beliefs. Something else will have to emerge to provide real insight.

The ways in which people have tried to answer life's questions and make sense of past, present, and future have varied. Some people seize upon a big idea that is said to answer everything and will light the way (they hope) into the future. Such an approach with all the eggs in the basket of one big idea may owe more to an ideology being promoted than a sober assessment of past and present, but it does make explanations simple and predictable. Other people opt for multi-causality when it comes to explaining the past – a safer way to go, since historical events and present circumstances usually seem to result from multiple factors.

Why did England have a Reformation? Because King Henry fell in love, if you take Voltaire's word for it. On reexamination, all sorts of reasons emerge: politics, yes, but also from the start come theology, economics, and other cultural factors, all joined in a particular way to make the movement what it was. A cursory look at church life seen already in the New Testament epistles and then followed by the rough and tumble times of early church councils and creeds makes plain that

6 The point also is driven home by another ally from within church ranks. Lamin Sanneh, *Translating the Message: The Missionary Impact on Culture* (Maryknoll, NY: Orbis, 1989; revised second edn, 2009), makes the point that part of Christianity's success, humanly speaking, came because those who first brought and taught the message then let go of it so that others could present it in their own culture, connect with people in their world in their own idiom. The shift is fraught with difficulty, but we see it done from the earliest days in the New Testament. In contrast, Islam, says Sanneh, insists that if the faith is to be embraced, the sending culture also must come with it. Christianity adapts itself to the situation rather than forcing itself on the situation with a one-size-fits-all approach.

from the beginning, theology has never floated above the fray but emerges from the crucible of history.

Sorting through multi-causality is messy business. The debates about the balance never seem to end. So finding a metanarrative, a mark, for example, of Modernism, has proved so attractive, allowing for loose ends on the micro scale, but then tying them all together on the macro/meta scale.[7] Narratives help organize, and a single metanarrative can be particularly tempting. But over time pressure mounts with more and more exceptions to the chosen rule, until the grand tale unravels. What is left are purely personal perspectives[8] or perhaps larger islands of semi-stability,[9] but the hope for the all-encompassing understanding is gone.[10]

Against this background, the question is worth repeating: Is it really possible to decipher the past, make sense of the present, and see a clear path into the future? Given the ceaseless efforts, people seem to think or at least to hope the answer is "yes," and who would not want that? But despite all the work put in by countless thinkers over hundreds of years, nothing has emerged that finally survives as *the* answer, although plenty of would-be "solutions" have been tried and even forced for a while, only later to come up short. "Never say never" the saying goes, but constant failures, revisions, and reboots are surely cause to wonder if ultimate answers are possible.

Maybe when those questions of past, present, and future are asked, instead of "yes" the real answer is "no" – no, it is not possible to put all the pieces together

---

7 That is not to say that seeking out big pictures with overarching explanations comes first with the modern world. But the multiplication of factors (perhaps a nice way of saying "the increasing apparent chaos") puts a premium on finding a way to make order and sense of things.

8 Jean-Francois Lyotard, *The Postmodern Condition: A Report on Knowledge*, Theory and History of Literature, vol. 10 (Manchester: Manchester University Press, 1979), introduced the term *postmodern* in the course of arguing that metanarratives are no longer possible and a thing of the past, leaving each person to form an individual perspective on life.

9 Zygmunt Bauman, *Liquid Modernity* (Cambridge: Polity Press, 2000), stops short of Lyotard and straddles the gap between modernism and postmodernism. Bauman concedes that under mounting pressure, modernity has so heated up that the old verities can no longer hold things together. What once was solid modernity has split apart, rather like an ice floe breaking up with pieces now floating – not as stable as the whole sheet once had been, yet still able to offer some support to those who find themselves on the various chunks.

10 Quentin Skinner, ed., *The Return of Grand Theory in the Human Sciences* (Cambridge: Cambridge University Press, 1990), looks at the efforts of theorists (Gadamer, Foucault, Kuhn, Habermas, and more) to provide a framework in which to understand humans and their history. The chapters are rather like those floating islands of ice: a larger place for some to stand with a vantage point that makes sense at least from there, but none really take everything in. The only way that would happen is to follow the tack taken by Hegel, whose flow of history works when the subject is put on Procrustes' bed and made to fit. Grand theory looks nice, so long as one ignores the cutting room floor.

for a clear understanding of times gone by, now present, and soon future. Of course, a "no" seems frustrating and exasperating, a sign of surrender and failure. After all the time and brainpower expended, failure should be unacceptable, right? And unacceptable to whom? Is that ours to decide?

Falling short of a grand overview has sent thinkers back to the drawing board again and again. Something must be missing. We need to know what that is, to know more and know it better. And when (not if) we find it, things will fall in place. But perhaps knowledge is not the right target either. The information explosion in the modern age has put the emphasis on the expert and on the professional, who tend to pile up knowledge within a narrow range rather than to reach widely across fields. Specialization – or is it compartmentalization? – at the expense of broader understanding can have not just practical but even ethical consequences.[11]

What results is what Erwin Chargaff once bemoaned as knowledge without wisdom.[12] Although Chargaff did not have in mind the big questions raised here about the ability to grasp past, present, and future, and while he had no interest in a theological angle (still coming) on the problem, his diagnosis nevertheless points in a different and a better direction to go: not off on yet another search for

11 *Uni*versity? Does is still function in the old unified way? In 1963 Clark Kerr, Chancellor of the University of California system, coined the term "multiversity" to accent the wide and varied range of activities. But since then, it signals an institution having intramural problems with wider consequences. Medieval universities were spurred by the twelfth-century Renaissance, a spurt in ideas that scholars and students sought to corral and organize for their own learning and the wider good of those they served. While the amount known has multiplied exponentially, up into recent times academics could still cross lines and communicate. Fine points were out of reach, but using critical thinking they still understood basics and asked good questions. That seems to have declined. Attempts to reach across disciplines can be dismissed as dabbling, not serious. But when people only stay in house, after a while they can only talk among themselves. No wonder outsiders (taxpayers) ask, "Who cares?" and parents with students have second thoughts about the costs. "Universities across the world in the early twenty-first century find themselves in a paradoxical position. Never before in human history have they been so numerous and so important, yet never before have they suffered from such a disabling lack of confidence and loss of identity." Stefan Collini, *What Are the Universities For?* (London: Penguin, 2012), 1. Collini also writes about multiversity issues.
A couple of decades earlier Bruce Wilshire challenged the concept of *uni*versity and warned of problems from packing more and more information into silos, into departments and schools that talked only to themselves. The lack of a broader perspective meant the university was losing its ability to speak in harmony or in chorus about life's problems, resulting, in effect, in a moral collapse of an institution that arose centuries ago not simply to collect information but to provide leadership and guidance. Bruce Wilshire, *The Moral Collapse of the University: Professionalism, Purity, and Alienation* (Albany: SUNY Press, 1990).

12 Erwin Chargaff, "Knowledge Without Wisdom," *Harper's* 260, no.1560 (May 1980): 41–48. Chargaff was a distinguished East European biochemist, first at the University of Vienna and then, after he fled in the Nazi era, at Yale. His work helped lead to the discovery of the DNA double helix. Chargaff certainly qualifies as an expert and a specialist, but hardly lived in his own little fact-filled world.

still more knowledge but rather on a quest for wisdom that would carry through, for judgment that would sustain even when knowledge at times is lacking.

Part of being wise is to know when to quit. The Law of Holes – it sounds more profound when it is called a "Law" – puts it bluntly: If you find yourself in a hole, stop digging.[13] There is a tendency in modern thought to assume we are (or ought to be) always moving onward and upward, but that may not be the case. It could be better to stop, back up a bit, and even call a halt. To halt is not necessarily to lose. It may prove to be the wise thing to do. Far from being wasted effort, taking a second look could be the wise thing to do, as long as the second time around is not just seeing again but rather seeing more. This from "Little Gidding" by T.S. Eliot:

> We shall not cease from exploration
> And the end of all our exploring
> Will be to arrive where we began
> And to know the place for the first time.[14]

Full circle back to the start is not failure because we now *know* the place. That is, we do not just look at, we actually *see*, and that is a wise thing.

The problem is that seeing is neither automatic nor easy. Ernest Hemingway (to stay in the literary vein) wrote: "This looking and not seeing things was a great sin." Serious business, this failing to see. Yet how often have we not heard, "You're looking right at it. Don't you see?" Why is that? "*Das Auge sieht, was es sucht*" goes the aphorism from the German artist Max Slevogt.[15] As an Impressionist, Slevogt knew that while the eye takes in one thing – perhaps dots and dashes on canvas – the mind would seek and see another if it so wanted. The eye finds what it wants to search for, as if it had a mind of its own. That is not very open-minded, but it often happens.

And the problems can deepen. What if this is not a matter just of seeing something from a different vantage point and putting some spin on it? What if what the eye looks for is not really there, what then? Hemingway again:

> In Africa a thing is true at first light and a lie by noon and you have no more respect for it than for the lovely, perfect weed-fringed lake you see across the sun-baked salt plain.

13 The adage has a longer history, but this present rendition was dug up in "Is That Dirt Being Shovelled?" *The Bankers Magazine* 166 (1964): 61.

14 "Little Gidding" is the last of Eliot's *Four Quartets*, finished in 1942, named for a small village in Cambridgeshire with an Anglican community centered around high liturgical worship. The poem is filled with images such as a rose or fire that, when understood, spark a higher vision or knowing stemming from what is all around.

15 Petra Kipphoff, "*Die Auge sieht, was es sucht,*" *Zeit Online*, August 7, 1992. Found here: http://www.zeit.de/1992/33/das-auge-sieht-was-es-sucht.

> You have walked across that plain in the morning and you know that no such lake is there. But now it is there absolutely true, beautiful and believable.[16]

Even when we know better – the lake is not there – the eye can deceive and the mind creates a picture. This is not looking at the wrong thing but rather looking at something not even there. Patterns appear that seem to put life in order, but are they truly there? We know (or should know) they could just as well be of our own making from eye to mind, especially as the first light gives way over time, and the heat of the day bends the light. Yet we forge ahead under the circumstances, because it is hard to ignore what we think we see and what we want and hope we will find. But it gets worse. The hopes already rest on shaky impressions from without, and then comes this from within, as Hemingway confessed in a moment of honesty: "I make the truth as I invent it truer than it would be."[17] Does it seem wise to press ahead?

When it comes to knowing, to this point nothing really has passed muster, although it is not for lack of trying. Past failures and complex problems have not dampened efforts, and for good reason. "Knowledge is power," as the saying goes.[18] Imagine the power multiplied by knowing everything. So attempts to arrive at a "killer app" connecting and explaining all will continue – continue to be sought and continue to fall short.

It might be wise to pull back and halt or to try another approach. Erwin Chargaff, cited earlier, urged a search for wisdom to go along with knowledge. That seems to be a good direction to go, but with a slight change in course. Wisdom is sought not merely by first light or the light around that shines on the liberal arts at work through history. There is much to learn from that, but there also is a theological angle, a way not just to look but to see, and to do so thanks to a higher light from above.

The collapse of modernism's metanarratives left behind a postmodern age marked by uncertainty with the rejection of absolutes along with the possibility of picking up the pieces and returning to modernity's optimism and confidence. This hardly exhausts the traits of either era, but it is enough to show that postmodernism is within hailing distance of Skepticism. That phenomenon arose in

16 Ernest Hemingway, *True at First Light* (New York: Scribner, 1999). The lines are Hemingway's epigram. (And in truth, the book, edited posthumously by his son, was not enthusiastically received.)

17 Hemingway, *True at First Light*, 94.

18 That is often attributed to Francis Bacon, although that precise phrase is not in his works. Close is the line "ipsa scientia potestas est" or "knowledge herself is power," found in Francis Bacon's *Meditationes Sacrae* (London: Hooper, 1597). It is used when Bacon is discussing heresies with true knowledge being God's alone. The simpler "knowledge is power" comes from the Latin version (1681) of Thomas Hobbes, *Leviathan*, in chapter 10, *De homine*. See, for example, *Opera philosophica* (London: John Bohn, 1841), vol. 3, 69.

classical antiquity when the fourth century BC Greek Pyrrho of Elis and then the Academic Skeptics at Plato's Academy sowed seeds of radical doubt. From individual facts and perceptions to overarching explanations, they had no confidence either in those explanations or in their own personal ability to make sense of anything. "All I know is that I know nothing," went the famous line from the Academic Skeptics, a saying that called even itself into question.[19]

The classical era's various approaches to making sense of the world – Ionians, Pythagoras, or Plato, for example – all have advantages, but none seems to answer everything. When questions move into the metaphysical realm, the systems look good on paper, but is there hard proof? And so the door is open to the "how do you know?" and "can you be sure?" questions, and Skepticism steps up. Deductive approaches need accepted givens to start, but when they are challenged...? Inductive empirical approaches, on the other hand, have issues with quantity. (Do we have everything that matters? Have we missed a case that proves us wrong?) And there are questions with quality. (How good is the evidence?) Those issues were lurking in the wings for those early philosophers, but fortunately they do not all come on stage.

The same basic issues and questions continue to hide in the weeds, ready to threaten, at some times more than others. Modernism's efforts to find or build a grand framework have proved a tempting target, with critics rejecting the possibility and introducing postmodernism instead with reduced expectations and more personal, limited perspectives. In history, one age or approach will overlap with the next, and the transition may last a long time. That seems to be the case now, with elements of modernism still carrying on and still working toward a metanarrative, even as postmodernism continues to criticize and seeks to put its own stamp on things.[20]

---

19 Beginning around 266 BC, Plato's Academy entered a period when Skepticism held sway, beginning with Arcesilaus and then Carneades and lasting into the first century BC. Sources with information on the arguments of the Skeptics include Cicero, Augustine, Diogenes Laertius, and Sextus Empiricus. Cicero's treatise *De natura deorum* saw a Stoic, an Epicurean, and a Skeptic asking what they could know about the gods. By the end of the treatise, those questions had given way to deeper ones about the gods themselves. Augustine, who went through a skeptical phase before becoming Christian, wrote *Contra Academicos* in an effort to beat the Skeptics at their own game, but in the end he invokes higher authority that provides truth and stability. Sextus Empiricus in the fourth century AD works through ten tropes used by the Skeptics to make their case. John Greco, *The Oxford Handbook of Skepticism* (Oxford: Oxford University Press, 2011), has several chapters that lay out the different approaches under the basic label. More focused and detailed is Richard Bett, ed., *The Cambridge Companion to Ancient Scepticism* (Cambridge: Cambridge University Press, 2010).

20 Allan Hazlett, *A Critical Introduction to Skepticism*, Bloomsbury Critical Introductions to Epistemology (London: Bloomsbury Academic, 2014), is an argumentative apology for the position's value now as much as ever.

The issues and questions that challenge grand theories are always around somewhere, perhaps just simmering on the back burner and at other times heating up to a boil. The stove seems turned up today. The Renaissance/Reformation era, a table-setter for Modernity (and hence its other name, the Early Modern era) was also a pot boiler and is worth a look.

Between Late Antiquity and Renaissance, the Middle Ages were not unaware of Skepticism, but it was largely ignored or confined to a rather small circle, posing little threat. Augustine's shot at the Academic Skeptics seems to have satisfied most that the problem had been handled. With the Renaissance, however, keen interest arose in various philosophical schools, and the heat was turned up. A revival of Platonism and Neo-Platonism along with a fresh look at Aristotle stirred the intellectual pot. The overlap of fourteenth-century Nominalism put questions to Aquinas and the Moderate Realists about their ability to move smoothly from nature to supernature. ideas and transcendent absolutes are said to be existing on a higher level, but where is the proof? It takes time, however, before things collapse.[21]

Then came a really dangerous development as skeptical texts from antiquity gained circulation in Renaissance humanist circles.[22] Dusting off the writings of Cicero, Diogenes Laertius, and Sextus Empiricus was just part of the larger Renaissance revival of classical texts. Plato and Neo-platonism along with Aristotle captured the lion's share of the attention, and it would be some time before the texts for classical Skepticism moved from manuscript to print.[23] However,

21 While Nominalists had their doubts, they also upheld divine revelation as a norm, and so transcendent absolutes held on because of the inertia of Christian culture. It takes time to sink in and have an effect. With everything steeped in that worldview, it would take several centuries until the ethos weakened. Today the damage is obvious. So argues Richard M. Weaver, *Ideas Have Consequences* (Chicago: University of Chicago Press, 1948). Weaver tried to help modern culture reverse the degeneration. He begins by criticizing the turn taken in the fourteenth century with the criticism of Moderate Realism, setting up the eventual erosion of higher absolutes. (Of course, it could be asked of Weaver if the the Moderate Realists really did not invite the challenge by maintaining they could climb up and down the nature/supernature ladder, so to speak, with Aristotle meshing with and verifying revelation. And when they cannot satisfactorily deliver…? But the subsequent decline would take time.) Weaver tried to reestablish moral absolutes by arguing that to have private property, there must be a self-evident "metaphysical right" of ownership, or the world becomes a grab bag where the strongest will prevail. How persuasive that is can be debated, but it is an interesting non-theological approach.

22 On the Renaissance revival of Skepticism, see, for example, Richard Popkin, *The History of Scepticism from Savonarola to Bayle*, rev. edn (Oxford: Oxford University Press, 2003). The first version of the book published in 1960 by the University of California Press ran from Erasmus to Descartes. A 1979 revision from the same publisher stretched the study to Spinoza. Charles B. Schmitt, *Cicero Scepticus: A Study of the Influence of the* Academica *in the Renaissance* (The Hague: Martinus Nifhoff, 1972).

23 Sextus Empiricus, for example, did not appear in print and in Latin until his *Outlines of*

manuscript copies were read and discussed by influential scholars. For example, Giovanni Pico della Mirandola and his nephew Gianfrancesco both had access to the texts, and they corresponded with Desiderius Erasmus and Philipp Melanchthon. The Picos much preferred Platonism, but references to Skepticism are also found in their correspondence, which they kept private.

The ideas of the Skeptics appeared in public in *De incertitudine et vanitate scientiarum et artium, atque excellentia Verbi Dei, declamatio invective*, as Agrippa of Nettesheim made use of their arguments to ridicule the arts and sciences for the vanity displayed despite much uncertainty. Agrippa would influence Michel Montaigne, who would pick up the standard for Skepticism for a time with his essay *Apology of Raymonde Sebond* that used the ten tropes in Sextus Empiricus to undercut certainty when it came to knowing and understanding the world. Montaigne half-joked in the *Apology* (Book 2, chapter 12), "When I play with my cat, who knows if I am not a pastime to her more than she is to me?" But he dealt with serious issues about the cosmos and the human soul, and so debilitating are the challenges that in mid-essay Montaigne bluntly asked, "What do I know?" For himself, he manages to avoid prosecution and persecution by turning at the essay's end to Christianity. What did he know? – but divine relation is greater and the church knows much and will persevere. Still, raising questions like this, like those posed earlier about making sense of the world, is playing with fire and is serious business.

Montaigne's essay later in the sixteenth century shows that Skepticism was not a flash in the pan. It was not for lack of trying that the ideas stayed alive. Decades earlier the Lutheran Reformation had three encounters with Skepticism involving three prominent theologians – Martin Luther, Johannes Brenz, and Philip Melanchthon – with each, interestingly, using the Old Testament book of Ecclesiastes for support.[24] Much could be said about all three, but a few paragraphs will have to do to illustrate how each dealt with the problem of radical doubt in different contexts.[25]

Pyrrhonism appeared in 1562, followed by his compete works in 1569. Richard Popkin, *The Columbia History of Western Philosophy* (New York: Columbia University Press, 2006), 330.

24 The texts for each are found most easily here:
Martin Luther, *Vorlesung über den Prediger Salomo, 1526; Annotationes in Ecclesiasten, 1532*, in WA 20: 1–203.
Johannes Brenz, *Der prediger Salomo* (Hagenau: Johann Setzer, 1528). Frommann-Holzboog issued a facsimile edition in 1970, the 400th anniversary of Brenz's death.
Philipp Melanchthon, *Enarratio brevis concionum libri Salomonis, cuius titulus est Ecclesiastes*, in *Philip Melanchthonis Opera*, ed., Karl Gottlieb Bretschneider and Heinrich Ernst Bindseil, in Corpus Reformatorum, vol. 14 (Braunschweig: Schwetschke, 1926), 89–160.

25 For more on what made Skepticism such a problem, along with the way Ecclesiastes was enlisted in reply, see Robert Rosin, *Reformers, The Preacher, and Skepticism: Luther, Brenz, Melanchthon, and Ecclesiastes*, Veröffentlichungen des Instituts für Europäische Geschichte, vol. 171 (Mainz: Verlag Philipp von Zabern, 1997).

When Martin Luther and Erasmus exchanged public salvos over the human will – free or bound – and the ability to respond to God's Law when it came to matters of salvation, Skepticism was also part of the argument. Erasmus felt uncomfortable with Luther's asserting what he believed Scripture said, and so Erasmus chose instead to side with the Skeptics and avoid bold declarations. He would rather rest in the arms of the church, Erasmus wrote. Falling back on the church echoed the Skeptics' approach to life.

Consistent doubt should drive one into the corner to curl up for safekeeping – that is, if the corner exists. To carry on in daily life skeptics would go with the flow of common convention. If others cross the street on the walk signal, then cross as well, but don't be surprised if you are run over by an Airbus 380 coming in to land. Ridiculous? You never know, but what else can one do? In Erasmus's case, stick with the church. (Remember, this is a Christian age with well over a millennium of the church caring for its own.)

Luther would have none of it. First, the institutional church was a poor authority compared with the biblical Word. Second, biblical texts were not a dark and confusing maze but the clear voice of God.

But invoking the Skeptics is not merely rhetorical introduction by Erasmus. There is the twist that enlisted Skepticism as his frontline ally, and made Luther furious. Luther knew that to avoid commitments, the classical era Skeptics taught that the will was free because that kept them uncommitted. Hence Luther to Erasmus: the Holy Spirit is no Skeptic but has written assertions into our hearts. Take those away, those assertions, and you take away Christianity.

Erasmus complained about Luther's rough rhetoric and repeated his arguments, which only angered Luther more. He intended to write again, but colleagues persuaded him to use his energies on other problems, and it seemed the moment had passed. Then the plague hit Wittenberg, and many left town, but Luther decided to stay and let God do what he wanted. In the interim Luther needed something to do in class for students who also remained, so he spent a semester lecturing on Ecclesiastes.

Why is that important? In 1523 Luther had written a preface to Ecclesiastes to help people understand a challenging book. He commented already then at some length on the Preacher opposing the notion of free will, an idea some foolishly maintained. Luther never mentioned Erasmus, but there was no doubt about the target, and Erasmus struck back the next year with the diatribe on free will. Now a few years later, still irritated by Erasmus, Luther went back to Ecclesiastes, once again never mentioning his counterpart, but repeatedly lashing out against free will that some foolishly championed, but in Ecclesiastes Luther expanded the debate.

The 1524/1525 exchange was over faith and salvation, matters in the so-called Kingdom (or Realm) of the Right Hand. Now Luther insisted that there is no free will also in the Kingdom of the Left, the realm of daily life. We appear to make choices every day, but morally and in terms of ordering the world, all is God's doing, not human choice.

Luther feared that Skepticism would turn believers away from confidence in and dependence on God, with the course of this life put instead squarely on their shoulders. That burden is impossible to bear and would crush them in despair. (Today: good luck holding all things together in a Modernist metanarrative.) On the other hand, while they cannot tell where and how God directs life's events, his people know things are in his hands, that God is love, and that he has promised to never drop them.

Their response is to live out their lives in faith, taking on whatever God puts on them in their various callings and roles. Their task is to do the best job they know how, but then to let go and leave the outcome to God. They can plan perfectly and act properly, yet if God chooses to direct things in some other direction for his purposes than he usually does, then that is how life goes. The race is not always to the swift, says Ecclesiastes, nor is the battle always to the strong. Those looking for a big picture in which they are involved actively organizing and pursuing life are bound to be confounded, to plunge into anxiety and fear, and be driven to distraction.

Luther knew that from Right-Hand-Kingdom experience when he tried to shoulder the load of pleasing God in the cloister. And in the Left he knew he could not orchestrate the Gospel's spread. What then? Heed the lesson at the close of the Preacher's book: Fear God and keep his commandments. In other words, trust and then get on with one's vocations as best one can. Trying to look beyond or above breeds despair and skepticism. It is enough to know one's place as a redeemed creature, as a tool or hands or mask of God – *larva Dei* is the theologian's term. It is a relief not to be saddled with more. It is a joy and a privilege to be entrusted with that.

That basic framework is echoed in the other two Lutheran theologians who also tackled Skepticism. The message is essentially the same, although the problems encountered would tailor basics for the case at hand.

The second Lutheran Reformer who felt it necessary to identify and fight Skepticism, also with Ecclesiastes in his arsenal, is Johannes Brenz. Brenz, a contemporary of Luther, worked in his native Swabia, a territory in the southwest part of the German lands. As the Reformation movement grew, the city officials in Schwäbish Hall sought an evangelical preacher for St. Michael's. Brenz was called to the parish, but his work extended far beyond, as he brought evangelical theology to a good part of south Germany.

Part of his approach involved writing, authoring a catechism long used in the region, along with commentaries on biblical books. Brenz had planned to do a study for each one (which he never managed to do). Ecclesiastes came early, the second one done. We might expect more prominent books to be at the top of the list – Romans or Galatians – but in the second half of the 1520s he turned to the Preacher? Why? Like Luther, there was a practical reason, but Brenz's was different, as the introduction to his book explains.

Swabia had experienced peasant uprisings in mid-decade. The peasants had hitched their demands about taxes, land access, and more to the Reformation cause. They called for the right to choose and remove their parish preacher at the start, and then followed with demands about taxes, land access and more after that, and finished by saying they would concede any of the above if they could be proved contrary to the word of God.

Leave aside the fact that Scripture says little about late medieval fishing rights in Swabia. A larger issue is the fundamental misunderstanding by the peasants that their claims were an expression of freedom brought by the Gospel. Confused theology for sure! And why did that happen? Brenz argues at the start that the fault lies with ruling officials who have failed to press for the Evangelical Reformation to be adopted more quickly and widely. (Brenz, like Luther, would prefer that bishops act, but if they failed, then ruling authority could step in, not to preach but to facilitate good preaching.) The failure to promote reform meant confused theology. No good would come of that, but plenty of frustration, alienation, and rebellion would likely come. It would lead to what A.G. Dickens called "tavern unbelief."[26] Before things escalated (or degenerated), right preaching and teaching had to do their work to build up, so that people understood first what the Gospel was and then what difference that made, not just for forgiveness but for their daily lives. They may not get those foresting rights and inheritance taxes may still sting, but they know that God has them in hand regardless and sees better and beyond.

It was a message Brenz found in Ecclesiastes and drove home in many ways over hundreds of pages.[27] No one knows the future, and no one can manage the present and guarantee results. Brenz knew that about his own work and writing, but it was something he had to do in his role, his vocation. How that all would end

---

26 A.G. Dickens, *Lollards and Protestants in the Diocese of York, 1509–1558* (London: Oxford University Press, 1959), 12–13, notes how theological doubts arose among the English without any formal philosophical prompting. Out of confusion that persists comes complaining about all sorts of little things. The alehouse conversation becomes grumbling and then a more serious challenge to church and doctrine. "What do *they* know?" is tantamount to skepticism.

27 Luther lectured on Ecclesiastes in the 1526–1527 semester and then wanted his lectures cleaned up quickly for publication. Erasmus had written round two in 1526 and this would be Luther's answer. But events conspired to delay publication until 1532. Meanwhile, Brenz published his Ecclesiastes commentary in 1528 with a preface by Luther, who noted that his own work was not done and so he was most happy to have the excellent book from Brenz. That was no empty endorsement. Luther also spoke of the "Rotten," the rabble or rebellious peasants that had prompted Brenz.

is up to God, who has promised faithfulness. The basic message appears again: fear God and keep his commandments.

Philipp Melanchthon, Luther's Wittenberg co-worker, also used Ecclesiastes as a defense against Skepticism. After Luther's 1546 death, the mantle fell to Melanchthon, though many in the Lutheran movement were not pleased or supportive. While Melanchthon shared a commitment to the Evangelical message and reform, he also had different interests than Luther from the start. If being happy with liberal arts learning for its own sake was a mark of a humanist, then Luther would not qualify. Melanchthon likely would, although he certainly used it in the cause of reform, as did Luther.

They also diverged on some theological points. For example, Melanchthon tried to go deeper into the matter of the human will and conversion to understand more what went on, while Luther was happy to confess he did nothing and it was out of his hands and in God's. When explaining justification, Melanchthon tried to stretch the tent as widely as possible in discussions at Regensburg, making room for some irenic Roman counterparts, even as they reached out to him. They were happy with each other, but they found no support in their camps back home. But perhaps it is unreasonable to expect a faculty to be in lockstep. The question is whether the differences can be worked out or if they matter. As far as Luther was concerned, Melanchthon was an ally and a friend.

After Luther's death, things went south. Melanchthon was neither the personality Luther was, nor the leader needed at the time. The Smalcaldic War quickly went badly for the Evangelicals. Until things could be wrapped up, the Augsburg and then Leipzig Interims were to serve temporarily. Melanchthon had a hand in the latter that many Lutherans considered a betrayal. Broader language on justification by faith (no "alone" mentioned), Communion with both bread and cup, and Lutheran preachers keeping their wives was all they got. Criticism rained, but what was Melanchthon to do? He was rather like a fighter covering up in the corner, waiting for the bell to regroup and try later for a comeback. It was easy to criticize from afar where the war was not, and easy also in hindsight. It was not a happy time.[28]

It not only was hard to be a theologian in those tumultuous times, but it was also challenging to be in government. The 1530 Augsburg Confession was a theological statement to prove a political point: We Lutherans are church and thus entitled to carry on in the German Empire. When Brenz pressed officials to promote reform, he knew from his own upbringing as the son of a *Schultheiß*, a

28 Melanchthon would also be accused of Calvinist sympathies for having reworded the Augsburg Confession article on the Lord's Supper. But the vocabulary used could be found elsewhere in Lutheran writings, and no one seemed to balk until continued discussions in the 1560s over what was Lutheran and what was Reformed prompted some to be critical of Melanchthon's *Variata*.

kind of mayor, that politics rarely go as one would like. Officials everywhere, especially in Evangelical lands under the Interims, were already under pressure to follow the law, and if imperial Catholic troops were nearby to encourage, well …

In 1552 Melanchthon wrote a short explication on Ecclesiastes, done for Joachim Moeller, family friend and newly elected member of the Hamburg city council. Hamburg had become an imperial city (1510), a move granting privileges for past service and continued loyalty. But it also joined the pro-Reformation Smalcaldic League in 1536. In the war, although fighting was elsewhere, Hamburg was no backwater, and ruling the city was still difficult. Melanchthon used Ecclesiastes to urge young Moeller to do his duty. "Commit your way to the Lord and he will bring it to pass," from a Psalm verse, was Melanchthon's conclusion voiced over and over again. There is no telling which way life will go, no marshaling events simply to Hamburg's benefit. Being an administrator (in government as in church) grants no special insight. So prepare, take up the calling given, and then do what is right as God gives insight. Work with what God gives and move on – another way to look at the basic message from the Preacher.

But there could be a twist to this treatise. Melanchthon may be preaching the Preacher not just for Moeller but also for himself. By 1552 the long knives were out and many were tired of Melanchthon. Gnesio-Lutherans wanted the genuine stuff and Melanchthon did not deliver, at least in their eyes. But in his own eyes, he had carried out his vocation. He is not without flaws, as one sees in his letters at times with remarks that cut some and build up others. But a betrayer of the Gospel? He did not see himself that way. So much scorn, it could be that Melanchthon writes also for himself. Fear God and keep his commandments is for him as well.

Three examples from the sixteenth century of how to live without the metanarrative still offer food for thought with lessons to be learned. Other ways to look at life do not all fall victim to historical materialism (ala Benjamin), nor to religion, at least of the Žižek variety with religion simply a tool to sweep away. But religion or theology is also nothing to build grand theory on. The theories all exist under the sun (to crib from the Old Testament Preacher), and as such, no matter how grand, they are always limited not simply in the quantity and quality of what they include but also in perspective and scope. Christian theology cannot be domesticated that way, as if we have things in hand and understand it all in a way that will guarantee success.

There is a saying attributed to Luther: "*Wenn zur Theologie kommt, eine gewiße Bescheidenheit gehört dazu*," that is, "When it comes to theology a certain modesty is called for." Some pontificate with grand plans for church or world, ignorant of their inabilities. Better to interject a little *Bescheidenheit.* Žižek is certainly right on this point: religion must not bind itself to one form and then foist that on all. The form, the culture, is not the essence of religion and its message. Rather let the message go as it comes to a new place. Let it settle in and find its level among people.

The Reformation worked in a very different world – not always easy, but it worked in the culture it had. The task today is the same, although the context is different. No one has the grand plan, the foolproof approach. No one has the final word. Instead we learn from the ongoing conversation.

And what of doubts and second thoughts? Skepticism is not finally beaten, at least in life as far as we can see. Rather it is warded off and held at arm's length – preferably God's arms, which are more than long enough. At the same time, the approach of Ecclesiastes that worked in the Old Testament and again in the Reformation culture can work still in ours. Fear God and keep his commandments.

That approach cannot be proved. It is theology – not Žižek's but biblical theology – and as such, while there are things to learn from texts, those facts come with promises that must simply be believed. To be convinced of this, thankfully, not ours to accomplish but is finally the Spirit's doing.

Fig. 3: Robert Kolb, Lutheran Missionary Retreat speaker, Jos, Nigeria, 1980

Ruth A. Mattson, Compiler

Robert Kolb Bibliography

2017–1968

Kolb, R./C.P. Arand. *The way of concord: From historic text to contemporary witness.* St. Louis, MO: Concordia Seminary Press, 2017.

Kolb, R./C. Trueman. *Between Wittenberg and Geneva: Lutheran and reformed theology in conversation.* Grand Rapids, MI: Baker Academic, 2017.

Wengert, T.J./R. Kolb, et al., ed. *Dictionary of Luther and the Lutheran traditions.* Grand Rapids, MI: Baker Academic, a division of Baker Publishing Group, 2017.

Kolb, R. *Bound choice, election, and Wittenberg theological method: From Martin Luther to the Formula of Concord.* Minneapolis: Fortress Press, 2017.

______. "Bound, freed, freed to be bound: Wittenberg understanding of justification." *Unio cum Christo* 3 (2017) 43–54.

______. "*Innerprotestantische Streitigkeiten.*" Pp. 109–124 in *Philipp Melanchthon: Der Reformator zwischen Glauben und Wissen: ein Handbuch.* Edited by G. Frank and A. Lange. Berlin: De Gruyter, 2017.

______. "*Rechtfertigungslehre.*" Pp. 347–362 in *Philipp Melanchthon: Der Reformator zwischen Glauben und Wissen: ein Handbuch.* Edited by G. Frank, and A. Lange. Berlin: De Gruyter, 2017.

______. "*Schwärmerei* as original sin: Luther's view of doubt and defiance of God's Word as the root of sin." *Modern Reformation* 26/5 (2017) 42–51.

______. "Albrecht of Mainz, Amsdorf, Augsburg, etc." Pp. various in *Dictionary of Luther and the Lutheran traditions.* Edited by T.J. Wengert, R. Kolb, et al. Grand Rapids, MI: Baker Academic, a division of Baker Publishing Group, 2017.

______. "*Ars vivendi and ars dolendi:* Mathesius' Jesus Syrach commentary as catechetical instruction." Pp. 317–333 in *Johannes Mathesius (1504–1565). Rezeption und Verbreitung der Wittenberger Reformation durch Predigt und Exegese.* Edited by Armin Kohnle and Irene Dingel. Leipzig: Evangelische Verlagsanstalt, 2017.

______. "*Bibelauslegung in der Via Wittenbergensis: Die Volkshermeneutik von Johann Mathesius als Vertreter von Luthers Homiletik.*" Pp. 255–269 in *Johannes Mathesius (1504–1565). Rezeption und Verbreitung der Wittenberger Reformation durch Predigt und Exegese.* Edited by Armin Kohnle and Irene Dingel. Leipzig: Evangelische Verlagsanstalt, 2017.

______. "Foreword." Pp. ix–x in *Martin Luther on reading the Bible as Christian scripture: The Messiah in Luther's biblical hermeneutic and theology.* Edited by W. Marsh. Princeton theological monograph series. Eugene, OR: Pickwick Publications, 2017.

______. *"Johann Gerhards Anteil am Ernestinischen Bibelwerk."* in *Konfession, Politik und Gelehrsamkeit: Der Jenaer Theologe Johann Gerhard (1582–1637) im Kontext seiner Zeit.* Edited by M. Friedrich, S. Salatowsky, and L. Schorn-Schütte. Kulturwissenschaften Band 11. Stuttgart: Franz Steiner Verlag, 2017.

______. *"Lutherbilder der Frühen Neuzeit."* Pp. 25–46 in *Luthermania. Ansichten einer Kultfigur.* Edited by H. Rößler. Wolfenbüttel: Herzog August Bibliothek, 2017.

______. "The Church." Pp. 577–608 in *Reformation theology: A systematic summary.* Edited by M. Barrett, and M.S. Horton. Wheaton, IL: Crossway, 2017.

______. "How Martin Luther revolutionized Bible study." *Bible Study* 9/6 (2017) 13–17.

______. "'The armor of God and the might of His strength': Luther's sermon on Ephesians 6 (1531/1533)." *Concordia Journal* 43/1-2 (2017) 59–73.

______. "Luther's suggestions for preaching." *Concordia Journal* 43/1–2 (2017) 109–114.

______. "Review: *Ablass und Reformation: erstaunliche Kohärenzen.* Berndt Hamm." *Lutheran Quarterly* 31/2 (2017) 218–220.

______. "Review: *Nicolaus von Amsdorf. Ausgewählte Schriften der jarhe 1550 bis 1562 aus der ehemaligen Eisenacher Ministerialhihliothek.* ed., Hagen Jäger." *Lutheran Quarterly* 31/2 (2017) 208–210.

______. The many sides of Luther: Review: Martin Luther: Renegade and prophet. Lyndal Roper, 2017. https://www.thegospelcoalition.org/article/book-review-martin-luther-renegate-prophet (accessed 27 September 2017).

______. To preach like Luther, you must listen like Luther, 2017. https://www.thegospelcoalition.org/article/to-preach-like-luther-you-must-listen-like-luther (accessed 27 September 2017).

Kolb, R. *Martin Luther and the enduring Word of God: The Wittenberg school and its scripture-centered proclamation.* Grand Rapids, MI: Baker Academic, 2016.

Kolb, R., et al., ed. *The Oxford handbook of Martin Luther's theology.* Reprint edition. Oxford: Oxford University Press, 2016.

Kolb, R. "Martin Luther today: The reformer and his heritage." Preface in *Martin Luther's travel guide: 500 years of the ninety-five theses: On the trail of the Reformation in Germany.* Edited by C. Dömer. New York, NY: Berlinica Publishing LLC, 2016.

______. "Preface to the Latin works, 1545." Pp. 489–503 in *Pastoral writings.* Edited by M.J. Haemig. The annotated Luther volume 4. Minneapolis: Fortress Press, 2016.

______. "The Lutheran Confessions: A genre to define the church." Pp. 350–358 in *Martin Luther and the Reformation. Essays, catalog of the United States exhibit.* Edited by State office for heritage management and archaeology Saxony-Anhalt et al. Dresden: Sandstein, 2016.

______. "'A time of shadows and signs': Johann Gerhard's use of the Old Testament in early homiletical and devotional writings." Pp. 147–162 in *Konfession, Politik und Gelehrsamkeit: Der Jenaer Theologe Johann Gerhard (1582–1637) im Kontext seiner Zeit.* Edited by Markus Friedrich, Sascha Salatowsky, Luise Schorn-Schütte. Stuttgart: Steiner, 2016.

______. "God, creation and providence." 17 Pp. in *The Oxford handbook of early modern theology, 1600–1800.* Edited by U.L. Lehner. New York City: Oxford University Press, 2016.

______. "Introduction." Pp. 9–24 in *Lives and writings of the great fathers of the Lutheran Church.* Edited by T. Schmeling. St. Louis, MO: Concordia Pub. House, 2016.

______. "Martin Luther." Pp. 217-234 in *T & T Clark companion to the doctrine of sin.* Edited by K.L. Johnson and D. Lauber. Bloomsbury companions. London, New York: Bloomsbury T&T Clark, 2016.

______. "*Memoria Melanchthoniana* 1560: The public presentation of Philip Melanchthon at his death." Pp. 89–102 in *Memoria – theologische Synthese – Autoritätenkonflikt: Die Rezeption Luthers und Melanchthons in der Schülergeneration.* Edited by I. Dingel. Spätmittelalter, Humanismus, Reformation 90. Tübingen: Mohr Siebeck, 2016.

______. "The enduring word of God, in Wittenberg." *Lutheran Quarterly* 30/2 (2016) 193–204.

______. "Free-standing altars. A reformation ideal." Logia forum: short studies and commentary. *Logia* 25/no. 3 (2016) 61–62.

______. "Review: *Ordnungen für die Kirche – Wirkungen auf die Weh. Evangelische Kirchen Ordnungen des. 16. Jahrhunderts.* Sabine Arend and Gerald Dorner." *Lutheran Quarterly* 30/2 (2016) 214–216.

______. "Review: Otto Scheel (1876–1954): *Eine biographische Studie zu Lutherforschung, Landeshistoriographie und deutsch-dänischen Beziehungen.* Carsten Mish." *Lutheran Quarterly* 30/4 (2016) 442–444.

______. "Review: *Dona Gratis Donata:* Essays in honor of Norman Nagel on the occasion of his 90th birthday. Collver, Albert, Bart Day, et al." *Concordia Journal* 42/3 (2016) 263–264.

______. "Review: Luther's works 68: Sermons on Matthew, chapters 19–24. Concordia." *Concordia Journal* 42/1 (2016) 89–91.

______. "Review: Luther's works 77: Church postil III. Concordia." *Concordia Journal* 42/1 (2016) 89–91.

______. "*Das Kreuz – die wirkliche Befreiungstheologie.*" *Confessio Augustana IV* (2016) 43–54.

______. "The Bible in the Reformation and Protestant Orthodoxy." Pp. 89–114 in *The Enduring Authority of the Christian Scriptures.* Edited by D. Carson. Grand Rapids, MI: Eerdmans, 2016.

Kolb, R. "Believing, teaching, confessing: A vision for North American Lutherans." *Currents in Theology and Mission* 42 (2015) 273–278.

______. "Die pastorale Dimension des pädagogischen Wirkens Melanchthons.: Die Ausbildungspraxis der Pfarrer." Pp. 345–358 in *Institutionen und Formen gelehrter Bildung um 1550.* Edited by Matthias Asche et al. Leipzig: Evangelische Verlagsanstalt, 2015.

______. "Christianity: Lutheranism." Pp. 256–266 in *Worldmark encyclopedia of religious practices.* Edited by T. Riggs. Farmington Hills, MI: Gale, Cengage Learning, 2015.

______. "*Das Wirken des Heiligen Geistes im 21. Jahrhundert: Die Kontinentalverschiebung des Luthertums.*" *Lutherische Beiträge* 20/2 (2015) 105–115.

______. "Homiletical helps on LSB series B • Lent 2, Romans 5:1–11." *Concordia Journal* 41/1 (2015) 63–65.

______. "Foreword." Pp. xi–xv in *Fruit for the soul: Luther on the lament psalms.* Edited by D. Ngien. Minneapolis: Fortress, 2015.

______. "Foreword." Pp. 13–14 in Luther on the Christian life: Cross and freedom. Edited by C. Trueman. Theologians on the Christian life. Wheaton, IL: Crossway, 2015.

______. "Philipp Melanchthon's reading of Romans." Chapter 3 in *Reformation readings of Paul: Explorations in history and exegesis.* Edited by R.M. Allen. Downers Grove, IL: InterVarsity Press, 2015

______. "The New *Bekenntnisschriften der Evangelisch-Lutherischen Kirche.*" *Lutheran Quarterly* 29 (2015) 214–216.

______. "*Studienbuch Martin Luther: Grundtexte und Deutungen.*" *Lutheran Quarterly* 29/2 (2015) 230–232.

Kolb, R/C. Arand. "'I make these confessions my own': Lutheran Confessional subscription in the twenty-first century." *Concordia Journal* 41/1 (2015) 23–33.

______. "Homiletical helps on LSB series B • Baptism of Our Lord, Luke 3:15–22." *Concordia Journal* 41/4 (2015) 352–353.

______. "Jakob Andreae's preaching in the public arena (Augsburg, 1559)." *Lutheran Quarterly* 29/1 (2015) 10–32.

______. "*La prédication et le chant: Prêcher sur des textes de cantiques à l'époque de la Réformation luthérienne tardive.*" *Positions luthériennes* 63/2 (2015) 115–139.

______. "Luther's truths: then and now." *Journal of Lutheran Mission* 2/4 (2015) 5–15.

______. "Nowhere more present and active than in the holy letters: Luther's understanding of God's presence in scripture." *Lutheran Theological Journal* 49/1 (2015) 4–17.

______. "Review: A Christian in Toga: Boethius— interpreter of antiquity and Christian theologian. Claudio Moreschini." *Concordia Journal* 41/2 (2015) 180.

______. "Review: Luther and his world. Graham Tomlin." *Lutheran Quarterly* 29/1 (2015) 81–82.

______. "Review: Luther's fortress: Martin Luther and his Reformation under siege. James Reston." *Lutheran Quarterly* 29/3 (2015) 359–360.

______. "Review: Theologian of sin and grace: The process of radicalization in the theology of Matthias Flacius Illyricus. Luka Ilić." *Concordia Journal* 41/3 (2015) 279–280.

Kolb, R. "*Der grosse und der kleine Katechismus Martin Luthers. Einleitung.*" Pp. 841–850 in *Die Bekenntnisschriften der Evangelisch-Lutherischen Kirche.* Edited by I. Dingel. Göttingen: Vandenhoeck & Ruprecht, 2014.

Kolb, R., et al., ed. *The Oxford handbook of Martin Luther's theology.* Oxford: Oxford University Press, 2014.

______. "Luther's hermeneutics of distinctions: law and gospel, two kinds of righteousness, two realms, freedom and bondage." Pp. 168–186 in *The Oxford handbook of Martin Luther's theology.* Edited by R. Kolb, I. Dingel, and L. Batka. Oxford handbooks. Oxford, UK: Oxford University Press, 2014.

______. "*[...] da jr nicht trawrig seid wie die anderen, die keine Hoffnung haben: Der Gebrauch der Heiligen Schrift in Leichenpredigten der Wittenberger Reformation (1560–1600).*" Pp. 1–26 in *Leichenpredigten als Medien der Erinnerungskultur im europäischen Kontext: [... Vorträge, die 2012 anlässlich des fünften Marburger Personalschriften-Symposions gehalten wurden].* Edited by E.-M. Dickhaut. Geschichte Bd. 5. Stuttgart: Steiner, 2014.

______. "*Luthers Katechismen—Texte und Kontexte.*" Pp. 883–890 in *Von den altkirchlichen Symbolen bis zu den Katechismen Martin Luthers. Die Bekenntnisschriften der evangelisch-lutherischen Kirche: Quellen und Materialien.* Edited by I. Dingel and R. Kolb. *Auftr. der Evangelischen Kirche in Deutschland zus. mit Bastian Basse Bd. 1.* Göttingen [u. a.]: Vandenhoeck & Ruprecht, 2014.

Dingel I./R. Kolb, ed. *Von den altkirchlichen Symbolen bis zu den Katechismen Martin Luthers. Die Bekenntnisschriften der evangelisch-lutherischen Kirche: Quellen und Materialien. Auftr. der Evangelischen Kirche in Deutschland zus. mit Bastian Basse Bd. 1.* Göttingen [u. a.]: Vandenhoeck & Ruprecht, 2014.

______. "*Nicholaus von Amsdorf.*" Pp. 16–23 in *Das Reformatorenlexikon.* Edited by I. Dingel and V. Leppin. Darmstadt: Lambert Schneider, 2014.

______. "Orders for burial in the sixteenth century Wittenberg circle." Pp. 257–279 in *Gute Ordnung: Ordnungsmodelle und Ordnungsvorstellungen in der Reformationszeit.* Edited by I. Dingel and A. Kohnle. Leucorea-Studien zur Geschichte der Reformation und der Lutherischen Orthodoxie Band 25. Leipzig: Evangelische Verlagsanstalt, 2014.

______. "Paul Eber as preacher." Pp. 375–400 in *Paul Eber (1511–1569): Humanist und Theologe der zweiten Generation der Wittenberger Reformation.* Edited by D. Gehrt and V. Leppin. *Leucorea-Studien zur Geschichte der Reformation und der Lutherischen Orthodoxie* Band 16. Leipzig: Evangelische Verlagsanstalt, 2014.

______. "*Reformation und Ablass: Luthers 95 Thesen; Luthers Appell an Albrecht von Mainz: Sein Brief vom 31. Oktober 1517.*" Pp. 80–88 in *Meilensteine der Reformation: Schlüsseldokumente der frühen Wirksamkeit Martin Luthers.* Edited by I. Dingel and H.P. Jürgens. Gütersloh: Gütersloher Verlagshaus, 2014.

______. "The 'three kingdoms' of Simon Musaeus: A Wittenberg student processes Luther's thought." Pp. 297–321 in *Collaboration, conflict, and continuity in the Reformation: Essays in honour of James M. Estes on his eightieth birthday.* Edited by K. Eisenbichler. Essays and studies 34. Toronto: Centre for Reformation and Renaissance Studies, 2014.

______. "The Lutheran doctrine of original sin." Pp. 109–129 in *Adam, the fall, and original sin: Theological, biblical, and scientific perspectives.* Edited by H. Madueme. Grand Rapids, MI: Baker Academic, a division of Baker Publishing Group, 2014.

______. "Hieronymus Mencel," "Joachim Mörlin," "Simon Musäus," "Cyriakus Spangenberg." Pages various in *Aus erster Hand 95 Porträts zur Reformationsgeschichte.* Edited by Daniel Gehrt and Sascha Salatowsky. Gotha: Forschungsbibliothek, 2014.

______. "The printer's funeral sermon: recalling the contributions of the printer in the Wittenberg Reformation." Pp. 191–206 in *The German book in Wolfenbüttel and abroad: Studies presented to Ulrich Kopp in his retirement.* Edited by W.A. Kelly and J. Beyer. Studies in reading and book culture vol. 1. Tartu [Estonia]: University of Tartu Press, 2014.

______. "God's word produces faith and fruit: Reflections from Luther's understanding of the Sermon on the Mount." *Concordia Journal* 40 (2014) 217–224.

______. "*Die Kleinen Propheten als Zeitgenossen der Reformatoren: Zur Auslegung des Zwölfprophetenbuchs in der lutherischen Spätreformation.*" *Lutherische Theologie und Kirche* 38/1 (2014) 21–43.

______. "*Die Sterbe- und Ewigkeitslieder in deutschen lutherischen Gesangbüchern des 17. Jahrhunderts.*" *Lutheran Quarterly* 28/2 (2014) 235–238.

______. "How the doctrine of the incarnation shaped Western culture." *Church History* 83/2 (2014) 453.

______. "Homiletical helps LSB series A • Lent 4, Isaiah 42:14–21." *Concordia Journal* 40/1 (2014) 71–72.

______. *"Lutherische Homiletik um 1600: Die Unterweisungen von Siegfried Sack und Johann Gerhard." Lutherische Beiträge* 19/3 (2014) 139–152.

______. "Pastoral practice in the funeral sermons of Nikolaus Selnecker (1530–1592)." *Lutheran Quarterly* 28/1 (2014) 22–48.

______. "Review: *Religiosität im späten Mittelalter: Spannungspole, Neuaufbrüche, Normierungen.* Berndt Hamm." *Lutheran Quarterly* 28/1 (2014) 99–101.

______. "Review: *Die 'Passion-Betrachtungen' der Catharina Regina von Greiffenberg im Rahmen ihres Lebenslaufes und ihrer Frömmigkeit.*" *Lutheran Quarterly* 28/3 (2014) 370–372.

______. "Review: *Gotha macht Schule: Bildung von Luther bis Francke: Katalog zur Ausstellung der Universitäts- und Forschungsbibliothek Erfurt/Gotha in Zusammenarbeit mit der Stiftung Schloss Friedenstein Gotha.* Sascha Salatowsky." *Lutheran Quarterly* 28/3 (2014) 341–343.

______. "Review: *Konstruktion von Geschichte: Jubelrede — Predigt — protestantische Historiographie.* Klaus Tanner." *Lutheran Quarterly* 28/1 (2014) 120–122.

Kolb, R. "Did Luther's students hide the hidden God? *Deus absconditus* among Luther's first followers." Pp. 7–16 in *Churrasco: A theological feast in honor of Vitor Westhelle.* Edited by Mary Philip, John Arthur Nunes, and Charles M. Collier. Pickwick Publications, 2013.

______. "Inviting community: ecclesiology from the foundations up." Pp. 9–17 in *Inviting community.* Edited by R. Kolb and T.J. Hopkins. St. Louis, MO: Concordia Seminary Press, 2013.

Kolb, R./T.J. Hopkins, ed. *Inviting community.* St. Louis, MO: Concordia Seminary Press, 2013.

______. "Pastoral education in the Wittenberg way." Pp. 67–79 in *Church and school in early modern Protestantism: Studies in honor of Richard A. Muller on the maturation of a theological tradition.* Edited by Jordan J. Ballor and Jason Zuidema. Leiden, The Netherlands: Brill, 2013.

______. "Prophets of the German nations and other saint-sinner martyrs." Pp. 121–141 in *Calvin and Luther: The continuing relationship.* Edited by R. W. Holder. Refo500 academic studies volume 12. Göttingen: Vandenhoeck & Ruprecht, 2013.

______. "15 days of prayer with Dietrich Bonhoeffer." *Concordia Journal* 39/2 (2013) 179.

______. "Called to milk cows and govern kingdoms: Martin Luther's teaching on the Christian's vocations." *Concordia Journal* 39/2 (2013) 133–141.

______. "Homiletical helps on LSB series C • Lent 2, Philippians 3:17–4:1." *Concordia Journal* 39/1 (2013) 62–64.

______. "In memoriam Schwarzwäller, Klaus, 1935–2012." *Lutheran Quarterly* 27/2 (2013) 211–214.

______. "Die theologische Pilgerschaft von Viktorin Strigel 'gnesiolutherischen' Hoftheologe zum 'calvinistischen' Professor." Pp. 79–96 in *Calvinismus in den Auseinandersetzungen des frühen konfessionellen Zeitalters.* Edited by Herman J. Selderhuis, Martin Leiner, and Volker Leppin. Göttingen: Vandenhoeck & Ruprecht, 2013.

______. "Dynamics of party Conflict in the Saxon late Reformation, Gnesio-Lutherans vs. Philippists." Pp. 152–167 in *Calvinismus in den Auseinandersetzungen des frühen konfessionellen Zeitalters.* Edited by Martin Leiner. Göttingen: Vandenhoeck & Ruprecht, 2013.

______. "Review: *Die Bedeutung des Beziehungsgeflechts der Osnabrücker ev. luth. Pastoren für den Verlauf der Osnabrücker Kirchenpolitik 1907–1936.* Carsten Linden." *Concordia Journal* 39/3 (2013) 263–264.

______. "Review: Power of Faith: 450 Years of the Heidelberg Catechism. Karla Apperloo-Boersma and Herman J. Selderhuis, ed." *Renaissance Quarterly* 66/4 (2013) 1429–1430.

______. "Review: Reading Augustine in the Reformation: the flexibility of intellectual authority in Europe, 1500–1620. Arnoud Visser." *Lutheran Quarterly* 27/1 (2013) 120–122.

______. "Review: The great works of God. Parts one and two, The mysteries of Christ in the Book of Genesis, chapters 1–15. Valerius Herberger." *Concordia Journal* 39/3 (2013) 252–253.

______. "*Widerspricht sich die Bibel? Antworten aus dem Kreis um Luther.*" *Lutherische Beiträge* 18/1 (2013) 24–39.

Kolb, R. *Teaching God's children his teaching: A guide for the study of Luther's Catechism.* St. Louis, MO: Concordia Seminary Press, 2012.

______. *Luther and the stories of God: Biblical narratives as a foundation for Christian living.* Grand Rapids, MI: Baker Academic, 2012.

______. "The Marburg Articles: from Robert Kolb and James Nestingen, ed., *Sources and contexts of the Book of Concord* (Minneapolis: Fortress Press, 2001)." Pp. 88–93 in *Martin Luther's basic theological writings.* Edited by T. Lull and W.R. Russell. Minneapolis: Fortress Press, 2012.

______. "The pastoral dimension of Melanchthon's pedagogical activities for the education of pastors; Melanchthon's doctrinal last will and testament: the *responsiones ad articulos Bavaricae inquisitionis* as his final confession of faith; Melanchthon and the Establishment of confessional norms; The critique of Melanchthon's doctrine of the Lord's Supper by his 'Gnesio-Lutheran' students." Pp. various in *Philip Melanchthon: Theologian in classroom, confession, and controversy.* Edited by I. Dingel, R. Kolb, et al. Refo500 academic studies vol. 7. Göttingen, Bristol, CT: Vandenhoeck & Ruprecht, 2012.

Dingel, I./R. Kolb, et al., ed. *Philip Melanchthon: Theologian in classroom, confession, and controversy.* Refo500 academic studies vol. 7. Göttingen, Bristol, CT: Vandenhoeck & Ruprecht, 2012

______. "Human nature, the fall, and the will." Pp. 14–31 in *T&T Clark companion to Reformation theology.* Edited by D. M. Whitford. T&T Clark companions. London, New York: T & T Clark, 2012.

______. "Recultivation of the vineyard in sixteenth-century Lutheran exegesis and preaching." Pp. 305–319 in *The Reformation as Christianization: Essays on Scott Hendrix's Christianization thesis.* Edited by A.M. Johnson, and J.A. Maxfield. Spätmittelalter, Humanismus, Reformation Studies in the late Middle Ages, humanism and the Reformation 66. Tübingen: Mohr Siebeck, 2012.

______. "Those who are sent: Christ and his church: Christology, missiology, and ecclesiology in the gospel of John." *Missio Apostolica* 20/1 (2012) 11–15.

Arand, C.P./J.A. Nestingen/R. Kolb. *The Lutheran confessions: History and theology of the Book of Concord.* Minneapolis: Fortress Press, 2012.

______. "Matthias Flacius' *Glossa Compendiaria:* The Wittenberg Way of Exegesis in its Second Generation." Pp. 72–89 in *Matija Vlačić [III, …] Proceedings of the Third*

International Conference on Matthias Flacius Illyricus, Labin/Croatia, 2010. Edited by Marina Miladinov and Luka Ilić. Labin: Grad Labin, 2012.

______. "Nikolaus von Amsdorf, Buchstabe und Geist, etc." Pp. various in *Luther-Lexikon.* Edited by Volker Leppin and Gury Schneider-Ludorff. Regensburg: Bückle & Böhm, 2012.

______. "Preaching the people of Christ's Passion. Luther's depiction of the characters of John 18–19." *Lutheran Forum* 46/4 (2012) 38–41.

______. "Homiletical helps on LSB series B • Lent 3, Exodus 20:1–17." *Concordia Journal* 38/1 (2012) 66–68.

______. "Luther's preaching of the people of Christ's Passion." *Lutheran Forum* 46/4 (2012) 38–41.

______. "Remembering Bo Giertz." *Lutheran Quarterly* 26/1 (2012) 83–86.

______. "Review: *Das Wormser Schisma der Augsburger Konfessionsverwandten von 1557: protestantische Konfessionspolitik und Theologie im Zusammenhang des zweiten Wormser Religionsgesprächs.* Bjorn Slenczka." *Lutheran Quarterly* 26/3 (2012) 346–348.

______. "Review: Divine transcendence and the culture of change. David Hopper." *Concordia Journal* 38/1 (2012) 87–89.

______. "Review: Lazarus Spengler Schriften. Bd. 3, *Schriften der Jahre Mai 1529 bis März 1530.*" *Theologische Literaturzeitung* 137/3 (2012) 318–320.

Kolb, R. *Die Konkordienformel: Eine Einführung in ihre Geschichte und Theologie.* Oberurseler Hefte: [...], Ergänzungsbände Bd. 8. Göttingen, Niedersachs: Edition Ruprecht, 2011.

______. "The Lutheran theology of baptism." Pp. 53–75 in *Baptism: Historical, theological, and pastoral perspectives.* Edited by G. L. Heath and J.D. Dvorak. McMaster theological studies series. Eugene, OR: Pickwick Publications, 2011.

______. "Homiletical helps on LSB series A • Easter 2, John 20:19–31." *Concordia Journal* 37/1 (2011) 78–79.

______. "In memoriam Robert McCune Kingdon: (29 December 1927–10 December 2010)." *The Sixteenth Century Journal* 42/1 (2011) 3–7.

______. "*Luthers Gebrauch von Erzählungen in Predigt und Vorlesung.*" *Lutherische Theologie und Kirche* 35/3 (2011) 129–151.

______. "Luther's theology as a foundation for twenty-first century missiology." *Missio Apostolica* 19/2 (2011) 94–100.

______. "Publishing authority: the text of the Book of Concord." *Concordia Journal* 37/4 (2011) 285–291.

______. "Remembering Frederik Gabriel Hedberg (1811–1893)." *Concordia Journal* 37/4 (2011) 273–274.

______. "Resurrection and justification: Luther's use of Romans 4, 25." *Lutherjahrbuch* 78 (2011) 39–60.

______. "Review: Christ and culture revisited. Donald Carson." *Concordia Journal* 37/1 (2011) 88–89.

______. "Review: *Die Schmalkaldischen Artikel.* Werner Führer." *Lutheran Quarterly* 25/1 (2011) 94–96.

______. "Review: German histories in the age of reformations, 1400–1650. Thomas Brady." *Lutheran Quarterly* 25/1 (2011) 90–92.

______. "Review: Heinrich Heshusius and confessional polemic in early Lutheran orthodoxy. Michael Halvorson." *Lutheran Quarterly* 25/4 (2011) 456–458.
______. "Review: Humanist biography in Renaissance Italy and Reformation Germany: friendship and rhetoric. James Weiss." *Lutheran Quarterly* 25/2 (2011) 247–248.
______. "Review: *Interim und Apokalypse: die religiösen Vereinheitlichungsversuche Karls V. im Spiegel der magdeburgischen Publizistik 1548–1551/52.* Anja Moritz." *Lutheran Quarterly* 25/4 (2011) 472–474.
______. "Review: Inventing authority: the use of the church fathers in Reformation debates over the Eucharist. Esther Chung-Kim." *Lutheran Quarterly* 25/4 (2011) 445–447.
______. "Review: *Lutherische Gestalten—heterodoxe Orthodoxien. Historisch-systematische Studien.* Jörg Baur." *Lutheran Quarterly* 25/4 (2011) 486–488.
______. "Review: Natural law and the two kingdoms: a study in the development of Reformed social thought. David VanDrunen." *Church History* 80/2 (2011) 386–388.
______. "Review: Philip Melanchthon, speaker of the Reformation: Wittenberg's other reformer. Timothy Wengert." *Lutheran Quarterly* 25/4 (2011) 478–480.
______. "Review: *Philippismus und orthodoxes Luthertum an der Universität Wittenberg: die Rolle Jakob Andreäs im lutherischen Konfessionalisierungsprozess Kursachsens (1576–1580).* Ulrike Ludwig." *Lutheran Quarterly* 25/1 (2011) 114–116.
______. "Review: Piety and plague: from Byzantium to the baroque. Franco Mormando." *Church History* 80/1 (2011) 172–175.
______. "Review: Studies in law and gospel for the laity [electronic resource]. Stephen Stohlmann." *Concordia Journal* 37/3 (2011) 255–256.
______. "'So much began in Halle': the mission program that sent Mühlenberg to America." *Concordia Historical Institute Quarterly* 84/3 (2011) 26–35.
Kolb, R., ed. *The American mind meets the mind of Christ.* St. Louis, MO: Concordia Seminary Press, 2010.
______. "The American mind meets the mind of Christ" in *The American mind meets the mind of Christ.* Edited by Robert Kolb. St. Louis, MO: Concordia Seminary Press, 2010.
Kolb, R./D.J. Jagnow. *Comunicando o evangelho hoje.* Macomb, MI, Porto Alegre: Lutheran Heritage Foundation; Editora Concórdia, 2010.
Kolb, R. "The Relationship between Scripture and the Confession of the Faith in Luther's Thought." Pp. 53–62 in *Kirkens bekjennelse I historisk og aktuelt perspektiv.: Festskrift til Kjell Olav Sannes.* Edited by Torleiv Austad, Tormad Engelviksen, and Lars Østnor. Trondheim: Tapir Akademisk Forlag, 2010.
______. "The first Protestant 'Biblical theology': the syntagma of Johannes Wigand and Matthaeus Judex." Pp. 189–206 in *Hermeneutica Sacra: Studien zur Auslegung der Heiligen Schrift im 16. und 17. Jahrhundert. [Studies of the Interpretation of Holy Scripture in the sixteenth and seventeenth centuries].* Edited by T. Johansson, R. Kolb, and J.A. Steiger. Berlin: De Gruyter, 2010.
Johansson, T./R. Kolb/J.A. Steiger, ed. *Hermeneutica Sacra: Studien zur Auslegung der Heiligen Schrift im 16. und 17. Jahrhundert. Studies of the Interpretation of Holy Scripture in the sixteenth and seventeenth centuries.* Berlin: De Gruyter, 2010.
______. "Bishop Giertz's use of history in *Stengrunden.*" Pp. 71–88 in *A hammer for God: Bo Giertz: lectures from the centennial symposia, and selected essays by the bishop.* Edited by E. R. Andræ. Fort Wayne, IN: Lutheran Legacy, 2010.

______. "First Protestant 'Biblical theology'." Pp. 155–188 in *Melanchthon's rhetorical composition of the Apology*. Edited by C.P. Arand. Hermeneutica Sacra. Berlin/New York: De Gruyter, 2010.

______. "Models of the Christian life in Luther's Genesis sermons and lectures." Pp. 193–220 in *Lutherjahrbuch 76. Jahrgang 2009: Junghans, Helmar. Organ der Internationalen Lutherforschung*. Edited by Terrance Dinovo and Robert Kolb. Göttingen: Vandenhoeck & Ruprecht Gmbh & Co, 2010.

Dinovo, T./R. Kolb. *Lutherjahrbuch 76. Jahrgang 2009: Junghans, Helmar. Organ der Internationalen Lutherforschung*. Göttingen: Vandenhoeck & Ruprecht Gmbh & Co, 2010.

______. "The sheep and the voice of the shepherd: the ecclesiology of the Lutheran confessional writings." *Concordia Journal* 36/4 (2010) 324–341.

______. "David: king, prophet, repentant sinner: Martin Luther's image of the son of Jesse." *Perichoresis* 8/2 (2010) 203–231.

______. "Luther's recollections of Erfurt: The use of anecdotes for the edification of his hearers." *Luther-Bulletin* 19 (2010) 6–16.

______. "Luther's theology of the Cross fifteen years after Heidelberg: lectures on the psalms of ascent." *Journal of Ecclesiastical History* 61/1 (2010) 69–85.

______. "Recollections of a tourist missionary." *Missio Apostolica* 18/1 (2010) 5–10.

______. "Review: Transforming worldviews: an anthropological understanding of how people change. Paul Hiebert." *Concordia Journal* 36/1 (2010) 75–76.

______. "Four German Luther studies." *Lutheran Quarterly* 24/2 (2010) 188–196.

______. "Review: A history of biblical interpretation. vol. 2, The medieval through the Reformation periods. Alan Hauser; Duane Watson, ed." *Concordia Journal* 36/2 (2010) 194–196.

______. "Review: *Erfurter Annotationen 1509–1510/11*. Martin Luther." *Journal of Ecclesiastical History* 61/4 (2010) 848.

______. "Review: *Johannes Sturm (1507–1589): Rhetor, Pädogoge und Diplomat*. Matthieu Arnold." *Theologische Literaturzeitung* 135/12 (2010).

______. "Review: Partakers of the divine nature: the history and development of deification in the Christian traditions. Michael J. Christensen and Jeffery A. Wittung, ed." *Church History* 79/4 (2010) 906–908.

______. "Review: That all may believe: a theology of the gospel and the mission of the church. Carl Braaten." *Missio Apostolica* 18/1 (2010) 67–68.

______. "Review: The new faces of Christianity: believing the Bible in the global South. Philip Jenkins." *Missio Apostolica* 18/1 (2010) 68–69.

______. "Review: The new shape of world Christianity: how American experience reflects global faith. Mark Noll." *Missio Apostolica* 18/1 (2010) 69–70.

______. "Review: *Umstrittene Judenmission: das Leipziger Zentralverein für Mission unter Israel von Franz Delitsch bis Otto von Härling*. Thomas Küttler." *Missio Apostolica* 18/2 (2010) 153–154.

Kolb, R. *Martin Luther: Confessor of the faith*. Christian theology in context. Oxford, New York: Oxford University Press, 2009.

______. "Confessing the faith, the Wittenberg way of life." *Tidsskrift for Teologi og Kirke* 80 (2009) 247–65.

______. *Teaching God's children his teaching* (Latvian translation). Riga: Lutheran Heritage Foundation, 2009.

______. "The fathers in the service of Lutheran teaching: Andreas Musculus' use of patristic sources." Pp. 105–123 in *Auctoritas Patrum II: Neue Beitrage zur Rezeption der Kirchenvater Im 15. und 16. Jahrhundert / New Contributions on the Reception of the Church Fathers in the 15th and 16th centuries.* Edited by M. Wriedt. Göttingen: Vandenhoeck & Ruprecht Gmbh & Co, 2009.

______. "The theology of Justus Jonas." Pp. 103–120 in *Justus Jonas (1493–1555) und seine Bedeutung für die Wittenberger Reformation.* Edited by I. Dingel, J. Hund, and H.-O. Schneider. Leucorea-Studien zur Geschichte der Reformation und der Lutherischen Orthodoxie Bd. 11. Leipzig: Evangelische Verlagsanstalt, 2009.

______. "God's select vessel and chosen instrument: the interpretation of Paul in late Reformation Lutheran theologians." Pp. 187–211 in *A companion to Paul in the Reformation.* Edited by R.W. Holder. Brill's Companions to the Christian Tradition vol. 15. Leiden, Boston: Brill, 2009.

______. "Luther on the theology of the cross." Pp. 33–54 in *The pastoral Luther: Essays on Martin Luther's practical theology.* Edited by T.J. Wengert. Lutheran Quarterly Books. Grand Rapids, MI: William B. Eerdmans Pub., 2009.

______. "John Calvin's five hundredth birthday." *Concordia Journal* 35/3 (2009) 236–238.

______. "Luther on peasants and princes." *Lutheran Quarterly* 23/2 (2009) 125–146.

______. "*Bibelauslegung in der Via Wittenbergensis: Die Volkshermeneutik von Johannes Mathesius als Vertreter von Luthers Homiletik.*" *Lutherische Theologie und Kirche* 33/2 (2009) 93–110.

______. "Christian without denomination? reflection on the Asian situation from the perspective of Martin Luther." *Theology & Life* 32 (2009) 183–205.

______. "Comments." *Lutheran Quarterly* 23/1 (2009) 103–109.

______. "Homiletical helps on LSB series B • Resurrection of our Lord, Mark 16:1–8." *Concordia Journal* 35/1 (2009) 85–87.

______. "Luther's and Melanchthon's students: The Wittenberg circle and the development of its theology to 1600." *Religion Compass* 3/3 (2009).

______. "Models of the Christian life in Luther's Genesis sermons and lectures." *Lutherjahrbuch* 76 (2009) 193–220.

______. "Review: Christianity and its competitors: the new faces of old heresy. James McGoldrick." *Concordia Journal* 35/1 (2009) 97–99.

______. "Review: *Erinnerte Reformation: Studien zur Luther-Rezeption von der Aufklärung bis zum 20. Jahrhundert.* Christian Danz; Rochus Leonhardt, ed." *Lutheran Quarterly* 23/4 (2009) 489–491.

______. "Review: Life writing in Reformation Europe: lives of reformers by friends, disciples and foes. Irena Backus." *Lutheran Quarterly* 23/3 (2009) 355–357.

______. "Review: Luther's lectures on Genesis and the formation of evangelical identity. John Maxfield." *Concordia Journal* 35/2 (2009) 218–220.

______. "Review: The Cambridge history of Christianity. 6, Reform and expansion 1500–1660. R. Po-chia Hsia, ed." *Journal of Reformed Theology* 3/2 (2009) 227–228.

______. "*Seelsorge* for the Cranachs." *Lutheran Forum* 43/1 (2009) 34–37.

Kolb, R./C.P. Arand. *The genius of Luther's theology: A Wittenberg way of thinking for the contemporary church.* Grand Rapids, MI: Baker Academic, 2008.

Kolb, R., ed. *Lutheran ecclesiastical culture, 1550–1675.* Leiden, Boston: Brill, 2008.

Kolb, R./M.J. Haemig. "Preaching in Lutheran pulpits in the age of confessionalization." Pp. 117–157 in *Lutheran ecclesiastical culture, 1550–1675.* Edited by R. Kolb. Leiden, Boston: Brill, 2008.

Kolb, R. "Introduction." Pp. 1–14 in *Lutheran ecclesiastical culture, 1550–1675.* Edited by R. Kolb. Leiden, Boston: Brill, 2008.

______. "'*Bekentnis der reinen lere des Euangelij Vnd Confutatio der jtzigen Schwermer,*': *Nikolaus von Amsdorf und die Entfaltung einer neuen Bekenntnisform.*" Pp. 307–24 in *Nikolaus von Amsdorf (1483–1565) zwischen Reformation und Politik.* Edited by Irene Dingel. Leipzig: Evangelische Verlagsanstalt, 2008.

______. "*Die Josef-Geschichten als Fürstenspiegel in der Wittenberger Auslegungstradition.: 'Ein verständiger und weiser Mann' (Genesis 42,33).*" Pp. 41–55 in *Christlicher Glaube und weltliche Herrschaft. Zum Gedenken an Günther Wartenberg.* Edited by Michael Beyer, Jonas Flöter, and Markus Hein. Leipzig: Evangelische Verlagsanstalt, 2008.

______. "'Life is King and Lord over death': Martin Luther's view of death and dying." Pp. 23–45 in *Tod und Jenseits in der Schriftkultur der Frühen Neuzeit.* Edited by Marion Kobelt Groch and Cornelia Niekus Moore. Wiesbaden: Harrassowitz, 2008.

______. "Nikolaus von Amsdorf, Jakob Andreae, etc." Pp. various in *The New Westminster Dictionary of Church History.* Edited by Robert Benedetto. Louisville: Westminster/John Knox, 2008.

______. "Homiletical helps on LSB series A • Epiphany 2, John 1:43–51." *Concordia Journal* 34/4 (2008) 329–330.

______. "Review: *Gottes Nähe unmittelbar erfahren: Mystik im Mittelalter und bei Martin Luther.* Berndt Hamm, Volker Leppin, ed." *Journal of Reformed Theology* 2/1 (2008) 92–93.

______. "Review: *Konfession und Kultur: lutherischer Protestantismus in der zweiten Hälfte des Reformationsjahrhunderts.* Thomas Kaufmann." *Lutheran Quarterly* 22/2 (2008) 214–216.

______. "Review: Martin Luther as comforter: Writings on death. Neil R. Leroux." *Renaissance Quarterly* 61/2 (2008) 573–574.

______. "The *Summaria* of Veit Dietrich as an aid for teaching the faith." *Archiv für Reformationsgeschichte* 99 (2008) 97–119.

______. "'This is my customary procedure,' says God: Martin Luther's use of dialogue and monologue in lectures and sermons." Pp. 25–40 in *Teach these things: Essays in honor of Wallace Schulz.* Edited by E. Rottmann, B. Chisamore, and D. Mackey. Versailles, MO: Wild Boar Books, 2008.

Kolb, R. *A booklet of comfort for the sick; & On the Christian knight by Spangenberg, Johann.* Reformation Texts with Translation (1350–1650). vol. 11; Theology and piety series # 4. Milwaukee, WI: Marquette University Press, 2007.

______. "*Die Zweidimensionalität des Mensch-Seins: die zweierlei Gerechtigkeit in Luthers 'De votis monasticis Iudicium'.*" Pp. 207–220 in *Luther und das monastische Erbe.* Edited by C. Bultmann, V. Leppin, and A. Lindner. Tübingen: Mohr Siebeck, 2007.

______. "Foreword." Pp. ix–xvii in *The sacred scriptures and the Lutheran confessions.* Edited by P.J. Secker. Selected writings of Arthur Carl Piepkorn vol. 2. Mansfield, CT: CEC Press, 2007.

______. "Lutheran view: God's baptismal act as regenerative." Pp. 91–109 in *Understanding four views on baptism*. Edited by T.J. Nettles and J.H. Armstrong. Counterpoints Series. Grand Rapids, MI: Zondervan, 2007.

______. "*'Ein kindt des todts' und 'Gottes Gast': Das Sterben in Luthers Predigten.*" *Lutherische Theologie und Kirche* 31/1 (2007) 3–22.

______. "Forgiveness liberates and restores: the freedom of the Christian according to Martin Luther." *Word & World* 27/1 (2007) 5–13.

______. "God and his human creatures in Luther's sermons on Genesis: the reformer's early use of his distinction of two kinds of righteousness." *Concordia Journal* 33/2 (2007) 166–184.

______. "Homiletical helps on LW series C • Pentecost 19, Habakkuk 1:1–4, 2:1–4." *Concordia Journal* 33/3 (2007) 317–318.

______. "Review: Bartholomäus Ziegenbalg, the father of modern Protestant mission: An Indian assessment. Daniel Jeyaraj." *Lutheran Quarterly* 21/4 (2007) 469–471.

______. "Review: *Bildung und Konfession: Theologenausbildung im Zeitalter der Konfessionalisierung.* Herman J Selderhuis, Markus Wriedt, ed." *Lutheran Quarterly* 21/4 (2007) 473–475.

______. "Review: Christ present in faith: Luther's view of justification. Tuomo Mannermaa." *Interpretation* 61/1 (2007) 103–104.

______. "Review: *Compendium locorum theologicorum ex Scripturis Sacris et Libero Concordiae, lateinisch—deutsch—englisch.* Leonhard Hutter." *Concordia Journal* 33/2 (2007) 222–224.

______. "Review: *Der Augsburger Religionsfrieden.* Axel Gotthard." *Journal of Ecclesiastical History* 58/1 (2007) 146–147.

______. "Review: *Die Erfindung des Theologen: Wittenberger Anwiesungen zum Theologiestudium im Zeitalter von Reformation und Konfessionalisierung.* Marcel Nieden." *Lutheran Quarterly* 21/4 (2007) 473–475.

______. "Review: *FrömmigkeitTheologie—Frömmigkeitstheologie: Contributions to European church history: Festschrift für Berndt Hamm zum 60. Geburtstag.* Gudrun Litz, et al., ed." *The Sixteenth Century Journal* 38/3 (2007) 787–789.

______. "Review: *Medizinische Theologie: christus medicus und theologia medicinalis bei Martin Luther und im Luthertum der Barockzeit: mit Edition dreier Quellentexte.* Johann Steiger." *Church History and Religious Culture* 87/1 (2007) 110–112.

______. "Review: *Reformatoren im Mansfelder Land: Erasmus Sarcerius und Cyriakus Spangenberg.* Stephan Rhein and Gunther Wartenberg, ed." *Journal of Ecclesiastical History* 58/3 (2007) 570–571.

______. "'The noblest skill in the Christian church': Luther's sermons on the proper distinction of law and gospel." *Concordia Theological Quarterly* 71/3–4 (2007) 301–318.

______. "The three-hundredth anniversary of Lutheran mission in India." *Lutheran Quarterly* 21/1 (2007) 95–101.

Kolb, R. *Luther's way of thinking: introductory essays: collected essays.* Trivandrum, India: Luther Academy India, 2006.

____. "Lutheranism." Pp. 196–203 in *Worldmark encyclopedia of religious practices.* Edited by T. Riggs. Detroit: Thomson Gale, 2006.

______. "*Controversia perpetua. Die Fortsetzung des adiaphoristischen Streits nach dem Augsburger Religionsfrieden.*" Pp. 191–209 in *Politik und Bekenntnis. Die Reaktionen*

Auf das Interim von 1548. Edited by Irene Dingel and Günther Wartenberg. Leipzig: Evangelische Verlagsanstalt, 2006.

______. "*Historiksa perspektiv I Stengrunden.*" in *Talet om korset - Guds kraft. Till hundraårsminnet av biskop Bo Giertz födelse.* Edited by Rune Imberg. Göteborg: Din Bok, 2006.

______. "*Luther und seine Studenten erziehen zu Christlicher Lebensweise: Die reformatorische Predigt über Lukas 6,36–42 als Beispiel zur Ermahnung.*" *Lutherische Beiträge* 11 (2006) 106–122.

______. "The unsearchable judgments of God: Luther's uses of Romans 11:33–36." *Luther-Bulletin Tijdschrift voor interconfssioneel Lutheronderzoek* 15 (2006) 30–49.

______. "Facing missiology: the prosopography of the mission work of the Lutheran Church—Missouri Synod." *Missio Apostolica* 14/2 (2006) 97–102.

______. "Here we stand: confessing the faith in Luther's footsteps from Worms to Smalcald." *Concordia Journal* 32/2 (2006) 175–188.

______. "Homiletical helps on LW series B • Pentecost 3, 2 Corinthians 4:13–18." *Concordia Journal* 32/2 (2006) 227–228.

______. "Late Reformation Lutherans on mission and confession." *Lutheran Quarterly* 20/1 (2006) 26–43.

______. "Lutheran theology in seventeenth-century Germany." *Lutheran Quarterly* 20/4 (2006) 428–456.

______. "Review: Lutheran Reformation and the Law. Virpi Mäkinen, ed." *Renaissance Quarterly* 59/3 (2006) 905–907.

______. "Review: A history of biblical interpretation. v 1, The ancient period. Alan J. Hauser, Duane F. Watson, ed." *Concordia Journal* 32/1 (2006) 118–119.

______. "Review: *Luther neu gelesen: Modernität und ökumenische Aktualität in seiner letzten Vorlesung.* Ulrich Asendorf." *Lutheran Quarterly* 20/4 (2006) 462–465.

______. "Review: *Melanchthon und der Calvinismus.* Günter Frank and Herman J. Selderhuis, ed." *Renaissance Quarterly* 3 (2006) 910–912.

______. "The Formula of Concord as a model for discourse in the church." *Concordia Journal* 32/2 (2006) 189–210.

______. "The verbs of the great commissions." *Missio Apostolica* 14/1 (2006) 6–7.

Kolb, R./T.J. Wengert. "The future of Lutheran confessional studies: reflections in historical context." *Dialog* 45/2 (2006) 118–126.

Kolb, R. *Bound choice, election, and Wittenberg theological method: From Martin Luther to the Formula of Concord.* Lutheran Quarterly Books. Grand Rapids, MI: William B. Eerdmans Pub., 2005.

______. "*Jeder Christ ist in die Pflicht genommen, Zeugnis vom Glauben abzulegen: Die Verkündigung der Lutheraner in der Spätreformation zu Mission und Bekenntnis.*" Pp. 127–142 in *Gottes Wort in der Zeit: verstehen - verkündigen - verbreiten. Festschrift für Volker Stolle.* Edited by Werner Klän and Christoph Barnbrock. Münster: LIT, 2005.

______. "Law and gospel, Predestination, Two kingdoms doctrine." Pp. various in *The Encyclopedia of Christianity.* Edited by Erwin Fahlbusch. Grand Rapids/ Leiden: Eerdmans/Brill, 2005–2008.

______. "From hymn to history of dogma: Lutheran martyrology in the Reformation era." Pp. 295–313 in *More than a memory: Discourse of martyrdom and construction of a*

Christian identity in the history of Christianity. Edited by J. Leemans. Leuven, Paris, Dudley, MA: Peeters, 2005.

______. "Georg Major as preacher." Pp. 93–121 in *Georg Major (1502–1574): Ein Theologe der Wittenberger Reformation*. Edited by I. Dingel, G. Wartenberg, and M. Beyer. Leucorea-Studien zur Geschichte der Reformation und der Lutherischen Orthodoxie Bd. 7. Leipzig: Evangelische Verlagsanstalt, 2005.

______. "A 'Missourian' reaction to the abiding differences and ecumenical blessings of 'unsettled discussions' on the doctrine of justification." *Dialog* 44/3 (2005) 285–289.

______. "Homiletical helps on LW series A • Day of Pentecost, John 16:5–11." *Concordia Journal* 31/2 (2005) 162–163.

______. "Melanchthon's doctrinal last will and testament: The *Responsiones ad articulos Bavaricae inquisitionis* as his final confession of faith." *The Sixteenth Century Journal* 36/1 (2005) 97–115.

______. "On the move ever yet." *Missio Apostolica* 13/1 (2005) 2–3.

______. "When the Lord hides: witnessing of an unprogrammable God." *Missio Apostolica* 13/1 (2005) 16–21.

______. "Review: Ancient-future evangelism: making your church a faith-forming community. Robert Webber." *Concordia Journal* 31/4 (2005) 455–456.

______. "Review: *Anfechtung und Trost bei Sigismund Scherertz: ein lutherischer Theologe im Dreissigjährigen Krieg*. Alexander Bitzel." *Lutheran Quarterly* 19/1 (2005) 101–104.

______. "Review: *Die Vernunft des Gottendankens: Religionsphilosophische Studien zur frühen Neuzeit*. Günter Frank." *Renaissance Quarterly* 58/2 (2005) 625–626.

______. "Review: *Johann Heermann (1585–1647): Prediger in Schlesien zur Zeit des Dressighährigen Krieges*. Bernhard Liess." *Lutheran Quarterly* 19/4 (2005) 479–481.

______. "Review: Luther's lives: two contemporary accounts of Martin Luther. E. Vandiver, R. Keen, T. Frazel." *Lutheran Quarterly* 19/2 (2005) 245–248.

______. "Review: *Orthodoxie als Konsensbildung: das theologische Disputationswesen an der Universität Wittenberg zwischen 1570 und 1710*. Kenneth Appold." *Lutheran Quarterly* 19/3 (2005) 354–356.

Kolb, R. "The Braunschweig Resolution: The *Corpus Doctrinae Prutenicum* of Joachim Mörlin and Martin Chemnitz as an interpretation of Wittenberg theology." Pp. 67–89 in *Confessionalization in Europe, 1555–1700: Essays in honor and memory of Bodo Nischan*. Edited by J. M. Headley and H.J. Hillerbrand. Aldershot, Hants, England, Burlinton, VT: Ashgate, 2004.

______. "*Caspar Peucers Abendmahlsverständnis*." Pp. 111–144 in *Caspar Peucer (1525–1602): Wissenschaft, Glaube und Politik im konfessionellen Zeitalter; [Beiträge des wissenschaftlichen Kolloquiums in Bautzen 25.–28. September 2002]*. Edited by H.-P. Hasse and G. Wartenberg. Leipzig: Evang. Verl.-Anst., 2004.

______. "Confessional Lutheran theology." Pp. 66–80 in *The Cambridge companion to Reformation theology*. Edited by D.V.N. Bagchi and D.C. Steinmetz. Cambridge Companions to Religion. Cambridge, UK, New York, NY: Cambridge University Press, 2004.

______. "Contemporary Lutheran understandings of the doctrine of justification." Pp. 153–176 in *Justification: What's at stake in the current debates*. Edited by M. Husbands and D.J. Treier. Downers Grove, IL, Leicester, England: InterVarsity Press; Apollos, 2004.

______. "Human performance and the righteousness of faith: Martin Chemnitz's anti-Roman polemic in Formula of Concord III." Pp. 125–139 in *By faith alone: Essays on justification in honor of Gerhard O. Forde*. Edited by J.A. Burgess, and M. Kolden. Grand Rapids, MI: William B. Eerdmans Pub., 2004.

______. "Luther on the two kinds of righteousness." Pp. 38–55 in *Harvesting Martin Luther's reflections on theology, ethics, and the church*. Edited by T.J. Wengert. Lutheran Quarterly Books. Grand Rapids, MI: William B. Eerdmans Pub., 2004.

______. "Lutheranism; Martyrs and Martyrologies; The Book of Concord; Flacius Matthias Illyricus (1520–1575); Luther, Martin (1483–1546)." Pp. various in *The encyclopedia of Protestantism*. Edited by Hans J. Hillerbrand and Robert Kolb. New York, London: Routledge, 2004.

Hillerbrand, H.J./R. Kolb, ed. *The encyclopedia of Protestantism*. New York, London: Routledge, 2004.

Kolb, R. "*Johann Spangenbergs 'Christlicher Ritter' als Beispiel der frühlutherischen Erbauungsliterature*." *Lutherische Theologie und Kirche* 28 (2004) 57–80.

______. "Martin Luther and the German nation." Pp. 39–55 in *A companion to the Reformation world*. Edited by R. Po-chia Hsia. Blackwell Companions to European History. Malden, MA: Blackwell Pub., 2004.

______. "The Gerhards and their orthodox library." *Lutheran Quarterly* 18/1 (2004) 91–96.

______. "Opening doors to intercultural missiological exchange." *Missio Apostolica* 12/1 (2004) 2–3.

______. "Review: Historical method and confessional identity in the era of the Reformation (1378–1615). Irena Backus." *Church History* 73/1 (2004) 204–206.

______. "Review: *Joachim Mörlin, Luthers Kaplan—'Papst der Lutheraner': ein Zeit - und Lebensbild aus dem 16 Jahrhundert*. Jürgen Diestelmann." *Lutheran Quarterly* 18/1 (2004) 97–99.

______. "Review: *Reichstag und Reformatio: Kaiserliche und ständische Religionspolitik von den Anfängen der Causa Lutheri bis zum Nürnberger Religionsfrieden*. Armin Kohnle." *Lutheran Quarterly* 18/4 (2004) 483–485.

Kolb, R., et al. *30th anniversary Concordia Seminary walkout [sound recording]: panel discussion*. St. Louis, MO: Concordia Seminary Media, 2004.

Kolb, R. "Luther's function in an age of confessionalization." Pp. 209–226 in *The Cambridge companion to Martin Luther*. Edited by D.K. McKim. Cambridge Companions to Religion. Cambridge, U.K, New York: Cambridge University Press, 2003.

______. "That God's kingdom may advance with power throughout the world." Pp. 66–72 in *Witness and worship in pluralistic America*. Edited by J. Johnson. St. Louis, MO: Concordia Seminary, 2003.

______. "Christian witness and service." *Missio Apostolica* 11/2 (2003) 76–77.

______. "Homiletical helps on LW Series B • St. Bartholomew, John 1:43–51." *Concordia Journal* 29/3 (2003) 308–310.

______. "Melanchthonian method as a guide to reading confessions of faith: the index of the Book of Concord and late Reformation learning." *Church History* 72/3 (2003) 504–524.

______. "'A hammer against free choice,' Johannes Wigand's interpretation of Luther's *De servo arbitrio*." Pp. 131–146 in *Vanha ja nuori. Juhlakirja Simo Heinisen tädyttäessä 60 vuotta*. Edited by Kaisamari Hintikka, Hanna-Maija Ketola, and Päivi Salmesvuori. Helsinki: Luther-Agricola-Seura, 2003.

______. "Justification by the forgiveness of sins: Late Reformation Lutheran exposition of the Third Article of the Creed." Pp. 123–133 in *Nåd och sanning. Församlingsfakulteten 10 år*. Edited by Rune Imberg and Torbjörn Johansson. Göteborg: Församlingsförlaget, 2003.

______. "On the character and characteristics of witnesses to the gospel." *Missio Apostolica* 11/1 (2003) 2–3.

______. "Review: *Apologetik und Mission: Die missionarische Theologie Karl Heins als Beitrag für eine Misisonstheologie der Gegenwart*. Thomas Kothmann." *Missio Apostolica* 11/1 (2003) 72–73.

______. "Review: Beyond maintenance to mission: a theology of the congregation. Craig Nessan." *Missio Apostolica* 11/1 (2003) 61–62.

______. "Review: The Bible as book: The Reformation. Orlaith O'Sullivan, Ellen Herron." *Church History* 72/3 (2003) 652–654.

______. "The plan behind the promise: Luther's proclamation of predestination." *Reformation & Revival* 12/2 (2003) 41–52.

Kolb, R. *Make disciples, baptizing: God's gift of new life and Christian witness*. Latvian translation. Rīga, Macomb, MI: Lutheran Heritage Foundation, 2002.

______. "Divine determination and human responsibility: David Chytraeus (1531–1600) on *necessitas*." Pp. 221–238 in *Lord Jesus Christ, will you not stay: Essays in honor of Ronald Feuerhahn on the occasion of his sixty-fifth birthday*. Edited by J.B. Day, and Al Collver. Houston, TX, St. Louis, MO: Feuerhahn Festschrift Committee; Available through Concordia Pub. House, 2002.

______. "Preaching the Christian life: ethical instruction in the postils of Martin Chemnitz." Pp. 133–154 in *Caritas et Reformatio: Essays on church and society in honor of Carter Lindberg*. Edited by D.M. Whitford. St. Louis, MO: Concordia Academic Press, 2002.

______. "The legal case for martyrdom: Basilius Monner on Johann Friedrich the Elder and the Smalcald War." Pp. 145–160 in *Reformation und Recht: Festgabe für Gottfried Seebass zum 65. Geburtstag*. Edited by I. Dingel, et al. Gütersloh: Chr. Kaiser/Gütersloher Verlagshaus, 2002.

______. "Martin Chemnitz." Pp. 140–154 in *The Reformation theologians: An introduction to theology in the early modern period*. Edited by C. Lindberg. The great theologians. Oxford, Malden, MA: Blackwell, 2002.

______. "'Nothing but Christ crucified': the autobiography of a cross-cultural communicator." Pp. 37–53 in *The theology of the cross for the 21st century: Signposts for a multicultural witness*. Edited by A.L. García and A.R.V. Raj. St. Louis, MO: Concordia Pub. House, 2002.

______. "Christ's descent into hell as Christological locus in the era of the Formula of Concord." *Lutherjahrbuch* 69 (2002) 101–118.

______. "Confessing the creator to those who do not believe there is one." *Missio Apostolica* 10/1 (2002) 24–36.

______. "God's mission: command and promise." *Missio Apostolica* 10/1 (2002) 2–3.

______. "Homiletical helps on LW Series A • Easter 6, 1 Peter 3:15–22." *Concordia Journal* 28/2 (2002) 192–193.

______. "Luther on the theology of the cross." *Lutheran Quarterly* 16/1 (2002) 443–466.

______. "Review: *Luthertum und Demokratie: deutsche und amerikanische Theologen des 19. Jahrhunderts zu Staat, Gesellschaft und Kirche.* Angelika Dőrfler-Dierken" *Lutheran Quarterly* 16/3 (2002) 358–362.

______. "Preaching predestination: Martin Chemnitz's proclamation of God's election of believers." *Concordia Journal* 28/1 (2002) 23–40.

______. "Preaching the Christian life: Ethical instruction in the postils of Martin Chemnitz." *Lutheran Quarterly* 16/3 (2002) 275–301.

______. "Protestant scholasticism: essays in reassessment. Carl R. Trueman and R.S. Clark, ed." *Church History* 71/1 (2002) 203–204.

______. "Review: *Ad fontes Lutheri:* toward the recovery of the real Luther: essays in honor of Kenneth Hagen's sixty-fifth birthday. Kenneth Hagen, Timothy Maschke, et al." *Lutheran Quarterly* 16/3 (2002) 356–358.

______. "Review: *Diaskepsis theologica:* a theological examination of the fundamental difference between Evangelical Lutheran doctrine and Calvinist or Reformed teaching. Nicolaus Hunnius." *Concordia Journal* 28/4 (2002) 473–474.

______. "Review: Pierre Bayle's reformation: conscience and criticism on the eve of the Enlightenment. Barbara Tinsley." *Concordia Journal* 28/4 (2002) 466–467.

______. "Review: Planting missions across cultures. Kenneth Behnken." *Concordia Journal* 28/2 (2002) 220–221.

______. "Review: The revolution of the candles: Christians in the revolution of the German Democratic Republic. Jörg Swoboda." *Concordia Journal* 28/4 (2002) 475–476.

Kolb, R./C. Neddens/W. Klän. *Gottes Wort vom Kreuz: Lutherische Theologie als kritische Theologie.* Oberurseler Hefte Heft 40. Oberursel: Oberurseler Hefte, 2001.

Kolb, R./J.A. Nestingen. *Sources and contexts of the Book of Concord.* Minneapolis, MN: Fortress Press, 2001.

Kolb, R. {L?} "Review: Martin Luther's theology: its historical and systematic development. Bernhard Lohse." *Calvin Theological Journal* 36/1 (2001) 186–188.

______. "*Das Erbe Melanchthons im Bekenntnis der ungarischen Bursa an der Universität Wittenberg (1568).*" Pp. 223–239 in *Melanchthon und Europa.* Edited by G. Frank, and M. Treu. Melanchthon-Schriften der Stadt Bretten Bd. 6. Stuttgart: J. Thorbecke Verlag, 2001–.

______. "The chief controversy between the papalists and us: grace, faith, and human righteousness in sixteenth-century ecumenical exchange." Pp. 62–82 in *2001, a justification odyssey: papers presented at the Congress on the Lutheran Confessions.* Edited by J.A. Maxfield. St. Louis, MO: Luther Academy, 2001.

______. "Review: A new tool for the study of the history of missions: Gerald Anderson's biographical dictionary of Christian missions." *Missio Apostolica* 9/1 (2001) 46–49.

______. "Another challenge for Lutheran missiologists: the ethics of Christian witness." *Missio Apostolica* 9/1 (2001) 2–3.

______. "Confessing at Augsburg: a model for contemporary evangelistic and ecumenical witness." *Reformation & Revival* 10/2 (2001) 63–74.

______. "On an August Sunday in Ugale ... on the blessings and challenges of church fellowship with the new partners of the LCMS." *Concordia Journal* 27/4 (2001) 292–295.

______. "Review: The Trinity and Martin Luther: a study on the relationship between genre, language and the Trinity in Luther's works (1523–1546). Christine Helmer." *Calvin Theological Journal* 36/1 (2001) 175–177.

______. "Sources and contexts of the Lutheran confessional writings." *Lutheran Quarterly* 15/2 (2001) 125–141.

______. "The Book of Concord: co-editor response." *Dialog* 40/1 (2001) 72–75.

______. "The Formula of Concord and contemporary Anabaptists, Spiritualists, and Anti-Trinitarians." *Lutheran Quarterly* 15/4 (2001) 453–482.

Kolb, R., et al. *12th Theological Symposium: Courageous confession [sound recording]: shaping the life of the church.* St. Louis, MO: Concordia Seminary Media Services, 2001.

Kolb, R. *Make disciples, baptizing: God's gift of new life and Christian witness.* Malayalam translation, 2001.

______. "*Seelsorge und Lehre in der Spätreformation am Beispiel von Nikolaus Selneckers Abhandlung zur Prädestinationslehre.*" *Lutherische Theologie und Kirche* 25 (2001) 14–34.

Kolb, R. "*Andreas Musculus: Katechismus aus den Vätern: Patristik im Dienst der Polemik und der Erbauung in der Spätreformation.*" *Lutherische Theologie und Kirche* 24 (2000) 114–134.

______. "Hermann Sasse's 'Theses on the question of Church fellowship and altar fellowship' of 1537.'" *Concordia Journal* 26 (2000) 104–114.

Kolb, R./T.J. Wengert. *The Book of Concord: The confessions of the Evangelical Lutheran Church.* Minneapolis: Fortress Press, 2000.

______. "*Ars moriendi lutherana: Andreas Poachs Schrift 'Vom Christlichen Abschied aus diesem sterblichen Leben [...] Matthei Ratzenbergers' (1559).*" Pp. 95–112 in *Vestigia pietatis: Studien zur Geschichte der Frömmigkeit in Thüringen und Sachsen; Ernst Koch gewidmet.* Edited by G. Graf. Herbergen der Christenheit Sonderband 5. Leipzig: Evang. Verl.-Anst., 2000.

______, "C.F.W. Walther and August R. Suelflow, theologians and churchmen; Walther and the Epitome of the Formula of Concord; C.F.W. Walther's sermons on mission: a contribution to Lutheran history of mission and theology of mission / Volker Stolle; translated by Robert Kolb." Pp. 45–60; 177–202 in *Soli Deo gloria: Essays on C.F.W. Walther in memory of August R. Suelflow.* Edited by A.R. Suelflow. St. Louis, MO: Concordia Pub. House, 2000.

______. "Theology and mission. The five great commissions and contemporary Christian witness." Pp. 95–102 in *The Lutherans in Mission: Essays in honor of Won Yong Ji.* Edited by A. Scott. Ft. Wayne, IN: Lutheran Society for Missiology, 2000.

______. *The Christian faith.* Translated into Russian by A. Inshakov. Sterling Heights, MI: Lutheran Heritage Foundation, 2000.

______. *Speaking the Gospel today.* Translated into Latvian by L. Lapa, and A. Smilgdrīvs. Riga: Lutheran Heritage Foundation, 2000.

______. *The Christian faith: A Lutheran exposition.* Translated into Ukrainian by Iryna Tkach. Sterling Heights, MI: Lutheran Heritage Foundation, 2000.

______. "In the Lord's century." *Missio Apostolica* 8/1 (2000) 2–3.

______. "Nikolaus Gallus' critique of Philip Melanchthon's teaching on the freedom of the will." *Archiv für Reformationsgeschichte* 91 (2000) 87–110.

______. "Reality rests on the word of the Lord: Martin Luther's understanding of God's word." *Reformation & Revival* 9/4 (2000) 47–63.

______. "Review: '*Mutter der Kirchen' im 'Haus des Islam': Gegenseitige Wahrnehmungen von arabischen Christen und Muslimen im West- und Ostjordanland.* Andreas Feldtkeller." *Missio Apostolica* 8/1 (2000) 45–46.

______. "Review: *Es Begann in Halle … Missionwissenschaft von Gustav Warneck bis heute.* Dieter Becker, ed." *Missio Apostolica* 8/1 (2000) 46–47.

______. "Review: *Missionstheologie bei Wilhelm Löhe: Aufbruch zur Kirche der Zukunft.* Christian Weber." *Missio Apostolica* 8/1 (2000) 44–45.

______. "Review: Outside the fold: conversion, modernity, and belief. Gauri Viswanathan." *Missio Apostolica* 8/1 (2000) 48–49.

______. "Review: *Theologie der Bekenntnisschriften der evangelisch-lutherischen Kirche: eine historische und systematische Einführung in das Konkordienbuch.* Bd 1. Gunther Wenz." *Lutheran Quarterly* 14/2 (2000) 238–240.

______. "Schwiebert, Ernest G, 1895–2000." *Lutherjahrbuch* 67 (2000) 19–21.

Kolb, R. *Martin Luther as prophet, teacher, hero: Images of the reformer, 1520–1620.* Texts and studies in Reformation and post-Reformation thought. Grand Rapids, MI: Baker Books; Paternoster Press, 1999.

______. "Niebuhr's 'Christ and culture in paradox' revisited: The Christian life, simultaneous in both dimensions." Pp. 104–125 in *Christ and culture in dialogue: Constructive themes and practical applications.* Edited by A.J.L. Menuge. St. Louis. MO: Concordia Academic Press, 1999.

______. "Introduction; Patristic citation as homiletical tool in the vernacular sermon of the German late Reformation." Pp. various in *Die Patristik in der Bibelexegese des 16. Jahrhunderts: [Vorträge, gehalten anläßlich eines Arbeitsgespräches vom 20. bis 23. März 1994 in der Herzog-August-Bibliothek].* Edited by D.C. Steinmetz and R. Kolb. Wolfenbütteler Forschungen Bd. 85. Wiesbaden: Harrassowitz, 1999.

Steinmetz, D.C./R. Kolb, ed. *Die Patristik in der Bibelexegese des 16. Jahrhunderts: [Vorträge, gehalten anläßlich eines Arbeitsgespräches vom 20. bis 23. März 1994 in der Herzog-August-Bibliothek].* Wolfenbütteler Forschungen Bd. 85. Wiesbaden: Harrassowitz, 1999.

______. "The devil & the well-born. Proclamation of the law to the privileged in the late Reformation." Pp. 161–171 in *Let Christ be Christ: Theology, ethics & world religions in the two kingdoms: Essays in honor of the sixty-fifth birthday of Charles L. Manske.* Edited by D. N. Harmelink. Huntington Beach, CA: Tentatio Press, 1999.

______. "Altering the agenda, shifting the strategy: The *Grundfest* of 1571 as Philippist program for Lutheran concord." *The Sixteenth Century Journal* 30/3 (1999) 705–726.

______. "Belief in a personal creator cannot be taken for granted." *Missio Apostolica* 7/1 (1999) 2–3.

______. "Christian witness and God's gift of academic disciplines." *Missio Apostolica* 7/2 (1999) 128–129.

______. "Luther on the two kinds of righteousness; reflections on his two-dimensional definition of humanity at the heart of his theology." *Lutheran Quarterly* 13/4 (1999) 449–466.

______. "Martin Luther: The man and his mind." *Reformation & Revival* 8/1 (1999) 11–33.

______. "Review: Having ears that hear: Bible studies for adults and confirmation youth on the nature and functions of the word of God. Stephen Stohlmann." *Concordia Journal* 25/2 (1999) 213–214.

______. "Review: Law and gospel: Philip Melanchthon's debate with John Agricola of Eisleben over *poenitentia*. Timothy Wengert." *Church History* 68/2 (1999) 455–456.

______. "Review: *Religiöse Konversion: systematische und fallorientierte Studien in soziologischer Perspektive*. Monika Wohlrab, et al." *Lutheran Quarterly* 13/2 (1999) 243-246.

______. "Review: *Theologie der Bekenntnisschriften der evangelisch-lutherischen Kirche: eine historische und systematische Einführung in das Konkordienbuch*. Bd 1. Gunther Wenz." *Lutheran Quarterly* 13/3 (1999) 351–353.

______. "Review: Transforming culture: a challenge for Christian mission. Sherwood Lingenfelter." *Concordia Journal* 25/3 (1999) 323–324.

______. "Review: *Veröffentlichte Kirchenpolitik: Kirche im publizistischen Streit zur Zeit der Religionsgespräche, 1538–1541*. Georg Kuhaupt." *Church History* 68/4 (1999).

______. "The autobiography of the new believer: Shaping personal confession of the faith for the newborn children of God." *Missio Apostolica* 7/2 (1999) 94–101.

______. "'What benefit does the soul receive from a handful of water?' Luther's preaching on baptism, 1528–1539." *Concordia Journal* 25/4 (1999) 346–363.

______. "*Jednosc wyznania – droga do 'Formuly zgody'* [introduction to the Formula of Concord]." Pp. 373–86 in *Ksiegi Wyznaniowe Kosciola Luteranskeigo [The Confessional Books of the Lutheran Church]*. Bielsko-Biala: Augustana, 1999.

______. "Johannes Oecolampadius." in *The Encyclopedia of the Renaissance*. Edited by Paul F. Grendler. New York: Scribners, 1999.

Kolb, R. "*Kollege und Schüler. Nikolaus von Amsdorffs Einsatz für die Theologie Martin Luthers auf dem Hintergrund des Wittenberger biblischen Humanismus.*" *Lutherische Theologie und Kirche* 22 (1998) 137–150.

R.B. Barnes/R. Kolb, et al., ed., *Habent sua fata libelli, [or], Books have their own destiny: Essays in honor of Robert V. Schnucker*. Sixteenth Century essays & studies vol. 50. Kirksville, MO: Thomas Jefferson University Press, 1998.

Kolb, R. "Flacius Illyricus, Matthias (1520–1575)." Pp. 190–195 in *Historical handbook of major biblical interpreters*. Edited by D. McKim. Downers Grove, IL: InterVarsity Press, 1998.

______. "The book trade as Christian calling: Johann Friedrich Coelestin's admonition to printers and bookdealers." Pp. 61–72 in *Habent sua fata libelli, [or], Books have their own destiny: Essays in honor of Robert V. Schnucker*. Edited by R.B. Barnes, R. Kolb, et al. Sixteenth Century essays & studies vol. 50. Kirksville, MO: Thomas Jefferson University Press, 1998.

______. "The fathers in the service of Lutheran teaching: Andreas Musculus' use of patristic sources." Pp. 105–123 in *Auctoritas patrum II: Neue beitrage zur Rezeption der Kirchenväter im 15 und 16 Jahrhundert*. Edited by M. Wriedt, Leif Grane, et al. Mainz: Zabern, 1998.

______. "All Lutherans as missionaries; editorial." *Missio Apostolica* 6/1 (1998) 2–4.

______. "Forms and facets of faith: Factors in witness and assimilation." *Concordia Journal* 24/4 (1998) 319–336.

______. "God kills to make alive: Romans 6 and Luther's understanding of justification (1535)." *Lutheran Quarterly* 12/1 (1998) 33–56.

______. "Review: Church under the pressure of Stalinism: the development of the status and activities of the Soviet Latvian Evangelical Lutheran Church during 1944–1950. Jouko Talonen." *Lutheran Quarterly* 12/3 (1998) 364–368.

______. "Review: *Gesetz und Heil: eine Untersuchung zur Vorgeschichte und zum Verlauf des sogenannten zweiten antinomisitischen Streits.* Matthias Richter." *The Sixteenth Century Journal* 29/1 (1998) 308–310.

______. "Review: Luther's theological testament: The Schmalkald articles. William Russell." *Lutheran Forum* 32/2 (1998) 50–51.

Kolb, R. *Make disciples, baptizing: God's gift of new life and Christian witness.* Concordia Seminary Publication. Fascicle Series no. 1. St. Louis, MO: Concordia Seminary, 1997.

______. "Melanchthon's influence on the exegesis of his students: the case of Romans 9." Pp. 194–215 in *Philip Melanchthon (1497–1560) and the commentary.* Edited by T.J. Wengert, and M.P. Graham. Sheffield: Sheffield Academic Press, 1997.

______. "Tileman Hesshus: his doctrine of the pastoral office and influence on the Missouri Synod." Pp. 113–144 in *The office of the ministry.* Edited by C. C. Boshoven. The Pieper Lectures vol. 1, 1996. St. Louis, MO: Concordia Historical Institute, 1997.

______. "*Die Anordnung der Loci Communes Theologici: der Aufbau der Dogmatik in der Tradition Melanchthons.*" *Lutherische Theologie und Kirche* 21/3 (1997) 168–190.

______. "Philipp Melanchthon: Reformer and theologian." *Concordia Journal* 23/4 (1997) 309–316.

______. "Review: *Gesammelte Schriften. Bd 2, Nachrufe, autobiographische Schriften, Cosmoxenus.* Johann Andreä." *The Sixteenth Century Journal* 28/1 (1997) 246–247.

______. "Review: Protestant history and identity in sixteenth-century Europe, vol. 1: the medieval inheritance. Bruce Gordon." *Church History* 66/3 (1997) 597–598.

______. "Review: Protestant history and identity in sixteenth-century Europe, vol. 2: the later Reformation. Bruce Gordon." *Church History* 66/3 (1997) 597–598.

______. "Review: Whether secular government has the right to wield the sword in matters of faith: a controversy in Nürnberg in 1530 over freedom of worship and the authority of secular government in spiritual matters: five documents. James Estes, ed." *Church History* 66/1 (1997) 194–195.

______. "The Ordering of the *Loci Communes Theologici:* The structuring of the Melanchthonian dogmatic tradition." *Concordia Journal* 23/4 (1997) 317–337.

______. "C.F.W. Walther." in *Makers of Christian Theology in America.* Edited by Mark G. Toulouse and James O. Duke. Nashville: Abingdon, 1997.

______. "*Keresztyének és az élet politikai vonatkozásai – egy lutheránus perspektiva.*" *Lelkipásztor, Evangélikus Lelkészi Szakfolyóirat (Budapest)* 72 (1997) 122–126.

Kolb, R. "*Gott tötet, um lebendig zu machen. Das Taufmotiv von Römer 6 in Luthers Verständnis der echtfertigung in Galaterkommentar von 1535.*" *Lutherische Theologie und Kirche* 20 (1996) 153–175.

______. "*O jednosc wyznania droga do Formuly Zgody,*" [Unity in Confession – the Way to the Formula of Concord]." *Teologia i ambona* 11 (1996) 9–20.

______. "*Spór osiandryjski i Fomuly Zgodz nauka o usprawiedliwieniu* [The Osiandrian controversy and the doctrine of justification in the Formula of Concord]." *Teologia i ambona* 11 (1996) 21–19.

______. *Luther's heirs define his legacy: Studies on Lutheran confessionalization.* Collected studies CS539. Alsershot: Variorum, 1996.
______. "Amsdorf, Andreaes, Book of Concord, Martin Luther, etc." Pp. various in *The Oxford encyclopedia of the Reformation.* Edited by H.J. Hillerbrand. 4 vol. New York: Oxford University Press, 1996.
______. "The doctrine of Christ in Nikolaus Selnecker's interpretation of Psalms 8, 22, and 110." Pp. 313–332 in *Biblical interpretation in the era of the Reformation: Essays presented to David C. Steinmetz in honor of his sixtieth birthday.* Edited by R.A. Muller and J.L. Thompson. Grand Rapids, MI: William B. Eerdmans Pub., 1996.
______. "*Passionsmeditation. Luthers und Melanchthons Schüler predigen und beten die Passion.*" Pp. 267–296 in *Humanismus und Wittenberger Reformation: Festgabe anlässlich des 500. Geburtstages des Praeceptor Germaniae Philipp Melanchthon am 16. Februar 1997: Helmar Junghans gewidmet.* Edited by M. Beyer and G. Wartenberg. Leipzig: Evangelische Verlagsanstalt, 1996.
______. "Mission in today's world: Implications for the congregations." *Missio Apostolica* 4/2 (1996) 95–102.
______. "Niebuhr's 'Christ and culture in paradox' revisited." *Lutheran Quarterly* 10/3 (1996) 259–279.
______. "Tag team evangelism: Congregations helping members with Christian witness in daily life." *Missio Apostolica* 4/1 (1996) 11–18.
______. "Witnessing in our vulnerability." *Missio Apostolica* 4/1 (1996) 48–50.
Kolb, R. *Speaking the Gospel today: A theology for evangelism.* Second edition. St. Louis, MO: Concordia Pub. House, 1995.
______. "Law and gospel in the Lutheran confessions." Pp. 44–53 in *The beauty and the bands: papers presented at Congress on the Lutheran Confession, Itasca, Illinois, April 20–22, 1995.* Edited by John R. Fehrmann, Daniel Preus, Bruce Lukas. Crestwood, MO/ Minneapolis: Luther Academy/ Association of Confessional Lutherans, 1995.
______. "God's gift of martyrdom: The early Reformation understanding of dying for the faith." *Church History* 64/3 (1995) 399–411.
______. "Review: *Gesammelte Schriften. Bd 7, veri Christianismi solidaeque philosophiae libertas.* Johann Andreä." *The Sixteenth Century Journal* 26/4 (1995) 937–938.
______. "'That I may be His own': The anthropology of Luther's explanation of the Creed." *Concordia Journal* 21/1 (1995) 28–41.
Kolb, R./T.J. Wengert. "Translating the Book of Concord for the twenty-first century." *Concordia Journal* 21/3 (1995) 305–311.
Kolb, R. "Burying the brethren: Lutheran funeral sermons as life writing." Pp. 97–113 in *The Rhetorics of life-writing in early modern Europe, Forms of biography from Cassandra Fedele to Louis XIV.* Ann Arbor, MI: University of Michigan Press, 1995.
______. "*Luthers Auslegung des ersten Gebots als Impuls für ein lutherisches Bekenntnis heute.*" *Lutherische Theologie und Kirche* 19 (1995) 50–60.
Kolb, R. "Learning to drink from the foundations of Israel, Cyriakus Spangenberg learns hermeneutics from Luther; On eternal predestination and God's election by grace, The exegetical basis of the Lutheran teaching in Cyriakus Spangenberg's commentary on Romans 8 & 9; Preaching and hearing in Luther's congregations, village pastors and peasant congregations." *Lutheran Synod Quarterly* 34 (1994) 2–91.

______. "Confessing the faith: Our Lutheran way of life." *Concordia Journal* 20/4 (1994) 356–367.

______. "Review: Anselm and Luther on the atonement: Was it necessary? Burnell Eckardt." *Calvin Theological Journal* 29/2 (1994) 556–558.

______. "Review: Communal Reformation: The quest for salvation in 16th-century Germany. Peter Blickle." *Religious Studies Review* 20/2 (1994) 156.

______. "Review: *Die Erlanger Theologie.* Karlmann Beyschlag." *Lutheran Quarterly* 8/4 (1994) 452–454.

______. "Review: *Die ganze Christenheit auf Erden: Martin Luther und seine ökumenische Bedeutung zum 65. Geburtstag des Verfassers.* Gottfried Maron." *Religious Studies Review* 20/2 (1994) 155.

______. "Review: *Dominus narrabit in scriptura populorum:* A study of early 17th-century Lutheran teaching on preaching and the *Lettische lang-gewünschte Postill of Georgius Mancelius.* Jānis Krēsliņš." *Lutheran Quarterly* 8/1 (1994) 77–80.

______. "Review: Fountainhead of federalism: Heinrich Bullinger and the covenantal tradition; with a translation of *De testamento seu foedere Dei unico et aeterno (1534).* J. Wayne Baker." *Concordia Theological Quarterly* 58/2–3 (1994) 204–205.

______. "Review: Gasparo Contarini: Venice, Rome, and reform. Elisabeth Gleason." *Religious Studies Review* 20/3 (1994) 245.

______. "Review: *Johannes Bugenhagen zwischen Reform und Reformation: die Entwicklung seiner frühen Theologie anhand des Matthäuskommentars und der Passions- und Auferstehungsharmonie.* Anneliese Bieber-Wallmann." *The Sixteenth Century Journal* 25/3 (1994) 744–745.

______. "Review: *Novis Linguis Loqui: Martin Luthers Disputation über Joh 1:14 'Verbum Caro Factum est' aus dem Jahr 1539.* Stefan Streiff." *Religious Studies Review* 20/2 (1994) 155–156.

______. "Review: Philip Melanchthon's rhetorical construal of biblical authority: *Oratio Sacra.* John Schneider." *Calvin Theological Journal* 29/2 (1994) 529–531.

______. "Review: Preaching in the last days: the theme of two witnesses in the 16th and 17th centuries. Rodney Petersen." *Religious Studies Review* 20/3 (1994) 244–245.

______. "Review: Problems of authority in the Reformation debates. Gillian Evans." *Church History* 63/3 (1994) 452–453.

______. "Review: Protestants: The Birth of a Revolution. Steven Ozment." *Religious Studies Review* 20/2 (1994) 156.

______. "Review: The colloquy of Montbéliard: Religion and politics in the 16th century. Jill Raitt." *Fides et historia* 26/3 (1994) 79–81.

______. "Review: The conversion of Henri IV: politics, power, and religious belief in early modern France. Michael Wolfe." *Religious Studies Review* 20/2 (1994) 155.

______. "Review: The phoenix and the flame: Catalonia and the Counter Reformation. Henry Kamen." *Religious Studies Review* 20/3 (1994) 245.

______. "Review: Venice's hidden enemies: Italian heretics in a Renaissance city. John Martin." *Religious Studies Review* 20/2 (1994) 156.

______. "The five great commissions and contemporary Christian witness." *Missio Apostolica* 2/2 (1994) 75–82.

Kolb, R. *The Christian faith: A Lutheran exposition.* St. Louis, MO: Concordia Pub. House, 1993.

______. "'Not without the satisfaction of God's righteousness': The atonement and the generation gap between Luther and his students." Pp. 136–156 in *Die Reformation in Deutschland und Europa: Interpretationen und Debatten: Beiträge zur gemeinsamen Konferenz der Society for Reformation Research und des Vereins für Reformationsgeschichte, 25–30 September 1990 im Deutschen Historischen Institut, Washington, D.C.* Edited by H.R. Guggisberg, G.G. Krodel, and H. Füglister. Gütersloh: Gütersloher Verlagshaus, 1993.

______. "Christian civic responsibility in an age of judgment." *Concordia Journal* 19/1 (1993) 10–34.

______. "Review: (Em)bodying the word: Textual resurrections in the martyrological narratives of Foxe, Crespin, de Beze and d'Aubigné. Catharine Coats." *The Sixteenth Century Journal* 24/4 (1993).

______. "Review: Memoirs in exile: confessional hope and institutional conflict. John Tietjen." *Lutheran Quarterly* 7/1 (1993) 106–109.

______. "Review: The shaping of the reformed baptismal rite in the 16th century. Hughes Old." *Lutheran Quarterly* 7/2 (1993) 220–222.

______. "The influence of Luther's Galatians commentary of 1535 on later sixteenth-century Lutheran commentaries on Galatians." *Archiv für Reformationsgeschichte* 84 (1993) 156–184.

Kolb, R./S. Arnold. *The software of service: Lutheran presupposition and perspective on the public ministry and the office of teacher.* Lutheran Education Association Monographs. River Forest, IL: Lutheran Education Assoc., 1993.

Kolb, R. *Teaching God's children his teaching: A guide to the study of Luther's Catechism.* Hutchinson, MN: Crown Publishing, 1992.

______. "Foreword to the book." Pp. 5–7 in *Commentary on Romans.* by P. Melanchthon, Edited by F. Kramer. St. Louis, MO: Concordia Pub. House, 1992.

______. "Philipp's foes, but followers nonetheless: late humanism among the Gnesio-Lutherans." Pp. 159–177 in *The Harvest of humanism in Central Europe: Essays in honor of Lewis W. Spitz.* Edited by M.P. Fleischer. St. Louis, MO: Concordia Pub. House, 1992.

______. "*Umgestaltung und theologische Bedeutung des Lutherbildes im späten 16. Jahrhundert.*" Pp. 202–231 in *Die lutherische Konfessionalisierung in Deutschland: Wissenschaftliches Symposion des Vereins für Reformationsgeschichte 1988.* Edited by H.C. Rublack. Schriften des Vereins für Reformationsgeschichte Bd. 197. Gütersloh: G. Mohn, 1992.

Dinovo, T./R. Kolb, ed. *Martin Luther in two centuries: the sixteenth and the twentieth: Lectures of Helmar Junghans presented during a tour of the United States, March-April 1991.* St. Paul, MN: Lutheran Brotherhood Foundation Reformation Research Library, Luther Northwestern Theological Seminary, 1992.

Kolb, R. *Confessing the faith: Reformers define the Church, 1530–1580.* Concordia Scholarship Today. St. Louis, MO: Concordia Pub. House, 1991.

______. *Luther: Pastor of God's people.* St. Louis, MO: Concordia Pub. House, 1991.

______. "'Saint John Hus' and 'Jerome Savonarola, confessor of God': The Lutheran "canonization" of late medieval martyrs." *Concordia Journal* 17/4 (1991) 404–418.

______. *Christian civil responsibility in an age of judgment [sound recording]: Convocation recorded on November 6, 1991, Concordia Seminary, St. Louis.* St. Louis, MO: Concordia Seminary Media Services, 1991.

Kolb, R. "The doctrine of the ministry in Martin Luther and the Lutheran confessions." Pp. 49–66 in *Called and ordained: Lutheran perspectives on the office of the ministry.* Edited by T.W. Nichol and M. Kolden. Minneapolis: Fortress Press, 1990.

______. "Sixteenth-century Lutheran commentary on Genesis and the Genesis commentary of Martin Luther." Pp. 243–258 in *Théorie et pratique de l'exégèse, Actes du troisième colloque international sur l'histoire de l'exégèse biblique au XVIe siècle.* Edited by Irena Backus and Francis Higman. Geneva: Droz, 1990.

______. "Festivals of the Saints in the Late Reformation Lutheran Preaching." *The Historian* 53 (1990) 613–626.

______. "Lutheran Church–Missouri Synod; Franz Pieper; C.F.W. Walther." Pp. various in *The Dictionary of Christianity in America.* Edited by Daniel G. Reid. Downers Grove, IL: InterVarsity Press, 1990.

______. "Review: The Churches and the Third Reich, V 2. The year of disillusionment, 1934: Barmen and Rome. Klaus Scholder." *Lutheran Quarterly* 4/2 (1990) 238–239.

Kolb, R. "Review: Ordinary saints: An introduction to the Christian life. Robert Benne." *Lutheran Quarterly* 3/2 (1989) 232–233.

______. "Review: Prophecy and Gnosis. Apocalypticism in the wake of the Lutheran Reformation. Robin Bruce Barnes." *Renaissance Quarterly* 42/3 (1989) 560–562.

Kolb, R. "Hit men and midwives: Christian witness at work and at worship." Pp. 17–41 in *Sent forth by God's blessing: the 1987 Institute of Liturgical Studies.* Edited by D.G. Truemper. Valparaiso, IN: Institute of Liturgical Studies, 1988.

______. "Luther's Smalcald Articles: Agenda for testimony and confession." *Concordia Journal* 14/2 (1988) 115–137.

______. "Singing the Lord's song in a new land: Luther's influence on C.F.W. Walther's *The proper distinction of Law and Gospel.*" *Lutheran Synod Quarterly* 28 (1988) 1–36.

Kolb, R. "Matthias Flacius Illyricus." in *The Encyclopedia of Religion.* Edited by Mircea Eliade. New York: Macmillan, 1987.

______. "Teaching the text, The commonplace method in Sixteenth Century Lutheran biblical commentary." *Bibliothèque d'Humanisme et Renaissance* 49 (1987) 571–585.

______. "Review: *Zur Bilanz des Lutherjahres.* Peter Manns, ed." *Church History* 57/2 (1988) 256.

______. *For all the saints: Changing perceptions of martyrdom and sainthood in the Lutheran Reformation.* Macon, GA: Mercer University Press, 1987.

______. "The advance of dialectic in Lutheran theology: the role of Johannes Wigand (1523–1587)." Pp. 93–100 in *Regnum, religio et ratio: Essays presented to Robert M. Kingdon.* Edited by J. Friedman. Sixteenth century essays & studies vol. VIII. Kirksville, MO: Sixteenth Century Journal Publishers, 1987.

______. "C.F.W. Walther, interpreter of Luther on the American frontier." *Lutheran Quarterly* 1/4 (1987) 469–485.

______. "Review: *Les dissidents du 16ue siècle entre l'Humanisme et le Catholicisme.* Marc Lienhard, ed." *Lutheran Quarterly* 1/3 (1987) 393–395.

______. "Review: Luther the reformer: the story of the man and his career. James Kittelson." *Concordia Theological Quarterly* 51/2-3 (1987) 234–235.

Kolb, R. "*Martin Chemnitz, Gnesio-Lutheraner.*" Pp. 115–129 in *Der zweite Martin der Lutherischen Kirche: Festschrift zum 400. Todestag vom Martin Chemnitz.* Edited by W.A. Junke. Braunschweig: Ev.-luth. Stadtkirchenverband und Propstei, 1986.

______. "The age of confessionalism: Luther, Augsburg, and the late reformation concept of confession." Pp. 33–50 in *Controversy and conciliation: The Reformation and the Palatinate, 1559–1583.* Edited by D. Visser. Pittsburgh theological monographs, new ser. 18. Allison Park, PA: Pickwick Publications, 1986.

Kolb, R. "'Perilous events and troublesome disturbances': The role of controversy in the tradition of Luther to Lutheran orthodoxy." Pp. 181–201 in *Pietas et Societas, New trends in Reformation social history: Essays in memory of Harold J. Grimm.* Edited by Kyle C. Sessions and Phillip N. Bebb. Kirksville, MO: Sixteenth Century Journal Publishers, 1985.

______. "Luther as Seelsorger." *Concordia Journal* 11/1 (1985) 2–9.

Kolb, R., ed. *Christian wisdom in service to God's world.* Saint Paul, MN: Concordia College, 1984.

______. *Speaking the Gospel today: A theology for evangelism.* St. Louis: Concordia Pub. House, 1984.

______. "The German Lutheran reaction to the third period of the Council of Trent." *Lutherjahrbuch* 51 (1984) 63–95.

Kolb, R. "Luther for the German Americans. The Saint Louis edition of Luther's Works." *Concordia Historical Institute Quarterly* 56 (1983) 98–110.

______. "Luther the master pastor: Conrad Porta's *Pastorale Lutheri*, handbook for generations." *Concordia Journal* 9/5 (1983) 179–187.

Kolb, R. "God calling, 'Take care of my people': Luther's concept of vocation in the Augsburg Confession and its Apology." *Concordia Journal* 8/1 (1982) 4–11.

______. "God, faith, and the devil: Popular Lutheran treatments of the first commandment in the era of the Book of Concord." *Fides et historia* 15/1 (1982) 71–89.

Kolb, R./D.A. Lumpp. *Martin Luther, companion to the contemporary Christian.* St. Louis, MO: Concordia Pub. House, 1982.

Kolb, R. "The Flacian rejection of the Concordia: Prophetic style and action in the German Late Reformation." *Archiv für Reformationsgeschichte* 73 (1982) 196–217.

Kolb, R. "Martin Luther; Lutheran Churches; Reformation, Protestant." Pp. various in *Abingdon Dictionary of living religions.* Edited by Keith Crim. Nashville: Abingdon, 1981.

______. "Matthaeus Judex's condemnation of princely censorship of theologians' publications." *Church History* 50/4 (1981) 401–414.

Kolb, R. *Confessing Christ before the world [sound recording]: 16th century views of Augsburg, 1530.* St. Louis, MO: Concordia Seminary Media Services, 1980.

______. "Augsburg 1530: German Lutheran interpretations of the Diet of Augsburg to 1577." *The Sixteenth Century Journal* 11 (1980) 47–61.

______. "Good works are detrimental to salvation: Amsdorf's use of Luther's words in controversy." *Renaissance and Reformation/Renaissance et Réforme* 4 (O.S. 16) (1980) 136–151.

______. "Jakob Andreae (1528–1590)," Pp. 53–68 in *Shapers of religious traditions in Germany, Switzerland, and Poland.* Edited by Jill Raitt. New Haven: Yale University Press, 1980.

Kolb, R. "'A beautiful, delightful jewel': Cyriakus Spangenberg's plan for the Sixteenth Century noble's library." *The Journal of Library History* 24 (1979) 129–159.

______. [Insight and substance to this popular account of Luther's Small Catechism] in *What does this mean? In observance of the 450th anniversary of Martin Luther's Small Catechism 1529–1979.* by M. Luther. Appleton, WI: Aid Association for Lutherans, 1979.

______. "The layman's Bible: the use of Luther's catechisms in the German late reformation." Pp. 16–26 in *Luther's catechisms—450 years: Essays commemorating the Small and Large Catechisms of Dr. Martin Luther.* Edited by D.P. Scaer and R.D. Preus. Ft. Wayne, IN: Concordia Theological Seminary Press, 1979.

Kolb, R. "Historical background of the Formula of Concord." Pp. 12–87 in *A contemporary look at the Formula of Concord.* Edited by W. Rosin and R.D. Preus. St. Louis, MO: Concordia Pub. House, 1978.

______. *Nikolaus von Amsdorf (1483–1565): Popular polemics in the preservation of Luther's legacy.* Bibliotheca humanistica & reformatorica vol. 24. Nieuwkoop: De Graaf, 1978.

______. "Jakob Andreae's concern for the laity." *Concordia Journal* 4/2 (1978) 58–67.

______. "The theologians and the peasants: Conservative evangelical reactions to the German peasants' revolt." *Archiv für Reformationsgeschichte* 69 (1978) 103–131.

Kolb, R. *Andreae and the Formula of Concord: Six sermons on the way to Lutheran unity.* St. Louis, MO: Concordia Pub. House, 1977.

______. "Cyriakus Spangenberg's *Adelspiegel*, A theologian's view of the duties of the nobleman." Pp. 12–21 in *Social groups and religious ideas in the Sixteenth Century.* Edited by Miriam U. Chrisman and Otto Grundler. Kalamazoo: The Medieval Institute, 1977.

______. "Dynamics of party conflict in the Saxon Late Reformation, Gnesio-Lutherans vs. Philippists." *The Journal of Modern History* 49 (1977) D1289–1305.

Kolb, R./John Jay Hughes. *Sixteenth century bibliography: The Center for Reformation Research microform holdings from all periods.* 8 vols. St. Louis, MO: Center for Reformation Research, 1977–1979.

Kolb, R. *Caspar Peucer's library: portrait of a Wittenberg professor of the mid-sixteenth century.* St. Louis, MO: Center for Reformation Research, 1976.

______. "Georg Major as controversialist: Polemics in the late reformation." *Church History* 45/4 (1976) 455–468.

______. "Nikolaus von Amsdorf on vessels of wrath and vessels of mercy: A Lutheran's doctrine of double predestination." *Harvard Theological Review* 69/3–4 (1976) 325–343.

Kolb, R. "Review: Luther and the peasants' war: Luther's actions and reactions. Robert Crossley." *Church History* 44/1 (1975) 116.

Kolb, R. "Review: The world of the Reformation. Hans Hillerbrand." *Concordia Theological Monthly* 45/1 (1974) 69.

Kolb, R. *Nikolaus von Amsdorf, knight of God and exile of Christ: piety and polemic in the wake of Luther.* PhD dissertation. Madison: University of Wisconsin, 1973.

______. "Parents should explain the sermon: Nikolaus von Amsdorf on the role of the Christian parent." *Lutheran Quarterly* 25/3 (1973) 231–240.

______. "Six Christian sermons on the way to Lutheran unity." *Concordia Theological Monthly* 44/4 (1973) 261–274.

Kolb, R. "Conversation between Pasquil and German: Theological mood and method, 1537." *Concordia Theological Monthly* 41/3 (1970) 131–145.

Kolb, R. *Pauline paidology: the use of the suffering servant of God image of Isaiah 52/53 for Jesus Christ in the Pauline corpus.* STM thesis. Concordia Seminary (St. Louis, MO) 1968.

______. *The paidology of Acts: Isaiah 53 in the theology of the early church.* Seminary class paper, Concordia Seminary (St. Louis, MO) 1968.

The Editors and Authors

Charles P. Arand, PhD., is the Eugene E. and Nell S. Fincke Graduate Professor of Theology and Systematic Theology at Concordia Seminary, St. Louis, MO, USA.

L'ubomír Batka, Dr. Theol., is Dean of the Evangelical Lutheran Theological Faculty of Comenius University in Bratislava, Slovak Republic.

Amy Nelson Burnett, PhD., is Paula and D.B. Varner University Professor of History at the University of Nebraska-Lincoln, NE, USA.

Prof. Dr. phil. theol. habil. Irene Dingel is Director of the Leibniz-Institute for European History (Department of History of Occidental Religion), Mainz, Germany.

Mary Jane Haemig, ThD., JD, is Professor of Church History and Director of the Reformation Research Program at Luther Seminary, St. Paul, MN, USA.

Scott Hendrix, PhD., is Professor Emeritus of Reformation History and Theology at Princeton Theological Seminary, USA.

Erik H. Herrmann, PhD., is Associate Professor of Historical Theology and Director of the Center for Reformation Research at Concordia Seminary, Saint Louis, MO, USA.

Guntis Kalme, PhD., is Instructor at Luther Academy in Riga, Latvia.

Werner Klän, Prof. Dr. Theol., is Professor of Systematic Theology at Lutherische Theologische Hochschule, Oberursel and Extraordinary Professor at the Theological Faculty of the University of Pretoria, Republic of South Africa.

David A. Lumpp, ThD., is Professor of Theology and Ministry at Concordia University, St. Paul, MN, USA.

Mark C. Mattes, PhD., is Professor of Theology and Philosophy at Grand View University in Des Moines, IA, USA.

Daniel L. Mattson, PhD., is retired from World Mission of the Lutheran Church—Missouri Synod and serves in the Academic Staff at Concordia Seminary, St. Louis, MO, USA.

Richard A. Muller, PhD., is P.J. Zondervan Professor Emeritus of Historical Theology at Calvin Theological Seminary in Grand Rapids, MI, USA.

Paul W. Robinson, PhD., is Professor of Historical Theology at Concordia Seminary, St. Louis, MO, USA.

Robert Rosin, PhD., is Eugene E. and Nell S. Fincke Graduate Professor of Theology Emeritus at Concordia Seminary, St. Louis, MO, USA.

Timothy J. Wengert, PhD., is Ministerium of Pennsylvania Professor Emeritus of Reformation History at the Lutheran Theological Seminary, Philadelphia, PA, USA.